Scottish Fiction

and the British Empire

Douglas S. Mack

Edinburgh University Press

First published 2006 by
Edinburgh University Press Ltd
22 George Square, Edinburgh

ISBN 0 7486 1814 7 (paperback)

Typeset by Douglas S. Mack

Printed and bound in Great Britain by
Antony Rowe Ltd, Chippenham, Wilts

A CIP record for this book is available from the British Library

Acknowledgements

The writing of this book has been a long-term project. Earlier versions of some passages in it appeared in articles which I have contributed to *Studies in Hogg and his World* and *The Journal of Stevenson Studies*, and earlier versions of other passages formed part of my Introduction to the 1999 Penguin Classics edition of Scott's novel, *The Tale of Old Mortality*. I wish to express my gratitude to the Trustees of the British Museum for permission to reproduce *Sawney in the Boghouse* and *The English-Irish Highlander*. While working on *Scottish Fiction and the British Empire* I have been helped in various ways by very many people, and, for their comments and advice, I record with pleasure my particular thanks to Janette Currie, Ian Duncan, Peter Garside, Suzanne Gilbert, Scott Hames, Gillian Hughes, Wilma Mack, Robin MacLachlan, and Eric Massie. During the later stages of the writing of the book I had some health problems, and for helping me through these I express heart-felt thanks to my wife Wilma, and to Maureen Hamill of Falkirk Royal Infirmary.

Contents

ONE

Introduction: 'Can the Subaltern Speak?'

Scotland and the British Empire

In the early 1980s Ranajit Guha made what has proved to be a fruitful and influential distinction between what he called the 'elite' and what he called the 'subaltern classes'. Writing about Indian society in the days of British Imperial rule, Guha suggested that a dominant elite then operated in tune with the interests of the British raj, and contained 'foreign as well as indigenous' groups. The foreign elements included British officials, industrialists, merchants, financiers, planters, landlords, and missionaries, while the indigenous elements (at an all-India level) included 'the biggest feudal magnates, the most important representatives of the industrial and mercantile bourgeoisie and native recruits to the uppermost levels of the bureaucracy'. At a more local level, the indigenous portion of the dominant elite could also include people belonging to 'hierarchically inferior' social strata, who nevertheless acted in the interests of the elite *and not in conformity to interests corresponding truly to their own social being* [Guha's italics]. Guha stresses that the 'subaltern classes', on the other hand, consisted of the 'people', the dominated mass of the population in town and country. *Scottish Fiction and the British Empire* will argue that, in Scotland as in India, the 'elite' and the 'subaltern classes' had significantly different experiences of the impact of the British Imperial project.[1]

Guha's distinction has been taken up and developed by Gayatri Chakravorty Spivak and other postcolonial theorists, and one focus of the resulting debate has been an exploration of whether the expression of subaltern concerns and insights was always and inevitably either silenced or distorted during the Imperial era by the power of the Imperial elite: 'can the subaltern speak?', as Spivak's famous question puts it. The official Imperial account of the process of colonisation was a story in which the Empire brought the light of 'progress' and 'civilisation' to 'dark' places still enmeshed in 'savagery'. Subaltern people on the receiving end of Imperial power might well wish to tell a different story about the arrival of Empire—but it was not in the Imperial interest to allow potentially subversive alternative stories to gain a hearing. Edward Said makes the point as follows in *Culture and Imperialism* (1993):

> A great deal of recent criticism has concentrated on narrative fiction, yet very little attention has been paid to its position in the history and world of empire. Readers of this book will quickly discover that narrative is crucial to my argument here, my basic point being that stories are at the heart of what explorers and novelists say about strange regions of the world; they also become the method colonized people use to assert their own identity and the existence of their own history. The main battle in imperialism is over land, of course; but when it came to who owned the land, who had the right to settle and work on it, who kept it going, who won it back, and who now plans its future—these issues were reflected, contested, and even for a time decided in narrative. As one critic has suggested, nations themselves *are* narrations. The power to narrate, or to block other narratives from forming and emerging, is very important to culture and imperialism, and constitutes one of the main connections between them.[2]

Scottish Fiction and the British Empire will argue that, in the Scotland of the Imperial era, there was a vigorous contest over the Imperial elite's power to narrate and to block other narratives from forming and emerging. Furthermore, it will be argued that this contest generated a remarkable and widely influential flowering of Scottish fiction during the British Imperial heyday. This flowering consists partly of novels and other fictional narratives through which Scottish writers like Sir Walter Scott and John Buchan (operating within the structures of Imperial Britain's elite) did much to shape and focus Imperial Britain's sense of itself. However, it also consists partly of novels and other fictional narratives in which subaltern Scottish writers like James Hogg and Lewis Grassic Gibbon challenge and subvert some of Imperial Britain's assumptions, by trying to gain a hearing for the subaltern voice.

What forms did elite / subaltern tensions take in the Scotland of the Imperial era, and in what ways did these tensions help to generate the vigorous pro-Imperial and anti-Imperial strands that can be identified in Scottish narratives of the British Imperial period? In seeking to answer these questions, it will be useful to consider the circumstances in which Scotland first became involved as a participant in the British Imperial project. During the final years of the seventeenth century Scotland was still an independent country, and was actively engaged in an attempt to establish itself as a significant Imperial power in its own right. At this period, William of Orange occupied both the throne of Scotland and the throne of England. The two countries had shared the same monarch since 1603, when the reigning King of Scots, James VI, inherited the

English throne on the death of the unmarried and childless English queen, Elizabeth. In spite of the century-old Regal Union, however, Scotland and England were still very much separate entities during William's reign. In the course of a lucid account of the economic and other tensions that existed between the two countries during the 1690s, the historian T. M. Devine has suggested that these tensions, paradoxically, helped to pave the way for the Parliamentary Union that, in 1707, united England and Scotland and thus brought into being a new multi-nation state called 'Britain'. Devine describes the tensions of the 1690s as follows:

> Between 1689 and 1697 William's wars with France were having serious effects on Scottish commerce while the Royal Navy was implementing the Navigation Laws with full rigour against illicit Scottish trade with England's American colonies. Conflict in the economic sphere was intensified by the collapse of the Company of Scotland's ill-fated expedition to Darien in central America. This enterprise was launched in a mood of great national optimism in 1695, but by March 1700 the attempt to found a Scottish colony on the Isthmus of Panama to trade with the Pacific and Atlantic simultaneously had ended in total disaster. The reasons for the catastrophe were many, ranging from poor planning to the lethal effects of tropical disease on the first settlers. But the blame was also laid squarely at England's door. English investment had been withdrawn from the original undertaking as a result of mercantile and political pressure from London, while the possibility of bringing relief to the Scottish settlement in 1699 had come to naught, in large part because the London government, conscious of the vital diplomatic need to maintain Spanish support against France, refused to send provisions or succour. The Darien failure had a serious economic impact because of the enormous national investment that had gone into it, but the political fall-out was just as significant. The disaster directly hit the pockets of the noblemen, lairds and merchants represented in the Scottish parliament precisely at the time when many landowners were already suffering from a collapse of rental income as a result of calamitous harvest failures in the 1690s. Simmering discontent gave way to strident criticism that Scotland's miseries were all rooted in the Regal Union of 1603.[3]

As Devine points out, Scotland was not allowed to trade with England's American colonies under the Regal Union. Equally, Scotland's attempt to set up its own American colony in Darien was hindered by no less a figure than the King of Scots himself, because this person (in his other capacity as King of England) found it in his interest to discourage Scottish success in this crucial project. In the resulting mood of Scottish discontent with the Regal Union, Devine goes on to argue, it came to seem that Scotland's future lay either in ending that Union, or in a still closer Union with England. Steps were duly taken towards ending the Regal Union when the 1703 session of the Scottish Parliament, under Jacobite influence, adopted measures designed to ensure that future decisions about the succession to the Scottish throne would be taken within Scotland, rather than being imposed from England. These moves opened the way for the eventual restoration to the Scottish throne of the exiled Catholic Stuart dynasty, in spite of English determination to maintain a Protestant succession to the thrones of both countries. The ending of the Regal Union by the restoration of the Stuarts to the Scottish throne would have been decidedly unhelpful for Protestant England in its ongoing struggle with pre-Revolutionary France, the great Catholic European power of the period. Faced with this potentially dangerous situation, the English government took active and vigorous measures to promote Union with Scotland.[4] In the event, when the Union of 1707 duly established the new state called 'Britain', this did much to consolidate a secure home base within the island of Great Britain for what became the 'British' (no longer simply the English) Imperial project. The home base of the British Empire was in due course further strengthened by the Union of 1801 between Britain and Ireland. Secure in its domination of all the British Isles in the years that followed Union with Ireland, Britain was well placed to move towards the world hegemony it established as the nineteenth century advanced.

However, the internal political stability of the British Isles had been much less secure in the early decades of the eighteenth century, thanks in part to the existence of rival claimants to the British throne. This destabilising situation can be traced back to events that took place almost two decades before the Union of 1707. In the 'Glorious Revolution' of the late 1680s the Roman Catholic King James VII (in Scotland) and II (in England) was deposed first in England (in 1688) and then in Scotland (in 1689), to be replaced in both countries by his Protestant son-in-law William of Orange (who at first reigned jointly with his wife, James's daughter Mary, who had been brought up as a Protestant). As T. C. Smout points out in *A History of the Scottish People 1560–1830*, this deposition of a Stuart King of Scots was for many people in Scotland 'a shattering break with their national history, for it was the deposition of a dynasty that had ruled since 1371'.[5]

Following his wife's death in 1694, William reigned in his own right in both Scotland and England. When William himself died in 1702, the Protestant succession was maintained in both countries by Anne, another Protestant daughter of James VII. Meanwhile James VII had died in 1701, at which point his son (also James, a half-brother of Queen Anne) became the exiled Catholic claimant to the two thrones, a man regarded by his Jacobite followers as the *de jure* King James VIII and III. The Union of 1707 was negotiated and implemented during Queen Anne's reign with a view to safeguarding the Protestant succession, and after this queen's death in 1714 the British throne passed to a Protestant German aristocrat, the Elector of Hanover, one of whose ancestors, some generations previously, had married a daughter of the Scottish King James VI. These were the circumstances in which, in 1714, George I came somewhat precariously to the throne of the seven-year-old British state, as the first of what proved to be a long succession of Hanoverian British monarchs.

From the 'Glorious Revolution' onwards Jacobites dreamed of and worked for a return to power of the exiled Stuart dynasty, and in the early decades of the eighteenth century it was assumed by Scottish Jacobites that the hoped-for return would end the still-fragile Union of 1707. An unsuccessful Jacobite rising of 1715 followed Queen Anne's death in 1714, and in 1745 Prince Charles Edward (a grandson of James VII) arrived in Scotland in order to lead another rising. The Prince came with few companions, but with promises of support from pre-Revolutionary France. Charles found a ready response among his mainly Episcopalian or Catholic Scottish supporters, although he was strongly opposed by Scottish Presbyterians. A Jacobite army was raised which quickly gained control of Scotland, and subsequently began an invasion of England. The Hanoverian British government in London was thoroughly frightened by the initial successes of the Jacobites, but lack of widespread English support when the Prince's army invaded England resulted in a retreat into Scotland by Charles and his followers. An insurrection becomes much less formidable once it begins to retreat, and the Jacobite cause met a devastatingly final defeat at the Battle of Culloden in 1746. Ruthless reprisals followed as the Hanoverian regime took decisive action to end the Jacobite threat once and for all. This bloody aftermath of Culloden firmly established the Union settlement of 1707 for the foreseeable future, and ended the threat posed to the Protestant British Empire by the Scottish Jacobite allies of pre-Revolutionary Catholic France.

The 1707 Union between Scotland and England and the defeat of the Jacobite rising of 1745–46 were thus crucial in creating the conditions in which the British Empire could flourish. Indeed, during the long heyday of the British Empire the *Union* Flag (popularly known as the Union Jack) became a familiar and imposing sight in many a far-flung corner of the world, from India to Nigeria. In her seminal book *Britons: Forging the Nation 1707–1837*, Linda Colley goes out of her way to stress the *Britishness* of the British Empire:

> The English and the foreign are still all too inclined today to refer to the island of Great Britain as 'England'. But at no time have they ever customarily referred to an *English* empire. While it existed, as in retrospect, the empire has always been emphatically British. In terms of self-respect, then, as well as for the profits it could bestow, imperialism served as Scotland's opportunity.[6]

As Colley also makes clear, this British Empire was to be a Protestant enterprise, defining itself through its opposition to what it saw as the backwardness and superstition of Catholicism, and through its opposition to what it saw as the tyrannical nature of the Catholic powers of Europe: this was to be an Empire of Progress and Liberty.[7]

What, then, did the Union and involvement in the British Imperial project mean for

Scotland? For one thing, the Union allowed Scotland (if one may so express it) to get its snout in the trough of European Imperial expansion, in spite of the Darien disaster. Because of Darien, Scotland did not achieve this rewarding situation as an independent player like Belgium or Portugal. Instead, it had to settle for a significant (albeit distinctly junior) partnership in a British Empire in which the centre of real power lay in England, in the Imperial capital, London. Substantial rewards were nevertheless available for Scotland in its role as the smaller and poorer junior partner in the British Imperial project. In *Britons*, Linda Colley writes that 'burrowing into the very heart of the *civilian* establishment in London was rarely possible for Scots before 1780', but she goes on to argue that, for 'Scots from a wide variety of social backgrounds', post-Union Imperial Britain offered 'two arenas in which life was still sufficiently hard or uncertain to repel the more pampered and overbearing English patricians, and opportunities were consequently much more open'. These arenas were 'the less fashionable regiments of Britain's army, and the coal-face of its empire'. Colley continues:

> Ever since the Union, the British army had been one of the few departments of the state wide open to Scottish ambition. Perhaps one in four regimental officers in the mid-eighteenth century was a Scot. Like their English, Welsh and Irish counterparts, these men needed money and contacts to get to the very top of their profession. But if they possessed these attributes, as well as proven loyalty [i.e. loyalty to the Hanoverian Protestant succession], there were no barriers to what they might achieve.

With regard to the coal-face of Empire, Colley writes:

> More than a quarter of the East India Company's army officers were Scotsmen; so, by mid-century, were a good proportion of its civilian officers in Madras and Bengal—the Scottish bankers and stockholders who had a strong grip on the Company made sure of that. [...] In the decade after 1775, some 47 per cent of the 249 men appointed to serve as writers in Bengal were Scots; and so were 60 per cent of the 371 men allowed to reside in Bengal as free merchants.[8]

Large numbers of Scots eagerly grasped the splendid opportunities offered by 'the less fashionable regiments of Britain's army, and the coal-face of its Empire'. Nevertheless, the Imperial centre of gravity remained firmly in England. In the British Imperial project, the Scottish tail was never going to be allowed to wag the English dog, and, as a result, Scots who wished to seize the opportunities offered by the British Empire had to learn how to operate acceptably and successfully within Britain's Imperial power structures. This learning process necessarily involved them in an adjustment to English cultural and linguistic norms, and in a consequent dilution of their own Scottish cultural identity. Clearly, this placed post-Union Scots in a dilemma. Was dilution of one's cultural identity a price worth paying in order to gain access to the rewards of Empire? Some Scots embraced the new Britishness with enthusiasm, while others (less willing, perhaps, to pay the full price for getting their snouts into the Imperial trough) actively sought to sustain and revive Scotland's old indigenous pre-British ways in the face of pressure to adjust to English cultural and linguistic norms. At the end of the day, however, most Scots of the Imperial era were doubtless motivated both by a desire to gain access to the material rewards of Empire, and by a desire to preserve Scotland's cultural identity—in spite of the fact that these desires tended to pull in opposite directions. In the resulting crisis of identity, the need to adjust to the new British norms was likely to be most keenly felt by members of the Scottish elite who were closest to the British levers of Imperial power and wealth. Equally, the impulse to retain and sustain Scottish identity was likely to come most naturally to the poor and the dispossessed of subaltern Scotland, that is to say to those with little direct access to the material rewards of Empire. This complex and problematic situation might perhaps be summed up by saying that Scotland, as junior partner in the British Imperial project, took a coloniser's role within Britain's external Empire, but shared with Ireland and Wales the experience of being colonised within a process Katie Trumpener has described as 'British internal colonialism'.[9]

The post-Union and post-Culloden Scottish elite adjusted to the demands of the British Imperial era in ways that are noticeably similar to Guha's picture of the Indian elite during the British raj. In Scotland as in India the indigenous elements of the Imperial elite included 'the biggest feudal magnates, the most important representatives of the industrial and mercantile bourgeoisie and native recruits to the uppermost levels of the bureaucracy'. Other parallels can be drawn. For example, in Scotland as in India many of the most highly-placed indigenous members of the elite aspired to send their children to the great English public schools and universities, where the patterns of behaviour of the English gentry could be acquired. Likewise, in India and Scotland alike, a mastery of the English language was essential for those who aspired to a secure and rewarding place within the Imperial elite. Thus children educated within Scotland during the Imperial period were forcefully encouraged during the educational process to reject Scots and Gaelic, the indigenous languages of Scotland, in favour of 'the King's English', the standard language through which the business of Empire was carried on. This process of linguistic re-education was necessary to equip talented Scots to operate efficiently within the Empire's world-wide structures. Scots, the language of Lowland Scotland, was sufficiently close to English to allow mutual comprehension, but only with some difficulty on both sides, and with real possibilities of failures of communication. Gaelic, the language of Highland Scotland, presented a still greater problem, being as impenetrable to a monoglot English-speaker as one of the indigenous languages of India. Clearly, monoglot Gaelic-speakers were ill equipped to make a contribution to the smooth running of the Imperial machine, and Highlanders who aspired to a rewarding place within the Imperial power structures had perforce to master the English language. A difficult and unrewarding future lay in store for Highlanders unwilling or unable to make this and other necessary cultural adjustments to the demands of the post-Union British Imperial state.

Highlanders, Empire, and *Waverley*

Collisions between Highlanders and the British Imperial state loom large in one of the nineteenth century's most powerfully influential stories, Sir Walter Scott's *Waverley* (1814). In this novel Edward Waverley is a young English cavalry officer in the army of the Hanoverian British government, who happens to journey north into Highland Scotland in 1745 just as Prince Charles's rising is about to begin. Introduced to the Prince by his Highland host, the complex, heroic, but deeply flawed Jacobite plotter Fergus Mac-Ivor, Edward is enthused by the romance of his situation, and he is persuaded to change sides and join the Prince's insurgent army. However, the wavering Waverley in due course extricates himself from his Jacobite commitment, in time to change sides again before Culloden. This allows him to make his peace with the Hanoverian British government, and after Culloden he goes on to marry a sweet and docile bride from an aristocratic Scottish Jacobite family. The Union between England and Scotland having thus been happily re-enacted on a domestic level, Scott's novel concludes when Edward and his Scottish Rose enter a fruitful future under the benign auspices of an enlightened British Imperial state. *Waverley* can thus be seen as an endorsement, by an author writing from within the ranks of the Scottish elite, of the British constitutional status quo of the 1810s, the period of the novel's publication.

It is well worth remembering that *Waverley* was published in July 1814, less than a year before the Battle of Waterloo (June 1815). Waterloo was the final and decisive battle of the Napoleonic Wars, that long and titanic struggle between Imperial Britain and post-Revolutionary Imperial France. Given the acute importance of questions of Imperial power in 1814, it is not particularly surprising that *Waverley* is much concerned with Scotland's place within the British Imperial state. Indeed, Scott's novel actively seeks not only to endorse, but also to enhance, Scotland's place within that state. This emerges strongly in *Waverley*'s presentation of Evan Dhu (Gaelic for 'Black-haired Evan') Maccombich, a Highlander who is a loyal follower of his clan chieftain Fergus Mac-Ivor. Fergus is known to his followers as Vich Ian Vhor, that is to say 'the son of John the Great', John the Great being the heroic founder of the clan. Towards the end of Scott's novel the Jacobite adventure has come to grief at Culloden, and Fergus and Evan Dhu are on trial for treason at the English city of Carlisle, watched by their former comrade-in-arms Edward Waverley. After Fergus has duly been condemned to death, Evan Dhu's attention is focused on his Chief:

Evan Maccombich looked at him with great earnestness, and, rising up, seemed anxious to speak, but the confusion of the court, and the perplexity arising from thinking in a language different from that in which he was to express himself, kept him silent. There was a murmur of compassion among the spectators, from the idea that the poor fellow intended to plead the influence of his superior as an excuse for his crime. The judge commanded silence, and encouraged Evan to proceed.

"I was only ganging to say, my lord," said Evan, in what he meant to be an insinuating manner, "that if your excellent honour, and the honourable court, would let Vich Ian Vhor go free just this once, and let him gae back to France, and no to trouble King George's government again, that ony six o' the very best of his clan will be willing to be justified in his stead; and if you'll just let me gae down to Glennaquoich, I'll fetch them up to ye mysell, to head or hang, and you may begin wi' me the very first man."

Notwithstanding the solemnity of the occasion, a sort of laugh was heard in the court at the extraordinary nature of the proposal. The judge checked this indecency, and Evan, looking sternly around, when the murmur abated, "If the Saxon gentlemen are laughing," he said, "because a poor man, such as me, thinks my life, or the life of six of my degree, is worth that of Vich Ian Vhor, it's like enough they may be very right; but if they laugh because they think I would not keep my word, and come back to redeem him, I can tell them they ken neither the heart of a Hielandman, nor the honour of a gentleman."

There was no farther inclination to laugh among the audience, and a dead silence ensued.[10]

The people in the crowded court laugh at someone who is, in their eyes, a comic subaltern buffoon from a barbarous and outlandish region, a man who is barely able to speak intelligibly, and who seems to be exhibiting a particularly transparent kind of low cunning. It is easy to imagine an Imperial court in Africa or India in which an accused subaltern 'native' might be perceived in a similar way. Very properly, however, the judge in *Waverley* checks the 'indecency' of the laughter in court. Clearly, Scott's narrative is challenging reductive stereotypes about barbarous Highland Scotchmen by exhibiting a Highlander who is fully worthy of respect, in spite of the indecent laughter of the spectators at his trial. Nevertheless, Black-haired Evan and the Son of John the Great have undoubtedly been in armed rebellion against the British Imperial state. They have been brought before the court for this 'crime', and have been found guilty. The Judge therefore pronounces 'upon both prisoners the sentence of the law of high treason, with all its horrible accompaniments'. But he then attempts to offer Evan a way out:

"For you, poor ignorant man," continued the judge, "who, following the ideas in which you have been educated, have this day given us a striking example how the loyalty due to the king and state alone, are, from your unhappy ideas of clanship, trans-

ferred to some ambitious individual, who ends by making you the tool of his crimes—
for you, I say, I feel so much compassion, that if you can make up your mind to petition for grace, I will endeavour to procure it for you—otherwise—"

"Grace me no grace," said Evan; "since you are to shed Vich Ian Vhor's blood, the
only favour I would accept from you, is to bid them loose my hands and gie me my
claymore, and bide you just a minute sitting where you are."

"Remove the prisoners," said the judge; "his blood be upon his own head."[11]

Manifestly, Scott's narrative values Evan Dhu's fierce loyalty to his chieftain. However, the Judge's comments and commands also make it clear that Evan's loyalty to clan
and chieftain is ultimately misplaced: such loyalty is due only to 'the king and state'. All
this suggests that Highlanders like Evan Dhu are capable of becoming valuable servants of the [Hanoverian] king and the [Imperial] state, once they have been re-
educated and once they have learned to re-direct their striking loyalty into the proper
channels. Evan Dhu himself is too bound up in the old ways to make the necessary
adjustment, however, and as a result he duly suffers 'the sentence of the law of high
treason, with all its horrible accompaniments'. Nevertheless, the first readers of
Waverley in 1814 would be well aware that, during the seven decades between Culloden
and the publication of Scott's novel, Highland Scotland had in fact seen a transfer of
loyalty of the kind desired by the novel's Judge. Highland regiments had been successfully recruited to serve in the British army, and these regiments had fought for Britain
with great valour and distinction during the Napoleonic Wars. Indeed, their value to
the British cause was soon to be further confirmed at Waterloo. The trial scene in
Waverley thus serves not only to assert that Highlanders are worthy of respect; it also
serves as a reminder that their indigenous traditions and culture can, with proper re-
focusing, be directed with potent effect to the service of 'the king and state'. In making
these points with great emotional force, Scott's narrative is actively helping to generate
and to sustain English acceptance of an Imperial British identity that is not exclusively
English. In this new and complex British identity, Scott hopes, the Scottish Highlander
will be permitted to occupy an honourable and honoured place, and will no longer be
subjected to the 'indecency' of a ridicule based on cultural incomprehension. And
Scott's hopes were to bear fruit. *Waverley* made a deeply influential contribution to the
early stages of a process that has produced (among many other things) the British royal
family's continuing love affair with Highland Scotland—a love affair symbolised by
Queen Victoria's Highland residence at Balmoral.

It is also worth remembering, however, that the Napoleonic Wars had their origins
in the French Revolution, and that the British elite of the 1810s was deeply worried
about the possibility of subaltern revolutionary activity in Britain: there were lively fears
of a radical enemy within, as well as fears of an external French enemy. When the trial
scene in *Waverley* is seen in this context, one cannot but feel that Scott's narrative is

offering Evan Dhu's notable loyalty as an admirable example of how subaltern people ought to behave towards their natural leaders in the elite. Evan, after all, is not only prepared to give up his life for his chief, but he is also properly humble. He says: 'If the Saxon gentlemen are laughing […] because a poor man, such as me, thinks my life, or the life of six of my degree, is worth that of Vich Ian Vhor, it's like enough they may be very right'. To what extent does Scott's narrative here offer a credible picture of how a subaltern Highlander would actually have felt and spoken in the dire circumstances in which so many of them found themselves in 1746, after Culloden? Does Scott's narrative show what someone like Evan Dhu would really have felt and said? Or does it show what Scott (as a member of the British Imperial state's Scottish elite) would like to believe that 'a poor man' like Evan Dhu would have felt and said? In short, can the subaltern speak within a narrative such as *Waverley*? Could it be that, when Evan Dhu speaks at his trial at Carlisle, what we are hearing is not an authentic subaltern voice but the voice of an elite ventriloquist?

In spite of such lurking questions, during the nineteenth century Scottish Highland soldiers were no longer generally regarded as backward savages, but came to be seen as heroes of the British Empire and as symbols of Britain's Imperial power—and this change came about in part because perceptions had been changed by *Waverley* and other Scott narratives. The Waverley Novels could be, and were, interpreted and appropriated in all sorts of ways for all sorts of political positions, but one of the crucial aspects of their political potency was their symbolic legacy in the master-narrative of British Empire. When one thinks of Victoria (Queen and Empress) at Balmoral, or of her kilted and bagpipe-playing Highland soldiers sustaining the British raj in India, Scott's legacy is powerfully present in the background.

Nevertheless, this Scott-inspired strand is not the whole story of bagpipes and tartan during the Imperial period. Another aspect of the story can be traced in Fiona Stafford's account of the 'scenes of appalling violence' through which, in the period after Culloden, the British state sought to impose 'systematic cultural destruction' on Highland Scotland.[12] Here Stafford is focusing on a process described as follows by the historian Michael Lynch:

> Cumberland's savage orders to harry, burn and kill men, women and children alike in a campaign of mass-reprisal after Culloden was unusual in eighteenth-century warfare but it was no more than a repeat performance of the final Elizabethan conquest of Ireland after 1601, when (as here) the bloodletting came after forty years of frustration and failure in dealing with a Celtic people. It was one more act in the long drama of the consolidation of an English Empire.[13]

Stafford's account describes how, after the initial post-Culloden blood-letting, 'a series of measures were implemented to crush the distinctive Highland way of life'. These measures involved attempts to replace the use of Gaelic with English, and in addition 'the tartan plaid was banned, and no Highlander allowed to carry arms or play the bag-pipes'.[14] All this bore heavily on the subaltern population, and provoked an outpour-ing of vigorous and sparky Gaelic poetry composed by sometimes illiterate subaltern poets for the subaltern audience of the ceilidh-house. One thinks, for example, of Iain Mhic Fhearchair's 'Oran Mu 'n Eideadh Ghaidhealach' ('Song to the Highland Dress'), and Rob Donn MacAoidh's splendidly outrageous 'Briogais MhicRuaridh' ('MacRory's Trousers'), both of which were composed during the post-Culloden period when it was illegal to wear Highland dress.[15]

These poems give voice to subaltern Scotland's experience of British Imperial power in one of the sets of circumstances in which that experience was interestingly and illu-minatingly different from the experience of the Scottish elite. Another text that gives voice to the experiences and concerns of subaltern Scotland is *The Three Perils of Woman* (1823), a novel through which James Hogg ('The Ettrick Shepherd') entered into con-scious dialogue and debate with the baronet Sir Walter Scott. In this outrageously sub-versive novel, Hogg eloquently questions certain silences in the stories told by Scott in narratives such as *Waverley*, silences about the sufferings of subaltern Highland Scot-land not only in Cumberland's post-Culloden atrocities, but also in the notorious Sutherland Clearances of the 1810s.[16] The present book will argue that, in texts such as *The Three Perils of Woman*, Hogg sought out the role of Robert Burns's successor as spokesman for subaltern Scotland. This is not to suggest that working-class writers like Burns (the 'ploughman-poet') and Hogg (the shepherd-novelist) were free from complicity in the Imperial project. On the contrary, *Scottish Fiction and the British Empire* will explore the implications of the fact that Burns was preparing to go to Jamaica to become 'a driver of negroes' when the success of the Kilmarnock edition of his poems enabled him to stay in Scotland. Likewise, it will explore the implications of Hogg's participation in elite imperialist cultural formations such as *Blackwood's Edinburgh Maga-zine*. However, this book will also argue that Burns, Hogg, and later writers such as Lewis Grassic Gibbon contrived to find creative and ground-breaking ways in which to allow the subaltern voice to be heard—and thus to question some of the attitudes and assumptions that sustained the master-narrative of the British Empire.

In *Scottish Fiction and the British Empire* the main focus will be on the novel, although poetry and other genres will also be considered from time to time. After *Waverley* the novel established itself as the pre-eminent literary genre of the Britain of the Imperial era, and the novels of Walter Scott, John Buchan, and other Scottish novelists of the nineteenth and twentieth centuries did much to shape and sustain the Imperial master-narrative. However, *Scottish Fiction and the British Empire* will suggest that there is a con-tinuing vitality in the alternative Hogg / Gibbon Scottish tradition of fiction, a tradi-tion that sets out to articulate the experiences and insights of non-elite people. This vitality, it will be argued, continues to manifest itself not only in the writings of post-

Imperial Scottish authors like Jackie Kay and James Kelman, but also in the fictions of post-Imperial writers of the Scottish Diaspora such as Alistair MacLeod and Alice Munro.

Notes

1 Ranajit Guha's 'On Some Aspects of the Historiography of Colonial India' was first published in 1982 in the first volume of *Subaltern Studies*. It is quoted here from *Selected Subaltern Studies*, ed. by Ranajit Guha and Gayatri Chakravorty Spivak (New York: Oxford University Press, 1988), pp. 37–44 (p. 44).

2 Edward Said, *Culture and Imperialism* (London: Chatto & Windus, 1993), p. xiii.

3 T. M. Devine, *The Scottish Nation 1700–2000* (London: Allen Lane, 1999), pp. 5–6.

4 For lucid accounts of the 1707 Union, see Devine, *The Scottish Nation*, pp. 3–30, and Michael Lynch, *Scotland: A New History* (London: Pimlico, 1992), pp. 310–26.

5 T. C. Smout, *A History of the Scottish People 1560–1830* (London: Fontana, 1972), p. 195.

6 Linda Colley, *Britons: Forging the Nation 1707–1837* (London: Vintage, 1996), pp. 136–37.

7 See Colley's discussion in *Britons*, pp. 10–58.

8 Colley, *Britons*, pp. 132–34.

9 Katie Trumpener, *Bardic Nationalism: The Romantic Novel and the British Empire* (Princeton: Princeton University Press, 1997), p. xiii.

10 Scott, *Waverley; or, 'Tis Sixty Years Since*, ed. by Claire Lamont (Oxford: Clarendon Press, 1981), p. 320.

11 *Waverley*, ed. Lamont, pp. 320–21.

12 James Macpherson, *The Poems of Ossian and Related Works*, ed. by Howard Gaskell with an Introduction by Fiona Stafford (Edinburgh: Edinburgh University Press, 1996), pp. ix–x.

13 Michael Lynch, *Scotland: A New History* (London: Pimlico, 1992), pp. 338–39.

14 *The Poems of Ossian*, ed. Gaskell, pp. ix–x.

15 For these poems (with English translations), see *The Poetry of Scotland: Gaelic, Scots and English 1380–1980*, ed. by Roderick Watson (Edinburgh: Edinburgh University Press, 1995), pp. 278–85 and 295–97. For the remarkable flowering of Gaelic poetry in eighteenth-century Scotland, see also *Gaelic Poetry in the Eighteenth Century: A Bilingual Anthology*, ed. by Derick S. Thomson (Aberdeen: ASLS, 1993), and *An Lasair: Anthology of 18th Century Scottish Gaelic Verse*, ed. by Ronald Black (Edinburgh: Birlinn, 2001).

16 For a fuller discussion see the 'Historical and Geographical Note' in the paperback edition of Hogg, *The Three Perils of Woman*, ed. by Antony Hasler and Douglas S. Mack (Edinburgh: Edinburgh University Press, 2002).

TWO

Opening the Boarded Window

Tha bùird is tàirnean air an uinneig
troimh 'm faca mi an Aird an Iar

[*The window is nailed and boarded
through which I saw the West*]

Sorley MacLean, 'Hallaig'

Hogg and Wilson

With the colonised Indian subaltern in mind, Ania Loomba has given a concise and lucid indication of the issues raised by the question 'Can the subaltern speak?':

> To what extent did colonial power succeed in silencing the colonised? When we emphasise the destructive power of colonialism, do we necessarily position colonised people as victims, incapable of answering back? On the other hand, if we suggest that the colonial subjects can 'speak' and question colonial authority, are we romanticising such resistant subjects and underplaying colonial violence? In what voices do the colonised speak—their own, or in accents borrowed from their masters? Is the project of recovering the 'subaltern' best served by locating her separateness from dominant culture, or by highlighting the extent to which she moulded even those processes and cultures which subjected her? And finally, can the voice of the subaltern be represented by the intellectual?[1]

In approaching these questions in a Scottish context, it will be useful to consider rival attempts by two of Sir Walter Scott's contemporaries, John Wilson and James Hogg, to represent the voice of subaltern Scotland through their competing portrayals of Hogg's public persona, 'The Ettrick Shepherd'. Many of the complex elite / subaltern exchanges and tensions of early-nineteenth-century Scotland surface in the edgy, strained, but potent friendship of Wilson and Hogg. As a result, this friendship has generated a fair amount of discussion recently, as has its notable fictionalised echo, the relationship between 'Christopher North' (representing Wilson) and 'The Ettrick Shepherd' (representing Hogg) in the well-known *Noctes Ambrosianae* dialogues written by Wilson and others for *Blackwood's Edinburgh Magazine* in the 1820s and 1830s.[2] The continuing resonance of the 'Shepherd' of the *Noctes* seems to derive, at least in part, from the fact that Hogg was seen by Wilson (and by other contemporaries such as Scott) as someone who represented and embodied subaltern Scotland. Wilson himself, on the other hand, was very much a product of the Scottish elite.

John Wilson (1785–1854) grew up in the west of Scotland. His mother was a woman of aristocratic pretensions, acutely conscious of her descent (by the female line) from one of the major figures of seventeenth-century Scotland, the great Marquis of Montrose. Wilson's father was a wealthy gauze manufacturer in Paisley, and it is therefore clear that (in Guha's terms, discussed in the Introduction), Wilson's roots lay with the elite: partly with 'the biggest feudal magnates' of Scotland, and partly with that country's 'most important representatives of the industrial and mercantile bourgeoisie'. After concluding his studies at the University of Glasgow, the young Wilson went on to complete his education at the University of Oxford. In following this course, he confirmed that the indigenous Scottish elite of the British Imperial era (like the indigenous Indian elite of that period) had a lively sense of the value of an education at the top-ranking educational institutions of England.

Returning to Scotland after his time at Oxford, Wilson went on to become a poet and a novelist, beginning to establish his reputation in 1812 when his modestly successful book-length narrative poem *The Isle of Palms* was published in Edinburgh by John Ballantyne. Narrative verse romances had been the dominant British literary genre during the Napoleonic Wars. However, after the publication of *Waverley* (1814) and the decisive battle of Waterloo (1815) the novel established itself as the dominant postwar genre, and in due course the author of *The Isle of Palms* began to produce works of elegant and sentimental prose fiction. He also became one of the moving spirits behind the widely-read *Blackwood's Edinburgh Magazine* (founded in 1817), and he came to act in some ways as the magazine's Editor (although not officially so named). In 1820 Wilson's influential position in Scotland's intellectual and social elite was confirmed when he was elected Professor of Moral Philosophy in the University of Edinburgh.[3]

Like Wilson, James Hogg (1770–1835) was a frequent contributor to *Blackwood's*, but the backgrounds of the two men were very different. Hogg's parents were both descended from shepherding families in the remote sheep-farming district of Ettrick Forest in the Scottish Borders. His mother's family were noted carriers of Ettrick's rich oral tradition of ballads and stories, and at the time of his birth in 1770 his father (a former shepherd) was tenant of a modest Ettrick sheep farm. The young James began to attend the local parish school around 1775, but his formal education ceased after a few months when his father became bankrupt, and for the remainder of his childhood Hogg had to earn his keep by working on various farms in the district, often living in conditions of real hardship and deprivation. This emerges clearly enough in his 'Memoir of the Author's Life', when he writes about his childhood experiences as follows:

> From some of my masters I received very hard usage; in particular, while with one shepherd, I was often nearly exhausted by hunger and fatigue. […] Every little pittance that I earned of wages, was carried directly to my parents, who supplied me with what cloaths I had. These were often scarcely worthy of the appellation; in particular, I remember of being exceedingly scarce of shirts. Time after time I had but two; which grew often so bad, that I was obliged to quit wearing them altogether; for, when I put them on, they hung down in long tatters as far as my heels. At these times I certainly made a very grotesque figure; for, on quitting the shirt, I could never induce my breeches to keep up to their proper sphere. When fourteen years of age, I saved five shillings of my wages, with which I bought an old violin. This occupied all my leisure hours, and hath been my favourite amusement ever since. I had commonly no spare time from labour during the day; but, when I was not over fatigued, I generally spent an hour or two every night in rubbing over my favourite old Scottish tunes;—my bed being always in stables and cow-houses, I disturbed nobody but myself.[4]

This musical young Scottish sansculotte eventually got access to books in his late teens when working as a shepherd in Ettrick Forest, and from that point onwards he read voraciously. Throughout his twenties (that is to say, during the 1790s, the decade that followed the French Revolution) Hogg worked as a shepherd in congenial and intelligent company at the farm of Blackhouse in Ettrick Forest, where he had extensive access to books. Around this time he began to write poems which circulated within the Ettrick community, gaining him the local nickname 'Jamie the Poeter'. In September 1802 Hogg had a meeting with Walter Scott (with whom he had previously corresponded),[5] when Scott was in Ettrick collecting traditional ballads for the third volume of *Minstrelsy of the Scottish Border*. This meeting led to a friendship between the two men which, although sometimes turbulent, nevertheless lasted until Scott's death thirty years later.

Following his meeting with Scott in September 1802, Hogg began (with Scott's help) to make serious attempts to establish himself both as an author and as a tenant-farmer. He had some success as an author with a book of poems called *The Mountain Bard* (1807), and with 'a practical treatise on the diseases of sheep' called *The Shepherd's Guide* (also 1807). These two very different books helped to provide the capital for sheep-farming projects in Dumfriesshire, but Hogg's farming ventures were unsuccessful and in the autumn of 1809 he absconded, leaving debts and illegitimate children behind him. His native community regarded the failed farmer as being in disgrace, and he was unable to find employment in Ettrick as a shepherd. As a result, this product of subaltern Scotland moved to Edinburgh in 1810 in a brave if not entirely promising attempt to earn his living as a professional writer. Fame and recognition did arrive in 1813, however, when his long poem *The Queen's Wake* was published. The success of this poem led to his friendship with Wilson, who had started to establish his own reputation in the previous year with *The Isle of Palms*.[6] Later in the 1810s both Hogg and Wilson were to become significant figures in the group of writers associated with *Blackwood's Edinburgh Magazine*, and this connection (with interruptions caused by quarrels) continued into the 1830s.

Famously, the number of *Blackwood's* for October 1823 contains a ferociously unfavourable review by Wilson of Hogg's *The Three Perils of Woman*, which had been published in August that year. A cornucopia of pig puns on Hogg's name, this review seems to draw energy from the elite / subaltern tensions of the years that followed the Peterloo Massacre of 1819. At Peterloo, a Radical political meeting in Manchester was violently dispersed by cavalry in a brutal over-reaction that can be seen as a manifestation of the elite's deeply-rooted fears about the perceived threat of violent Jacobin revolution in England. Similar tensions made themselves manifest in Scotland in the 'Radical War' of 1820,[7] and these elite / subaltern tensions form one part of the context in which Wilson's 1823 review presents Hogg as a talented but barely housetrained subaltern writer. For Wilson in this review, Hogg's occasional flashes of highsouled and naïve genius co-exist with the deplorably low-souled boorishness of an uncultivated peasant. Here is an extract:

> It is indeed this rare union of high imagination with homely truth that constitutes the peculiar character of his writing. In one page, we listen to the song of the nightingale, and in another, to the grunt of the boar. Now the wood is vocal with the feathered choir; and then the sty bubbles and squeaks with a farm-sow, and a litter of nineteen pigwiggins. [...] Now enters bonny Kilmenie, or Mary Lee, preparing to flee into Fairyland, or beat up the quarters of the Man in the Moon; and then, lo and behold, some huggered, red-armed, horny-fisted, glaur-nailed Girrzy, removing on the day before term, from the Hen-coop to the sign of the Kilt, on an advance of six shillings on the half-year's wage. Never was there such a bothering repast set down before the reading public by any other caterer. [...] If you suffer your plate for a single moment to escape from the shelter of your own bosom, a hundred to one but you see one of the Tweeddale Yeomanry licking it up with a tongue half a yard long, and as rough as a bison's.[8]

A complex elite / subaltern interaction is at work here. After quoting the above extract in his seminal article 'Hogg's Body', Ian Duncan comments as follows:

The reviewer's explosion of satirical indignation goes well beyond the standard sneer at Hogg's peasant origins. For Wilson is fascinated by what he derides. [...] The riotous hotchpotch of style and substance, troped as Hogg's intractable *hoggishness*, energises Wilson's own writing.

The other striking feature of Wilson's writing is its insistent, obsessive, devolution to the physical—to gross, if not monstrous, bodily presences. Again, the red-armed, horny-fisted Girzzy and the member of the Tweeddale Yeomanry, 'with a tongue half a yard long, and as rough as a bison's', are Wilson's memorable inventions, not Hogg's.[9]

What, then, is it about Hogg that energises Wilson's writing? And what drives Wilson's obsessive concern with gross bodily presences? Duncan goes on to quote a passage from Wilson's review in which Hogg himself emerges as a monstrous bodily presence:

What with his genius, and what with his buck-teeth; what with his fiddle, and what with his love-locks lolling over his shoulders as he 'gaed up the Kirk,' tastily tied with a blue ribbon; what with his running for prize-hats up the old avenue of Traquhair, 'with his hurdies like twa distant hills,' to the distancing of all competitors; and what with his listering of fish and grewing of mawkins, a gentler and more irresistible shepherd was not to be found from Moffat to Mellerstain.[10]

Duncan comments:

The tone of this writing is curiously hard to place. It wants to be contemptuous, certainly, and is not lacking in a bullying sort of affection; it is also definitely excited, exhilarated, by the vision of the 'gentle and irresistible shepherd' with his shameless pretensions to being minstrel, sportsman and lover. Wilson's rhetoric mimics an excessive comic outrage at the usurpation of pastoral conventions by a real shepherd, but it expresses something else besides: beyond the burlesque roar, a strange overtone of yearning. (A yearning, I shall argue presently, for a lost self of Wilson's own.) The desire to crush Hogg, to put him down, is so exaggerated as to have the opposite effect, of celebrating him, building him up, into a mythic figure—the Comus of Scottish letters. This monstrous shepherd presides over the imaginary farmyard of Wilson's review, heaving and teeming with anarchic life, like some kind of pansexual nature-spirit, whose avatars include the bison-tongued yeoman and the sow with her 'litter of nineteen pigwiggins'.[11]

This yearning 'for a lost self of Wilson's own' also emerges in the *Noctes Ambrosianae* in Christopher North's frequent hints that he too has had an athletic youth, both sporting and sexual. But such exploits are long over for the now-lame North.

As they attempted to adjust to post-Union realities, members of the Scottish elite (feeling themselves to be awkward and provincial) tried to emulate the enviable urbanity and elegance of their English counterparts. As part of this process, they tried to free their speech and writing of what they called 'Scotticisms', and they also began to think of themselves as inhabitants, not of 'Scotland', but of 'North Britain'. Such aspirations could co-exist with a certain regret and sense of loss over one's increasing detachment from the gross and earthy but vigorous culture of subaltern Scotland, a culture that came to be personified by Hogg in his role as the 'Ettrick Shepherd'. This was the cultural context in which Wilson's sentimental fiction aspired to high-souled refinement and rejected boorish, Hoggish coarseness in a process that can be interpreted (as Ian Duncan aptly puts it) as a kind of

> high-minded castration—a literary equivalent of the disciplinary self-mutilation practised by certain cults and sects. No wonder, after such drastic recourse, that tears flow so readily. [12]

For Ian Duncan, Wilson in his sentimental fiction consciously rejects an atavistic energy and coarseness to which he is nevertheless deeply attracted, an energy, indeed, which had driven his own youthful exploits as sexual athlete and pugilist. In the *Noctes Ambrosianae* these brutish energies are projected by the mature Wilson onto the figure of the Ettrick Shepherd, that coarse and uncultivated man of the people. When this happens Wilson's writing is distinctly energised, in his *Blackwood's* review of *The Three Perils of Woman* as well as in the *Noctes*.

This begins to suggest that the elite / subaltern distinction does not operate as a neat and uncomplicated binary opposition in the circumstances of early-nineteenth-century Scotland. Furthermore, if Wilson's elite writing could on occasion be energised by contact with Hogg's Ettrick subaltern world, it can also be argued that Hogg's writing was energised by his contact with the world of the Edinburgh elite, the world of Wilson and Scott. In one of the most valuable books on Hogg so far published, Douglas Gifford makes a celebrated distinction between what he calls 'Ettrick Hogg' and 'Edinburgh Hogg'.[13] I would like to focus on a similar but not identical distinction, between 'Hogg's Ettrick world' and 'Hogg's Edinburgh world'. In order to open this matter out, it will be useful to quote from that wonderful book, David Daiches's *Two Worlds: An Edinburgh Jewish Childhood*. One of Daiches's two worlds was the Scotland he experienced as an Edinburgh schoolboy, and later as a student at Edinburgh University. The other was the Jewish culture he experienced through growing up in the home of his father, Dr Salis Daiches, Rabbi of the Edinburgh Hebrew Congregation from 1919 till 1945 and one of the most important figures in the religious life of Scotland during the twentieth century. In *Two Worlds*, David Daiches writes that the competing claims of his two worlds became strongly felt during his years as a university student:

The change which resulted in my life when I left school and entered Edinburgh University was enormous, and had far-reaching consequences. At school I had done my work and gone home, taking no part in sports or other extra-curricular activities. But the University was different. There was a great variety of social and intellectual life outside the lecture room, and it was not mostly confined, as non-academic school activities were, to Friday night and Saturday; I found myself joining societies, writing for the student magazine, making friends among my non-Jewish fellow students. [...] The sense of liberation was intoxicating. I had not realised before how narrow and indeed lonely my life had previously been.[14]

Nevertheless, the pull of the Jewish world remained strong; and Daiches writes of returning one winter evening from a happy and lively meeting of a university society to attend a Friday night service at the synagogue.

There was only a handful of people, old men mostly, at the service, and as the slow and melancholy notes of the concluding hymn *Yigdal* rose thinly up to the roof, I thought of the centuries during which this hymn had been sung, of long dead Jewish congregations in Provence, the Rhineland and Poland, who had held so steadfastly to their Jewish way of life and passed their heritage unchanged on to their children. I thought of the long roll of Jewish martyrs, those who had given their lives for 'the sanctification of the Name'. I thought of my own ancestors, of my grandfather and of *his* father, Aryeh Zvi Daiches, whose picture I had seen on the wall of my grandfather's study, a noble looking man in a fur-trimmed cap, one of the innumerable Jewish scholars and teachers from whom I was descended.[15]

Hogg, like Daiches, put down roots that drew nourishment from two very different worlds. In Hogg's case, one of these worlds was the post-Enlightenment Edinburgh of the heyday of Sir Walter Scott, the Edinburgh of *The Edinburgh Review* and of *Blackwood's Edinburgh Magazine*. This elite Edinburgh world can fairly be described as one of the major centres of cultural production in early-nineteenth-century Europe, and it liked to claim for itself the title of 'the Athens of the North'. Devoutly wishing to have this claim taken seriously in the British Imperial capital, members of Edinburgh's intellectual and social elite anxiously sought to divest themselves of any traits that would appear narrow, coarse, or provincial to London eyes, in a process of 'high-minded castration', to repeat Ian Duncan's apt phrase. This Edinburgh—brilliant although somewhat lacking in self-confidence—provided the mature Hogg with the core of his audience, and it was through this world that he got in contact with the institutions that published his writings. Access to this intellectually vibrant world no doubt brought Hogg the same kind of liberating excitement that Edinburgh University provided for the young David Daiches just over a century later. It seems clear that, for Hogg, this elite Edinburgh world came to be embodied and personified by the two men with whom he formed his most significant intellectual friendships: John Wilson and Walter Scott.

In the final analysis, however, Hogg's loyalty to his roots in the subaltern society of Ettrick meant that he could not wholly share the assumptions of the elite Edinburgh intellectual world of Wilson and Scott. Indeed, it can be argued that Hogg's best writing is driven by his need to explore his areas of disagreement with that elite Edinburgh world. The nature of these areas of disagreement can be traced in Hogg's response to Wilson's *Lights and Shadows of Scottish Life* (1822), a collection of sentimental short stories in which the characters tend to shed tears copiously. Wilson's book seeks to generate a similar flow of sentimental tears among its readers, and goes out of its way to celebrate qualities much admired within the Scottish elite: qualities such as refinement, purity, sensibility, and delicacy of feeling. Here as elsewhere this author sets out to remove any hint of distressing provincial coarseness, in an act of 'high-minded castration'. *Lights and Shadows of Scottish Life* also has a strong Tory agenda. Published a couple of years after the Radical War of 1820, Wilson's stories emerge from a period during which highly-charged radical anti-establishment political agitation had deeply alarmed a panicky British elite, in Scotland and England alike. Fears about radical and revolutionary political agitation thus form part of the context in which *Lights and Shadows of Scottish Life* sets out its approving depictions of a strikingly pious and docile Scottish peasantry, who are presented as being affectionately loyal and obedient to their social superiors. Here Wilson tries to represent the Scottish subaltern voice, but he proves to be a deeply unconvincing ventriloquist.

Wilson's book was published by William Blackwood, and on 24 May 1822 Blackwood sent a copy to Hogg's wife Margaret, along with other recently-published books (Galt's *The Provost* and Gillespie's *Sermons*) intended for Hogg himself. Hogg responded as follows on 14 June 1822:

> I think very highly of both the books you have sent me but far most highly of *Lights and Shadows* in which there is a great deal of very powerful effect purity of sentiment and fine writing but with very little of real nature as it exists in the walks of Scottish life The feelings and language of the author are those of Romance Still it is a fine and beautiful work.[16]

This stops well short of being an unequivocal endorsement, and Hogg's next book, *The Three Perils of Woman* (1823), can be read as a riposte to *Lights and Shadows of Scottish Life*. For example, when *The Three Perils of Woman* was published in three volumes by the London publisher Longman in 1823, the final paragraph of the opening Chapter (or 'Circle') asserted:

I like that way of telling a story exceedingly. Just to go always round and round my hero, in the same way as the moon keeps moving round the sun; thus darkening my plot on the one side of him, and enlightening it on the other, thereby displaying both the *lights* and *shadows* of Scottish life. And verily I hold it as an incontrovertible truth, that the moon, descending the western heaven on an evening in autumn, displays these lights and shadows in a much more brilliant and delightful manner, than has ever been done by any of her brain-stricken votaries. There we see nature itself; with those it is nature abominably sophisticated.[17]

Wilson is called to mind here, not only by the reference to 'the *lights* and *shadows* of Scottish life' (the italics are Hogg's), but also by the mention of the moon, because invocations of the moon and descriptions of moonlit scenes are characteristic features of *The Isle of Palms* (1812). For example, the first Canto of Wilson's poem contains extended descriptions of a ship on a moonlit sea. A happy island landfall is expected, but the moon sets and the ship thereafter is wrecked. (There will be only two survivors, a young man and a young woman, left alone together on the Isle of Palms.) The second Canto opens as follows:

> O Heavenly Queen! By Mariners beloved!
> Refulgent Moon! when in the cruel sea
> Down sank yon fair Ship to her coral grave,
> Where didst thou linger then? Sure it behoved
> A Spirit strong and pitiful like thee
> At that dread hour thy worshippers to save.[18]

Hogg included some parodies of Wilson's poetry in *The Poetic Mirror* (1816). One of these is 'Hymn to the Moon', in which Wilson is presented as an absurd votary of the moon whose bombastic flow of overblown rhetoric comes to a disconcertingly abrupt stop when the moon sets: it is rather as if a tap has been turned off. Just before this happens the Wilson-figure of Hogg's parody is addressing both the moon itself and its reflection in a lake:

> Ye both are beautiful—therefore both, hail,
> Now and for ever—first, thou watery Moon,
> And then, thou Moon aërial! haply one,
> But, whether one or two, still beautiful,
> Too beautiful by far not to be view'd,
> Waning or full, without a gush of tears!
>
> Where art thou gone? all of a sudden gone?
> Why hast thou left thy pensive worshipper

Sitting in the darkness on the mossy stump
Of an old oak-tree?—Hark! the owl! the owl!
He is a living clock that tells the hour
To visionary men who walk by nights
Composing poesy! […] [19]

It begins to appear that *The Three Perils of Woman* is driven by Hogg's need to question what he sees as the false and unreal picture of subaltern Scottish life offered in Wilson's writings. Indeed, Hogg's book pointedly suggests that Wilson's sentimental narratives are merely the windy and insubstantial effusions of a 'brain-stricken' votary of the moon. The stories in *Lights and Shadows of Scottish Life*, Hogg asserts, construct a picture that bears little relation to lived and felt experience. By stressing that the real moon looks down on the realities of Scottish life 'in a much more brilliant and delightful manner', *The Three Perils of Woman* suggests that real Scottish life is much more interesting than Wilson's fictional version. Will Hogg's own book offer the real Scottish life that is falsified in Wilson's stories? *The Three Perils of Woman* stops short of making this claim, perhaps recognising that it is itself a fiction, a construction or picture of reality rather than reality itself. Nevertheless, in the '*lights* and *shadows*' passage quoted above, Hogg contrives to imply that his book will offer a picture of Scottish life that *does* connect with lived and felt experience. *The Three Perils of Woman*, that is to say, will try to tell it like it is, will try to present 'nature itself' while demonstrating that Wilson's fictions merely offer 'nature abominably sophisticated'. Hogg's book, in short, sets out to send up the account of 'the *lights* and *shadows* of Scottish life' offered by Wilson's fictions, and sets out to replace that account with something better and truer. Here, Hogg hopes, the real voice of subaltern Scotland will be able to speak, and to be heard.

Aspects of Hogg's subversive response to Wilson can be seen in the opening pages of *The Three Perils of Woman*, in a conversation between the Scots-speaking Border sheep-farmer Daniel Bell and his English-speaking wife. In the post-Union and post-Culloden Scotland of the Imperial era, choice of language was a resonant matter. To choose English was to align oneself with the new British order being embraced by the elite, while to choose Scots (in the Lowlands) or Gaelic (in the Highlands) was to align oneself with the unreconstructed old ways surviving in subaltern Scotland. During the eighteenth century the Lowland county of Ayrshire produced two writers of international repute. One (James Boswell) was a member of the social elite, and the other (Robert Burns) was a subaltern 'peasant-poet'. When Boswell chose to write in English and Burns chose to write much of his poetry in Scots, these choices had a significance that went far beyond mere linguistic preference.

With regard to the conversation between the Bells in Hogg's novel, it quickly becomes clear that Mrs Bell disdains her husband's coarse and hoggish loyalty to the old ways of subaltern Scotland, aspiring instead to a notably frigid version of the modern and cultivated proprieties celebrated by Wilson's fictions. (The Bells' daughter Gatty exemplifies other aspects of Wilsonian values, namely extreme sensibility and delicacy of feeling.) The conversation between Gatty's parents focuses on Daniel's successful sale of a ram:

> "Mr Bell, that's astonishing; did you actually sell a single sheep for fifty pounds?" said the good dame.
>
> "I did that, hinney; but then it was a toop, ye maun recollect, and nae common toop either."
>
> "A toop! What do you mean by a toop?"
>
> "What do I mean by a toop! Heard ever ony body the like o' that? Have ye been a farmer's wife these twa-an'-twenty years, an dinna ken what a toop means? A toop is just a male-sheep, hinney. A toop and a ewe are exactly the same in a hirsel, as a man and a woman are in society."
>
> "Well, Mr Bell, I conceived it so. But might you not as easily denominate the animal a ram, as he is called in Scripture, and then every body would understand you?"
>
> "A ram! a snuff o' tobacco! Na, na, it's an unco ramstamphish name that for sic a bonny dooce-looking animal as Duff."
>
> "At all events, Mr Bell, I conceive it a more proper name than tupe."
>
> "It's no tupe, hinney, nor tup, nor tip, nor ram; nor ony o' thae dirty cuttit words; it's just plain downright toop, the auld Scots word, and the auld Scots way o' saying it."
>
> "Well, my dear, it makes little difference the name; but since it is a fact that you can breed a tupe, as you call it——"
>
> "I never ca'd it sic a name in my life."
>
> "To the value, I say, of fifty pounds, why not keep all your sheep tupes?" (pp. 6–7)

Here the voice of the old subaltern Scotland seems to be alive and well and speaking through Daniel, while Mrs Bell speaks in the accent of one who aspires to membership of the elite. In this linguistic and cultural contest it is clear that Mrs Bell's aspirations to Wilsonian refinement have detached her not only from her linguistic roots, but also from a willingness to understand the realities of sheep-farming. By implication, furthermore, her refusal to understand the roles of a toop and a ewe in a hirsel (*flock*) suggests what subsequent events will confirm: that she is likely to be equally wide of the mark in her understanding of the roles of 'a man and a woman […] in society'. Daniel, on the other hand, exhibits a certain coarse but vigorous contact with reality in his comments about the functions of a 'toop'.

So far, this is a victory for Hogg's coarse old subaltern Ettrick world over the kind of refinement valued by Wilson's fictions. Nevertheless *The Three Perils of Woman* does not set out to paint a romanticised picture of the old sheep-farming world of the Borders. This book's project is to tell it like it is, and a lively sense of the limitations of the pastoral world of Hogg's youth emerges from the words with which the narrator concludes the first volume:

> There is no life so easy as that of a sheep farmer, but there is none so monotonous. No stirring, no animation; but the same routine from day to day, and from year to year; looking at tups; taking a glass of toddy; talking of rents, dogs, and shepherds; buttoning and unbuttoning; lying down in bed, and rising up again, from generation to generation. There is more interest excited by farming seven acres of arable land, sown with various crops of grain, than seventeen hundred of pasture land on both sides of the Border.   (p. 128)

For Hogg the vibrant intellectual life of elite Edinburgh, as personified by his friends Wilson and Scott, represented an escape-route from a subaltern life restricted to the concerns of sheep-farming, a life of 'the same routine from day to day, and from year to year; [...] buttoning and unbuttoning; lying down in bed, and rising up again, from generation to generation'. Nevertheless, as he grew more and more familiar with intellectual Edinburgh, Hogg increasingly wished to question and subvert some of its assumptions, and he also increasingly wished to assert the validity of aspects of the values of his own native community. As a result of these pressures *The Three Perils of Woman* develops into a glorious and outrageous send-up of Wilson's fiction, at the same time as providing Hogg's own alternative (and subversively subaltern) view of 'the *lights* and *shadows* of Scottish life'. Hogg scholars have often expressed outrage at Wilson's review of *The Three Perils of Woman*—and the review is, indeed, pretty outrageous. Nevertheless, one can see why Hogg's book would infuriate Wilson. It is, after all, a devastatingly effective send-up of Wilson's sentimental fiction. For Wilson the case would no doubt be made even worse by Hogg's lowly social origins: the uppity peasant needed to be put firmly in his place, and the *Blackwood's* review of *The Three Perils of Woman* provided a mouth-watering opportunity to do just that.

Hogg and Scott

John Wilson was not the only member of Edinburgh's intellectual elite to receive attention in *The Three Perils of Woman*. In its final volume, Hogg's 'series of domestic Scottish tales' contains a powerful critique of Scott's *Waverley*.[20] Tellingly, this section of Hogg's narrative does not follow *Waverley* in focusing on the Jacobite rising of 1745-46 as experienced by the officer class. Instead, Hogg's focus is on the experiences of people (including, very notably, a servant girl and a blacksmith) who would have been reductively pigeonholed by Scott and Wilson as mere members of 'the lower orders'. *Waverley* had presented the experiences of subaltern Scotland in 1746 in terms of (for example) Evan Dhu's gallant loyalty to his chieftain. *The Three Perils of Woman*, on the other hand, shows the lives of Sally Niven and Peter Gow (the servant girl and the blacksmith) being desolated and torn apart by a brutal civil war driven by the self-serving schemes of two rival elites, Jacobite and Hanoverian. Scott and Hogg write about subaltern suffering and deprivation from different perspectives. Scott's writings frequently observe the poor with an impressive decency and compassion, and he ventriloquises the Scots speech of subaltern Scotland with sympathy, vigour, and energy. When Hogg tries to represent the subaltern voice, however, he does so not as a sympathetic and intelligent elite observer, but as someone who has been there, as someone who has felt the cold and the hunger.

Scott was in many ways the leader and personification of Edinburgh's social and intellectual elite, and he makes a significant personal appearance in the first volume of *The Three Perils of Woman*, as a character in the modern story of the Bell family. This happens shortly after the conversation about 'tupes' quoted above, at a point in the narrative at which Daniel is advising his daughter about how she should speak and behave when she goes to Edinburgh to complete an education designed to equip her to become a member of the elite. Daniel says:

> But mind aye this, my woman,—that good sense is weelfaurd and becoming, in what-ever dialect it be spoken; and ane's mother-tongue suits always the lips of either a bonny lass or an auld carl the best. And mair than that, the braid Scots was never in sic repute sin' the days of Davie Lindsey, thanks to my good friend Wattie Scott,—I may weel ca' him sae, for his father was my father's law-ware, and mony a sound advice he gae him.   (p. 11)

'Davie Lindsey' is Sir David Lindsay (1490–1555) who was a prominent figure at the court of James V, both as court poet and as Lord Lyon, King of Arms. Lindsay's great play *Ane Satyre of the Thrie Estaitis*, written in 'the braid Scots', was and is remembered with affection as a powerful articulation of the grievances and concerns of sixteenth-century subaltern Scotland. Clearly, Daniel sees 'Wattie Scott' as a new 'Davie Lindsey', as another admired and well-connected writer who writes in Scots to give voice to the insights and concerns of the poor.

Daniel goes on to tell Gatty that, when she goes to Edinburgh, she can see Scott 'every day from the gallery of the Parliament-House'. Scott was a lawyer as well as an author, and he did indeed make regular appearances in Edinburgh's Parliament House while performing his professional duties as a Clerk of Session. Gatty, it seems, will recognise him easily: he has 'hair of a pale silver grey, a head like a tower, braid shoul-ders, and long shaggy e'e-brees—the very picture of an auld, gruff Border Baron,—that's Wattie Scott' (p. 11). Daniel continues by saying that he knew Scott as a boy. This claim, although at first sight surprising, is not implausible: during his childhood Scott did indeed spend an extended period in the Borders, having been sent for health reasons to live with his grandfather, a Border sheep-farmer. Scott's imagination was undoubtedly fired by the strand in his ancestry that connected him with one of Scotland's leading aristocratic families (the Scotts of Buccleuch), and he would no doubt have felt comfortable about being perceived as 'the very picture of an auld, gruff Border Baron'. However, Daniel's words also serve as a reminder that Sir Walter also had roots in Hogg's own subaltern world of Border sheep-farming.

Daniel remembers the young Scott as

> a bit hempy callant, wi' bare legs, and the breeks a' torn off him wi' climbing the linns and the trees for the nests o' corbie-craws and hunting-hawks. And then he was so sanguine, that he was finding them every day; but there was ane o' his hunting-hawks turned out a howlet, and another o' them a cushat-dow. And as for his ravens, his grandfather told old Wauchope out of his own mouth, that 'as for his Wat's grand ravens, there was never ane o' them got aboon the rank of a decent respectable hoody-craw.' But these sanguine, keen-edged chaps are the lads for making some figure in life, for they set out determined either to make a spoon or spill a horn. And ye see, though Wat, when he was young, clamb mony a tree in vain, and rave a' his breeks into the bargain, he continued climbing on, till he found a nest wi' gouden eggs at the last. Weel, God bless him! he's turned out an honour to Scotland. (p. 12)

Clearly, this passage conveys an affectionate admiration for Scott—but a certain edge can also be detected, lurking in a possible suggestion that self-interested careerism may have been involved in Scott's climb to the substantial financial rewards of 'a nest wi' gouden eggs'. Furthermore, this account of boyhood adventures can be read, on one level, as a comment on the nature of Scott's writings. When the passage is seen in this way, a strong suggestion emerges that Scott's fictions, while powerfully attractive, are nevertheless like Wilson's in that they do not always have the firmest of grips on reality. Hogg had already poked fun at Scott's writings on these grounds about a decade earlier, in his own weekly periodical *The Spy*. The number of *The Spy* for 1 June 1811 contains an account by one 'Malise' of a visit to 'the Trossacks', scene of Scott's hugely popular poem *The Lady of the Lake* (1810). In Scott's poem 'Malise' is the henchman of the Highland chieftain Roderick Dhu, and in *The Spy* Hogg's Malise asserts that the 'greatest fault' of 'the delightful poem of the *Lady of the Lake*' is its failure to affix 'the stamp of reality' on its incidents. He goes on to declare:

> The soul of man thirsts naturally and ardently for truth; and the author that ceases to deceive us with the appearance of it, ceases in a proportional degree to interest our feelings in behalf of the characters which he describes, or the fortunes of the individuals to which these characters are attached.[21]

According to Hogg's Mailse, unless a visitor to 'the Trossacks' is stimulated by both Scott's poetry and some Highland whisky, 'he may as well stay at home; he will see little, that shall either astonish or delight him'. Reality, in short, will not match the expectations generated by 'the delightful poem of the *Lady of the Lake*', unless assisted by artificial stimulants. Addressing 'The Spy', Malise illustrates his point as follows:

> This is no chimera, Sir, I can attest its truth from experience. I once went with a friend to view the Craig of Glen-Whargen in Nithsdale,—it was late before we reached it;—we were hungry and wearied, having fished all day;—it was no rock at all!—the Cat-Craig at the back of our house was much more striking!—it was a mere trifle,—we sat down by a well at its base;—dined on such provisions as we had, and by repeated applications to a bottle full of whisky, emptied it clean out;—the rock continued to improve;—we drank out of the bottle alternately, and in so doing were obliged to hold up our faces towards the rock of Glen-Whargen,—it was so grand and sublime, that it was not without an effort we could ever bring our heads back to their natural position.—Still as the whisky diminished the rock of Glen-Whargen increased in size and magnificence; and by the time the bottle was empty, we were fixed to the spot in amazement at that stupendous pile; and both of us agreed that it was such a rock as never was looked upon by man![22]

In an acute discussion of this passage from *The Spy*, Antony Hasler writes:

> The staging of the Highlands through the manipulation of realia here extends into the more subjective theatricals achieved with the help of Scott and another artificial stimulant. As Hogg points to the constructedness of the Highlands and Scott's role in their construction, he also erects a platform on which to play out his own anxiety of influence, glancing over his shoulder, as he so frequently does, at the more famous author. The speciously tumescent Border crag allegorises the covert deflation of a potent literary precursor.[23]

In March 1823 Scott discovered his appearance as a nest-raiding 'bit hempy callant' in *The Three Perils of Woman* when he accidentally picked up proofs of Hogg's novel from James Ballantyne's printing office, instead of proofs of his own *Quentin Durward*, which was also in the process of being printed at that time. Following this mistake he wrote as follows to Ballantyne:

> I send Copy galore—by some mistake instead of the duplicate of sheet Q. I fetched the inclosed of Hogg & naturally looking at it I found my self introduced with singular vulgarity & bad taste. However it is needless to say any thing about it—As Spenser says/ Let Grill be Grill, & have his *hoggish* mind/ Or in an adage more appropriate for

the occasion "The more you stir the more it will stink"/ I shall be desirous to have my own sheet & so soon as that can be gotten a copy of the first Vol. as printed.[24]

Scott here resorts to pig puns as he reacts to the 'singular vulgarity & bad taste' of the indelibly '*hoggish*' Hogg. The *hoggish* quotation from Spenser comes from the final stanza of Book II Canto 12 of *The Faerie Queene*, and refers to Grille, the companion of Ulysses who was transformed by Circe into a hog. This condition suited Grille so well that he refused to be changed back to human shape.[25] Clearly, Scott's irritated response here to *The Three Perils of Woman* has something in common with John Wilson's response to Hogg's novel in the notorious *Blackwood's* review.

Gurth and Ivanhoe

The Three Perils of Woman was published in August 1823. A year later, in August 1824, Scott produced a further flow of porcine puns when he wrote as follows in a letter to William Stewart Rose:

> The great Hogg found his lair at Abbotsford on Friday, Lockhart bringing him here like a pig in a string, for which the lady of the mansion sent him little thanks, she not thinking the hog's pearls (qu. Perils) an apology for his freedoms.[26]

John Gibson Lockhart (1794–1854) was a friend of John Wilson, with whom he worked closely during the early years of *Blackwood's Edinburgh Magazine*. Lockhart had much in common with Wilson: his roots (like Wilson's) lay in the west of Scotland, and (again like Wilson) he had been educated at the Universities of Glasgow and Oxford. Lockhart was also Scott's son-in-law, having married Scott's daughter Sophia in 1820. Five years before bringing Hogg to Abbotsford 'like a pig in a string' in 1824, Lockhart had described a somewhat boar-like Hogg in *Peter's Letters to his Kinsfolk* (1819):

> Although for some time past he has spent a considerable portion of every year in excellent, even in refined society, the external appearance of the man can have undergone but very little change since he was 'a herd on Yarrow.' His face and hands are still [in 1819] as brown as if he lived entirely *sub dio*. His very hair has a coarse stringiness about it, which proves beyond dispute its utter ignorance of all the arts of the friseur; [...] his teeth have been allowed to grow where they listed, and as they listed, presenting more resemblance, in arrangement, (and colour too,) to a body of crouching sharpshooters, than to any more regular species of array. The effect of a forehead, towering with a true poetic grandeur above such features as these, and of an eye that illuminates their surface with the genuine lightnings of genius,— [...] these are things which I cannot so easily transfer to my paper.[27]

Here we have the same incongruous mixture of high-souled nobility and peasant boorishness described by Wilson in his review of *The Three Perils of Woman*. Commenting on Lockhart's description of Hogg in *Peter's Letters*, Ian Duncan writes in 'Hogg's Body':

> Lockhart establishes the two features that identify Hogg's grotesque physiognomy: the Shepherd's long hair, which is here transformed from gracefully luxuriant to coarse and stringy, and, above all, his irregular, projecting *teeth*—emblems of bestial appetite and oral aggression, the tusks of the Boar of Ettrick. (Lockhart's bizarre simile of the 'body of crouching sharp-shooters' hints at a revolutionary dangerousness in popular vitality, perhaps, in this year 1819.)[28]

Duncan goes on to remark:

> In *Ivanhoe* (1820) Scott may have been paying a compliment to Hogg, *de haut en bas*, in the person of Gurth the swineherd, the hoggish shepherd of his English romance of chivalry. Gurth's valour and loyalty to Ivanhoe earn him his manumission from serfdom; internal bonds of fealty replace the external shackles of the slave's collar. Thus Scott rehearses, elegantly enough, the roles of patron and 'faithful shepherd' with which he and Hogg had commenced their relationship—and even allows for Hogg's limited progress in a literary career of his own, in Scott's shadow.[29]

Perhaps 'Gurth's valour and loyalty to Ivanhoe' provide an echo of Evan Dhu's valour and loyalty to Vich Ian Vhor. Be that as it may, the Edinburgh literary elite tended to think of Hogg as a representative figure, a talented embodiment of 'the peasantry' and 'the common people'. This being so, the faithful and valorous Gurth's devoted loyalty to the aristocratic knight Ivanhoe can be interpreted as a picture of what Scott (and Wilson) wanted Hogg (and 'the common people') to be like. In discussing the origins of the French Revolution in his *Life of Napoleon Buonaparte*, Scott writes:

> In La Vendée alone, the nobles had united their interest and their fortune with those of the peasants who cultivated their estates, and there alone were they found in their proper and honourable character of proprietors residing on their own domains, and discharging the duties which are inalienably attached to the owner of landed property. And—mark-worthy circumstance!—in La Vendée alone was any stand made in behalf of the ancient proprietors, constitution, or religion of France; for there alone the nobles and the cultivators of the soil held towards each other their natural and proper relations of patron and client, faithful dependents, and generous and affectionate superiors.[30]

In effect, Scott is suggesting that the horrors of the French Revolution could have been avoided, if only more of the French nobles had been like Ivanhoe, and more of the French peasants had been like Gurth. One can admire Scott's decency in wishing, on a personal level, to be a 'generous and affectionate superior' in his dealings with his 'faithful dependents', among whom could be numbered the peasants who cultivated his landed property at Abbotsford as well as the Ettrick Shepherd. Worryingly for the elite, however, in the Scotland of the 1820s Guha's 'subaltern classes' were no longer wholly at ease with what Scott saw as the 'natural and proper relations of patron and client'. For example, the Radicals involved in the Radical War of April 1820 did not intend to accept 'internal bonds of fealty' as the natural replacement of 'the external shackles of the slave's collar', as Ian Duncan aptly puts it with regard to Gurth. As the elite saw it, however, it was deplorable that these dangerous and deluded Radicals declined to offer faithful, valorous, and Gurth-like service to their superiors, absurdly and threateningly demanding instead the mob rule of democracy.

Tensions surrounding Peterloo and the Radical War are worth bearing in mind when we consider another possible representation of Hogg in Scott's fiction. Referring to the publication of *Ivanhoe* in 1820, Ian Duncan writes in 'Hogg's Body':

> Three years later, following Hogg's more aggressive 'homage' to Scott in *The Three Perils of Man* (1822), and contemporaneous with Hogg's thoroughly subversive inclusion of him in *The Three Perils of Woman*, the hero of Scott's *Quentin Durward* encounters a fearsome, carnivalesque figure of appetite, riot and misrule called 'the Wild Boar of the Ardennes'. [...] This creature commands a revolutionary violence that degrades men into beasts—not only himself and his mob, but the venerable Bishop of Liège, pole-axed like an ox in the shambles.[31]

Ian Duncan adds that the Wild Boar, 'whether or not he bears any intended reference to Hogg, is a sinister and repulsive monster'. Indeed he is. A product of the anxious imagination of the elite about the horrific potential of popular insurrection, it may be suggested that this monster personifies the nightmarish alternative to Gurth's faithful service to Ivanhoe. The Wild Boar's riot of appetite and misrule is in effect an enactment of what is to be expected if the subaltern classes ever take their assertiveness to the point of successful revolutionary violence. Like the Boar of Ettrick, the Boar of the Ardennes can be interpreted as a representative embodiment of the subaltern classes. Indeed, Scott's description of the Boar of the Ardennes seems to echo his son-in-law's description of the Boar of Ettrick in *Peter's Letters*. As we have seen, Lockhart presents a Hogg whose hair has 'a coarse stringiness about it', and who has projecting, tusk-like teeth, irregularly (and alarmingly) arranged like 'a body of crouching sharp-shooters'. Combined with 'such features as these', however, Lockhart describes 'an eye that illuminates their surface with the genuine lightnings of genius', and a forehead 'towering with a true poetic grandeur'. Scott's Boar of Ardennes is similarly equipped. His hair, we are told, resembles the 'rude and wild bristles' of a boar, while his face exhibits 'an unusual thickness and projection of the mouth and upper-jaw', combined with 'huge projecting side-teeth'. Nevertheless he has 'an open, high, and manly forehead' and 'large, sparkling, light-coloured eyes'. This promise of something 'valiant and generous' has been overpowered, however, by an 'expression of violence and insolence, which, joined to debauchery and intemperance, had stamped upon the features a character inconsistent with the rough gallantry which they would otherwise have exhibited'.[32] Here we do not quite have a fallen angel, but we do seem to have a fallen Shepherd, a fallen Gurth.

In the writings of Wilson and Scott, then, it seems that Hogg emerges as a figure representative of subaltern Scotland—as the Ettrick Shepherd, as the Wild Boar of Ettrick. Dissatisfied with these representations of himself, and with other attempts by Wilson and Scott to ventriloquise subaltern Scotland, Hogg set out (in *The Three Perils of Woman* and elsewhere) to create texts that would tell it like it is, and allow the real voice of subaltern Scotland to speak. The Hogg who produced these texts was very far from being a simple-minded peasant. He had suffered the hardships and deprivations of subaltern Scotland, and he had deep roots in the oral culture of the subaltern world of Ettrick, but the Hogg of the 1810s and the 1820s was also a product of wide reading, and of an immersion in the vibrant intellectual world of 'the Athens of the North'. This was, perhaps, a Scottish subaltern who was well equipped to speak.

In her ground-breaking book *Bardic Nationalism: The Romantic Novel and the British Empire* (Princeton University Press, 1997), Katie Trumpener makes some comments that throw light on differences of approach between Scott's fictions and Hogg's. Discussing new early-nineteenth-century genres of fiction (the national tale, the historical novel, the Gothic novel), Trumpener argues that these new genres

> analyze both Britain's constituent cultures and her overseas colonies. The early national tale evokes an organic national society, its history rooted in place; the historical novel describes the way historical forces break into and break up this idyll—and yet, through the very upheaval they cause, shape a new national community in place of the old. Nationalist Gothic and annalistic novels, however, refuse this happy ending to stress instead the traumatic consequences of historical transformation and the long-term uneven development, even schizophrenia, it creates in "national characters." Although such novels now seem prescient in their critique of colonialism and modernization, it is Walter Scott's historical novel, with its stress on historical progress, that won out as the paradigmatic novel of empire, appealing to nationalist, imperialist, and colonial readers alike. For Scott insists simultaneously on the self-enclosed character of indigenous societies (living idyllically, if anachronistically, outside of historical time), on the inevitability with which such societies are forcibly brought into history,

and on the survival of cultural distinctiveness even after a loss of political autonomy. As he enacts and explains the composition of Britain as an internal empire, Scott underlines the ideological capaciousness of empire, emphasizes the analogies between nation formation and empire building, and argues for the continued centrality of national identity as a component of imperial identity.[33]

For Trumpener, Scott in his historical novels 'enacts and explains the composition of Britain as an internal empire'. In these novels 'indigenous societies' such as Evan Dhu's Highland clan, having lived 'idyllically, if anachronistically, outside of historical time', are 'forcibly brought into history' by events such as Culloden. With their stress on 'historical progress', these novels insist that the anachronistic idyll of the old indigenous societies must be left behind, but they also insist on 'the survival of cultural distinctiveness even after a loss of political autonomy'. Evan Dhu is so bound up in the old ways that he has to die with his Chief at Carlisle, unable to make the transition to the modern world. Nevertheless, Scott's narrative in *Waverley* suggests that the 'cultural distinctiveness' of the Highlands has a continuing and valuable role in the modern world of Imperial, Hanoverian Britain—once the Highlanders have adjusted to the realities of 'the composition of Britain as an internal Empire', and their loyalty has been re-directed from chief and clan to the king and state.

As Trumpener indicates, 'Walter Scott's historical novel, with its stress on historical progress' had immense prestige and cultural influence in nineteenth-century Britain. Hogg's writings, on the other hand, can be linked with what Trumpener describes as 'nationalist Gothic and annalistic novels' that refuse the happy ending offered by Scott's historical novel, and 'stress instead the traumatic consequences of historical transformation'. Flourishing in Scotland alongside Scott's historical novel, writing of this kind tried (among other things) to give voice to the experiences of the subaltern as dispossessed outcast. As we shall see, this strand of the Scottish tradition finds expression in poetry in Scots and Gaelic, as well as in the 'nationalist Gothic and annalistic novels' of writers like James Hogg and John Galt.

Subaltern Gaels

Subaltern Highland Scotland had a great deal of painful experience of dispossession during the Imperial era, as a result of the notorious Highland Clearances. The Clearances took different forms in different parts of the Highlands, and occurred in various phases over a long period from the second half of the eighteenth century until the second half of the nineteenth century.[34] Prince Charles's Jacobite army had drawn much support from Highland Scotland, and the post-Culloden reprisals hastened the destruction of the traditional clan-based structures of Highland society. Having been (in Trumpener's terms) 'forcibly brought into history' by Culloden and its violent aftermath, the chieftains and people of the clans were in no position to aspire to live 'idylli-cally, if anachronistically, outside of historical time'. The realities of Imperial Britain's victory at Culloden hastened a process, already under way, through which Highland clan chieftains were increasingly becoming an integral part of the post-Union British landed elite, and were thus becoming modern British landowners as opposed to patriarchal leaders of their people in the Celtic tradition. Discussing this process, T. M. Devine comments:

> The roles of patriarchal chief and capitalist landlord were incompatible and there is evidence in the historical record of landed families agonizing over the conflicts be-tween these two functions. However, the forces making for the victory of landlord-ism over tribalism were eventually triumphant.[35]

Highland chieftains gradually ceased to feel constrained by their traditional role as guardians of the clan and its ancient territory. Furthermore, they began to see the clan lands as their own personal property, and they duly began to clear their property of its human population in order to facilitate the profitable activity of sheep-farming. And when profits from the sheep began to dwindle in due course, the now-empty land-scapes of depopulated Highland estates began to be turned over to gentlemanly Victo-rian country sports such as deer-hunting and grouse-shooting.

The change from traditional chieftain to modern landowner can be traced in the Hebrides, for example in the island of Barra and in the adjacent islands of South and North Uist. These islands enjoyed comparative economic stability during the Napo-leonic Wars, when there was a strong demand for kelp, an alkaline substance extracted from seaweed. Kelp was important in the manufacture of glass and soap, and the Heb-rides were well suited at that time to its large-scale production: there was plenty of sea-weed, and plenty of cheap labour to undertake the back-breaking work involved. How-ever, the coming of peace at the end of the Napoleonic Wars gave British manufactur-ers ready access to cheaper resources from overseas, and serious economic hardship came to Barra and the adjacent islands in the later 1810s as demand for Hebridean kelp fell away. Encouraged by emigration agents and by the availability of cheap fares to Canada, some Barra people responded to this economic hardship by emigrating volun-tarily. In 1817 their chief, Colonel MacNeill of Barra, expressed mixed feelings about this development:

> The loss of so many very decent people, is much to be regretted; at the same time, those that remain, will in time, be much better; this reflection always offers us some-thing consolatory when one reflects he has seen for the last time, those he has been accustomed to from early infancy.[36]

Colonel MacNeill's manifest decency helped to keep the full horror of the Clearances from Barra until the 1840s. Economic difficulties continued, however, and in 1841 the bankrupt estate of the MacNeills of Barra was sold to Colonel John Gordon of Cluny, a vastly wealthy member of an Aberdeenshire family that had prospered spectacularly in post-Union Scotland. In the early 1840s Gordon of Cluny had ambitious plans for the economic regeneration of his extensive and cheaply-acquired estates in Barra and the Uists. These plans did not give him the hoped-for profits, however, and during the famine of the 1840s he attempted to stem his losses from his island estates by resorting to a ruthless policy that combined eviction with forced emigration.[37] Drawing on contemporary newspaper reports to describe an episode of mid-1848 that resulted from this policy, Eric Richards records that Gordon of Cluny had organised

> an emigration from North and South Uist to Quebec, whence the people would rejoin relatives already settled on Cape Breton Island. The people were under some considerable pressure to leave the Uists. A vessel was arranged to arrive at Lochmaddy in North Uist, in July. The people had readied themselves, and Gordon, in conformity with his usual policy, had paid their passages and forgiven their arrears.

After long waiting at Lochmaddy the emigrant ship did not appear, and the people were told that a vessel would be provided for them in Glasgow. Two contingents duly got to Glasgow, but, Richards continues:

> 'Few of them were blessed with the possession of sixpence'; only two or three out of 150 knew any English; many were children and some were more than seventy years of age. Few could afford accommodation in Glasgow; the rest were turned into the streets. Of these, many became ill with measles and whooping cough and were taken to the Night Asylum. [...] Even at the best of times emigration was a trauma for the departing people; in times of famine and clearance it became a nightmare.[38]

During the Clearances the successors of Vich Ian Vhor in the Highland elite were liable to tell the successors of Evan Dhu to bugger off to Canada, sometimes going so far as to burn down their homes in order to encourage compliance with this injunction.

As we shall see in Chapter 8, the Canadian novelist Alistair MacLeod (himself a descendant of Highlanders who emigrated to Canada in the eighteenth century) has written movingly in his novel *No Great Mischief* (1999) of the post-Culloden Highland experience of exile to Cape Breton Island. It may be that the eighteenth-century Scottish subaltern speaks (albeit indirectly) through the pages of this Canadian novel, written at the end of the twentieth century. Highland subaltern experience of post-Culloden realities also finds a voice in Gaelic poetry from the eighteenth century onwards. During the seventeenth century, the period of the Regal Union, there had been some loss of vigour in the literary use of Scottish indigenous languages. Following the Union of 1707, however, there was a notable revival in the literary use of Scots and Gaelic, a project undertaken in conscious opposition to the British Imperial preference for the standard language, 'the King's English'. Robert Burns, the so-called 'plough-man-poet', was the most famous exponent of this attempt to give voice to the insights and concerns of the Scottish subaltern world, but Burns's eighteenth-century Scots-language predecessors Allan Ramsay and Robert Fergusson were also poets of real significance and stature. Eighteenth-century Gaelic poetry likewise gives voice to subaltern experiences and insights, two leading Gaelic poets of the time being Alasdair MacMhaighstir Alasdair and Duncan Ban Macintyre. This eighteenth-century Gaelic revival was continued into the nineteenth and twentieth centuries by poets like Mary Macpherson and Sorley MacLean. Mary Macpherson came to be known as 'Màiri Mhór nan Oran', which can be translated either as 'Big' or 'Great' 'Mary of the Songs': she was a large woman physically, but in Gaelic the connotations of *mhór* go well beyond mere physical size. At all events Màiri Mhór's poetry gave voice, within Queen Victoria's Imperial Britain, to Gaelic-speaking subaltern Scotland's abhorrence of the behaviour of the feudal magnates and other Scottish representatives of the Imperial elite responsible for the Highland Clearances. Because of memories of the Clearances, land ownership is still a topic capable of touching raw nerves in Scotland as the twenty-first century opens. Raw nerves were likewise touched when the Land Law Reform debate in the elections of 1885 was energised by Màiri Mhór nan Oran's articulation of the subaltern cause in her famous song 'Brosnachadh nan Gaidheal' ('Incitement of the Gaels'). A short extract is given below, together with an English translation by William Neill.[39]

'Sa' cheàrn 's na dh'àithneadh dhuinn le Dia,	*The place commanded us by God,*
Chan fhaod sinn triall air sliabh no gaineimh,	*where we can't travel moor or strand,*
A h-ùile nì 'n robh smear no luach,	*and every bit of fat or value,*
Gun spùinn iad uainn le lagh an fhearainn.	*they have grabbed with Land Law from us.*

Chan eil bileag ghorm no uaine,	*Neither stalk or blade of green,*
Far 'n robh dualachas mo sheanar,	*that was our fathers' heritage,*
Leis na bric tha snàmh fo'n chuan,	*nor the trout that swim the sea,*
Nach tug iad uainn, a dheòin no dh'aindeoin.	*they have not claimed in our despite.*

The Sioux were experiencing similar 'Land Law' troubles around this time in the American West, and so were the Igbo people of West Africa as we shall see in Chapter 3.

Eloquent responses to the Clearances are also to be found in the writings of Sorley MacLean. This twentieth-century Gaelic poet was born in 1911, and grew up on the remote Hebridean island of Raasay as a member of a talented family of Gaelic-speaking tradition-bearers. The young Sorley's parents eked out a living on the proceeds of a small croft and a small tailoring business, and the boy himself began his education at the primary school on Raasay. Here, as was customary, the teaching of Gaelic-speaking children was conducted in English, a language that perforce had to be mastered. Sorley's education continued at Portree High School on the neighbouring island of Skye, and then at the University of Edinburgh, where he became familiar with the advanced intellectual currents of twentieth-century Europe. Sorley MacLean is thus an example of the centuries-old Scottish tradition of making a cheap but first-rate university education available to a 'lad o' pairts', that is to say a talented subaltern boy. Like many other Scots of his class down the centuries, Sorley MacLean was able to establish himself in professional life because the ancient Scottish universities of St Andrews, Glasgow, Aberdeen, and Edinburgh welcomed the 'lad o' pairts'. After leaving university he spent most of his career working as a schoolteacher and headmaster, but he was also a man of strongly-held socialist convictions who joined the forces of the British Empire in order to be able to fight against fascism during the second world war. He was seriously wounded in the Battle of El Alamain.[40] This socialist Gaelic-speaking headmaster and soldier from the Western Isles of Scotland thus emerges as a man not only deeply loyal to his subaltern roots, but also very much in tune with the ideas of the intellectual *avant-garde* of Europe. As we have seen, Ania Loomba has posed the question 'can the voice of the subaltern be represented by the intellectual?', but it appears that in MacLean's case there is not a neat binary opposition between 'the subaltern' and 'the intellectual'. In this he is not unusual in the Scottish context. Several Scottish writers can plausibly be described as being simultaneously 'subalterns' and 'intellectuals': Robert Burns, James Hogg, and Alasdair MacMhaighstir Alasdair are three examples among the many that spring readily to mind.

Several competent judges regard Sorley MacLean as one of the major poets of twentieth-century Europe. His celebrated poem 'Hallaig' speaks for subaltern Scotland by confronting the post-Culloden and post-Clearances devastation of Gaelic culture. The poem does so by contemplating the fate of the village of Hallaig on MacLean's native island of Raasay. This village is now deserted and in ruins because its population was evicted by the local landowner in the 1850s during the Highland Clearances. MacLean in his youth knew Raasay people who had direct personal memories of the traumatic events of the Clearances, and 'Hallaig' is a lament for the people of a lost community. This poem reactivates the ancient bardic tradition of Gaelic poetry, not least in its reverence for the deer. In the traditional culture of the Scottish Highlands the deer has a place somewhat similar to that of the buffalo in the traditional culture of Native Americans of the Plains. As well as reactivating ancient Gaelic roots, however, 'Hallaig' is also (for example, in its condensed symbolism) a poem consciously in contact with the cutting edge of contemporary twentieth-century literary Modernism. MacLean himself has said: 'I came to maturity at the time of the great symbolist movement in European poetry, which you've got in Yeats, Eliot, MacDiarmid, Blok in Russia and Paul

Valéry in France, and my symbols came mostly from my immediate environment'.[41] Symbols drawn from the Raasay environment can be seen in the opening of 'Hallaig' (quoted below in the original Gaelic, together with the poet's own translation into English). In these lines, the lost society of the ruined and empty village is evoked through images of the deer, and of the native woodlands of the island:

'Tha tím, am fiadh, an coille Hallaig'	*'Time, the deer, is in the wood of Hallaig'*
Tha bùird is tàirnean air an uinneig	*The window is nailed and boarded*
troimh 'm faca mi an Aird an Iar	*through which I saw the West*
's tha mo ghaol aig Allt Hallaig	*and my love is at the Burn of Hallaig,*
'na craoibh bheithe, 's bha i riamh	*a birch tree, and she has always been*
eadar an t-Inbhir 's Poll a' Bhainne,	*between Inver and Milk Hollow,*
thall 's a bhos mu Bhaile-Chùirn:	*here and there about Baile-chuirn:*
tha i 'na beithe, 'na calltuinn,	*she is a birch, a hazel,*
'na caorunn dhìreach sheang ùir.	*A straight, slender young rowan.*
Ann an Screapadal mo chinnidh,	*In Screapadal of my people*
far robh Tarmad 's Eachunn Mór,	*where Norman and Big Hector were,*
tha 'n nigheanan 's am mic 'nan coille	*their daughters and their sons are a wood*
ag gabhail suas ri taobh an lóin.	*going up beside the stream.*

But as well as native woodland with its trees of birch, hazel, and rowan, Raasay also had a commercial plantation of pine trees. This wood was established on the hill Cnoc an Rà during the nineteenth century, in the time of the Clearances. The poem continues:

Uaibhreach a nochd na coilich ghiuthais	*Proud tonight the pine cocks*
ag gairm air mullach Cnoc an Rà,	*crowing on the top of Cnoc an Ra,*
dìreach an druim ris a' ghaelaich—	*straight their backs in the moonlight—*
chan iadsan coille mo ghràidh.	*they are not the wood I love.*
Fuirichidh mi ris a' bheithe	*I will wait for the birch wood*
gus an tig i mach an Càrn,	*until it comes up by the cairn,*
gus am bi am bearradh uile	*until the whole ridge from Beinn na Lice*
o Bheinn na Lice f' a sgàil.	*will be under its shade.*

The poem then turns to 'the Sabbath of the dead' at Hallaig, 'where the people are frequenting, every single generation gone'. Finally, there is an evocation of 'silent bands' of the girls of Hallaig, who 'go to Clachan as in the beginning', and return to Hallaig in the evening, 'in the dumb living twilight, [...] their laughter a mist in my ears,'

's am bòidhche 'na sgleò air mo chridhe   *and their beauty a film on my heart*
mun tig an ciaradh air na caoil,   *before the dimness comes on the kyles,*
's nuair theàrnas grian air cùl Dhùn Cana   *and when the sun goes down behind Dun Cana*
thig peileir dian á gunna Ghaiol;   *a vehement bullet will come from the gun of Love;*

's buailear am fiadh a tha 'na thuaineal   *and will strike the deer that goes dizzily,*
a' snòtach nan làraichean feòir;   *sniffing at the grass-grown ruined homes;*
thig reothadh air a shùil 'sa' choille: *his eye will freeze in the wood,*
chan fhaighear lorg air fhuil ri m' bheò.[42]   *his blood will not be traced while I live.*

Seamus Heaney has written that his experience of encountering Sorley MacLean's poetry in translations by Iain Crichton Smith 'was like opening the door on a morning of sea-filled brightness'. Heaney goes on to say that he first heard MacLean's poems spoken in Gaelic when he heard MacLean himself read them at the Abbey Theatre in Dublin: 'again, this had the force of revelation: the mesmeric, heightened tone; the weathered voice coming in close from a far place; [...] above all the sense of bardic dignity that was entirely without self-parade'. On this occasion Seamus Heaney was present on stage at the Abbey Theatre, his role being to read some of MacLean's poems in the poet's own English translations. Heaney comments:

> Reading 'Hallaig' on that occasion, in the poet's own English, and hearing it in the deep lamenting register of the Gaelic, extended and confirmed my sense of him as a major figure. This was the song of a man who had come through, a poem with all the lucidity and arbitrariness of a vision. [...] It held fast to a field of indigenous obsessions, but its effect was not merely to celebrate indigenous ground: it opened that 'nailed and boarded' window of the first line in such a way that a sense of loss became a sense of scope, and what might have been a pious elegy became a rich and strange ode to melancholy [...]. 'Hallaig' is a key poem because it is about haunting and loss and this mood is a persistent one all through the work, as is the theme of love and wounding: which arrests the fluent dreamscape at the end of the poem.[43]

Heaney writes of MacLean's 'bardic dignity', and this is entirely appropriate. In 'Hallaig', MacLean reactivates the bard's traditional role of speaking for a whole society. In *Bardic Nationalism* Katie Trumpener has written as follows of eighteenth-century conceptions of the bardic role:

The publication of Thomas Gray's poem "The Bard" (1757) and James Macpherson's *Poems of Ossian* (1760-65) would stir up English enthusiasm for bardic poetry and for the picturesque landscapes of Wales, Scotland, and Ireland. Yet its newfound popularity in England endangered the bardic tradition in a new way, as English poets tried to impersonate the bardic voice and to imitate bardic materials, without grasping their historical and cultural significance. For nationalist antiquaries, the bard is the mouthpiece for a whole society, articulating its values, chronicling its history, and mourning the inconsolable tragedy of its collapse. English poets, in contrast, imagine the bard (and the minstrel after him) as an inspired, isolated, and peripatetic figure.[44]

In its heyday, the British Empire sought, throughout the territories it controlled, to establish an acceptance of its own system of values, of its own view of the world: its own story, in short.[45] Clearly, in order to further this project, it was in the Empire's interest to 'nail and board' the windows that opened out on the alternative views of the world provided by the cultures of pre-Imperial indigenous communities. 'Hallaig' sets out to re-open one such 'nailed and boarded' window, and in doing so, this poem accepts the traditional bardic role of acting as 'the mouthpiece for a whole society, articulating its values, chronicling its history, and mourning the inconsolable tragedy of its collapse'.

Walter Scott was one of the Scottish writers who helped to shape the Grand Narrative that articulated Imperial Britain's sense of itself. On the other hand, Scottish subaltern writers like James Hogg and Sorley MacLean reacted against the Imperial Grand Narrative by attempting to open the 'nailed and boarded' window that looks out on the life and experiences of subaltern Scotland. In Chapter 3 we shall consider their debate within a wider context.

Notes

1   Ania Loomba, *Colonialism / Postcolonialism* (London: Routledge, 1998), p. 231.

2   A particularly valuable contribution to this discussion is Ian Duncan, 'Hogg's Body', *Studies in Hogg and his World*, 9 (1998), 1–15. Other notable contributions include J. H. Alexander, 'Hogg in the *Noctes Ambrosianae*', *Studies in Hogg and his World*, 4 (1993), 37–47; and Andrew Noble, 'John Wilson (Christopher North) and the Tory Hegemony', in *The History of Scottish Literature: Volume 3 Nineteenth Century*, ed. by Douglas Gifford, general editor Cairns Craig (Aberdeen: Aberdeen University Press, 1988), pp. 125–51. See also the 'Introduction' by Antony Hasler and the 'Afterword' by David Groves in James Hogg, *The Three Perils of Woman; or, Love, Leasing, and Jealousy: A Series of Domestic Scottish Tales*, ed. by David Groves, Antony Hasler, and Douglas S. Mack, The Stirling / South Carolina Research Edition of the Collected Works of James Hogg (Edinburgh: Edinburgh University Press, 1995).

3   For a detailed account of Wilson's life, see Elsie Swann, *Christopher North <John Wilson>* (Edinburgh: Oliver and Boyd), 1934.

4   Quoted from the version of Hogg's *Memoir of the Author's Life* that appeared in *The Mountain Bard* (Edinburgh: Constable; London, Murray, 1807), pp. v–vi; for the 1832 version of this passage, see Hogg's *Altrive Tales*, ed. by Gillian Hughes, The Stirling / South Carolina Research Edition of the Collected Works of James Hogg (Edinburgh: Edinburgh University Press, 2003), p. 14.

5   See *The Collected Letters of James Hogg*, ed. by Gillian Hughes, The Stirling / South Carolina Research Edition of the Collected Works of James Hogg (Edinburgh: Edinburgh University Press, 2004–   ), I, 1800–1819 (2004), pp. 15–20. Recent research by Peter Garside and Richard Jackson points to September 1802 as the date for this meeting between Hogg and Scott. I am indebted to Peter Garside for this information.

6   The account of Hogg's life given here draws on Hogg's autobiographical writings, and on material kindly supplied by Dr Gillian Hughes, who is working on a biography of Hogg.

7   For an account of the Radical War, see Devine, *The Scottish Nation*, pp. 226–30.

8   [John Wilson], 'Hogg's Three Perils of Woman', *Blackwood's Edinburgh Magazine*, 14 (1823), 427–37 (p. 427); cited in Ian Duncan, 'Hogg's Body', p. 1. Kilmeny and Mary Lee are pure and chaste heroines in Hogg's poems *The Queen's Wake* (1813) and *Pilgrims of the Sun* (1815).

9   Ian Duncan, 'Hogg's Body', pp. 1–2.

10   [John Wilson], 'Hogg's Three Perils of Woman', p. 428; cited in Ian Duncan, 'Hogg's Body', p. 2.

11   Ian Duncan, 'Hogg's Body', p. 2.

12   Ian Duncan, 'Hogg's Body', p. 10.

13   Douglas Gifford, *James Hogg* (Edinburgh: Ramsay Head, 1976), pp. 9–30.

14   David Daiches, *Two Worlds: An Edinburgh Jewish Childhood*, Canongate Classics, 7 (Edinburgh: Canongate, 1987), p. 142.

15   Daiches, *Two Worlds*, p. 146.

16   Both letters are cited in Antony Hasler's Introduction in *The Three Perils of Woman*, ed. by Groves, Hasler, and Mack, p. xviii.

17   *The Three Perils of Woman*, ed. by Groves, Hasler, and Mack, p. 25. Future references to this novel are to this edition, and are given in the text. These page references also apply to the Edinburgh University Press paperback edition (2002).

18   *The Poetical Works of Professor Wilson* (Edinburgh: Blackwood, 1865), p. 17.

19   James Hogg, *The Poetic Mirror; or, The Living Bards of Britain* (London: Longman; Edinburgh: John Ballantyne, 1816), pp. 271–72.

20   See *The Three Perils of Woman*, ed. Groves, Hasler, and Mack, pp. xxv, 449.

21   James Hogg, *The Spy*, ed. by Gillian Hughes, The Stirling / South Carolina Research Edition of the Collected Works of James Hogg (Edinburgh: Edinburgh University Press, 2000), p. 398.

22   Hogg, *The Spy*, ed. Hughes, pp. 401–02.

23   Antony J. Hasler, 'Reading the Land: James Hogg and the Highlands', *Studies in Hogg and his World*, 4 (1993), 57–82 (p. 58).

24   National Linrary of Scotland (hereafter NLS), MS 5317, fol. 61: quoted in Walter Scott, *Quentin Durward*, ed. by J. H. Alexander and G. A. M. Wood, The Edinburgh Edition of the Waverley Novels (Edinburgh: Edinburgh University Press, 2001), p. 445. I am grateful to Gillian Hughes for drawing my attention to this reference.

25   See Edmund Spenser, *The Faerie Queene*, ed. by A. C. Hamilton (London: Longman, 1977), p. 297.

26 Scott's letter to Rose is dated '[*August* 1823]' by H. J. C. Grierson, but James C. Corson asserts that 'the correct date of the letter is 1824'. See *The Letters of Sir Walter Scott*, ed. by H. J. C. Grierson, 12 vols (London: Constable, 1932–37), VIII, 64–65, and James C. Corson, *Notes and Index to Sir Herbert Grierson's Edition of the Letters of Sir Walter Scott* (Oxford: Clarendon Press, 1979), p. 224.

27 John Gibson Lockhart, *Peter's Letters to his Kinsfolk*, ed. by William Ruddick (Edinburgh: Scottish Academic Press, 1977), pp. 44–45

28 Ian Duncan, 'Hogg's Body', p. 3.

29 Ian Duncan, 'Hogg's Body', p. 4.

30 Scott, *The Life of Napoleon Buonaparte*, 9 vols (Edinburgh: Cadell; London: Longman, 1827), I, 30–31.

31 Ian Duncan, 'Hogg's Body', p. 4.

32 *Quentin Durward*, ed. Alexander and Wood, p. 237.

33 Katie Trumpener, *Bardic Nationalism: The Romantic Novel and the British Empire* (Princeton: Princeton University Press, 1997), pp. xii–xiii.

34 An account of the Highland Clearances is available in Eric Richards, *A History of the Highland Clearances: Agrarian Transformation and the Evictions 1746–1886* (London: Croom Helm, 1982); and Eric Richards, *A History of the Highland Clearances Volume 2: Emigration, Protests, Reasons* (London: Croom Helm, 1985).

35 T. M. Devine, *Scotland's Empire1600–1815* (London: Allen Lane, 2003), p. 122. Chapter 6 of Devine's book ('Exodus from Gaeldom', pp. 119–39) gives an excellent overview of these matters.

36 Quoted from Eric Richards, *The Highland Clearances: People, Landlords, and Rural Turmoil* (Edinburgh: Birlinn, 2000), p. 209.

37 See Richards, *The Highland Clearances* (2000), pp. 208–25.

38 Richards, *A History of the Highland Clearances* (1982), pp. 407–08.

39 Quoted from *The Poetry of Scotland: Gaelic, Scots and English 1380–1980*, ed. by Roderick Watson (Edinburgh: Edinburgh University Press, 1995), pp. 484–85.

40 See Joy Hendry, 'Sorley MacLean: The Man and his Work', in *Sorley MacLean: Critical Essays*, ed. by Raymond J. Ross and Joy Hendry (Edinburgh: Scottish Academic Press, 1986), pp. 9–38.

41 Donald Archie MacDonald, 'Some Aspects of Family and Local Background: An Interview with Sorley MacLean', in *Sorley MacLean: Critical Essays*, ed. Ross and Hendry, pp. 211–22 (p. 219).

42 Quoted from *The Poetry of Scotland*, ed. Watson, pp. 620–23.

43 Seamus Heaney, 'Introduction', in *Sorley MacLean: Critical Essays*, ed. Ross and Hendry, pp. 1–7 (pp. 1–3).

44 Trumpener, *Bardic Nationalism*, p. 6.

45 For a discussion of this process see Fredric Jameson, *The Political Unconscious: Narrative as a Socially Symbolic Act* (Ithaca: Cornell University Press, 1981), pp. 52–54, 87.

THREE

'We Too Might Have a Story to Tell': Competing Narratives and Imperial Power

The nationalist movement in British West Africa after the Second World War brought about a mental revolution which began to reconcile us to ourselves. It suddenly seemed that we too might have a story to tell. "Rule Britannia!" to which we had marched so unselfconsciously on Empire Day now stuck in our throat.

(Chinua Achebe, 'Named for Victoria, Queen of England')

Can Miss Swartz be Heard?

If the subaltern speaks, will her voice make a difference to the power structures of Empire? Will anyone listen? Will anyone be interested in what they hear, if they do listen? Who cares about what the subaltern has to say?

With such questions in mind, let us consider Thackeray's *Vanity Fair*, a novel that looks back from a vantage point in the middle of the nineteenth century in order to give an account of the forces that had been shaping and changing British society from the time of the Battle of Waterloo (1815) onwards. One of the great novels of Imperial Britain's Victorian heyday, *Vanity Fair* made its first appearance in monthly parts, beginning in January 1847 and coming to a conclusion (with a double number) in July 1848. As we saw in Chapter 2, during July 1848 a large group of emigrants, evicted from the Uists by Colonel Gordon of Cluny and destined for Cape Breton Island, were waiting in vain at Lochmaddy in North Uist for their emigrant ship. These unfortunate Highlanders went on to suffer great hardship in Glasgow before finally leaving fo Canada. *Vanity Fair* offers what purports to be a panoramic view of British society during the first half of the nineteenth century, but the famine and evictions on Barra and the Uists seem very remote from its pages. Centring its interest on the life of the London officer class, Thackeray's narrative has a powerful and interesting story to tell.

But it simply does not register the long and traumatic story of the Highland Clearances. Becky Sharp may be a much-travelled woman with a notable breadth of experience, but it is hard to imagine the pages of *Vanity Fair* taking her as far out of her usual round as North (or even South) Uist.

Thackeray's account of British Imperial society is sensitively attuned to various metropolitan English voices, but is not always equally successful in picking up other resonances. Let us, for example, consider the case of the West Indian heiress Miss Swartz, whose large fortune excites the avaricious interest of many of the characters of *Vanity Fair*. Indeed, the crass *nouveau riche* London merchant Mr Osborne becomes so interested in Miss Swartz's money that he instructs his son George to marry her. George proves to be less than enthusiastic about his father's plans, however, and this leads to the following after-dinner conversation:

> 'I ain't going to have any of this dam sentimental nonsense and humbug here, sir,' the father cried out. 'There shall be no beggar-marriages in my family. If you choose to fling away eight thousand a year, which you may have for the asking, you may do it: but by Jove you take your pack and walk out of this house, sir. Will you do as I tell you, once for all, sir, or will you not?'
>
> 'Marry that mulatto woman?' George said, pulling up his shirt-collars. 'I don't like the colour, sir. Ask the black that sweeps opposite Fleet Market, sir. *I'm* not going to marry a Hottentot Venus.'[1]

George is not immune to the attractions of money: he certainly enjoys spending it. But he can resist 'a Hottentot Venus', however rich. George's racist disdain for 'that mulatto woman' also emerges in a conversation with his childhood sweetheart Amelia Sedley:

> 'My sisters say she has diamonds as big as pigeons' eggs,' George said, laughing. 'How they must set off her complexion! A perfect illumination it must be when her jewels are on her neck. Her jet-black hair is as curly as Sambo's. I dare say she wore a nose-ring when she went to Court; and with a plume of feathers in her top-knot she would look a perfect Belle Sauvage.' (pp. 244–45)

This is bad enough, but there is more to come:

> '[...] Diamonds and mahogany, my dear! think what an advantageous contrast—and the white feathers in her hair—I mean in her wool. [...] Her father was a German Jew—a slave owner they say—connected with the Cannibal Islands in some way or other. He died last year, and Miss Pinkerton has finished her education. She can play two pieces on the piano; she knows three songs; she can write when Mrs. Haggistoun

is by to spell for her; and Jane and Maria [George's sisters] already have got to love her as a sister.'

'I wish they would have loved me,' said Emmy, wistfully. 'They were always very cold to me.'

'My dear child, they would have loved you if you had had two hundred thousand pounds,' George replied. (p. 246)

Miss Swartz is 'chaperoned' by her Scottish relative 'Mrs. Haggistoun, Colonel Haggistoun's widow', who is 'a relation of Lord Binkie, and always talking of him' (p. 245). Like Osborne *père* and George's sisters, this representative of the Scottish aristocracy knows how to value two hundred thousand pounds. Indeed, Thackeray's narrator records that in due course old Osborne (a widower) 'had proposed for Miss Swartz, but had been rejected scornfully by the partisans of that lady, who married her to a young sprig of Scotch nobility' (p. 535), the 'Honourable James McMull' (p. 537). Mrs Haggistoun, it would appear, is skilled in looking after her own.

[Thackeray's drawing of Miss Swartz, from *Vanity Fair*]

Clearly, George Osborne's comments on Miss Swartz are racist, but this does not seem to be simply a case of the dreadful George expressing his own dreadful views. At one point the narrator records that George

> had then been to pass three hours with Amelia, his dear little Amelia, at Fulham; and he came home to find his sisters spread in starched muslin in the drawing-room, the dowagers cackling in the background, and honest Swartz in her favourite amber-coloured satin, with turquoise-bracelets, countless rings, flowers, feathers, and all sorts of tags and gimcracks, about as elegantly decorated as a she chimney-sweep on May-Day.   (p. 252)

Miss Swartz rehearsing for the Drawing Room

[Thackeray's drawing, from *Vanity Fair*]

The narrator here seems almost as racist as George, and indeed the whole weight and authority of the text seems to be pointing the moral that Osborne *père* and the rapacious Scotch are so lost to human decency that their overwhelming greed makes them willing to ally themselves by marriage to a West Indian woman, the daughter (it seems) of a union between a 'German Jew' and an African slave. From this racist perspective, Miss Swartz (the 'she chimney-sweep on May-Day') is less than fully human. Her money may be very interesting, but this amiable simpleton is of little interest or worth in and for herself. The perceptions and experiences of this wealthy 'Hottentot Venus' do not engage the attention of Thackeray's narrator. She is presented as an intruder in the metropolitan world of officer-class London, finding a place there only because of her inherited wealth. Thackeray's narrative sees Miss Swartz as a primitive, exotic outsider—and, as a matter of course, it does not allow her to speak. In *Vanity Fair* we do not hear her voice, we are not allowed to see things from her point of view, we are not told her story.

Miss Swartz calls to mind the West Indian heiress of another novel of the late 1840s: Bertha Mason in *Jane Eyre* (1847). In Charlotte Brontë's novel, Bertha is the madwoman in the attic, the first Mrs Rochester, and Bertha is like Miss Swartz in that her story does not get a hearing. Famously, however, the madwoman's story *is* told in Jean Rhys's *Wide Sargasso Sea* (1966). Because it is willing to look at events from Bertha's point of view, Jean Rhys's novel is able to question and subvert aspects of *Jane Eyre*. In the process, these two texts become competing narratives. Each narrative offers its own perspective, its own version of events. Each narrative seeks to establish and validate its own version of the truth.

Much can be at stake when narratives compete for a hearing. In his essay 'Named for Victoria, Queen of England' Chinua Achebe writes:

> The nationalist movement in British West Africa after the Second World War brought about a mental revolution which began to reconcile us to ourselves. It suddenly seemed that we too might have a story to tell. "Rule Britannia!" to which we had marched so unselfconsciously on Empire Day now stuck in our throat.[2]

In a passage quoted in the opening pages of this book's first chapter, Edward Said argues that stories 'become the method colonized people use to assert their own identity and the existence of their own history', and he goes on to stress that 'the power to narrate, or to block other narratives from forming and emerging, is very important to culture and imperialism, and constitutes one of the main connections between them'. The events of the middle years of the twentieth century suggest that Said was entirely right about the importance of stories. For Achebe's people, the telling of 'our' story played its part in undermining the British Empire by opening a window on a forgotten perspective on the African past, a perspective from which the rule of Britannia could be seen to be an alien intrusion. Clearly, in this situation it was in the Empire's interest to seek to impose its own story. It was likewise in the Empire's interest to seek to silence 'our' story, to nail and board the window that offered a dangerous glimpse of an alternative to the Empire's version of events.

According to the British Empire's approved and official story, the rule of Britannia enforced Progress through a benign violence, as it took control over the lives of the child-like 'natives' of 'dark' and 'savage' places such as Africa. From the official perspective of the Empire, it seemed self-evident that Kipling's 'lesser breeds without the law' did not have a story of their own, and because the 'native' peoples were perceived to be less than fully human it was taken for granted that their history began with the arrival of 'civilisation' and the Empire. In 'An Image of Africa: Racism in Conrad's *Heart of Darkness*', a ground-breaking lecture given at the University of Massachusetts in 1975, Achebe summed up the institutional power behind such attitudes by asking: 'For did not that erudite British historian and Regius Professor at Oxford, Hugh Trevor Roper, also pronounce that African history did not exist?'[3] It begins to appear that the official Imperial story—and with it the Empire itself— will be destabilised, unless it continues to be widely assumed that Bertha Mason, Miss Swartz, and other people from the Empire's 'margins' have not become civilised enough to have a story of their own to tell. As a result, in Victorian novels like *Vanity Fair* and *Jane Eyre*, such people (like Victorian children) are seen but not heard.

Of course, narratives emerged from Imperial culture that were more complex than the simple official version of the Empire's story. As we shall see in a later chapter, the Scottish writer Robert Louis Stevenson, while living in the South Seas in the 1890s as a privileged European, broke new ground as he questioned various aspects of the Imperial Grand Narrative in *The Beach of Falesá* and *The Ebb Tide*. Likewise, Joseph Conrad's *Heart of Darkness* (1902) competes with the official Imperial story by offering a devastating critique of the situation created by European Imperial presence in the Belgian Congo towards the end of the nineteenth century, a situation Conrad had experienced at first hand during his visit to the Congo in 1890. In spite of the powerful anti-Imperial strand in Conrad's novel, however, Achebe has argued that racist Imperial assumptions are present, both in Conrad himself and in *Heart of Darkness*. In 'An Image of Africa: Racism in Conrad's *Heart of Darkness*', Achebe writes:

Conrad was born in 1857, the very year in which the first Anglican missionaries were arriving among my own people in Nigeria. It was certainly not his fault that he lived his life at a time when the reputation of the black man was at a particularly low level. But even after due allowance has been made for all the influences of contemporary prejudice on his sensibility there remains still in Conrad's attitude a residue of antipathy to black people which his peculiar psychology alone can explain. His own account of his first encounter with a black man is very revealing:

A certain enormous buck nigger encountered in Haiti fixed my conception of blind, furious, unreasoning rage, as manifested in the human animal to the end of my days. Of the nigger I used to dream for years afterwards.

Certainly Conrad had a problem with niggers. His inordinate love of that word itself should be of interest to psychoanalysts. (p. 258)

For Achebe, *Heart of Darkness* is 'a book which parades in the most vulgar fashion prejudices and insults from which a section of mankind has suffered untold agonies and atrocities in the past and continues to do so in many ways and many places today'. Achebe also argues that Africa, in *Heart of Darkness*, operates as a setting that 'eliminates the African as human factor', and he also writes of Conrad's novel's 'dehumanization of Africa and Africans' (pp. 259, 257).

It is possible to accept the thrust of Achebe's case with regard to Empire and Africa, while still feeling that a defence of *Heart of Darkness* is possible. For example, Wilson Harris has written:

Achebe's essay on "the dehumanisation of Africa and Africans" by "bloody racists" is, therefore, in the light of western malaise and postimperial hangover, a persuasive argument, but I am convinced his judgement or dismissal of *Heart of Darkness*—and of Conrad's strange genius—is a profoundly mistaken one.[4]

Whatever case might be made for *Heart of Darkness*, however, it seems clear that Achebe's hostility towards Conrad's novel draws its strength from an entirely convincing perception that *Heart of Darkness* does not show any willingness to recognise the existence of a valuable pre-Imperial African culture. Achebe does not necessarily demonstrate that *Heart of Darkness* is a failure as a work of art, but he does demonstrate that *Heart of Darkness* remains entangled in the crass old Imperial assumptions about the sub-human status of the 'lesser breeds without the law' who have not yet been civilised by the Imperial project. Conrad's novel fails to register that 'we too might have a story to tell'.

Hogg and Scott: An African Perspective

Achebe's questioning of Conrad offers interesting parallels with Hogg's questioning of Scott and Wilson in the years before and after the Battle of Waterloo. As we have seen, Scott and Wilson at this period ventriloquised the voice of subaltern Scotland in narratives based on the assumptions and world-view of the Imperial elite. Hogg, himself a subaltern Scot, felt that these narratives distorted the realities of subaltern Scotland, and in *The Three Perils of Woman* (1823) and other texts he set out to let the Scottish subaltern speak. In *Things Fall Apart* (1958) Achebe likewise sets out to show that 'we too might have a story to tell'. In conscious competition with Conrad's narrative in

Heart of Darkness, Achebe's novel tells the story of the Imperial conquest of Africa from the point of view of the African people. What emerges is not a story about the coming of the pure light of civilisation to the Dark Continent, but a story about how things fall apart, a story about the destruction of an old pre-colonial African oral culture that is complex, far from perfect, but worthy of great respect.

One result of the Imperial advance is the suicide of Okonkwo at the end of Achebe's novel. Okonkwo is the complex, imperfect, impressive embodiment of the old Igbo traditional oral culture, and relics of traditional practices with regard to the burial of the dead begin to emerge in the aftermath of his suicide. This kindles the interest of the District Commissioner, the local representative of Imperial power, and 'the resolute administrator in him gave way to the student of primitive customs'.[5] The final paragraph of *Things Fall Apart* reads as follows:

> The Commissioner went away, taking three or four of the soldiers with him. In the many years in which he had toiled to bring civilization to different parts of Africa he had learnt a number of things. One of them was that a District Commissioner must never attend to such undignified details as cutting down a hanged man from a tree. Such attention would give the natives a poor opinion of him. In the book which he planned to write he would stress that point. As he walked back to the court he thought about that book. Every day brought him some new material. The story of this man who had killed a messenger and hanged himself would make interesting reading. One could almost write a whole chapter on him. Perhaps not a whole chapter but a reasonable paragraph, at any rate. There was so much else to include, and one must be firm in cutting out details. He had already chosen the title of the book, after much thought: *The Pacification of the Primitive Tribes of the Lower Niger*. (pp. 147–48)

Things Fall Apart and *The Pacification of the Primitive Tribes of the Lower Niger* can be seen as competing narratives, as rival attempts to establish the meaning of the sequence of events that produced the Imperial conquest of Africa. By allowing the African story to be heard, Achebe's novel challenges and complicates the Imperial story. Okonkwo may be worth only a paragraph in the Empire's story of the pacification of the primitive tribes of the Lower Niger, but by the end of *Things Fall Apart* the reader has come to see that, in the competing African narrative of how things fall apart as the Empire advances, Okonkwo is well worth a whole book.

The telling of Okonkwo's a story is fraught with danger for the Empire. For Achebe's generation the telling of the African story of the arrival of Empire 'brought about a mental revolution which began to reconcile us to ourselves. [...] "Rule Britannia!" to which we had marched so unselfconsciously on Empire Day now stuck in our throat'. In effect, this development meant that the British Empire's days in Africa were numbered.

Like Okonkwo, *Vanity Fair*'s Miss Swartz has a story to tell. Thackeray's novel, however, is not particularly anxious to allow that story to be heard, and the unfortunate Miss Swartz still awaits the writing of her own equivalent of *Wide Sargasso Sea*. Whatever else it might or might not be, however, *Vanity Fair* is a highly sophisticated piece of narrative art, and Chapter 6 of Thackeray's novel speculates amusingly on the different kinds of story it might choose to tell. One possibility would be a tale of 'the supremely genteel', a tale of Lords and Ladies (p. 60). Another possibility would be a story of the 'terrible', which would produce 'a tale of thrilling interest, through the fiery chapters of which the readers should hurry, panting' (p. 61). Yet another possibility is described as follows:

> suppose we had resorted to the entirely low, and described what was going on in Mr. Sedley's kitchen;—how black Sambo was in love with the cook (as indeed he was), and how he fought a battle with the coachman in her behalf; how the knife-boy was caught stealing a cold shoulder of mutton, and Miss Sedley's new *femme de chambre* refused to go to bed without a wax candle; such incidents might be made to provoke much delightful laughter, and be supposed to represent scenes of 'life'. (pp. 60–61)

It appears, then, that the antics of 'black Sambo' and his fellow servants might generate 'much delightful laughter', but that such people are too 'low' to provide the subject-matter of a story that deserves a serious hearing: they are, after all, mere servants, and one of them is black, to boot. In Thackeray's novel, this inability to be taken seriously is a trait that the servants share with other characters who do not have a secure and accepted place within the charmed circle of the Imperial elite. One such character is Miss Swartz, as we have seen. Another is the young West Indian heiress's chaperone and relative, Mrs Haggistoun. The naming of characters can be uncomfortably pointed in *Vanity Fair*, and this applies to Miss Swartz and to her chaperone alike. As *Swartz* in German means 'black', the name of this daughter of 'a German Jew' and an African slave chimes with George Osborne's description of her as a 'Hottentot Venus'. *Haggistoun* likewise points to the *outré* origins of the lady concerned. Haggis, Scotland's national dish, has a certain notoriety, being concocted from the entrails of sheep, and calling a Scottish character 'Mrs Haggistoun' (that is to say, 'Mrs Haggis-town') is rather like calling a French character 'Mrs Frogeater'. The naming of Miss Swartz and Mrs Haggistoun seems to suggest that it is taken for granted that an account of the activities and concerns of these characters 'might be made to provoke much delightful laughter'. However, it also seems to be taken for granted that the lives, concerns, and insights of such characters cannot be expected to engage the serious and sympathetic interest and concern of a sophisticated metropolitan reader. In *Things Fall Apart*, the District Commissioner does not engage fully with Okonkwo. The narrator of *Vanity Fair*, likewise, does not engage fully with Miss Swartz, 'black Sambo', and Mrs

Haggistoun. Thackeray's novel is willing to laugh at the 'Hottentot Venus' and the money-obsessed lady from the Land of Haggis, but is not willing to give a hearing to the experiences and insights of these people from the Imperial margins.

Mrs Haggistoun, in *Vanity Fair*'s terms, is 'Scotch'. Those at the power-centre of British society in its Imperial heyday tended to use *Scotch* as a word (like *nigger* or *wog*) calculated to convey something rather different from respectful and affectionate accept- ance of the persons so described. Manifestly, the 'Scotch' were infinitely more comfort- able and infinitely better rewarded under the Empire than the 'niggers', but to be called either 'nigger' or 'Scotch' was to be reminded with some force that you were not 'one of us'. A late example of this Imperial usage of *Scotch* is to be found in a letter written by George Orwell to the novelist Anthony Powell on 8 June 1936. Orwell refers to Powell's verse satire *Caledonia* :

> I am glad to see you make a point of calling them "Scotchmen", not "Scotsmen" as they like to be called. I find this a good easy way of annoying them.[6]

Vanity Fair's Scotchwoman, Mrs Haggistoun, belongs to a generation in their prime when the Battle of Waterloo was fought in 1815, Waterloo being the great central event in Thackeray's novel. This means, of course, that she belongs to a generation from whom the first readers of *Waverley* (1814) were drawn. Scots of that generation oper- ated in a cultural situation that presents a number of parallels with (as well as a number of differences from) the cultural situation of Nigerians of Achebe's generation. *Things Fall Apart* was first published in 1958, and it looks back to the cataclysmic events experi- enced by the generation of Achebe's grandparents in the second half of the nineteenth century. As we have seen, Achebe writes in 'An Image of Africa' that 'Conrad was born in 1857, the very year in which the first Anglican missionaries were arriving among my own people in Nigeria'. Later in the same essay Achebe remarks that Conrad sailed 'down the Congo in 1890 when my own father was a babe in arms'.[7] The West African world in which Achebe wrote *Things Fall Apart* had been shaped by events that had taken place around sixty to a hundred years previously, and Achebe's novel tries to make sense of the present by coming to terms with these events of the past. Scots of the Waterloo generation likewise lived in a world shaped by events that had taken place around sixty to a hundred years before their time—that is to say, the Union with Eng- land of 1707, and the failure of the Jacobite rising of 1745–46. These events had paved the way for Scotland's complex involvement in the British Imperial project, and Scots of the Waterloo generation, like Africans of Achebe's generation, were faced with the necessity of coming to terms with the Empire's power structures.

The Scots had much more extensive access to the fruits of Empire than the Africans, and some Scots proved to be notably adept in taking advantage of their opportunities. This provoked some understandable resentment in England, as can perhaps be seen in

Thackeray's rendering of the character of the rapacious Mrs Haggistoun. Likewise, *Vanity Fair*'s Jos Sedley, having long been lucratively active in India on behalf of the Empire as Collector of Boggley Wollah, is 'very witty regarding the number of Scotchmen whom Lord Minto, the Governor-General, patronized' (p. 40). Nevertheless, Scots of the Waterloo generation operated in a post-Union world in which their social and economic opportunities depended on their ability to adapt to the cultural and linguistic norms of Imperial power; that is to say, the cultural and linguistic norms of polite England. Scottish members of the Imperial elite, like Indian members of the Imperial elite, had to detach themselves somewhat from their own culture, in order to adjust to the linguistic and social norms of London, the Imperial capital. Similar pressures were faced by Africans who wished to gain a comfortable and profitable place for themselves under Imperial rule.

It would appear, therefore, that the post-Union Scots of the Waterloo generation shared to some extent the predicament of the Africans of Achebe's youth, the Africans who had marched so unselfconsciously to 'Rule Britannia!' on Empire Day. Interestingly, 'Rule Britannia!' had been written by an eighteenth-century post-Union Scot, James Thomson. In 'Rule Britannia!' Thomson chose to write in accordance with the spirit of the official and approved Imperial story. This was part of his successful strategy for finding fame and fortune in London. For many impecunious post-Union Scots like the young Thomson, the road to economic and social advancement was the high road to England; this road being in the eighteenth century, according to Dr Johnson's famous phrase, 'the noblest prospect which a Scotchman ever sees'.[8] However, while Scots of the Waterloo generation were often happy to march to the Empire's tune, there was also an impulse (as with many Africans of Achebe's generation) to assert that 'we too might have a story to tell'—and Scott and Hogg, among others, set out in their own different ways to try to give voice to that story.

Scott Has an Enlightened Story to Tell

Scott undertook the task of telling Scotland's story from a position within the Scottish elite, and he undertook it as someone who shared the commitment of most Scots of his class and generation to Scotland's place within Britain and the British Empire. Such people tended to think of themselves as inhabitants of 'North Britain'—a new name to match a new post-Union Scottish identity. This context moulded and shaped Scott's attempt to get a hearing for Scotland's story, and as a result Scott's narratives seek to advance the cause of 'North Britain' by confirming and enhancing Scotland's role within the Empire's structures.

There is a valuable discussion of Scott's approach to these matters in the extended analysis of *Waverley* in Robert Crawford's seminal book *Devolving English Literature* (1992; 2nd ed. 2000). In the course of this analysis Crawford focuses on what he calls the 'cultural imperialism of the English Colonel Talbot'. The specific reference here is to Chapter 56 of Scott's novel, in which Colonel Talbot dismisses the Gaelic language of Scottish Highlanders as 'gibberish', and adds that 'even the Lowlanders talk a kind of English little better than the negroes in Jamaica'. Crawford remarks:

> Scott's text has set out to make intelligible to the sympathetic reader what to Talbot is only a provincial babel. The un-English parts of the novel are strikingly assertive, giving it much of its distinctive flavour; *Waverley* is a Scottish and a British book. Partly about the need to be able to cross the boundaries of prejudice which divide the societies within Scotland, it is not advocating the erasure of these distinctive societies, but celebrating their diversity. *Waverley* matters most as a multicultural novel. If it has a 'target', then that target is mainly the oppressive prejudice represented by Colonel Talbot. His speech condemning those whose barbaric speech he considers little better than that of 'the negroes in Jamaica' hints at the way in which the cultural and linguistic issues raised by the book are universal ones.[9]

As a member of the North British sub-section of the British Imperial elite, Scott wished to encourage the consolidation of the compound identity of the still comparatively new British state, and this provided a motivation for the writing of *Waverley*. In making Scotland's story readily accessible to an English audience, Scott's novel seeks to overcome and disarm the kind of anti-Scottish prejudice embodied in the text of *Waverley* by the otherwise admirable Englishman, Colonel Talbot. Scott thus directly challenges anti-Scottish prejudice of the kind exhibited by *Vanity Fair*'s Jos Sedley, and in doing so he operates in tune with the needs of the Imperial state. By encouraging English readers to move beyond Colonel Talbot's failure to understand the cultural situation of Scotland, *Waverley* seeks to strengthen British Imperial society by carving out an accepted, valuable, and valued role within it for Scotland and the Scots.

We have seen that Scott's hopes for the British future are given expression in *Waverley* through the marriage of the Englishman Edward Waverley and his Scottish bride Rose Bradwardine at the end of the novel: this marriage is, as it were, an enactment of the fruitful marriage of the 1707 Union. Earlier in the novel, however, Rose is one of two possible Scottish brides for Edward Waverley. Her rival is the fierce, enthusiastic Flora McIvor, an unreconstructed, and unreconstructable, Jacobite deeply in sympathy with the French and Catholic culture of the exiled Jacobite court, at which she has spent part of her childhood. In the world-view of the firmly Protestant British Imperial elite, someone of Flora's sympathies could only be regarded as an embodiment of the superstitious, 'Papist' old days before the Reformation, a throwback to the days of the fifteenth and sixteenth centuries when a Catholic Scotland was allied to France in a long struggle against the old enemy, England. The 'Papist' Flora undoubtedly has a glamorous and aristocratic appeal, but although this Jacobite loyalist is an attractive figure of romance, she will never be able to find a secure place in the sober realities of the Protestant British Empire—the Empire that, in Scott's eyes, embodies the future. In the end, Edward Waverley has to reject Flora if he is to take his place in that future. Flora is a powerful and attractive figure, but in Scott's novel she embodies aspects of the Scottish past that must be left behind if the British future is to be embraced. The mild, sweet, and unthreatening Rose, on the other hand, embodies aspects of the Scottish past that are capable of being preserved, and adjusted to the purposes of domesticity in the rational and enlightened prosperity of a flourishing Imperial Britain.

Scott's complex and subtle novel expresses real sympathy with its hero's open and enthusiastic response to the romantic appeal of Flora and the Jacobite cause, but nevertheless Edward Waverley, in the end, has to grow out of his Jacobite infatuations. He has to grow up, in short—and in order to grow up he has to choose reality rather than romance. In Chapter 60 of the novel Edward is separated from his Jacobite comrades in a skirmish at Clifton. He then experiences a period of quiet and sober reflection, during which he decides to abandon his Jacobite commitment, and to return to the rational, law-abiding world of modern Hanoverian Britain. In the final paragraph of Chapter 60 we read that, as a result of this choice, 'he felt himself entitled to say firmly, though perhaps with a sigh, that the romance of his life was ended, and that its real history had now commenced'. Edward thus carries the adaptable Rose rather than the threatening Flora into Scotland's British and Imperial future. In *Waverley*, Scott presents his case with his accustomed decency and persuasive rationality. Imperial Britain took this immensely popular best-selling novel to its heart, and *Waverley* became one of the key texts through which nineteenth-century Imperial Britain formulated its sense of its identity and mission. Scott's novel told a story in tune with Imperial Britain's projects and purposes, and it readily found a large and receptive audience.

In finding a place for Scotland's story within the post-Union context of Imperial Britain, *Waverley* sets up a pattern that involves a progression from a barbarous past to a civilised future. On this view, some valuable things are lost as the transition is made, but much more is gained. It is interesting and desirable to retain souvenirs from the past, and to preserve from the past whatever might usefully be adapted to the purposes of the modern Imperial world. However, what in the end really matters for the Scott of *Waverley* is not the preservation of souvenirs, but progress from barbarity to the high civilisation of Imperial Britain. The seductive but potentially dangerous energies of the past are persuasively embodied by Flora, but these energies must not be allowed to threaten the progress guaranteed by the rule of Britannia.

In tracing its patterns, *Waverley* was much influenced by the ideas of the Scottish Enlightenment of the eighteenth century, a movement through which writers like David Hume (1711–76) and Adam Smith (1723–90) developed a tradition of rational, objective, and scientific enquiry. This project brought spectacular intellectual results. For example, one writer of the Scottish Enlightenment, James Hutton (1726–97), has a strong claim to be regarded as the founder of modern geology; and another, Joseph Black (1728–99), did much to prepare the way for modern chemistry.

The writers of the Scottish Enlightenment took it for granted that human beings operate in a world of solid reality that can be mapped, measured, described, and understood. They assumed that James Hutton, having observed various rock formations and having made the appropriate deductions, was able to produce a *Theory of the Earth* that accurately explained the development of the planet's structures. Similarly, Scott's fictions operate on the assumption that the truth about the past can be established through an objective and unbiased sifting of the evidence. For Scott, the nature of the political forces at work in the Scotland of the 1740s can be known and understood, and *Waverley* sets out to give a lucid and accurate picture of the nature of these forces.

Much follows from the Enlightenment's assumptions. If it is believed that the *Theory of the Earth* has established the objective, measurable truth that lies out there in the world, then it would seem to follow that, if an unenlightened person takes a view different from the objective, measurable truth as articulated in the *Theory of the Earth*, then such a person is quite simply wrong. Undoubtedly the metaphor of 'Enlightenment' has something useful and valid to say about the intellectual changes that took place in the eighteenth century. Equally undoubtedly, persons disagreeing with the findings of the investigations of the Enlightenment were often, indeed, quite simply wrong. Having said that, however, something more remains to be said. If assumptions based on the metaphor of Enlightenment are pushed too far and too confidently, the resulting belief in 'Progress' might foster delusions among the Enlightened about their own infallibility. Unexpectedly and dangerously, this process might likewise foster racist delusions among the Enlightened about the worthlessness of unenlightened, 'primitive', 'marginal' people. From the perspective of the Enlightenment, it could be assumed that a 'savage' eighteenth-century Cherokee in the wilderness of the New World would have a theory of the earth that differed radically from Hutton's. Such 'savages', sunk in the darkness of their unenlightened beliefs, might imagine that the natural world is animated by a Great Spirit, and that it is important for human beings to respect and honour the natural world in which the Great Spirit manifests itself. For the Enlightenment, the 'savage' Cherokee is a fascinating specimen, a modern manifestation of a primitive world long left behind by the progress made by European society; but, for the Enlightenment, the Cherokee's ideas are quite simply wrong, being a manifestation of primitive, unenlightened superstition. Like the 'primitive' tribesmen of the Lower Niger, the Cherokees were felt to be in need of a process of 'pacification', a process that would lead them out of their dark savagery into the light of modern civilisation. This set of assumptions was confidently and sincerely held by many post-Enlightenment people of European descent, who assiduously engaged in various aspects of the European Imperial project. However it was not in the event a set of assumptions that turned out to be particularly good news for the Cherokees and other 'native' peoples.

Hogg Has a Subaltern Story to Tell

> He hath put down the mighty from *their* seats, and exalted them of low degree. He hath filled the hungry with good things; and the rich he hath sent empty away.   (Luke 1. 52–53: part of the Magnificat)

Hogg, like Scott, set out to assert on Scotland's behalf that 'we too might have a story to tell'. Hogg's attempt to tell this story was very different from Scott's, however. Unlike Scott, Hogg was not a member of the North British elite, and he was fully prepared to believe that the gentlemanly elite did not necessarily have a monopoly of wisdom. A self-educated farm worker, Hogg was a subaltern anxious to speak, a man of the margins well able to empathise readily with allegedly 'low' and unenlightened persons like Miss Swartz and 'black Sambo'. Hogg's fictions do not set out to reject and dismiss rational, objective enquiry of the kind that produced Hutton's *Theory of the Earth*—far from it, in fact, as we shall see. However, it seems clear that this shepherd from Ettrick was capable of imagining that his social superiors—well-educated, enlightened gentlemen—might sometimes be in error. He also appears to have been ready and willing to assert that 'low' people like Miss Swartz and 'black Sambo' might have an interesting and valuable story to tell.

These features of Hogg's writing emerge, for example, in 'Tibby Hyslop's Dream, and the Sequel', a story published in *Blackwood's Edinburgh Magazine* in 1827 as part of a sequence of stories by Hogg called 'The Shepherd's Calendar'.[10] It was as 'The Ettrick Shepherd' that Hogg contributed 'The Shepherd's Calendar' to *Blackwood's*, and the narrative voice of these stories is that of the Ettrick Shepherd speaking as a representative of the Ettrick community. Indeed, Hogg's 'Shepherd's Calendar' stories present themselves as a series of re-creations on paper of the manner and the content of traditional Ettrick oral story-telling. In tune with the pattern established by Scott in *Waverley*, old subaltern story-telling of this kind was seen as a relic of a primitive past, albeit a relic full of antiquarian interest for the genteel and civilised modern readers of *Blackwood's*. This attitude had something in common with the approach of Achebe's District Commissioner, that 'student of primitive customs'. Hogg's story, however, seeks to subvert such attitudes by raising the possibility that the 'primitive customs' of the old barbarous ways of subaltern Scotland might have a continuing life and validity.

Set in the south of Scotland towards the end of the eighteenth century, 'Tibby Hyslop's Dream' tells the story of Tibby Hyslop (a farm worker) and her employer Mr Gilbert Forret. When the story opens Tibby is a beautiful, pious, and simple-minded girl of eighteen who lives her life according to an old-fashioned and superstitious system of beliefs. Her employer, in contrast, is a man of the modern world, a gentleman-

farmer with an active interest in the possibilities for agricultural innovation that fascinated the land-owning elite of North Britain. Hogg's story was written for *Blackwood's*,
and this Tory periodical, read mostly by gentlemen, took an active interest in agriculture
and in country life. Its readers would have tended to identify with the sophisticated
agricultural innovator Gilbert Forret, rather than with his simple-minded and superstitious dairymaid, but Hogg's story unsettles these expectations by viewing matters
from Tibby's perspective. 'Tibby Hislop's Dream' seeks to give voice to the dairymaid's
insights and concerns: Tibby too might have a story to tell.

The opening of 'Tibby Hislop's Dream' focuses on the sexual pursuit of Tibby by
her employer. We are told that Forret 'was notorious in his neighbourhood for the
debauching of young and pretty girls, and was known in Dumfries market by the
name of Gibby Gledger, from the circumstance of his being always looking slyly after
them' (p. 143). To *gledge* is 'to give a sidelong glance, to leer'. In his pursuit of Tibby,
Gibby tries to bring matters to a crisis in the byre, and it would appear that he is prepared to use physical force in the process. He is interrupted by the unexpected approach
of Tibby's grandmother, however. In the aftermath of this crisis, the superstitious
dairymaid begins to show her mettle when she rebukes her master:

> It was a lesson to him—a warning of the most sublime and terrible description,
> couched in the pure and emphatic language of Scripture. Gibby cared not a doit for
> these things, but found himself foiled, and exposed to his family, and the whole world,
> if this fool chose to do it. He was, therefore, glad to act a part of deep hypocrisy,
> pretending the sincerest contrition, regretting, with tears, his momentary derange-
> ment, and want of self-control [...]. Poor Tibby readily believed and forgave him; and
> thinking it hard to ruin a repentant sinner in his worldly and family concerns, she
> promised never to divulge what had passed; and he knowing well the value of her
> word, was glad at having so escaped. (p. 148)

Much concerning 'value' is at stake here. Tibby may be a mere dairymaid, but her famili-
arity with 'the pure and emphatic language of Scripture' unexpectedly gives her a touch
of sublimity. On the other hand, the progressive and innovative gentleman-farmer
'cared not a doit for these things'. He does, however, know 'the value of her word',
and rendered secure by Tibby's promise the would-be rapist turns on his former favourite with real venom and viciousness. This development allows Hogg's short story
to raise searching questions about the values and assumptions of the powerful people
in the North British society of his day, and in doing so it focuses on an incident at a
communal meal. This focus is not accidental. Communal meals are a noticeable feature
of the gospel of Luke, and as we shall see 'Tibby Hyslop's Dream' is full of echoes of
Luke: signposting this, Hogg's narrator remarks that Tibby 'could repeat the book of
the Evangelist Luke by heart' (p. 142).

No longer her master's favourite after the attempted rape, Tibby loses her regular employment and begins to endure the deprivations that come with severe poverty: 'Times grew harder and harder. Thousands yet living remember what a time that was for the poor' (p. 149). Tibby, in short, is reduced to destitution, and one of her few moments of respite comes when she is offered a little food by Mrs Forret at a communal meal in the farm kitchen:

> However, it so happened that as Tibby was sitting behind backs enjoying her little savoury meal, Mr Forret chanced to come into the kitchen to give orders anent something that had come into his mind; and perceiving Tibby, his old friend, so comfortably engaged, he, without speaking a word, seized her by the neck with one hand, and by the shoulder with the other, and hurrying her out at the back-door into the yard, he flung her, with all his might, on a dunghill. "Wha the devil bade you come into my house, and eat up the meat that was made for others?" cried he in a demoniac voice, choking with rage; and then he swore a terrible oath, which I do not choose to set down, that "if he found her again at such employment, he would cut her throat, and fling her to the dogs." (p. 150)

Gibby's actions here diverge spectacularly from the advice given to the rich by Christ at Luke 14. 12–14:

> When thou makest a dinner or a supper, call not thy friends, nor thy brethren, neither thy kinsmen, nor *thy* rich neighbours; lest they also bid thee again, and a recompence be made thee. But when thou makest a feast, call the poor, the maimed, the lame, the blind; And thou shalt be blessed; for they cannot recompense thee; for thou shalt be recompensed at the resurrection of the just.[11]

In considering what is at stake in Tibby's expulsion from the communal meal in Hogg's story, it is useful to bear in mind the economic and social pressures that were at work in the Scotland of the 1820s. Hogg discusses these pressures in his essay 'On the Changes in the Habits, Amusements and Condition of the Scottish Peasantry', which he contributed to the *Quarterly Journal of Agriculture* in the early 1830s. In this essay, Hogg (by this date a man in his early sixties) asserts that modern-day shepherds and farm-workers 'are better fed, better clothed, and better educated than the old shepherds and hinds of my first acquaintance; but they are less devout, and decidedly *less cheerful and happy*'.[12] Hogg suggests that the 'change from gay to grave, from cheerfulness to severity' can be explained with reference to changes in 'the intercourse between master and servant' he has seen during his lifetime. In such matters, he says,

> there is a mighty change indeed, and to this I am disposed principally to attribute the manifest change in the buoyant spirit and gaiety of our peasantry. Formerly every mas-

ter sat at the head of his kitchen table, and shared the meal with his servants. The mistress, if there was one, did not sit down at all, but stood at the dresser behind, and assigned each his portion, or otherwise overlooked the board, and saw that every one got justice. The master asked a blessing, and returned thanks. [...] But ever since the ruinous war prices made every farmer for the time a fine gentleman, how the relative situations of master and servant are changed! Before that time every farmer was first up in the morning, conversed with all his servants familiarly, and consulted what was best to be done for the day. Now, the foreman, or chief shepherd, waits on his master, and, receiving his instructions, goes forth and gives the orders as his own, generally in a peremptory and offensive manner. The menial of course feels that he is no more a member of a community, but a slave; a servant of servants, a mere tool of labour in the hand of a man whom he knows or deems inferior to himself, and the joy of his spirit is mildewed. (pp. 43–45)

The radical change came, it seems, when 'the ruinous war prices made every farmer for the time a fine gentleman'. Farmers, Hogg suggests, have become much too grand to converse with the servants familiarly, as before, and the nature of the old communal meals has changed. Likewise, the mistress might now expect to be waited upon by the servants, where previously she would be actively in charge of the distribution of the food at the communal meal, her role being to ensure 'that every one got justice'. This was an important role, given that food was not always plentiful. Mrs Forret, in Hogg's story, has kept to the old ways in giving Tibby much-needed food. Her husband, however, adopts a different course.

It begins to appear that, in 'Tibby Hyslop's Dream', the economic and social changes that took place in rural Scotland around the time of the Napoleonic Wars do not necessarily add up to Progress. These changes may well have been good news for 'a fine gentleman' (a farmer or a landowner), but they can be seen as very bad news indeed for a 'menial' like Tibby, who has ceased to be 'a member of a community', and has become 'a slave; a servant of servants, a mere tool of labour'. Further light is thrown on these matters by a letter written by Sir Walter Scott on 1 October [1822]. In addition to being an author and a lawyer, Scott was also a businessman. He had a large financial stake in the Edinburgh printing firm James Ballantyne & Co., and his letter of 1 October 1822 discusses the proposed installation of a new labour-saving device, a steam-powered printing press, at the Ballantyne factory. Scott writes to James Ballantyne as follows:

The business of the printing machine is a weighty concern. I am, generally speaking, no friend to these improvements of mechanism which go to deprive the poor of their bread. It is plain they must be fed in one way or other, and that honest and industrious labour is the best way for all parties. On the other hand, individuals can not control the progress of improved mechanism in inventing new modes of abridging labour and certainly are entitled to take the full benefit of them since they would otherwise be forced to do it in the course of time.

We may start first and make something till others follow our steps, and should we want to be the last, we should be compelled to the same course when others had reaped the preliminary benefit. The final effect must be, sooner or later, a downfall in the price of printing, for your calculation gives too great and assured a profit to be allowed to subsist very long in your hands without rivalry. [...] Upon the whole, therefore, I think you may with safety embark in the concern, though I own I feel some repugnance to turning so many men adrift, and even somewhat afraid you may get your premises burned down, if you do not use double precaution. I beg you look to your insurances, and watch your office well, for in the present humour of the lower classes men are capable of strange things. [...] On the whole I incline to the experiment strongly, yet, to consider it minutely, I wish you could come over in the *Blucher* and spend a Sunday here bringing your documents with you.[13]

There is no reason to believe that Scott's 'repugnance to turning so many men adrift' was anything other than genuine, and one sympathises with his discomfort. Nevertheless his letter conveys rather starkly the potential consequences of the conflicting claims of economic pressure and communal feeling, as experienced by the North British elite during the years of recession that followed the end of the Napoleonic Wars. But if times were difficult for the Scottish elite, they could be even more harshly difficult for subaltern Scotland. Workers coping with the immediate consequences of 'these improvements of mechanism which go to deprive the poor of their bread' could face a situation almost as daunting as that faced by the victims of the evictions of the Highland Clearances.

The harsh circumstances of Hogg's childhood had given him direct personal experience of eviction and destitution. In 'Memoir of the Author's Life', his autobiography, he gives an account of the circumstances:

My father, like myself, was bred to the occupation of a shepherd, and served in that capacity until his marriage with my mother; about which time, having saved a considerable sum of money, for those days, he took a lease of the farms of Ettrick House and Ettrick Hall. He then commenced dealing in sheep—bought up great numbers, and drove them both to the English and Scottish markets; but, at length, owing to a great fall in the price of sheep, and the absconding of his principal debtor, he was ruined, became bankrupt, every thing was sold by auction, and my parents were turned out of doors without a farthing in the world. I was then in the sixth year of my age, and remember well the distressed and destitute condition that we were in. At length the late worthy Mr. Brydon, of Crosslee, took compassion upon us; and, taking a short lease of the farm of Ettrick House, placed my father there as his shepherd, and thus afforded him the means of supporting us for a time. This gentleman continued to interest himself in our welfare until the day of his untimely death, when we lost the best friend that we had in the world.[14]

Clearly, Hogg's own childhood experience of being in a 'distressed and destitute condition' would predispose him to empathise with Tibby Hyslop's sufferings. Equally, he had the most direct and personal of reasons for valuing practical compassion of the kind exhibited by 'the late worthy Mr. Brydon, of Crosslee'.

Hogg's essay 'On the Changes in the Habits, Amusements and Condition of the Scottish Peasantry' makes it clear that, in 'Tibby Hyslop's Dream', Mrs Forret's action in giving food to the famished Tibby forms part of the mistress's traditional task of ensuring that 'every one got justice'. Gibby, however, has rejected his traditional role of president at the communal meal. This man of the North British elite is much too fine a gentleman to eat with his servants. He comes into the kitchen simply 'to give orders anent something that had come into his mind', and his ejection of the needy Tibby onto the dunghill makes manifest his violation of the older system of communal values that had underpinned the timely help through which 'the late worthy Mr. Brydon, of Crosslee' saved the Hogg family from absolute destitution.

In 'Tibby Hyslop's Dream' this exploration of a contrast between an older and a more modern set of values is very far from asserting that this move from old to new amounts to the Progress so valued by the North British elite of the early nineteenth century. Gibby, operating in accordance with the new ways, is an exploiter. Just as he sought to rape Tibby, so he seeks to rape the farmland on which he is tenant. He exploits it by planting a succession of profitable but scourging crops, paying no heed to the conditions of his lease, or to the rotation of crops that the land needs. This being against Scots law, Gibby eventually has to defend himself in court.[15] However, his devious schemes to manipulate the evidence come unstuck because of Tibby's innocent simplicity and truthfulness, and the trial leads to the ruin and suicide of the previously prosperous farmer.

Gibby, the exploiter, is detached from any sense of community, and from any sense of religion: he 'cared not a doit for these things' (p. 148). On the other hand, Tibby's sense of community emerges in the care she takes of her aged relatives: her actions, like the behaviour of Mr Brydon of Crosslee to the Hogg family, can be read as a modern equivalent of the behaviour of the Good Samaritan in Christ's famous parable in Luke 10. 30–37. Tibby's connection with the old ways is further reflected in her rather old-fashioned and simple-minded attitude to the supernatural. Gibby and Tibby, then, embody a contrast between the new ways and the old; but, in presenting this contrast, Hogg's story unexpectedly subverts some of the assumptions of the new North Britain about the nature of progress and social change. Tibby is a superstitious dairymaid, not at all the kind of person by whom the enlightened gentlemen of North Britain were accustomed to be instructed. Likewise, in Christ's parable the Samaritan is a most unexpected object of admiration. For Jews, Samaritans were heretics who had departed from the true faith of the children of Israel. Nevertheless this despised outsider helps the man who has been robbed and beaten, while respected leaders of the Jewish people—the priest and the Levite—pass by on the other side. The story about Tibby, like the story about the Good Samaritan, offers a disconcerting challenge to the assumptions of a comfortable and self-satisfied elite.

As well as pointing to the parable of the Good Samaritan, 'Tibby Hyslop's Dream' also seems to echo Christ's parable of the Rich Fool (Luke 12. 16–21). In this parable the Rich Fool reaps a plentiful harvest from his land, stores up his wealth in abundance, and resolves to 'eat, drink, and be merry':

> But God said unto him, *Thou* fool, this night thy soul shall be required of thee: then whose shall those things be, which thou hast provided? So *is* he that layeth up treasure for himself, and is not rich toward God. (Luke 12. 20–21)

Explaining this parable to his disciples, Christ compares people endowed with riches to a steward 'whom *his* lord shall make ruler over his household, to give *them their* portion of meat in due season' (Luke 12. 42). A steward who performs this duty of distributing necessary food will be richly rewarded when his lord comes in judgement. However, a different fate awaits a steward who, like the Rich Fool, wants to keep all the goodies for himself so that he can 'eat, drink, and be merry'. A steward of this kind, the servant of his lord,

> shall begin to beat the menservants and maidens, and to eat and drink, and to be drunken; The lord of that servant will come in a day when he looketh not for *him*, and at an hour when he is not aware, and will cut him in sunder, and will appoint him his portion with the unbelievers. [...] For unto whomsoever much is given, of him shall be much required: and to whom men have committed much, of him they will ask the more. (Luke 12. 45–46, 48)

Gibby's treatment of Tibby at the communal meal becomes doubly resonant when seen in the context of this parable. This Scottish gentleman-farmer would appear to be a Rich Fool who 'layeth up treasure for himself', and who 'is not rich toward God'. Gilbert Forret, Esquire, refuses to give his dependant Tibby Hyslop her 'portion of meat in due season'. Instead he throws her on a dunghill, thus acting like one who 'shall begin to beat the menservants and maidens'. As Gibby discovers to his cost, an evil fate awaits such a man: God, his lord, 'will come in a day when he looketh not for *him*, and at an hour when he is not aware, and will cut him in sunder'. It appears from

Hogg's echoing of the parable of the Rich Fool that the rich have serious responsibilities: 'For unto whomsoever much is given, of him shall be much required'. The rich, in short, ought not to throw their dependants on the dunghill.

When Gibby throws Tibby onto the dunghill, one's mind turns naturally to the atrocities of the Highland Clearances. Equally, one thinks of Scott and Ballantyne in 1822, contemplating 'turning so many men adrift' in order to secure the 'great and assured […] profit' promised by the prompt installation of the steam press. It is odd to reflect that, when 'Tibby Hyslop's Dream' appeared in *Blackwood's Edinburgh Magazine* in 1827, it was printed in Ballantyne's printing-house. Given Hogg's close and friendly links with Edinburgh print workers,[16] it may even be that he was fully aware of the relevance of his story to events in the Ballantyne establishment.

Does all this imply that Hogg was a political radical, an advocate of violent revolutionary change? Gillian Hughes has demonstrated that Hogg had links with Whig and Radical political circles,[17] but he has more often been thought of as a Tory—a view that derives at least in part from his long-standing association with Tory circles through his links with *Blackwood's*, and through his friendships with Wilson and Scott. However, the emphasis on the parables of the Good Samaritan and the Rich Fool in 'Tibby Hyslop's Dream' suggests a Hogg who in the 1820s was not a rigid follower of either the Tory or the Radical party line, but who instead had something in common with George Orwell's account of the political position of Dickens and Blake. For Orwell, 'Dickens's criticism of society is almost exclusively moral'. Indeed, Orwell adds, Dickens's 'whole "message" is one that at first glance looks like an enormous platitude: If men would behave decently the world would be decent'. Orwell continues:

> Dickens is not *in the accepted sense* a revolutionary writer. But it is not at all certain that a merely moral criticism of society may not be just as "revolutionary"—and revolution, after all, means turning things upside down—as the politico-economic criticism which is fashionable at this moment. Blake was not a politician, but there is more understanding of the nature of capitalist society in a poem like "I wander through each charter'd street" than in three-quarters of Socialist literature. […] two viewpoints are always tenable. The one, how can you improve human nature until you have changed the system? The other, what is the use of changing the system before you have improved human nature? They appeal to different individuals, and they probably show a tendency to alternate in point of time. […] "If men would behave decently the world would be decent" is not such a platitude as it sounds.[18]

In its focus on the values of the parable of the Good Samaritan and the parable of the Rich Fool, 'Tibby Hyslop's Dream' exhibits a deeply-felt empathy with the plight of the destitute and the dispossessed, as well as an angry contempt for acts of callous cruelty. However, in Hogg these potentially radical instincts combine with a more conservative belief in the value of the old communal ways, and a distrust of glib ideas about Progress. One might say that, insofar as Hogg was a Tory, his Toryism had something in common with the One Nation approach that was later to drive Disraeli's *Sybil* (1845).

It will be remembered that Tibby's old-fashioned religion is manifested by the fact that she 'could repeat the book of the Evangelist Luke by heart' (p. 142). Luke's is the only gospel in which the parable of the Good Samaritan appears, and it is also the only gospel in which the parable of the Rich Fool appears. Furthermore, Luke's gospel, more than any of the others, gives emphasis to communication between heaven and humanity by means of visitations by angels. For example, Luke's is the only gospel which contains the story of the Annunciation, in which the angel Gabriel tells Mary of the coming birth of Jesus (Luke 1. 26–38), and it is the only gospel in which the birth of Jesus is announced by an angel to shepherds watching their flocks (Luke 2. 8–20).

There are strong hints in 'Tibby Hyslop's Dream' that Tibby's 'old aunty Douglas' has communication with an angel. Tibby's grandmother speaks about this.

> "But—lownly be it spoken—I think whiles there's ane speaks till her again that my een canna see."
>
> "The angels often conversed wi' good folks langsyne," said Tibby. "I ken o' naething that can hinder them to do sae still, if they're sae disposed. But weel wad I like to hear ane o' thae preevat apologies, (perhaps meaning apologues,) for my auntie has something in her aboon other earthly creatures." (p. 146)

It is as a result of one of these 'preevat apologies' that Tibby's grandmother is sent on the rescue mission that, it seems, is instrumental in foiling Gibby's attempt at rape. Likewise, before the great trial that leads to Gibby's ruin and suicide, Tibby has a strange and vivid dream based on a prophetic utterance of old aunty Douglas (p. 152). In her dream, Tibby sees the living body of the farmer being torn and eaten by a gathering of rooks and hooded crows, and at the trial, when she sees the various lawyers present, she at once recognises them 'as the birds that she saw, in her dream, devouring her master, and picking the flesh from his bones' (p. 157).

Is old aunty Douglas in communication with an angel who watches over Tibby, the holy fool? Or are the 'preevat apologies' simply the ramblings of senility, accepted as gospel by a silly and credulous simpleton? Adopting a strategy that is quintessentially characteristic of Hogg's fictions, the Ettrick Shepherd, with a twinkle in his eye and a deadpan expression, keeps both interpretations in play as he teases the gentlemanly readers of *Blackwood's Edinburgh Magazine* with the possibility that real 'Sense and Worth', in Burns's phrase, may lie with the half-witted and superstitious dairymaid rather than with that respectable and sophisticated agricultural innovator, Gilbert Forret, Esquire, of Drumlochie.

Robert Burns, King George IV, and Robert Wringhim

Unlike *Waverley*, 'Tibby Hyslop's Dream' was written against the grain of the assumptions and purposes of the Imperial British elite. In its own subtle, indirect, but deeply subversive way, however, 'Tibby Hislop's Dream' allows the Scottish subaltern to speak with a radical egalitarianism that has much in common with Burns's 'For a' that and a' that':

Ye see yon birkie ca'd, a lord,   [*youth*]
   Wha struts, and stares, and a' that;
Though hundreds worship at his word,
   He's but a coof for a' that.   [*fool*]
For a' that, and a' that,
   His ribband, star and a' that,
The man of independant mind,
   He looks and laughs at a' that.— [...]

Then let us pray that come it may,
   As come it will for a' that,
That Sense and Worth, o'er a' the earth
   Shall bear the gree, and a' that.   [*win the prize*]
For a' that, and a' that,
   It's comin yet for a' that,
That Man to Man the warld o'er,
   Shall brothers be for a' that.—[19]

The elite of Edinburgh aspired to be North British rather than Scotch, but they were happy to describe the peasant-poet Robert Burns as a 'Scotch bard'. In *Devolving English Literature* Robert Crawford argues that this 'served to categorize Burns rather patronizingly as a belated primitive curiosity—as if one were to describe someone today as "a Zumerzet provincial" '. One is tempted to interject the additional suggestion that the phrase 'a Scotch bard' carried something of the connotations of another unhappy old phrase, 'a nigger minstrel'. Be that as it may, Crawford continues:

> In adopting the description 'a Scotch bard' and calling it his 'highest pride', Burns attempts to valorize this patronizing term. It allows him again to side firmly with those supposedly rather primitive Ayrshire peasants from whose society he comes and whose language he often uses.[20]

Similarly, the stories of Hogg's 'Shepherd's Calendar' series in *Blackwood's* combine together to form a teasing game between the Shepherd and his gentlemanly Edinburgh audience, a game which allows Hogg to side with the supposedly rather primitive Ettrick peasants from whose society *he* comes.

Hogg likewise distanced himself from the assumptions of the North British elite when, in the summer of 1821, he was invited to accompany Scott to London in order to attend George IV's coronation. In a letter to Scott of 5 [July] 1821 Hogg replied to this invitation by saying that he could not go because he had to attend a local market fair to buy sheep to stock his farm:

> I recieved yours last night which has put me in a terrible puzzle so fain would I go to London. I have thought on it all this day and sometimes with the tear in my eye when I found on calm reflection the thing to be next to impracticable. That great day at London is the next after St. Boswel's fair if I were to run off privately and leave the market and my farm half stocked I were judged mad beyond all hope of recovery. *I may not do it!* [21]

Hogg adopts an apologetic tone as he respectfully declines Scott's invitation, and he expresses his admiration of the monarch in notably emphatic terms: 'there is no man in his majesty's dominions admires his great talents [...] so much as I do'. Perhaps it is possible to detect a hint of irony here, lurking not too far below the surface. Be that as it may, Hogg is writing to reject an opportunity to go to the coronation, in spite of a hint from Scott that the visit might be used to procure a pension at a time when Hogg was even more short of money than usual: 'If you were to procure me a pension from that society you talk of or any society; you will get it as well and better without me than with me'.

The Scottish poet Allan Cunningham, who was a stonemason and a friend of Hogg, was living in London at the time of the coronation, but he, like Hogg, did not choose to attend. Cunningham has recorded a conversation he had with Scott about this:

> 'Well, Allan,' he said, when he saw me at this last sitting 'were you at the coronation? it was a splendid sight.' 'No, Sir Walter,' I answered; 'places were dear and ill to get. I am told it was a magnificent scene; but having seen the procession of King Crispin at Dumfries, I was satisfied.' I said this with a smile. Scott took it as I meant it and laughed heartily.
>
> 'That's not a bit better than Hogg,' he said. 'He stood balancing the matter whether to go to the coronation or the fair of Saint Boswell, and the fair carried it.' [22]

In the summer of 1822, a year after the coronation in London, the new king visited Edinburgh. 'Sixty years since', in the aftermath of the Jacobite rising of 1745-46, kilts and tartan had been regarded as seditious Jacobite symbols, and the wearing of them had been prohibited by law. For the visit of George IV to Edinburgh in 1822, however, Sir Walter Scott stage-managed a spectacular tartan-draped celebration, designed to set the seal on a transfer of loyalties from a Scottish and Jacobite past to a British and Hanoverian future. The new monarch personally entered into the spirit of things with becoming enthusiasm, clothing his ample frame in a kilt in honour of the occasion. Famously (and prudently), however, he gave due regard to the demands of modesty by wearing pink tights underneath his kilt.[23] Hogg's decision to remain immersed in the sheep-farming concerns of St Boswell's fair, rather than go to the coronation, has often been told as an example of his absurdity. This decision no doubt was absurd, at any rate when seen from the perspective of the Imperial elite. However, Hogg's choice was not the only absurdity associated with the pageantry that marked the opening of the reign of George IV.

ENGLISH IRISH
HIGHLANDER.

George IV in Edinburgh in 1822: from
The English Irish Highlander (Covent Garden: J. L. Marks, [1822])
© The Trustees of The British Museum

In organising the royal visit as well as in writing *Waverley*, Scott was attempting to create a narrative that would allow Scotland to find an accepted place in Britain's Imperial power structures. In this project, Scott was active on Scotland's behalf: he was asserting that 'we too might have a story to tell'. This assertiveness, however, was designed to enhance, rather than to challenge, the British political status quo; it was designed to secure Scotland's place at the British Imperial table. Scott's writings thus connect powerfully with the insights and ambitions of the Imperial elite. Similarly, it seems clear that Hogg's writings (like those of Burns a generation earlier) set out in a somewhat different direction as they seek to articulate the insights and ambitions of subaltern Scotland.

It was in this context that Hogg responded to Scott's politically-charged storytelling (in *Waverley* and in the royal visit of 1822) by means of an equally politically-charged story of his own, *The Private Memoirs and Confessions of a Justified Sinner* (1824). Set around the time of the 1707 Union between Scotland and England, this novel carries forward the pro-subaltern project of Burns and Hogg by presenting two competing narratives about the life of one Robert Wringhim. In the first of these narratives, Robert's story is told by a fictional 'Editor'. There then follows the strikingly different competing account of Robert's life that is contained in his own 'Private Memoirs and Confessions'. It will be argued below that Hogg's novel is thus able to contain within itself the equivalent of both *Jane Eyre* and *Wide Sargasso Sea*, the equivalent of both *Things Fall Apart* and *The Pacification of the Primitive Tribes of the Lower Niger*.

Scott, Wilson, and *Confessions of a Justified Sinner*

How then do the competing narratives of *Confessions of a Justified Sinner* operate? The attitudes and narrative strategies of Hogg's Editor call to mind the attitudes and narrative strategies of Peter Pattieson, the fictional narrator of Scott's *Old Mortality* (1816). In this novel Scott focuses on the Scottish Covenanters, a religiously-motivated subaltern movement named for their support of the principles of the 'National Covenant' of 1638 and the 'Solemn League and Covenant' of 1643. These Covenants were based on widespread Scottish opposition to attempts by the state to control the Scottish church in the interest of Royal power. Following the Restoration of Charles II in 1660, there were major armed risings in 1666 and in 1679, in which the Covenanters attempted to assert the rights of the people. Peter Pattieson's narrative in *Old Mortality* centres around the rising of 1679—a politically-sensitive subject during the radical agitation of the second half of the 1810s, because most subaltern Lowland Scots of Scott's generation remembered the Covenanters with respect and affection as people prepared to die defending the rights of the people in the face of aristocratic oppression.[24]

Peter Pattieson, Scott's narrator, claims that his narrative in *Old Mortality* presents an 'unbiassed picture of the manners of that unhappy period', a picture based on his researches among 'the most authentic sources of tradition, afforded by the representatives of either party'.[25] In keeping with this measured tone, *Old Mortality* duly gives a sympathetic account of the actions of the gentlemanly and moderate Covenanter Henry Morton, as he opposes tyrannical abuses of royal power. However, Pattieson's narrative draws a sharp distinction between Morton's admirable moderation, and the position of extremist Covenanters like John Balfour of Burley and Habakkuk Meiklewrath, who are presented as murderously deranged fanatics. This aspect of *Old*

Mortality draws on Scott's visceral hostility to the kind of popular revolutionary energy that had found expression in the subversive forces liberated by the French Revolution. In attacking extremist Covenanters as murderous fanatics, Scott's novel articulated the fear and the antagonism felt by members of the British Imperial elite of the Waterloo generation when they contemplated the comparatively recent history of Revolutionary France: the storming of the Bastille, Robespierre, the Jacobins, and the Terror.

The titlepage of the first edition of Hogg's novel reads: *The Private Memoirs and Confessions of a Justified Sinner: Written by Himself: With a Detail of Curious Traditionary Facts, and Other Evidence, by the Editor.* It is possible to detect here an echo of the tone of detached objectivity adopted by Peter Pattieson, the narrator of *Old Mortality*. Clearly, Hogg's 'Editor', like Pattieson, will investigate traditions, and will then weigh up the evidence in order to arrive at his conclusions. Pattieson's approach is also echoed in the opening words of the text of Hogg's novel, when the Editor writes: 'It appears from tradition, as well as some parish registers still extant [...]'.[26] Furthermore, the Editor's contemptuous and unsympathetic picture of Robert Wringhim presents a murderous and deranged fanatic, another Habakkuk Mucklewrath. In short, 'The Editor's Narrative' echoes the narrative tone of Scott's *Old Mortality*, and tells the life-story of a man who is an heir of the fanatics of *Old Mortality*.

Hogg's Editor, then, can be linked with Scott. Furthermore, Peter Garside has argued convincingly that Hogg's Editor also carries echoes of John Wilson / 'Christopher North'. Indeed, after pointing out that 'Wilson's stinging review' of *The Three Perils of Woman* appeared in *Blackwood's* while Hogg was writing the *Justified Sinner*, Garside suggests that 'a now noticeably more Wilson-like Editor' appears in the final pages of Hogg's novel.[27] The 'Editor' of the *Confessions of a Justified Sinner* can thus be associated with the two leading figures of the North British literary elite of Hogg's day, and 'The Editor's Narrative', it would appear, is Robert's life-story as it would be understood and told by that elite. It is, one might say, the official and accepted story, an equivalent of *The Pacification of the Primitive Tribes of the Lower Niger*. In contrast, we find in Robert's own 'Private Memoirs and Confessions' a story of disintegration that emerges from an old, pre-Enlightenment world, a narrative that fits the title *Things Fall Apart*. In these 'Private Memoirs and Confessions' the Editor's monster is humanised into an incompetent and bewildered fool caught up in a sequence of events that he can neither control nor understand. Increasingly, it becomes clear that 'the Editor's Narrative' is not the only possible view of the events of Robert's life. Robert, too, has a story to tell.

What is at stake as the two major narratives of *Confessions of a Justified Sinner* compete to tell the story of Robert's life? Significantly, Hogg's novel concludes with a short final narrative, in which the Editor describes how, in September 1823, he and a group of companions open Wringhim's grave on a mountain in Ettrick Forest. A striking feature of this coda is that one James Hogg (an Ettrick shepherd) makes an appearance as a character within the fiction. Unusually, Hogg insisted to his publishers that this particular novel should appear anonymously. Had the novel appeared in 1824 with Hogg's name on the titlepage, it would have been easy for readers to jump to the conclusion that the Editor must be a manifestation of the familiar figure of James Hogg, the Ettrick Shepherd. As things stand, however, it is possible for a surly and unhelpful James Hogg to enter the fiction in order to decline to guide the Editor to Wringhim's grave. The Editor meets 'Hogg' at a market fair, but this Ettrick shepherd has more important matters in hand than the Editor's jaunt:

> "Od bless ye, lad! I hae ither matters to mind. I hae a' thae paulies to sell, an' a' yon Highland stotts down on the green every ane; an' then I hae ten scores o' yowes to buy after, an' if I canna first sell my ain stock, I canna buy nae ither body's. I hae mair ado than I can manage the day, foreby ganging to houk up hunder-year-auld banes." (p. 170)

This reads rather like a re-run of the famous story about Scott, Hogg, the 1821 coronation, and St Boswell's Fair. At all events it is clear that, in the scene at the fair in which the surly shepherd declines to go along with the Editor, 'James Hogg' enters the fiction in order to obstruct and oppose a figure who is in some sense an embodiment of Edinburgh's elite literary world of the time, a world dominated by Sir Walter Scott and Professor John Wilson. However, this involves something more complex than a simple confrontation between 'Hogg' on the one hand, and 'Scott / Wilson' on the other. The figure of another major Scottish author seems to be in some way involved in this conflict over the houking up of hunder-year-auld banes. The author in question is Robert Burns, radical ploughman-poet and iconic hero of the Scottish people. As we shall see, references to Burns in the *Justified Sinner* raise searching questions about the grave-robbing activities of the 'Scott / Wilson' figure of the Editor.

Robert Burns, Robert I, and Robert Wringhim

The *Justified Sinner* was published in 1824, and Carol McGuirk has suggested that the account of the grave-opening in Hogg's novel echoes accounts of an exhumation of the body of Robert Burns in Dumfries in 1815. McGuirk's brief but very valuable suggestion appears in an essay on 'Burns and Nostalgia';[28] and she points in particular to an account written in 1834 by Hogg's friend, John McDiarmid of Dumfries, of the 1815 opening of Burns's grave, at which McDiarmid had himself been present. McDiarmid's account is reprinted in full in Hogg's book-length *Memoir of Burns* (1835).

Burns died in 1796, and he was buried in St Michael's churchyard, Dumfries. A simple gravestone was erected by his widow, but when a proposal for a more elaborate memorial eventually bore fruit in 1815, the grave had to be opened to allow the body to be moved to its new, grander resting-place. In his account of the 1815 grave-opening, McDiarmid mentions the opening in 1818 of the grave of another Scottish national hero, King Robert I (the Bruce). Through his victory at the Battle of Bannockburn in 1314 Robert I had defeated an attempted imperial conquest of Scotland by Edward I of England, and the Scottish independence secured at Bannockburn survived until the Union of 1707. The body of the victor of Bannockburn had been buried in a marble tomb in the church of Dunfermline, following his death in 1329. Hogg, like McDiarmid, seems to have associated the opening of the grave of Robert I in 1818 with the opening of the grave of Robert Burns in 1815, and it may therefore be useful to quote an account of the opening of Robert I's grave as an introduction to McDiarmid's account of the opening of Burns's grave. The following account of the opening of the king's grave is taken from Scott's *Tales of a Grandfather : Being Stories Taken from Scottish History*. As is clear from Scott's account, the memory of Robert I was held in particular affection by what Scott calls 'the common people'.

Robert I's heart, having been removed from his body after his death, was eventually buried in Melrose Abbey. Scott mentions this, and continues:

> As for his body, it was interred in the midst of the church of Dunfermline, under a marble stone. But the church becoming afterwards ruinous, and the roof falling down with age, the monument was broken to pieces, and nobody could tell where it stood. But [...] when they were repairing the church at Dunfermline [in 1818], and removing the rubbish, lo! they found fragments of the marble tomb of Robert Bruce. Then they began to dig farther, thinking to find the body of this celebrated monarch; and at length they came to the skeleton of a tall man, and they knew it must be that of King Robert, both because he is known to have been buried in a winding sheet of cloth of gold, of which many fragments were found about this skeleton, and also because the breastbone appeared to have been sawed through, in order to take out the heart. So orders were sent from the King's Court of Exchequer to guard the bones carefully, until a new tomb should be prepared, into which they were laid with great respect. A great many gentlemen and ladies attended, and almost all the common people in the neighbourhood. And as the church would not hold the numbers, they were allowed to pass through it, one after another, that each one, the poorest as well as the richest, might see all that remained of the great King Robert Bruce, who restored the Scottish monarchy. Many people shed tears; for there was the wasted skull, which once was the head that thought so wisely and boldly for his country's deliverance; and there was the dry bone, which had once been the sturdy arm that killed Sir Henry de Bohun, between the two armies, at a single blow, on the evening before the battle of Bannockburn.[29]

Scott's underlying political agenda can be glimpsed when he describes the victor of

Bannockburn as 'the great King Robert Bruce, who restored the Scottish monarchy'. There is an implied reference here to the defeat of Napoleon that was finally secured at Waterloo in 1815, and which paved the way (to Scott's delight) for the restoration of the French monarchy. As a member of the North British elite, and as a supporter of monarchy and of the Union, Scott here gives his own spin to Robert I's achievement. However, the feelings of 'the common people' were no doubt more in tune with the sentiments of Burns's famous song 'Robert Bruce's March to Bannockburn', which begins 'SCOTS, wha hae wi' WALLACE bled, | Scots, wham BRUCE has aften led'. This rousing hymn to Liberty was written in 1793 at a time of stirring revolutionary events in France, and it contrives to be simultaneously a celebration of Robert I's victory at Bannockburn and a celebration of the principles of the French Revolution. In a letter to George Thomson written about 30 August 1793, Burns mentions the old air 'Hey tutti taitie', and continues:

> There is a tradition, which I have met with in many places of Scotland, that it was Robert Bruce's March at the battle of Bannock-burn.—This thought, in my yesternight's evening walk, warmed me to a pitch of enthusiasm on the theme of Liberty & Independance, which I threw into a kind of Scots Ode, fitted to the Air, [which (*deleted*)] that one might suppose to be the gallant ROYAL SCOT's address to his heroic followers on that eventful morning. [...] the accidental recollection of that glorious struggle for Freedom, associated with the glowing ideas of some other struggles of the same nature, *not quite so ancient*, roused my rhyming Mania.[30]

'Robert Bruce's March to Bannockburn' ends with the words 'Let us DO—OR DIE!!!', and, as Andrew Noble and Patrick Scott Hogg observe, this is the tennis court oath of the French revolutionaries.[31] It appears that Scott and Burns, in associating Bannockburn with events flowing from the French Revolution, drew diametrically and revealingly opposite conclusions about reasons for celebrating Robert I's victory.

However that may be, Scott made use of the opportunity afforded by the opening of King Robert's tomb in 1818, and obtained a cast of 'the wasted skull, which once was the head that thought so wisely and boldly for his country's deliverance'. This cast of Robert I's skull was kept as an interesting antiquarian relic on the mantelpiece of the Entrance Hall of Sir Walter's home at Abbotsford.[32] A similar desire to obtain souvenirs by disturbing the bones of the dead makes itself felt in John McDiarmid's eyewitness account of the opening of Burns's grave in 1815. McDiarmid writes:

> It is generally known that the remains of Burns were exhumed, privately, on the 19th September, 1815, and deposited with every regard to decency, in the arched vault attached to the Mausoleum, then newly-erected in honour of his memory. The principal actors, on that occasion, were the late Convener Thomson, and Mr Milligan, builders,

Mr Grierson, Secretary to the Monument Committee, and Mr Bogie, Terraughty. Originally, his ashes lay in the north corner of the churchyard; and as years elapsed before any general movement was made, his widow, with pious care, marked the spot by a modest monument, the expense of which she willingly defrayed out of her own slender means. In the first instance, attempts were made to enlarge the churchyard wall, and thus avert the necessity of a ceremony, in the highest degree revolting to the feelings of Mrs Burns; but the spot was so narrow, and interfered so closely with the property of others, that the idea was abandoned as utterly impracticable. On the day, therefore, already named, the committee chosen, proceeded to the spot before the sun had risen, and went to work so rapidly, that they had well nigh completed their purpose previous to the assemblage of any crowd. And it was fortunate their measures were so wisely taken; for though the gates of St Michael's were carefully locked, a few early risers, and accidental observers, communicated so speedily their suspicions to others, that before the entrance to the vault could be closed, an immense crowd besieged the churchyard walls, and, on leave being refused, readily found the means of admitting themselves. Still the individuals alluded to discharged, with the greatest sternness, their duty as sentinels, by repressing all attempts at obtaining bones, or indeed anything connected with the respective coffins of the Bard and his two sons.— As a report had been spread that the largest coffin was made of oak, hopes were entertained that it would be possible to remove it without injury, or public examination of any kind. But this hope proved fallacious; on testing the coffin it was found to be composed of ordinary materials, and liable to yield to the slightest pressure; and the lid partially removed, a spectacle was unfolded, which, considering the fame of the mighty dead, has rarely been witnessed by a single human being. There lay the remains of the great poet, to all appearance entire, retaining various traces of recent vitality; or, to speak more correctly, exhibiting the features of one who had newly sunk into the sleep of death. The forehead struck every one as beautifully arched, if not so high as might have been reasonably supposed, while the scalp was rather thickly covered with hair, and the teeth perfectly firm and white. Altogether the scene was so imposing that the commonest workmen stood uncovered, as the late Dr Gregory did at the exhumation of the remains of King Robert Bruce, and for some moments remained inactive, as if thrilling under the effects of some undefinable emotion, while gazing on all that remained of one 'whose fame is as wide as the world itself.' But the scene, however imposing, was brief; for the instant the workmen inserted a shell or wooden case beneath the original coffin, the head separated from the trunk, and the whole body, with the exception of the bones, crumbled into dust. Notwithstanding of the solemnity the occasion required, at least a few felt constrained to lift and examine the skull,—probably under the inspiration of feelings akin to those of Hamlet when he leant and moralized over Yorick's grave [...].

Every thing, as we have said, was conducted with the greatest propriety and care;

and after the second grave-bed of the poet and his offspring had been carefully prepared, the original tomb-stone was placed above their ashes, and the vault closed for a
period of nearly nineteen years,—that is, from the 19th September, 1815, till the 28th
March, 1834.[33]

Burns's widow died in 1834, and the vault was opened then to allow her body to be
placed beside her husband's. This second grave-opening happened around the time
that Hogg was writing his *Memoir of Burns*, but clearly it is the 1815 exhumation, described above by McDiarmid, that may be a significant presence in *The Private Memoirs
and Confessions of a Justified Sinner* of 1824. There can be little doubt that Hogg was
aware of the details of the 1815 grave-opening, at the time when he was writing the
Justified Sinner. He had lived in the Dumfries area from 1804 till 1810, and in his book-
length *Memoir of Burns*, Hogg records that in 1804 he 'was accustomed to sit in the seat
next to' Burns's widow 'in the old church of Dumfries'.[34] Furthermore, Hogg's wife's
family were Dumfries people, and after he left the area Hogg kept in contact with
friends there, including John McDiarmid.[35] In addition, Hogg was obsessively interested in his ambition to be the successor of Burns, wrongly convincing himself (for
example) that he shared Burns's birthday, 25 January. In his autobiographical 'Memoir
of the Author's Life' Hogg gives prominence to an account of his first encounter with
a poem by Burns, when a man called Jock Scott repeated 'Tam o' Shanter' to him.

> I was delighted! I was far more than delighted—I was ravished! I cannot describe my
> feelings; but, in short, before Jock Scott left me, I could recite the poem from begin-
> ning to end, and it has been my favourite poem ever since. [...] This formed a new
> epoch of my life. Every day I pondered on the genius and fate of Burns. I wept, and
> always thought with myself—what is to hinder me from succeeding Burns?[36]

In all the circumstances, it seems likely that Hogg quickly obtained detailed information about the 1815 exhumation of Burns's body. It comes as no great surprise, then,
that there are several points of detail with regard to the 1815 exhumation that appear
to find echoes in the accounts in the *Justified Sinner* of the burial and the exhumation
of Robert Wringhim's body. For example, the body of Robert Wringhim, like the
body of Robert Burns, appears entire when the grave is opened, but quickly crumbles
away. In both cases, the scalp is thickly covered with hair, and in both cases the head
becomes detached from the trunk. Likewise, the exhumation of Burns takes place hur-
riedly as sunrise approaches, and the burial of Wringhim takes place in similar circumstances. Equally, the exhumation of Burns takes place on 19 September; while
Wringhim's 'last day of mortal existence' is 18 September, and he is buried 'early next
morning', 19 September (*Justified Sinner*, pp. 165, 167). This matching of dates may of
course be a coincidence: but it seems more likely to be a signal to the alert reader. It is

also worth noting that it is in September 1823 that the Editor and his companions open Wringhim's grave (*Justified Sinner*, p. 169).

The suggestion in all this is not, of course, that Robert Wringhim is Hogg's portrait of either Robert Burns or Robert I. Rather, the suggestion is that the figure of Burns (the spokesman and hero of subaltern Scotland) is in some sense a significant presence as the Ettrick Shepherd refuses to assist the Editor's project, the houking up of hunder-year-auld banes.

Souvenirs and Opened Graves

What precisely is at stake in the houking up of hunder-year-auld banes? At the opened grave, the Editor and his companions divide up the loot they have taken from the body in the grave. The Editor writes:

> we had hard work to find out all his pockets, and our guide supposed, that, after all, we did not find above the half of them. In his vest pocket was a long clasp knife, very sharp; the haft was thin, and the scales shone as if there had been silver inside. Mr. Sc——t took it with him, and presented it to his neighbour, Mr. R——n of W——n L——, who still has it in his possession. (p. 173)

In the *Justified Sinner*, Mr. Sc——t and William Laidlaw are among the Editor's companions at the grave-opening. For the Ettrick Shepherd, who tries to block the Editor's path to the grave, Mr Sc——t is wrong to treat relics of the Ettrick past as mere antiquarian curiosities, as souvenirs to be exhibited alongside the cast of Robert I's skull on the mantelpiece at Abbotsford. Hogg first met Scott in 1802, more than twenty years before the publication of the *Justified Sinner*. This meeting took place when Sir Walter (then Mr) Scott was visiting Ettrick Forest with a view to collecting and publishing the fragments of old ballads that remained there in oral tradition. Mr Scott was a young Edinburgh lawyer of literary tastes, and he held the legal post of Sheriff in the Ettrick area. Earlier in 1802 he had published two volumes of *Minstrelsy of the Scottish Border*, his definitive collection of traditional ballads, and a third volume was in preparation.[37] On his visit to Ettrick in 1802 Mr Scott was accompanied by William Laidlaw, and one purpose of the visit was to investigate 'Auld Maitland', a ballad suspected to be a modern forgery.

Whatever the mature Hogg eventually came to think of Scott's ballad-collecting activities, it seems clear that in 1802 the young Hogg was flattered by the Sheriff's interest, and was happy to assist with the research for the third volume of the *Minstrelsy*. At all events, in 1802 Scott sought out Hogg's mother, to hear her sing 'Auld Maitland'. In his *Familiar Anecdotes of Sir Walter Scott* (1834), Hogg gives the following account of what happened next:

My mother chaunted the ballad of Old Maitlan' to him, with which he was highly delighted, and asked her if she thought it ever had been in print? And her answer was, "O na, na, sir, it never was printed i' the world, for my brothers an' me learned it an' many mae frae auld Andrew Moor, and he learned it frae auld Baby Mettlin, wha was housekeeper to the first laird o' Tushilaw. She was said to hae been another nor a gude ane, an' there are many queer stories about hersel', but O, she had been a grand singer o' auld songs an' ballads."

"The first laird of Tushielaw, Margaret?" said he, "then that must be a very old story indeed?"

"Ay, it is that, sir! It is an auld story! But mair nor that, excepting George Warton an' James Stewart, there war never ane o' my sangs prentit till ye prentit them yoursel', an' ye hae spoilt them awthegither. They were made for singing an' no for reading; but ye hae broken the charm now, an' they'll never be sung mair. An' the worst thing of a', they're nouther right spell'd nor right setten down."

"Take ye that, Mr. Scott," said Laidlaw.

Scott answered with a hearty laugh, and the quotation of a stanza from Wordsworth, on which my mother gave him a hearty rap on the knee with her open hand, and said, "Ye'll find, however, that it is a' true that I'm telling ye." My mother has been too true a prophetess, for from that day to this, these songs, which were the amusement of every winter evening, have never been sung more.[38]

Like the District Commissioner in the final chapter of *Things Fall Apart*, 'Mr Scott' is a member of the Imperial elite and a 'student of primitive customs'. In Achebe's novel, Okonkwo dies as his traditional culture falls apart in the face of an Imperial advance allegedly dedicated to 'the pacification of the primitive tribes of the Lower Niger'. In Ettrick in 1802 another traditional culture is in danger of falling apart in the face of the advance of the values of the Imperial elite of North Britain, and Mr Scott, Sheriff of Ettrick Forest, collects souvenirs of that culture for his *Minstrelsy of the Scottish Border*. All this is uncomfortably similar to the behaviour in Hogg's novel of the group consisting of the Editor, William Laidlaw, 'Mr Sc—t', and their companions as they dig up Robert Wringhim's bones and carry off their souvenirs. It is also uncomfortably similar to the deplorable activities of the various assorted souvenir-hunters in Dumfries in 1815, at the opening of Burns's grave. It will be remembered that McDiarmid remarks that 'the individuals alluded to discharged, with the greatest sternness, their duty as sentinels, by repressing all attempts at obtaining bones, or indeed anything connected with the respective coffins of the Bard and his two sons'. In the final pages of the *Justified Sinner* the Ettrick Shepherd adopts a similar role as sentinel, as he tries to obstruct the progress of the gang of souvenir-hunters towards Robert Wringhim's grave.

That grave can be seen as a shrine of the culture of an old pre-Union Scotland, a culture that pre-dated the North British elite's desire to integrate themselves into the life of the British Imperial centre. This old Scottish culture had once possessed its own confidently aristocratic aspects, but was now increasingly confined to the non-elite world of subaltern Scotland. Scott and other members of the North British elite entered this subaltern world *de haut en bas*, in order to collect survivals from the Scottish past, survivals which they then preserved as souvenirs—on the mantelpiece at Abbotsford, for example, or between the covers of *Minstrelsy of the Scottish Border* (where, however, we have good authority for believing that 'they're nouther right spell'd nor right setten down'). Hogg, on the other hand, was born into the old subaltern culture, and as his literary career unfolded, he sought to continue to inhabit that culture, and to revive and develop it.

Superstitious and bigoted, Robert Wringhim is the antithesis of the assumptions and values of the Editor's new post-Union world. This deranged fanatic is very far from being a product of the Scottish Enlightenment. For better or worse, however, Robert Wringhim and his grave embody important aspects of the old culture of Scotland. Likewise, Robert Burns can be seen as someone who speaks from a position rooted within an old Scottish culture different from, and in competition with, the culture of the North British Imperial elite. We have seen that, in *Devolving English Literature*, Robert Crawford writes:

> In adopting the description 'a Scotch bard' and calling it his 'highest pride', Burns attempts to valorize this patronizing term. It allows him again to side firmly with those supposedly rather primitive Ayrshire peasants from whose society he comes and whose language he often uses.

Crawford continues:

> As he negotiates with the term 'bard', Burns's invention of the mockingly inflated 'bardship', his deployment of the self-deprecating diminutive 'bardie', and his adoption and celebration of the term 'a Scotch bard' show him well able to cope with the values of the metropolitan world of literature, and able to avoid being trapped in the potentially patronizing or embalming bardolatry of being simply a 'bard'. It is just such tactical canniness which he was to exhibit in his face-to-face dealings with the literati of Edinburgh, subverting and redeploying the power of their culture while remaining on good terms with men whose linguistic and other ideals were very different from his own.[39]

Like Burns, Hogg was able to participate in the metropolitan North British literary culture of Edinburgh, redeploying its tools in order to subvert some of its assumptions. Ultimately, however, Hogg's loyalties (like Burns's) lie with 'those supposedly rather primitive [...] peasants from whose society he comes'. In short, Burns and Hogg are Scotch bards who set out to speak on behalf of subaltern Scotland. Chinua Achebe adopts a similar role in *Things Fall Apart*, as he sets out to speak on behalf of the old pre-Imperial oral culture of the Igbo people. In undertaking this role, Achebe (like Burns and Hogg) seeks to demonstrate that 'we too might have a story to tell'.

It is in his role as bardic guardian of his people's story that the Ettrick Shepherd, in the final pages of the *Justified Sinner*, attempts to protect the shrine of pre-North-British Scotland—the grave of Robert Wringhim; the grave of Robert Burns; the grave of Robert I, King of Scots; the shrine at the heart of Ettrick Forest; the shrine of the old pre-Imperial and pre-Enlightenment culture of subaltern Scotland. Hogg seeks to protect this shrine from a souvenir-hunting party of grave-robbing gentlemen from North Britain's literary elite.

As the Ettrick Shepherd thus lines up with Burns (the radical Ploughman-Poet) against the elite North British literary establishment embodied by Scott and Wilson, it is possible to trace various parallels with *Things Fall Apart*. Achebe's novel deals with what might be called the *Waverley* moment, the moment at which an old, traditional, oral culture is threatened by the advance of the modern world; the moment at which the singing of the old songs during the long dark winter evenings falls out of fashion. How can we look back on an old oral culture, after the fall? It is tempting to try to romanticise it and to possess it through souvenirs, while continuing to live in our very different modern world. That was, it seems, Scott's relationship to traditional Highland culture as he organised the tartan extravaganza which was George IV's visit to Scotland in 1822. That was, likewise, the souvenir-hunting approach of the Editor and his friends when robbing the grave in Ettrick Forest. It was also the approach that put a cast of Robert I's skull on display on the mantelpiece at Abbotsford.

Hogg's writings, in contrast, adopt an approach that has more in common with *Things Fall Apart*. Faced with demeaning and blinkered Euro-centric assumptions that pre-colonial African tribal society was 'primitive' and 'savage', Achebe's novel constructs an alternative view of that society. This alternative view tries to give an honest, clear-eyed account of the real nature of the old culture, an account in which the old culture can speak in its own voice. For this reason, Achebe's novel does not avert its gaze from such things as the routine abandonment of newly-born twins, the occasional violence of Okonkwo, the killing of Ikemefuna. Nevertheless, in *Things Fall Apart* the techniques of the novel—that manifestation of modern European literary culture—provide the tools that make possible the telling of a story that subverts blinkered Euro-centric assumptions about Africa, a story that articulates and celebrates the worth of traditional Igbo oral culture. Achebe's text, when it reaches its final paragraph, has thoroughly discredited the Euro-centric assumptions about Imperial civilisation embodied in the title of the District Commissioner's projected book: *The Pacification of the Primitive Tribes of the Lower Niger*.

Re-Connecting with the Past

In a sense, *Things Fall Apart* is an attempt to resurrect the past, in that it is an attempt to tell it like it was. However, Achebe's novel does not advocate a return to the kind of life that it presents as having existed among the Igbo people in pre-Imperial days. Instead, its attitude seems to have something in common with the general thrust of the outlook of Jawaharlal Nehru, as described by Ania Loomba, who writes of Nehru's 'Anglicisation, his belief in socialism, modernity, and Western science'. Nevertheless, Loomba continues, Nehru

> was passionately eloquent about the 'Idea of India' which had been shaped at the dawn of civilisation and had survived for thousands of years. Such an idea, he suggested had changed through the ages but still clung to some of its originary foundations. We can find similar resurrections of the past in many African, Arab, and other nationalisms. Such a going back is actually quite modern in itself —it is a product of a *present* need, which reshapes, rather than simply invokes the past.[40]

This, then, is the point of saying that 'we too might have a story to tell'. As one of the architects of post-Imperial India, Nehru sought to re-connect India's future with its past after the Empire's attempt to marginalise or silence the voice of India's pre-Imperial culture. *Things Fall Apart*, in like manner, seeks to re-connect Africa's future with Africa's past. A 'Scotch Bard' of the generations of Burns and Hogg could aspire to a similar role.

Things Fall Apart seeks to reshape the future's relationship to the past by subverting the Euro-centric assumptions articulated by the District Commissioner. Some of the assumptions of the North British elite are similarly subverted by the *Justified Sinner*'s contest between 'The Editor's Narrative' and Robert's 'Private Memoirs and Confessions'. In Hogg's novel, as in Achebe's, a voice that had been marginalised is once more able to get a hearing. Furthermore Hogg's novel, like Achebe's, seeks to be clear-eyed about the faults of the old culture: Robert Wringhim is hardly an exemplary character. Nevertheless, by the end of the *Justified Sinner*, the Editor's rendering of Robert as a dehumanised monster no longer seems to the reader to be adequate.

Scott's fictions take a complex view of the competing claims of Scotland and North Britain. For example, although *Waverley* is North British in its ultimate allegiance, this novel nevertheless gives a generally sympathetic account of the culture of eighteenth-century Highland Scotland. Furthermore, the anti-Union side of the debate on the events of 1707 gets a sympathetic articulation in another novel by Scott, *The Bride of Lammermoor* (1819), a novel written at a time when Scott was going through a period of disillusionment with Britain's power structures. Contemplating Scott's complex responses, Hogg doubtless saw much that he could wholeheartedly admire. But it likewise seems clear that there were elements in Scott's fictions that Hogg found uncongenial. Much of Hogg's best writing seeks to investigate the significance of his areas of disagreement with Scott, and in the *Justified Sinner* the contest between Robert's Private Memoirs and the Editor's Waverley Novel of a Narrative forms part of that investigation. One aspect of this investigation is a questioning of what might be called Scott's souvenir-hunting approach to subaltern Scottish culture. However, Hogg's *Justified Sinner* is not an outright rejection of the ideas of Scott and the North British elite. The Editor's view of the world is by no means wholly foolish, and Hogg's friendships and other interests meant that he engaged creatively with ideas at the cutting edge of modern, Enlightened Edinburgh's intellectual explorations. Indeed, Ian Duncan has convincingly argued that 'the Ettrick Shepherd turns out to be imaginatively more attuned to the intellectual currents of advanced modernity, including radical materialism, than any contemporary Scottish author'.[41] The *Justified Sinner* is not an attack on that kind of Enlightenment. Rather, Hogg's novel offers a sophisticated and ultimately devastating subversion of the Editor's obtuse failure to be fully open to the value and the vitality of the culture of the 'supposedly rather primitive' peasantry of Ayrshire, Ettrick, and the Highlands—or, one might equally say, to the value and the vitality of the culture of 'the primitive tribes of the Lower Niger', and of all other allegedly primitive and marginal tribes beyond the allegedly civilised Pale.

In the spring of 1995 there was much interest in Scotland in the fate of a souvenir of Sioux culture that had been kept in a Glasgow museum for about a century. By the late 1880s, the active resistance of the 'primitive' Native American tribes against the advance of 'civilisation' was dwindling, and that resistance suffered a catastrophic setback when the killing of the great war leader Sitting Bull was followed by the massacre of Big Foot and his followers at Wounded Knee in 1890. In the desperate days of the late 1880s, the old Native American culture flared to life in the Ghost Dance religion. Dancing in ghost shirts which gave them powerful protection, the Sioux and others looked forward to a new spring in which the whites would be swept away, the buffalo and other game would be restored in abundance, and the ghosts of dead Indians would return in all the vigour of youth.

A ghost shirt said to have been removed from the body of one of the massacre victims at Wounded Knee came into the possession of 'Buffalo Bill' Cody's Wild West Show, and following a visit of the Wild West Show to Glasgow in 1891 during a European tour, this ghost shirt was acquired by the local museum as an interesting relic. Just over a century later, in 1995, the ghost shirt was seen by chance in Glasgow by John Earl, a part-Cherokee lawyer from Georgia, and as a result moves were set in train by the Sioux people to reclaim the looted ghost shirt. A high-powered Sioux delegation visited Scotland in 1995 to press their case, and to judge from the correspondence columns of the *Scotsman* newspaper at the time, the Sioux case was welcomed with warm sympathy by many Scots. Happily, the city of Glasgow decided in November 1998 to return the ghost shirt to the Sioux people, and the return duly took place in the summer of 1999.[42]

When the ghost shirt made its way from the Wild West Show to the Glasgow museum, it was handed over as a trophy, an interesting relic, a souvenir. When the Sioux delegation came to reclaim it a century later, the ghost shirt was for them an object of profound cultural and spiritual significance, which had been looted from the dead body of an ancestor. That sums up the contrast of perceptions articulated in *The Private Memoirs and Confessions of a Justified Sinner*, in the confrontation between the Editor and the Ettrick Shepherd about the opening of a grave at the heart of Ettrick Forest.

But the title of Achebe's novel is *Things Fall Apart*, and Hogg's novel to some extent shares Achebe's sense that an old culture has fallen apart, that something valuable has been lost. As we have seen, Hogg takes the view that, since the publication of Mr Scott's *Border Minstrelsy*, the old songs 'which were the amusement of every winter evening, have never been sung more'. In fact, this states the case too absolutely: traditional ballads were still being collected in Scotland from oral tradition more than a century after Hogg's death. Nevertheless it seems clear that Hogg witnessed during his lifetime a sharp decline in the traditional orally-based culture of Ettrick. The old ways seemed to be falling apart, and perhaps Hogg's resulting sense of loss provides one reason why his fictions return again and again to scenes that involve the raising of dead bodies, whether from opened graves or elsewhere. Can the old culture be restored to life, in a modern version of the glorious resurrection of the Easter story? Or is the only resurrection now on offer that provided by the Edinburgh intellectual world's very own 'resurrection men' of the 1820s, men who robbed new graves in order to supply the dissecting theatres in which the heirs of the Scottish Enlightenment usefully advanced the cause of scientific research?

At the end of the *Justified Sinner* there is a strong sense that to some extent the old ways have come apart at the seams. In his essay of the early 1830s 'On the Changes in the Habits, Amusements and Condition of the Scottish Peasantry', Hogg writes about the pleasures of song in his Ettrick youth:

> I never heard any music that thrilled my heart half so much as when these nymphs joined their voices, all in one key, and sung a slow Scottish melody. Many a hundred times has it made the hairs of my head creep, and the tears start into my eyes, to hear such as the Flowers of the Forest, and Broom of Cowdyknows. Where are those melting strains now? Gone, and for ever! Is it not unaccountable that, even in the classic Ettrick and Yarrow, the enthusiasm of song should have declined in proportion as that of their bards has advanced? Yet so it is. I have given great annual kirns, and begun singing the first myself, in order to elicit some remnants, some semblance at least, of the strains of former days. But no; those strains could be heard from no one, with the exception of one shepherd, Wat Amos, who alone, for these twenty years, has been always ready to back me. I say, with the exception of him and of Tam the tailor, there seems to be no songster remaining. By dint of hard pressing, a blooming nymph will

sometimes venture on a song of Moore's or Dibdin's (curse them!), and gaping, and half-choking, with a voice like a cracked kirk-bell, finish her song in notes resembling the agonies of a dying sow.

The publication of the Border Minstrelsy had a singular and unexpected effect in this respect. These songs had floated down on the stream of oral tradition, from generation to generation, and were regarded as a precious treasure belonging to the country; but when Mr Scott's work appeared their arcanum was laid open, and a deadening blow was inflicted on our rural literature and principal enjoyment by the very means adopted for their preservation. (pp. 41–42)

The young Hogg had played his part in Scott's attempt to collect and preserve the minstrelsy of the Scottish Border, but it would appear that, by the time he was writing the *Justified Sinner* twenty years later, the mature Hogg had come to believe that Scott's ballad-collecting had, most unexpectedly, inflicted a 'deadening blow' to the 'precious treasure' of the traditional oral culture of Ettrick. In the *Justified Sinner*, the opening of Wringhim's grave is an enactment of the laying open of the arcanum of the traditional culture, and Hogg's novel sets out to explore the unexpectedly disturbing implications of cultural souvenir-hunting of this kind.

Hogg's lament for the death of the Scottish song tradition, as expressed in the passage quoted above, finds an eighteenth-century parallel in Robert Fergusson's 'Elegy, On the Death of Scots Music'.[43] Likewise, in the Introduction of *Minstrelsy of the Scottish Border* Scott expresses a sense that he is gathering up the last remnants of a rapidly vanishing tradition. Things were falling apart, it seemed, and if the *Justified Sinner* rejects what it regards as Scott's souvenir-hunting approach to preservation, it offers no easy optimism about the possibility of a revival of the old ways. In spite of his best efforts, the Ettrick Shepherd is unable to bar the path of the Editor and Mr Sc—t to Robert's grave. 'There's an end to an auld sang', to quote the Earl of Seafield's famous comment on the apparently permanent adjournment of the Scottish parliament at the time of the Union in 1707. But it is always possible to hope that in the end there will be a joyful resurrection. In the event, the Scottish Parliament re-opened on 1 July 1999, after an interval of almost 300 years: the beginning of a new sang, as many people said at the time. And, famously, during the opening ceremony the newly-elected members of the revived Scottish Parliament spontaneously joined in the singing of Burns's radical and egalitarian anthem, 'For a' that and a' that'.[44] Hogg, of course, was not in a position to predict the events of the summer of 1999, but he seems to have been eager to hold on to hope for the possibility of resurrection, as may be shown by another quotation from his essay 'On the Changes in the Habits, Amusements and Condition of the Scottish Peasantry'.

With regard to all the manly exercises, had it not been for my own single exertions I think they would have been totally extinct in the Border districts. For the last forty years I have struggled to preserve them in a local habitation and a name, and I have not only effected it, but induced more efficient bodies to follow the example; such as the Great St Ronan's Border Club, the gallant Six Feet Club, &c. I have begged, I have borrowed of my rich Edinburgh friends, I have drawn small funds reluctantly from the farmers who attended, for the purpose of purchasing the prizes; but more frequently I have purchased them all from my own pocket; and though these prizes were necessarily of small value, yet by publishing annually all the victors' names in the newspapers, and the distance effected by each, and the competitor next to him, a stimulus was given for excellency in all these manly exercises, such as appears not to have existed for a century and more,—indeed, never since the religious troubles in Scotland commenced. (p. 43)

In his Gothic country house and estate at Abbotsford, Sir Walter Scott attempted to create a world in which he could live out a sustainable modern version of the life of a feudal landowner. The St Ronan's Border Games can be regarded as Hogg's equivalent attempt to regain contact with a departed pre-Union, pre-Imperial past: Hogg's attempt, to repeat his own phrase, 'to elicit some remnants, some semblance at least' of the days of the auld sangs.[45] Happily, at the beginning of the twenty-first century Hogg's St Ronan's Border Games continue in boisterous health as an annual event in Ettrick Forest. Arguably, in this achievement as well as in his writings, Hogg has demonstrated not only that the Scottish subaltern can 'speak', but also that the Scottish subaltern has something valuable to say.

Notes

1   William Makepeace Thackeray, *Vanity Fair: A Novel without a Hero*, ed. by John Sutherland, World's Classics (Oxford: Oxford University Press, 1983), p. 259. Subsequent page references are to this edition, and are given in the text. In this edition, John Sutherland provides the following note on Miss Swartz (p. 884): 'Commentators have noted Thackeray's animus against wealthy mulattoes. (See also "Miss Pye" later in *Vanity Fair*, or—most odious—Captain Woolcomb in *Philip*.) George P. Davies ascribes the hostility to Thackeray's resentment at his half-sister, Sarah Blechynden, the illegitimate offspring of his father's Eurasian mistress, Charlotte Rudd. (See "The Miscegenation Theme in the Works of Thackeray", *(Modern Language Notes)*, 1961, pp. 326–31.)'.

2   Chinua Achebe, 'Named for Victoria, Queen of England', in Chinua Achebe, *Hopes and Impediments: Selected Essays*, Anchor Books (New York: Doubleday, 1989), pp. 30–39 (p. 38).

3   Chinua Achebe, 'An Image of Africa: Racism is Conrad's *Heart of Darkness*', in Joseph Conrad, *Heart of Darkness*, Norton Critical Editions, 3rd edn (New York: Norton, 1988), pp. 251–62 (p. 258).

4   Wilson Harris, 'The Frontier on which *Heart of Darkness* Stands', in Joseph Conrad, *Heart of Darkness*, Norton Critical Editions, 3rd edn (New York: Norton, 1988), pp. 262–68 (p. 263).

5   Quoted from Chinua Achebe, *Things Fall Apart* (London: Heinemann, 1986). The novel was first published in 1958.

6   *The Collected Essays, Journalism and Letters of George Orwell*, ed. by Sonia Orwell and Ian Angus, 4 vols (London: Secker & Warburg, 1968), I, 223. The *Oxford English Dictionary* has a good article on the word 'Scotch' and its use.

7   Achebe, 'An Image of Africa', p. 259.

8   *Boswell's Life of Johnson*, ed. by George Birkbeck Hill, rev. by L. F. Powell, 6 vols (Oxford: Clarendon Press, 1934–50), I, 425.

9   Robert Crawford, *Devolving English Literature*, 2nd edn (Edinburgh: Edinburgh University Press, 2000), p. 130.

10 James Hogg, 'Tibby Hyslop's Dream, and the Sequel', forms part of James Hogg, *The Shepherd's Calendar*, ed. by Douglas S. Mack, Stirling / South Carolina Research Edition of the Collected Works of James Hogg (Edinburgh: Edinburgh University Press, 1995: paperback reprint 2002), pp. 142–62. Page references are to this edition, and are given in the text.

11 Quotations from the Bible are taken from the King James version, the version familiar to Hogg and his contemporaries.

12 James Hogg, 'On the Changes in the Habits, Amusements and Condition of the Scottish Peasantry', in *A Shepherd's Delight: A James Hogg Anthology*, ed. by Judy Steel (Edinburgh: Canongate, 1985), pp. 40–51 (p. 41). Subsequent page references are to this edition, and are given in the text.

13 Quoted from Nan Jaboor and B. J. McMullin, *James Ballantyne and Press Figures*, Monash Occasional Papers in Librarianship, Recordkeeping and Bibliography, 4 (Melbourne: Ancora Press, 1994), p. 22; see also p. 8. This part of Scott's letter is also quoted in James F. Leishman, 'Scott and the Ballantynes', *History of the Berwickshire Naturalists' Club*, 25 (1923–25), pt. 1 (1923), 115–28 (pp. 124–25). However, this part of Scott's letter is omitted from Sir Herbert Grierson's standard edition of Scott's *Letters*. To cover the omission, Grierson prints '[*Discusses the instalment of a new printing machine.*]'. See *The Letters of Sir Walter Scott 1821–1823*, ed. by H. J. C. Grierson (London: Constable, 1934), p. 255.

14 Quoted from the version of the 'Memoir of the Author's Life' that appears in Hogg, *Altrive Tales*, ed. by Gillian Hughes, Stirling / South Carolina Research Edition of the Collected Works of James Hogg (Edinburgh: Edinburgh University Press, 2003: paperback reprint 2005), p. 12.

15 This provision of Scots law is discussed in *Green's Encyclopædia of the Law of Scotland*, ed. by John Chisholm, 14 vols (Edinburgh: William Green, 1896–1904), IV, 2.

16 See Peter Garside, 'Printing Confessions', *Studies in Hogg and his World*, 9 (1998), 16–31.

17 See Gillian Hughes, 'James Hogg, *The Spy*, and the Edinburgh Whigs', *Studies in Hogg and his World*, 10 (1999), 48–58.

18 *The Collected Essays, Journalism and Letters of George Orwell*, ed. by Sonia Orwell and Ian Angus, 4 vols (London: Secker & Warburg, 1968), I, 416, 417, 427–28.

19 Robert Burns, 'For a' that an' a' that', in *The Poems and Songs of Robert Burns*, ed. by James Kinsley, 3 vols (Oxford: Clarendon Press, 1968), II, 762–63.

20 Crawford, *Devolving English Literature*, p. 95.

21 See *The Collected Letters of James Hogg*, ed. by Gillian Hughes, The Stirling / South Carolina Research Edition of the Collected Works of James Hogg (Edinburgh: Edinburgh University Press, 2004–), II, 1820–1831 (2006), where this letter is included at the appropriate point of the chronological sequence.

22 Quoted from M. G. Garden, *Memorials of James Hogg* (Paisley: Alexander Gardner, [1884]), pp. 146–47.

23 See Michael Lynch, *Scotland: A New History* (London: Pimlico, 1992), p. 355.

24 For a concise and lucid account, see David Stevenson, *The Covenanters: The National Covenant and Scotland* (Edinburgh: Saltire Society, 1988).

25 Walter Scott, *The Tale of Old Mortality*, ed. by Douglas S. Mack, Edinburgh Edition of the Waverley Novels (Edinburgh: Edinburgh University Press, 1993), p. 13.

26 James Hogg, *The Private Memoirs and Confessions of a Justified Sinner*, ed. by P. D. Garside, Stirling / South Carolina Research Edition of the Collected Works of James Hogg (Edinburgh: Edinburgh University Press, 1995: paperback reprint 2002), p. 3. Subsequent page references to the text of the novel are to this edition, and are given in the text.

27 Peter Garside, 'Hogg's *Confessions* and Scotland', *Studies in Hogg and his World*, 12 (2001), 118–38 (p. 125); see also *The Private Memoirs and Confessions of a Justified Sinner*, ed. Garside, pp. xxxii–liv.

28 Carol McGuirk, 'Burns and Nostalgia', in *Burns Now*, ed. by Kenneth Simpson (Edinburgh: Canongate Academic, 1994), pp. 31–69 (pp. 50-52).

29 Scott, *Tales of a Grandfather: Being Stories Taken from Scottish History*, 3 vols (Edinburgh: Cadell; London: Simpkin and Marshall; Dublin: Cumming, 1828), I, 210–11. *Tales of a Grandfather* was planned and written as a book for children, but Scott became deeply engaged with this exploration of his country's history.

30 J. De Lancey Ferguson, *The Letters of Robert Burns*, 2nd edn, ed. by G. Ross Roy, 2 vols (Oxford: Clarendon Press, 1985), II, 235–36.

31 *The Canongate Burns*, ed. by Andrew Noble and Patrick Scott Hogg, Canongate Classics, 104 (Edinburgh: Canongate, 2001), p. 467.

32 See James C. Corson, *Notes and Index to Sir Herbert Grierson's Edition of the Letters of Sir Walter Scott* (Oxford: Clarendon Press, 1979), p. 210. In an error that makes a ghoulish episode appear still more ghoulish, Scott's biographer John Sutherland asserts that Scott kept an actual skull purporting to be Robert I's (rather than a cast of Robert I's skull) on display at Abbotsford: see John Sutherland, *The Life of Walter Scott* (Oxford: Blackwell, 1995), p. 3.

33 McDiarmid's account is quoted from Hogg, 'Memoir of Burns', in *The Works of Robert Burns*, ed. by the Ettrick Shepherd and William Motherwell, 5 vols (Glasgow: Archibald Fullarton, 1834–36), V, 1–263 (pp. 253–56). According to Hogg (p. 246), McDiarmid's account had appeared in the *Dumfries Courier* at the time of the death of Burns's widow in 1834.

34 See Hogg, 'Memoir of Burns', p. 246.

35 For Hogg's friendship with John McDiarmid, see *The Collected Letters of James Hogg*, ed. Hughes, I, 403–04.

36 This passage first appeared in the 1832 version of the 'Memoir of the Author's Life': see Hogg, *Altrive Tales*, ed. Hughes, pp. 18, 220. Hogg, dates his encounter with Jock Scott shortly after Burns's death, that is to say in 1796. By that time Hogg was in his late twenties, and he would almost certainly have known about Burns. However, it may be that an incident of the kind described took place around 1790, when 'Tam o' Shanter'

was written. Hogg was nineteen at that time, and during his teenage years he had been semi-literate and had suffered real hardship scraping a living as a farm worker in an unfrequented district. If an incident of the kind described did indeed take place around 1790, Hogg would no doubt be tempted to transfer this event to the immediate aftermath of Burn's death, in order to dramatise his claim to be accepted as Burns's successor. Here, as it were, Jock Scott passes on the torch.

37 *Minstrelsy of the Scottish Border*, 2 vols (Kelso, 1802); 2nd edn, 3 vols (Edinburgh, 1803).

38 James Hogg, *Anecdotes of Scott*, ed. by Jill Rubenstein, Stirling / South Carolina Research Edition of the Collected Works of James Hogg (Edinburgh: Edinburgh University Press, 1999: paperback reprint 2004), pp. 37–38. Writing about thirty years after the event, Hogg here mistakenly dates this event in 1801 rather than 1802.

39 Crawford, *Devolving English Literature*, p. 95.

40 Ania Loomba, *Colonialism / Postcolonialism* (London: Routledge, 1998), p. 195.

41 Ian Duncan, 'The Upright Corpse: Hogg, National Literature and the Uncanny', *Studies in Hogg and his World*, 5 (1994), 29–54 (p. 43).

42 The story of the ghost shirt that found its way to Glasgow is conveniently summarised in two newspaper articles written to report moves to return it to the Sioux people: Dani Garavelli, 'Peace Pipe out in Ghost Shirt Row', *Scotland on Sunday*, 12 April 1998, p. 9; and Jim McBeth, 'Sioux Prepare to Celebrate Return of Ghost Shirt', *Scotsman*, 15 April 1998, p. 24. The decision to return the Ghost Shirt is recorded in Deborah Anderson, 'Lakota Sioux Win Battle to Take Warrior's Ghost Shirt to Homeland', *Scotsman*, 20 November 1998, p. 10; and the return itself is recorded in Phil Miller, 'Sacred Shirt Returned to Sioux Chiefs' *Scotsman*, 2 August 1999, p. 28.

43 See Matthew Wickman, 'Tonality and the Sense of Place in Fergusson's "Elegy, on the Death of Scots Music"', in *'Heaven-Taught Fergusson': Robert Burns's Favourite Scottish Poet*, ed. by Robert Crawford (East Linton: Tuckwell Press, 2003), pp. 163–78. Wickman writes (p. 163): 'Reacting against educational programmes and political agendas that seemed designed to ostracise the use of Scots, Fergusson's "Elegy" deploys a vernacular that is as demotic as it is educated, modulating between an orotund pastoral and ironic counterpastoral'.

44 For a valuable discussion of the significance of this incident, see Liam McIlvanney, *Burns the Radical: Poetry and Politics in Late Eighteenth-Century Scotland* (East Linton: Tuckwell Press, 2002), pp. 1–2.

45 For a discussion of Hogg and the St Ronan's Border Games, see David Groves, *James Hogg and the St Ronan's Border Club* (Dollar: Douglas S. Mack, 1987).

FOUR

The Journey North: Competing Narratives about the Scottish Highlands

> Stories are at the heart of what explorers and novelists say about strange regions of the world; they also become the method colonized people use to assert their own identity and the existence of their own history.
>
> (Edward Said, *Culture and Imperialism*)

From Culloden to Lucknow

The siege of Lucknow in 1857, during the uprising that the Empire chose to call 'the Indian Mutiny', was one of most resonant, traumatic, and disturbing incidents of Britain's Imperial high noon. Tennyson's poem 'The Defence of Lucknow' imagines the feelings of a member of the besieged garrison:

> Handful of men as we were, we were English in heart and in limb,
> Strong with the strength of the race to command, to obey, to endure,
> Each of us fought as if hope for the garrison hung but on him;
> Still—could we watch at all points? we were every day fewer and fewer.
> There was a whisper among us, but only a whisper that past:
> 'Children and wives—if the tigers leap into the fold unawares—
> Every man die at his post—and the foe may outlive us at last—
> Better to fall by the hands that they love, than to fall into theirs!'

The women and children were indeed saved (in the Victorian phrase) from a fate worse than death, but in the event this was achieved by the arrival of Scottish Highland soldiers. Tennyson's poem ends:

> Hark cannonade, fusillade! is it true what was told by the scout,
> Outram and Havelock breaking their way through the fell mutineers?

Surely the pibroch of Europe is ringing again in our ears!

All on a sudden the garrison utter a jubilant shout,

Havelock's glorious Highlanders answer with conquering cheers,

Sick from the hospital echo them, women and children come out,

Blessing the wholesome white faces of Havelock's good fusileers,

Kissing the war-harden'd hand of the Highlander wet with their tears!

Dance to the pibroch!—saved! we are saved!—is it you? is it you?

Saved by the valour of Havelock, saved by the blessing of Heaven!

'Hold it for fifteen days!' we have held it for eighty-seven!

And ever aloft on the palace roof the old banner of England blew.[1]

'Havelock's glorious Highlanders', with their 'wholesome white faces', and with their bagpipes playing 'the pibroch of Europe', are here presented as heroes of Empire. However, just over a century earlier Scottish Highlanders had themselves been seen as 'fell mutineers' from a backward and savage land who were threatening the civilized values represented by the Empire. The Jacobite rising of 1745, which drew much of its strength from Highland Scotland, was an attempt to restore the Catholic Stuarts to the British throne. As such, it posed a serious threat to an eighteenth-century Imperial Britain that defined itself (as Linda Colley has shown in *Britons*) as an emphatically Protestant entity willing and able to defend its ideals of 'progress' and 'liberty' against the threat posed by what it perceived to be the tyrannical power of a backward-looking, superstitious, and Catholic pre-Revolutionary France. Responding to the Jacobite rising of 1745, the British elite of the 1740s tended to see Highlanders as dangerous and primitive, as people to be both feared and despised, as a pro-French enemy within. This chapter will explore some of the ways in which the telling of stories helped to shape the remarkable change in Imperial Britain's attitude towards Scottish Highlanders that took place during the century after Culloden.

In 1745 there was real consternation in London when a Jacobite army emerged from the Highlands and began to advance south. This state of affairs can be powerfully sensed from *Sawney in the Boghouse*, a piece of propaganda from 1745 reproduced overlaf.[2] *Sawney* (a variant of 'Sandy') is a derogatory name for a Scotsman—and this particular Highland Sandy, having come to London, is having difficulty in coping with one of the amenities of civilised life, a 'boghouse'. In his native land, it seems, Sawney has been in the habit of dropping his 'Folio Cates on Mother-Earth', *Folio Cates* being 'choice morsels of the largest size'. But in spite of his *faux pas* in thrusting his 'brawny thighs' down the double ventholes that were apparently in vogue in London in the 1740s, Sawney is discovering what the bright lights of the great British metropolis have to offer: 'Neer did he naably disembaage [nobly pour forth] 'till now'.

In 'An Image of Africa: Racism in Conrad's *Heart of Darkness*', Achebe writes of Conrad's novel's 'dehumanization of Africa and Africans',[3] and *Sawney in the Boghouse*

Sawney in the Boghouse:

To London Sawney come, Who, from his Birth,
Had dropt his Folio Cates on Mother-Earth;
Shewn to a Boghouse, gaz'd with wond'ring Eyes;

Then, down each Venthole, thrust his brawny Thighs,
And Squeezing, cry'd — Sawney's a Laird. I trow.
N'eer did he naably disembrauge 'till now.

Publish'd June 17th 1745. price 6d

would appear to represent a similar dehumanisation of Highland Scotland and Highland Scots. This process of dehumanisation is not, of course, confined to Imperial Africa and eighteenth-century Britain: it is liable to come into play whenever one group seeks to dominate another group which it despises, resents, and fears. In the third chapter of the present book we saw this process of dehumanisation at its evil work in George Osborne's comments on Miss Swartz in *Vanity Fair*, as well as in Conrad's comments (as quoted by Achebe) on an 'enormous buck nigger' encountered in Haiti.[4] It was also to be encountered, to take some examples at random, in attitudes towards Jews that emerged within Nazi Germany; in attitudes towards West Indian and Asian immigrants that emerged within Britain at the end of Empire; and in attitudes towards Catholic Irish immigrants that emerged within nineteenth-century Scotland.

The ridicule of Highlanders manifest in *Sawney in the Boghouse* seems to be driven by a hatred born of fear: Sawney is depicted as having a rather dangerous-looking sword beside him as he attempts to negotiate the mysteries of the London boghouse. In 1745 Sawney's Jacobite 'rebellion' posed a real threat to the British Imperial state, and in *Sawney in the Boghouse* this fell mutineer is cast as a modern equivalent of Attila the Hun, a Dracula-figure ready to emerge from a backward and outlandish margin to deploy his potent and dangerous energies in an attempt to gain power in the Imperial capital. In short, like the Indian 'mutineers' a century later, this 'rebel' is seen as a barbaric, primitive, archaic threat to civilisation.

The racist thrust of *Sawney in the Boghouse* draws its vicious energy from the real panic generated in London in 1745 by the advance of the Jacobite army. This panic also helps to explain the ferocity of the reprisals exacted by the victorious Duke of Cumberland after the final defeat of the Jacobites at Culloden near Inverness in 1746. Reprisals after the 'Indian Mutiny' were similarly ferocious. To adapt a phrase from the conquest of the American West, in 1746 Cumberland's victorious forces sometimes acted on the assumption the only good Highlander was a dead Highlander. In or out of the boghouse, Sawney was seen as being both sub-human and dangerous. Emerging from his remote and barbarous homeland in 1745, he had posed a frightening threat to the London government, and he was not going to be allowed a second attempt to bring down the Empire.

Let us turn for a moment to another Sawney, a soldier called Sandy (or Alexander) MacDonald (*c.*1700–1770) who marched south with the Jacobite army in 1745. This Sawney's Gaelic name was Alasdair MacMhaighstir Alasdair, and a case can be made for regarding him as one of the major British poets of the eighteenth century. An educated man who had been a student at Glasgow University, Alasdair MacMhaighstir Alasdair was fluent in English as well as in his native Gaelic. A staunch Jacobite, this son of an Episcopalian clergyman eventually converted to Roman Catholicism. Along with Donnchadh Bàn Mac an t-Saoir / Duncan Ban Macintyre (1724–1808), Alasdair MacMhaighstir Alasdair helped to lead the Gaelic aspect of the eighteenth-century Vernacular Revival in Scottish poetry, the Scots-speaking equivalents of these men being Allan Ramsay, Robert Fergusson, and Robert Burns. The Vernacular Revival sought the recovery of a distinctive Scottish voice after the Union with England in 1707, and as part of this project the poetry of Alasdair MacMhaighstir Alasdair and Donnchadh Bàn Mac an t-Saoir contributes to an eighteenth-century revival and continuation of the ancient Gaelic bardic tradition. The poetry of these two men is thus of great relevance for discussions of the issues raised by Katie Trumpener's seminal book *Bardic Nationalism: The Romantic Novel and the British Empire* (Princeton University Press, 1997).

In the superb 'Moladh Beinn Dóbhrain' ('Praise of Ben Dorian'), Donnchadh Bàn Mac an t-Saoir echoes the complex and sophisticated rhythms and structure of traditional pibroch music. Alasdair MacMhaighstir Alasdair's 'Birlinn Chlann Raghnaill' ('Clanranald's Galley'), another praise-poem in the bardic tradition, celebrates the galley of the poet's clan, and describes its storm-tossed voyage from Scotland to Carrickfergus in Ireland. Ronald Black has noted this poem's emphasis on the heroic conduct of the crew in the storm, and has suggested that an allegorical reading is possible: 'if it is an allegory, the storm that nearly destroyed them is the '45, and the heroes and sufferers of the clan are not its leaders but its people'. Black also suggests that the voyage of the poem 'may take us back via the Islay-based kingdom of the Isles to the Irish origins of the Gael, or forward to a dream of Gaelic unity, or both.'[5]

For Roderick Watson, 'Birlinn Chlann Raghnaill' is 'a heroically extended *tour de force* of descriptive and poetic intricacy',[6] and the sophistication of the poetry of Alasdair MacMhaighstir Alasdair (also known as Sawney MacDonald) suggests that *Sawney in the Boghouse* does less than full justice to the Gaelic culture of the Scottish Highlands. In the eighteenth century, British metropolitan circles tended to be unaware of the existence of Gaelic poets like Alasdair MacMhaighstir Alasdair and Donnchadh Bàn Mac an t-Saoir. However, these circles were to become very well aware of the celebrated post-Culloden *Ossian* prose-poems of James Macpherson (1736–96), texts said to be translations of ancient Gaelic epics.

Scotland's Homer?

The circumstances of James Macpherson's early years provide an insight into the cultural and social context from which his *Ossian* poems emerged. Macpherson had been born in the Highland district of Badenoch in 1736, in the territory of his uncle, the clan chief Ewan Macpherson of Cluny. He was therefore a child of an impressionable age when the Jacobite rising of 1745–46 took place. Macpherson of Cluny and his followers were prominent in Prince Charles's Jacobite army, and the young James would have shared in the exultant hopes of his relatives in 1745. However, he also had to share the experience of seeing things fall apart after their catastrophic defeat at Culloden in 1746.

In her Introduction to an edition of Macpherson's *Poems of Ossian* published in

1996 by the Edinburgh University Press, Fiona Stafford has summed up James Macpherson's personal experience of the aftermath of Culloden:

> With defeat came disgrace for Clan Macpherson, as Cluny Castle was razed and much of the local community destroyed by the violence of the victorious army. [...] Between the ages of ten and eighteen, James Macpherson thus lived through scenes of appalling violence, and saw his home and family under the constant threat of further oppression. During this period, a series of measures were implemented to crush the distinctive Highland way of life, and render the region safe for ever. After 1746, the tartan plaid was banned, and no Highlander allowed to carry arms or play the bagpipes. The estates of prominent rebel chiefs (including Cluny) were forfeited to the Crown, while the ancient systems of ward-holding and heritable jurisdiction were abolished. Such measures were a more Draconian development from the earlier, relatively peaceful, attempts to open communications and transport networks in the Highlands, and to encourage the use of English rather than Gaelic. But it is in the context of systematic cultural destruction that Macpherson's efforts to collect old heroic poetry can be seen; they were, at least in part, an attempt to repair some of the damage to the Highlands sustained in the wake of the Jacobite Risings.[7]

In 1752 the teenage James Macpherson became a student at the University of Aberdeen. At Aberdeen, he encountered the theories of the philosophers of the Scottish Enlightenment, theories that placed great value on the epic poetry of allegedly 'primitive' societies like the one into which Macpherson himself had been born. For example, Thomas Blackwell of Aberdeen University had produced a pioneering *Enquiry into the Life and Writings of Homer* (1735); and, naturally enough, ideas like Blackwell's encouraged the young Macpherson to see potential value in the oral poetry and traditions of his own native Gaelic culture. That culture, having recently suffered military conquest, was now desolated and despised, and it is easy to understand why Macpherson would be fired by a desire to reassert its dignity and worth. With a mixture of motives typical of the eighteenth-century Scottish experience, Macpherson doubtless also saw his *Ossian* project as a possible passport to fame and fortune in London

Poems and traditions concerning the ancient warrior-bard Ossian held an important place in Macpherson's native Gaelic culture, and Macpherson imaginatively re-created and embellished this traditional material in texts which he presented as his own translations of third-century Gaelic poems by Ossian. Fiona Stafford gives the following account of the processes involved:

> In the years following Macpherson's death in 1796, the Highland Society of Scotland set up a Committee of investigation which concluded that, although Macpherson had not produced close translations of individual poems, he had nevertheless drawn on the

traditional tales collected in his tours, using certain recognisable characters, plots and episodes. He also developed his own very distinctive measured prose as the medium for presenting the Gaelic material in English, and while this was indebted to the prose tales of Gaelic Scotland, it also reflected Macpherson's academically influenced pre-conceptions about the nature of early poetry. For while he undoubtedly came across a large number of heroic ballads in the Highlands, he seems to have regarded his sources somewhat dismissively as the broken remains of great Celtic epics, and to have seen the task of recovery in the light of sympathetic restoration, rather than as a painstaking translation of the miscellaneous mass.[8]

Understandably, given the circumstances of their composition in the wake of devastating military defeat in 1746, Macpherson's *Ossian* poems are imbued with a deep melancholy that is redolent of desolating loss, of heroism in the face of defeat. Ossianic melancholy proved to be attractive to readers in a period in which Romanticism was beginning to develop, and Macpherson's *Ossian* poems took Europe by storm. Indeed, Ossian came to be widely regarded throughout Europe as the peer of Homer as an epic poet. Barbarous Sawney, it began to appear, might be the inheritor of a traditional culture that was ancient and worthy of respect. Given the eloquence and sophistication of the poetry of Alasdair MacMhaighstir Alasdair and Donnchadh Bàn Mac an t-Saoir, it is far from self-evident that this view of the matter was entirely foolish and ill-conceived. Like Achebe's Igbo people, Sawney too might have a story to tell.

Dr Johnson Visits the Highlands

In the latter part of the eighteenth century the long-established view of Highland Scotland as a wild, dangerous place populated by savages began to be challenged by an *Ossian*-influenced vision of Highland Scotland as a romantic and exotic place populated by an ancient people with a noble culture. However, in 1745 this development still lay in the future. In that year Dr Samuel Johnson, a man of Jacobite sympathies, was living in London while Prince Charles, Alasdair MacMhaighstir Alasdair, and the rest of the Jacobite army advanced southwards. It would be fair to say that Dr Johnson tended towards the *Sawney in the Boghouse* rather than the 'Sawney is Homer' view of Highland Scotland, and it seems clear that this particular London Jacobite was not excessively enthused by the prospect of being liberated by a triumphant and conquering Sawney. Johnson's friend and biographer James Boswell writes:

> I have heard him declare, that if holding up his right hand would have secured victory at Culloden to Prince Charles's army, he was not sure he would have held it up; so little confidence had he in the right claimed by the house of Stuart, and so fearful was he of the consequences of another revolution on the throne of Great-Britain; [...]. He no

doubt had an early attachment to the House of Stuart; but his zeal had cooled as his reason strengthened.[9]

This move from romance to reason is reminiscent of Scott's Edward Waverley, and (again like Waverley) Johnson undertook a journey north from the security and civilisation of England, and visited that wild, exotic, and barbarous place, the Scottish Highlands. Johnson travelled north in 1773, and in *A Journey to the Western Isles of Scotland* he writes about Gaelic, Sawney's native language:

> Of the *Earse* [Gaelic] language, as I understand nothing, I cannot say more than I have been told. It is the rude speech of a barbarous people, who had few thoughts to express, and were content, as they conceived grossly, to be grossly understood. After what has lately been talked of Highland Bards, and Highland genius, many will startle when they are told, that *Earse* never was a written language; that there is not in the world an Earse manuscript a hundred years old; and that the sounds of the Highlanders were never expressed by letters, till some little books of piety were translated, and a metrical version of the Psalms was made by the Synod of *Argyle*.[10]

This makes it abundantly clear that Johnson was not disposed to give credence to 'what has lately been talked of Highland Bards, and Highland genius' in the debate about Macpherson's *Ossian*. When he journeyed north to the Highlands, Johnson heard what he expected to hear: the barbarous Earse sounds through which his Highland hosts sought to communicate what he assumed to be their few thoughts and their gross conceptions.

Johnson was a complex and justly much-admired man, but he is not perhaps seen to best advantage in his dealings with Scotland and the Scots. When he dismisses Gaelic as 'the rude speech of barbarous people', his view has something in common with that of *Waverley*'s Colonel Talbot, who, it will be remembered, regards the Gaelic speech of the Scottish Highlands as 'gibberish'. At all events, both *Sawney in the Boghouse* and Johnson's comment on Gaelic are in their different ways as demeaning and dehumanizing as Conrad's phrase about the 'enormous buck nigger'. Johnson, however, does not leave matters there in his *Journey to the Western Isles*. Assuming that Highlanders inherit the language and culture of a barbarous people of few thoughts and gross conceptions, he puts this belief to work as the basis for an argument in justification of Cromwell's military conquest of Scotland in the 1650s:

> Yet what the Romans did to other nations, was in a great degree done by Cromwell to the Scots; he civilized them by conquest, and introduced by useful violence the arts of peace. I was told at *Aberdeen* that the people learned from Cromwell's soldiers to make shoes and to plant kail.[11]

This is a familiar argument of Imperialism: we must conquer those savage Redskins, so that we can make them stop scalping people, wear proper clothes, and take up farming. Modern Scotland evolved in that northern part of the British Isles which had remained unconquered by the Roman Empire, and Johnson's suggestion here is that Cromwell carried on the Imperial task, begun by the Romans, of civilising the British Isles through the 'useful violence' of conquest. One cannot but think here of Cromwell's activities in Ireland, activities which left a deep and traumatic mark on Irish society. As R. F. Foster puts it, 'Cromwellian Ireland has become a subject of more balanced and analytical historical inquiry than used to be the case, but Oliver Cromwell's record in Ireland is still inextricably identified with massacre and expropriation'.[12]

Johnson's line of thought has much in common with the assumptions of Achebe's District Commissioner about the pacification of the primitive tribes of the Lower Niger, and such assumptions made it natural to regard Culloden and its aftermath as a continuation of Cromwell's 'useful violence'. According to this view of the matter, Cromwell had civilised Lowland Scotland by conquest in the 1650s, and in 1746 the useful violence of Cumberland's conquering army had carried on Cromwell's work by bringing about the pacification of the primitive tribes of the Scottish Highlands. This set of assumptions takes it for granted that the role of the modern British Empire is to carry on the Roman Empire's work of civilization by conquest, through acts of 'useful violence' directed against primitive tribes wherever they might be found.

In this spirit, Johnson's *Journey to the Western Islands of Scotland* takes pleasure in the progress of work on a military road from a fort that 'was not long ago taken by the Highlanders':

> We soon came to a high hill, which we mounted by a military road, cut in traverses, so that as we went upon a higher stage, we saw the baggage following us below in a contrary direction. To make this way, the rock has been hewn to a level with labour that might have broken the perseverance of a Roman legion. [...] Passing on through the dreariness of solitude, we found a party of soldiers from the fort, working on the road, under the superintendence of a serjeant. We told them how kindly we had been treated at the garrison, and as we were enjoying the benefit of their labours, begged leave to shew our gratitude by a small present.[13]

The garrison, it seems, is working to good effect to carry on the civilising work of the old Roman legions; and although the barbarous Highlanders had managed to take the fort 'not long ago' during the rising of 1745, the process of forced pacification continues apace. The threat offered by the primitive clansmen is receding as the military road advances, and the soldiers to whom Johnson gives a small present are to be congratulated for following up the benign work of the 'useful violence' of Butcher Cumberland and his troops. All this seems entirely plausible, so long as we do not focus too clearly on the nature of Cumberland's 'savage orders to harry, burn and kill men, women and children alike in a campaign of mass-reprisal after Culloden'.[14]

At all events, Johnson sees England as the new Rome, spreading civilisation to barbarous nations by 'useful violence'. This allows him to make satisfactory sense of the post-Culloden events, but it is a strategy that can only work if Sawney, the Scottish Highlander, really *is* a sub-human barbarian. In this context, it is easy to understand the strength of Johnson's desire to disprove Macpherson's claims about *Ossian*. It would be difficult to justify Cumberland's policy if Sawney really were the moral equivalent of Homer.

Of course, Johnson did have a point: Macpherson presented his *Ossian* texts as direct translations of ancient Gaelic epics, and this was not the case. Nevertheless, there is merit in the view of the matter taken by Ian Haywood in his book *The Making of History* (London and Toronto: Associated University Presses, 1986). Haywood suggests that Macpherson's *Ossian* poems can best be understood as an early manifestation of the kind of historical fiction that was to flourish in the nineteenth century. Crucially, Haywood argues that, in Macpherson's eighteenth-century generation, retrospectively-imagined historical fictions (as later written by the Author of *Waverley* and his many followers) had still to become established as an accepted literary genre—and, as a result, Macpherson's *Ossian* texts sought to present themselves to their first readers as historical relics, rather than as self-proclaimed historical fictions.

That said, it should also be remembered that Macpherson's *Ossian* poems are more firmly rooted in traditional Gaelic culture than even Haywood's account would suggest. Fiona Stafford has summed up what is emerging as the modern scholarly consensus as follows:

> To take Dr Johnson's line on *Ossian*, then, and see it as the concoction of a charlatan is to ignore the complexities of Macpherson's achievement, and indeed the circumstances under which he worked. *Fingal* may not be a direct translation of Gaelic poems that had survived intact since the third century, but neither is it a "fake" or "forgery", because of Macpherson's peculiar situation at the confluence of very different cultures. As a Highlander, he was at liberty to draw on the common pool of stories and characters, whose chronologies had become mixed in the oral tradition centuries before he began to listen to them, and to recreate his own versions of the old tales (it was also common in the Highlands to attribute poems to Ossian, without worrying greatly about questions of transmission and appropriation). As a gentleman with a university education, he was inclined to view the oral tradition as the unreliable medium of a people yet to experience "civilisation", and to share his patrons' hopes that the early poetry of Scotland should have resembled that of Homeric Greece, surviving along with the ancient Gaelic language, as a result of the local geography. Macpherson's *Ossian* is thus a text belonging exclusively to neither Gaelic nor English

culture, and can only be understood sympathetically as an attempt to mediate between the two.[15]

Looked at unsympathetically, Macpherson's *Ossian* appears to be a forgery manufactured by a charlatan. Looked at sympathetically, it can be read as an imaginative attempt to re-create lost epic poetry of the Highlands from fragments surviving in the oral tradition of the people.

Scott and the Journey North

Born some thirty-five years after Macpherson, the generation of Scott and Hogg enjoyed a cultural inheritance that included the competing narratives of Macpherson and Johnson about the Highlands, and both Scott and Hogg wrote with an awareness of these competing narratives. Scott's *The Lady of the Lake* (1810) represented the first major attempt by a writer of his generation to provide an alternative to the Highland narratives of Johnson and *Ossian*. Written during the Napoleonic Wars, and making its appearance some four years before *Waverley*, Scott's poem belongs to the wartime genre of the long metrical romance, which was to be superseded by the historical novel in the post-war period.

The sixteenth-century Highlanders of *The Lady of the Lake* exhibit both the vices and the savage virtues of an early stage of society, and Ellen Douglas (the Lady of the Lake) points to these characteristics as she explains why she cannot marry Roderick Vich Alpine Dhu, the wild and lawless Highland chieftain under whose protection she is living while sharing her father's exile from the court of James V:

> I grant him brave,
> But wild as Bracklinn's thundering wave;
> And generous—save vindictive mood,
> Or jealous transport chafe his blood; [...]
> I grant him liberal, to fling
> Among his clan the wealth they bring,
> When back by lake and glen they wind,
> And in the Lowland leave behind,
> Where once some pleasant hamlet stood,
> A mass of ashes slaked with blood.[16]

What emerges here seems to be something of a mixture of Johnson's savages and the nobility of the ancient Highlanders of Macpherson's *Ossian*, and both the savagery and the nobility are confirmed when Roderick calls his clan together for battle. The summons is prepared in semi-pagan rites by the hermit who is the clan's Druid-like holy man, and these rites have something of the quality of nineteenth-century Britain's nightmares about African 'witch-doctors'. Nevertheless there is a heroic response to this summons: when the unwelcome call of duty comes, the son is prepared to leave his father's funeral and the newly-married bridegroom is willing to leave his bride to fight for the clan.

The poets of the eighteenth-century Scottish Vernacular Revival (Burns, Alasdair MacMhaighstir Alasdair, and the others) had attempted to reassert a subaltern Scottish voice in the aftermath of the Union of 1707. Writing a generation later and more than a century after the Union, Scott had a subtly different agenda. As a member of the Scottish elite, he shared with most of his generation and class a desire to make the Union work—and a desire to make it work to Scotland's advantage. Scott sought in his fictions to help to create a new sense of Britishness, a new and complex identity which would be more than simply Englishness continuing, and which would allow room for a distinctive Scottish contribution. In this way he sought, as it were, to secure a place for Scotland at the British Imperial top table.

As part of this project Scott accepts in *The Lady of the Lake* that traditional Highland society contains savage and primitive elements that must be left behind as modern post-Union British civilisation advances. However, he also asserts that traditional Highland society contains features that could serve Britain well, once harnessed to the Imperial cause. As we have seen, such ideas also find expression in the description of the trial of Evan Dhu Maccombich in *Waverley*. This novel, like *The Lady of the Lake* and the Scott-organised visit of George IV to Edinburgh in 1822, seeks to replace the old story featuring a de-humanised and demonised Highland Sawney with a new story in which Highlanders are transformed into Ossianic warriors who are noble and romantic, albeit (as Scott sees it) in need of some corrective re-education.

The need for re-education of Highlanders is a crucial part of Scott's new story. This begins to emerge comparatively early in *Waverley*, when a Highlander first makes an appearance in the pages of Scott's novel. As it happens, the Highlander in question is none other than Evan Dhu Maccombich, dressed 'in his full national costume', and carrying 'a long Spanish fowling-piece' as well as a Sawney-like broadsword (pp. 73–74). Enthused by his encounter with this exotic warrior, the impressionable Edward Waverley sets out to penetrate the Highlands with Evan as his guide—and as they enter the Highlands by the pass of Bally-Brough, Evan speaks to Waverley:

> "[...] See, there is an earn, which you southrons call an eagle—you have no such birds as that in England—he is going to fetch his supper from the laird of Bradwardine's braes, but I'll send a slug after him."
>
> He fired his piece accordingly, but missed the superb monarch of the feathered tribes, who, without noticing the attempt to annoy him, continued his majestic flight to the southward. A thousand birds of prey, hawks, kites, carrion crows, and ravens,

disturbed from the lodgings which they had just taken up for the evening, rose at the report of the gun, and mingled their hoarse and discordant notes with the echoes which replied to it, and with the roar of the mountain cataracts. Evan, a little disconcerted at having missed his mark, when he meant to have displayed peculiar dexterity, covered his confusion by whistling part of a pibroch as he reloaded his piece, and proceeded in silence up the pass. (p. 76)

Edward's entry into the Highlands by the pass of Bally-Brough will lead to his involvement in the Jacobite rising of 1745; and the firing of Evan's Spanish gun provides a memorable image that encapsulates the view that Scott's novel takes of the nature and significance of the Jacobite rising. Evan fires at 'the superb monarch of the feathered tribes'; but he misses, and the monarch of the skies soars on his way, untroubled. According to *Waverley*, in 1745–46 the Spanish gun of an outmoded Highland society can and does stir up a good deal of unpleasantness by rousing up many hawks and carrion crows; but it cannot begin to disturb the secure and serene authority of the eagle, the embodiment of the majesty and power of the Hanoverian monarchs of modern Imperial Britain. Scott's novel takes the view that the Jacobites, in their rising, are attempting to hit a target well beyond their range. On this view, the clock cannot be turned back, and the modern world is secure from Evan's archaic threat.

It is significant that it is a *Spanish* gun that Evan fires. The Spanish connection conjures up memories of the Spanish Armada, which, like Prince Charles's French-supported venture of 1745–46, was widely seen as an attempt by Catholic Europe to wrest power from a Protestant government in London. In Scott's fictions, Catholicism, and a Jacobite movement deeply sympathetic to Catholicism, tend to be associated with a superstitious and unenlightened past. In Scott's view, this world of the past can at times have a certain romantic attraction, but its romance has to be outgrown if entry is to be achieved into the mature, well-ordered rationality of the modern world. For this reason, Edward Waverley has to learn in due course to outgrow the romantic Jacobite infatuation to which he succumbs when he enters Evan's archaic Highland world by the pass of Bally-Brough.

In the old story about the Highlands put forward in different ways by Dr Johnson and by *Sawney in the Boghouse*, Sawney and his people (like the Cherokees and the primitive tribes of the Lower Niger) were presented as barbarians who had to be civilised by the useful violence of conquest. In *The Lady of the Lake* and in *Waverley* Scott constructs a new story that is much more sympathetic to Highlanders than the old one, but this new story (like the old one) assumes that Highland Scotland is backward and must undergo radical change in order to enter the modern world. In Scott's story the old order represented by Evan's Spanish gun is not sustainable, and its defeat is inevitable. Evan may be a much more attractive figure than Sawney in the boghouse, but an unreconstructed Evan is no better able than Sawney to cope with the modern world.

Waverley's new story, like Johnson's, is a call for the imposition of Progress. In Scott's story, however, the old world of Highland Scotland is not presented as being merely brutal and backward. On the contrary, it is seen as having much of great value to bring to the service of Imperial Britain. Once they have jettisoned outmoded aspects of their culture, the successors of Evan Dhu are well equipped to fulfil their potential in the modern world and become the heroic servants of Empire—for example on the Plains of Abraham in Quebec 1759, at Waterloo in 1815, and at Lucknow in 1857.

Hogg and the Journey North

The Lady of the Lake (1810) and *Waverley* (1814) were both hugely successful, and Scott's account of the nature, flaws, and potential value of Highland society came to be widely accepted. Responding to this, Hogg continued his consistent attempts to give voice to the experiences and concerns of subaltern Scotland by constructing his own alternative Highland narratives. For example, *Mador of the Moor* is a book-length poem, written in 1813 but not published until 1816, in which *The Lady of the Lake* is 'made o'er' or made over. In *Mador* Hogg attempts to tell it like it is by shaping a narrative in which Scott's aristocratic young Lady of the Lake becomes Ila Moore, an enterprising and self-reliant young Highland woman of low social standing who (unusually for a nineteenth-century heroine) retains sympathy and esteem in spite of becoming pregnant out of wedlock. At the end of *Mador's* Introduction Hogg warns his readers not to expect an idealised picture of human behaviour. To use the language of Hogg's discussion of *The Lady of the Lake* in *The Spy* (see Chapter 2), this passage makes it clear that *Mador of the Moor* will not, as it were, be offering an inflated picture of 'the rock of Glen-Whargen'. Instead, Hogg (as 'Nature's simple Bard') will be trying to tell it like it is:

> But ween not thou that Nature's simple Bard
>   Can e'er unblemish'd character define;
> True to his faithful monitor's award,
>   He paints her glories only as they shine.
>   Of men all pure, and maidens all divine,
> Expect not thou his wild-wood lay to be;
>   But those whose virtues and defects combine,
> Such as in erring man we daily see—
> The child of failings born, and scathed humanity.[17]

In *Mador*, 'Nature's simple Bard' presents a world in which real value is located in unexpected places—for example in an uppity peasant girl who, as the old phrase has it, is no better than she should be. Hogg undertakes a somewhat similar project in *Queen Hynde*

(1824), a wonderfully exuberant poem in the epic manner that pays tribute to the pro-subaltern poems of Alasdair MacMhaighstir Alasdair and Donnchadh Bàn Mac an t-Saoir, while also questioning aspects of the accounts of Highlanders to be found in Scott's narratives and in Macpherson's *Ossian* poems. Hogg's epic revisits the early period, the scenes ('Selma'), and the topics of *Ossian*, but humanises Macpherson's idealised view of the nobility of ancient Highlanders. Even the great St Columba, while admirable, is not impossibly noble in Hogg's epic: he too is someone in whom 'virtues and defects combine, | Such as in erring man we daily see.'[18]

Likewise, *Waverley*'s account of Highland Scotland comes under scrutiny in Hogg's *The Three Perils of Woman*, first published in 1823 in three volumes. This text describes itself as 'a series of domestic tales', and it consists of two groups of interlocking stories. The first group is set in the Lowland Scotland of Hogg's own day, and occupies the first two volumes. The second group is set in Highland Scotland in 1746 around the time of Culloden, and occupies the third volume. Taken together, these two groups of interlocking stories follow *Waverley* in exploring the relationship between Scotland's present situation and the events of 1745–46.

In *The Three Perils of Woman* as in *Waverley* a protagonist from the south moves north into the Highlands, but Hogg's Sally Niven is very different from Edward Waverley: Edward is an officer and an English gentleman, while Sally is a lower-class Lowland Scottish woman, who has come to the Highlands to work as a maidservant in a manse. In short, Hogg's text offers itself as an alternative to *Waverley* by exploring Culloden and its aftermath from the perspective of subaltern Scotland. *Waverley* tells its story of the events of 1745–46 by focusing on the experiences of members of the officer class. *The Three Perils of Woman* constructs its alternative account of these events by focusing on the experiences of a Lowland maidservant and a Highland blacksmith.

There are numerous points of contact between *The Three Perils of Woman* and *Waverley*. For example, in both texts a Spanish gun is fired at the point at which the narrative enters the Highlands. We have seen that, in *Waverley*, the firing of the Spanish gun provides a concrete image that sums up the text's view of the nature of the events of 1745–46: the majestic Imperial eagle of modern Britain soars away, untroubled by the firing of the puny and archaic Spanish gun of an outmoded Highland Jacobitism. The firing of the Spanish gun in *The Three Perils of Woman* provides an alternative image that questions and subverts the image offered by *Waverley*.

In Hogg's text the firing of the Spanish gun takes place in the Highland churchyard of Balmillo, by night, a few weeks before the battle of Culloden. A grave is being dug for a secret burial, and the digger is daft Davie Duff, the local sexton, who is acting under compulsion from Henning, an armed Lowland stranger. Henning, a large man, watches Davie complete the deep grave. Meantime the minister's bay horse, which Davie had been taking to the river for a drink, is roaming nearby.

While all this is going on, Peter Gow, the local blacksmith, is making his way to an assignation with his sweetheart Sally Niven. Peter is returning from an unsuccessful night's deer-hunting, and as he approaches Balmillo he catches a glimpse of what he thinks is a magnificent stag. What Peter sees, however, is not a stag, but the minister's bay horse. Peter then continues his journey towards Sally.

> As Peter went up by the corner of the garden, to reconnoitre whether the minister's maid was sleeping or waking, a thought entered Peter's head in one moment, and he stood still to consider of it.—"The churchyard lies straight in the line that this princely buck was pursuing," thinks Peter to himself—"Perhaps he may stop to take a snack as he goes through that,—the grass is very soft and green that grows out of them dead chaps. And if he should not have halted there, the doe is sure to be feeding at no great distance from him at this time of the year.—It is but a step—I'll go and see, any way."
>
> Peter went along by the south garden-wall, the very road that Davie Duff had ridden in the evening; and, peeping cautiously over at the end of the stile, his eyes were almost struck blind by the glorious object that he descried. Peter's head descended again below the cape of the dike, with an imperceptible motion, while his heart played thump, thump in his bosom, like an apprentice smith working at a stithy. "I declare," said Peter, in his heart, for his lips durst not so much as come together, for fear of making a noise,—"I declare yonder is the very monster feeding in the middle of the church-yard! Now, Patie Gow, acquit yourself like a man for once! Lord, what a prize is here!" (pp. 276–77)

In the darkness of night Peter thinks he sees the stag which he imagined he saw when he glimpsed the minister's bay horse; but what he sees in Balmillo churchyard is neither a stag nor a horse, but Henning, who is looking into the grave in which Davie Duff is digging. In all good faith, however, Peter fires his 'tremendous Armado-gun' at what he believes is a stag.

> The mark being near, the shot took effect, and a terrible effect it was!—Instead of a stag tumbling on the sward, or floundering away with a deadly wound, there sprung up a gigantic human figure at full length, and roaring out, "Murder!, murder!" dived at once into the bowels of the earth, and disappeared.
>
> Peter Gow fainted! actually went away in a faint—And none of your cold water and hartshorn faints either—none of your lady faints, where everything is seen and heard all the while, but a true, genuine, blacksmith's faint.—He fell, as dead as if he had been knocked down with a forehammer, back over at his full length on the minister's glebe; and the huge Spanish Armado-gun fell backwards above him, at her full length too. (p. 277)

Henning, having been killed by Peter's shot, falls into the grave. His body, as it falls, stuns Davie; and the dead man lies with 'his whole huge weight above the poor beadle' (p. 278). The clandestine burial party expected by Henning now arrives, and the grave is examined.

> One of the men with the lantern went forward to the grave, and as suddenly recoiled; but these were men not to be daunted; they gathered round the grave, and astonishment giving energy to their voices, the dialogue became loud and confused, for they were all speaking at once.
>
> "It is Henning!" said one.
>
> "Yes, by ——, it is!" said another. "Who can have done this deed?"
>
> "That must be searched into," said he who appeared to be the chief. "And dearly shall the aggressor pay for his temerity!"
>
> "He *shall* pay for it," said two or three voices at once; and with that they hauled the body out of the grave, and began to examine how the wounds appeared to have been given, when one cried out that there was another. They looked into the deep grave, and there lay the most revolting sight of all. The body of their friend was a little striped with blood, but this undermost corpse was actually swathed and congealed in it. They hauled the body out, and the coagulated masses of blood came along with it, which so much disfigured the whole carcase, that it could hardly be taken for a human frame; while at the same time there were clots of gelid clay hanging at the hair, on each side of the face, nearly as big as the face itself. The whole group was manifestly much shocked at the sight; but how much more so, when this horrible figure bolted up amongst their hands, and after saying in a hurried voice—"Uasals, bithidh mi anmoch," (gentles, I shall be too late,) ran off towards the minister's house and vanished. (p. 281)

The firing of the Spanish gun in Hogg's novel produces an image that is very different from the image produced by the firing of the Spanish gun in Scott's novel. *The Three Perils of Woman*'s alternative image offers a picture of war as incompetent confusion, in which violence, horror, degradation, and death go hand in hand with the ludicrous and the absurd. There is no discernible usefulness in this violence. In its attempt to offer an alternative to *Waverley*'s story of the events of 1745–46, Hogg's text does not present war as a necessary stage in the pacification of the primitive tribes of the Lower Niger. Instead, war is seen as a nightmare experience, both horrific and ludicrous, which has the power to overwhelm, disrupt, and destroy the everyday lives of ordinary people.

Because it sees the events of 1745–46 from a subaltern perspective, *The Three Perils of Woman* does not present these events as an unsuccessful attempt by an outmoded society to disrupt the serene and confident power of the modern world, but rather as a destructive and futile exercise in which both sides are equally enmeshed in incompetent, ludicrous, destructive horror. This view is confirmed in other parts of Hogg's text, not least in the part of his narrative that is based closely on 'the rout of Moy', an historical event that took place early in 1746, shortly before Culloden. At that time the Jacobite army was retreating northwards towards Inverness, and Prince Charles went ahead of his troops in order to spend time at the home of Lady Anne Mackintosh of Moy, an ardent admirer. Learning of this, the commander of the Government forces in Inverness advanced on Moy by night with a strong body of troops, with a view to capturing the Prince; but this plan was foiled when the shooting and shouts of a handful of people led by the local blacksmith caused panic and headlong flight in the ranks of the army of the British Government. In *The Three Perils of Woman*'s rendering of these events, Moy becomes Balmillo, and Lady Anne Mackintosh of Moy becomes the novel's Lady Balmillo. In Hogg's novel Peter Gow is the local blacksmith who puts the British army to flight, and Sally Niven also plays a major part in saving the Prince. The rout involves confusion, darkness, violence, absurdity, death; and this powerfully reinforces Hogg's novel's alternative image of war, as expressed in the firing of Peter Gow's Spanish gun.

The Three Perils of Woman competes with *Waverley* by seeking to give voice to the experiences of lower class, subaltern Scotland, and Hogg's Culloden narrative conveys its view of the meaning of the events of 1745–46 by telling the story of how these events tear apart the lives of Sally and Peter. Hogg's text asserts on behalf of subaltern Scotland that we too might have a story to tell about the events of 1745–46. It is a story that involves suffering and devastation, and Sally's appalling death at the end of the narrative represents and sums up the post-Culloden sufferings inflicted on Highland Scotland by the Duke of Cumberland and the army of the British Government. In the final paragraph of *The Three Perils of Woman*, the narrator refers to Sally's death, and asks 'Is there human sorrow on record like this that winded up the devastations of the Highlands?' (p. 407). After Culloden, Sally wanders through a nightmare landscape:

> all was ruin and desolation. Hamlet, castle, and villa, had shared the same fate; all were lying in heaps of ashes, and not a soul to be seen save a few military, and stragglers of the lowest of adverse clans scraping up the poor wrecks of the spoil of an extirpated people. (p. 362)

Eventually Sally witnesses the brutal deaths of her husband Alaster and of Peter Gow, at the hands of a detachment of British soldiers. Deranged through distress and grief, she spends the night alone, 'sitting raving and singing her lullaby, beside the bodies of her murdered husband and former lover' (p. 404). In this text, however, horror and pathos are not permitted to exist unqualified by intrusions of the ludicrous. Here, the ludicrous enters after the arrival of daft Davie Duff, who is finding ample employment in the post-Culloden world as 'cheneral purial mhaker to Khing Shorge, his Mhachesty' (p. 363). Here, as elsewhere, Davie's speech is set down in the text in accordance with a well-established convention for the rendering of the English speech of native Gaelic speakers.[19]

Davie receives payment from King George's troops on production of the severed ears of the bodies he has buried; and he therefore has a professional interest in the scene of carnage over which Sally has been mourning:

> The next morning, before the sunrising, who should come to the spot but Davie Duff, carrying his spade over his shoulder, and bringing also some cordials and refreshments for his old friends. He had been inured to scenes of carnage; and, indeed, they were become so familiar to him, that he delighted in them. But natural affection, though blunted in him, was not obliterated. The sight of his old familiar acquaintances lying stretched in their blood together was too much for his philosophy, or rather for his natural and acquired apathy, to bear; and poor Davie absolutely gave way to the kinder feelings of his nature, and stood leaning upon his spade and weeping over the remains of his once kind and indulgent friends, while his homely lamentation was not destitute of a rude pathos.
>
> "Ochon, a shendy Righ! and pe tis te way tey pe guide poor Highlandmans and vomans still? Och! but hersel pe fery sorry and woful! And now, fan no pody pe hearing, I will say, 'Cot tamn my mhaister, te Tuke of Cohumperland!' Now tat kif some relhief to her cood heart. Och, poor crheatures! te tays haif shanged sore! I haif seen you so full of te merry, and te happy, and te whanton luff, tat it was fery plhaisant; and nhow to see you all lhying kill't trou te pody! Och, ineed, it is mhore pad tan all tings in te whoule world! Well, I nheed nhot carry my whines and my prheads any mhore. Here's to your cood sleep, khind mustress Sally, and a cood lhong eferlhasting to you. The same to you, Peader Gobhadh; you shall haif cood grave, and dhecent dheep purial; and you shall lhye in ane anhoder's bhosoms, and te tevil a ane of te hears shall go out of yhour heads. As for tis yhoung sparker, hersel shall nhot say so fery mhooch. Poor mustress Sally! you haif something to pay your shot, forepy kiffing your hears. It would pe pad folly to pury cood rhed ghold in a plack moss, where it would pe all spoiled." (pp. 405–06)

Parts of this speech read like a parody of the kind of sentimental, regretful rumination over a grave that can by encountered in many eighteenth-century texts, for example Blair's *The Grave*, Gray's 'Elegy, Written in a Country Churchyard', and Young's *Night Thoughts*. In such texts the departed past may engender deeply-felt emotions, but it is securely contained within the grave. This is not the closure towards which *The Three Perils of Woman* is travelling, however. Much to Davie's alarm, Sally refuses to stay quietly and conveniently dead.

David had seen from whence Sally took the pieces of gold which she had given him to lay out, and, after this long apostrophe, he began a-loosing her bodice and fumbling about her breast. In a moment the dead woman seized him by the hand with a frightened and convulsive grasp, setting her nails into his wrist. Davie was stooping over her when this occurred, and the fright made him roar out and fall forward, tumbling quite over her and the body of her husband, on which she raised herself above him, held him down, and looked him madly in the face. But the scene that then occurred for a short space was too ludicrous to be described at the close of a tale so lamentably unfortunate in all its circumstances.   (pp. 405–06)

This brings us full circle, back to the firing of Peter Gow's Spanish gun at Balmillo churchyard in the opening scene of Hogg's Culloden story. Once again we have events that combine the horrific and the ludicrous, played out in the darkness of night. The final scene, like the opening scene, has three bodies covered in blood. The opening scene's double grave is echoed when Sally and Davie, after their distressing and ludicrous encounter, dig a double grave for the bodies of Sally's husband and her former lover. Equally, both scenes involve the startling re-animation of an apparently dead body. This final image, like the image generated by the firing of the Spanish gun, encapsulates the view taken by Hogg's novel of the nature and significance of the events of 1745–46.

The debate between *Waverley* and *The Three Perils of Woman* raises complex and resonant issues. Scott's novel offers a linear narrative in which a civilised future replaces a backward past. In contrast, *The Three Perils of Woman* offers a circular narrative, a fact which is stressed by the division of the narrative into 'Circles' rather than the expected 'Chapters'. This circular narrative is not about a world emerging from a dark past into a sunlit future. Instead, it envisages a world in which the same old follies are perpetrated again and again, from generation to generation: like spring and autumn, the old follies will all come round again, in their turn, to be repeated in a different set of circumstances. It is for this reason that *The Three Perils of Woman* narrates its tales of the 1740s, 'sixty years since', *after* its account of the Scotland of the Waterloo era, its own present day. To have dealt with the past first, and then the present, would have been to set up expectations of a pattern of progression along the same lines as *Waverley*. This would have allowed Sally's death to be comfortably contained in the departed past of the bad old days. As things stand, however, Sally's death ends *The Three Perils of Woman*, and the reader leaves this text face to face with the powerfully disturbing questions raised by Sally's death during the post-Culloden holocaust.

The progress envisaged by *Waverley* involves a contrast between an advanced, enlightened, and civilised society which is threatened (in the end, ineffectually) by forces that unexpectedly emerge from a marginal and backward old world. In *Waverley*, progress and modernity win the day, and this outcome is seen as inevitable. Hogg's circular narrative subverts and questions such notions of progress, and seeks to locate value in the allegedly backward and inferior margins of subaltern Scotland. Sally may be a mere servant-girl, but in the context of Hogg's subaltern and circular narrative she is far from being insignificant. After the double grave for Sally's husband and her former lover has been dug, Davie Duff contrives to get Sally to safety, in the house of a widow. But 'in the month of December following she was lost, and could nowhere be discovered' (p. 406). We are now about nine months on from Sally's brief marriage; and her final fate is described on the last page of Hogg's novel:

> a young shepherd, one of the M'Phersons before-mentioned, chanced to be out on the heights of Correi-Uaine gathering in some goats late one afternoon. The ground was slightly covered with snow, the air calm, and the frost intense; and, to his great aston-ishment, he heard a strain of music rise on the breeze, of such a sweet and mournful cadence, that he took it for an angel's coronach.[20] He listened and kept aloof for a good while, but at length, owing to the whiteness of the ground, he perceived that there was something living and human sitting on the grave in the correi. He ap-proached; and, horrible to relate! there was the poor disconsolate Sally actually sitting rocking and singing over the body of a dead female infant. He ventured to speak to her in Gaelic, for he had no other language; but she only looked wildly up to heaven, and sung louder. He hasted home; but the road was long and rough, and before his brothers reached the spot the mother and child were lying stretched together in the arms of death, pale as the snow that surrounded them, and rigid as the grave-turf on which they had made their dying bed. Is there human sorrow on record like this that winded up the devastations of the Highlands? (p. 407)

Can a Scotch maidservant of somewhat loose morals be taken seriously as a tragic heroine? In *The Three Perils of Woman* she most certainly can: in this text Sally's death is a matter of cataclysmic significance. In Hogg's novel the allegedly backward, marginal, and insignificant lives of the people of subaltern Scotland are taken seriously, and are allowed to move centre stage. Sally's death occurs in the north, in the wild territory to which Samuel Johnson and Edward Waverley journey before returning south to the safety and normality of the modern world. In *The Three Perils of Woman*, Sally's life, and her death, assert that the modern world of the south is not the only place in which reality, significance, and value are to be found. In *Things Fall Apart*, Achebe disturbs prevalent Euro-centric assumptions by asserting that it is possible to encounter signifi-cance and value in the pre-Imperial world of Okonkwo as well as in the Imperial world of the District Commissioner. In *The Three Perils of Woman* Hogg likewise asserts on behalf of subaltern Scotland that 'we too might have a story to tell', by locating signifi-cance and value in an allegedly backward and uncivilised world.

A similar point emerges in a rather different way in Robert Wringhim's abortive journey south towards the end of *The Private Memoirs and Confessions of a Justified Sinner*. A hunted outcast suspected of the murder of his mother, the disguised Robert journeys south towards the Border with England and reaches 'a small miserable inn in the village of Ancrum'. He finds he has to satisfy the curiosity of the people at the inn:

> I said I was a poor student of theology, on my way to Oxford. They stared at one another with expressions of wonder, disappointment, and fear. I afterwards came to learn, that the term *theology* was by them quite misunderstood, and that they had some crude conceptions that nothing was taught at Oxford but the *black arts*, which ridiculous idea prevailed over all the south of Scotland. For the present I could not understand what the people meant, and less so, when the man asked me, with deep concern, "If I was serious in my intentions of going to Oxford? He hoped not, and that I would be better guided."
>
> I said my education wanted finishing;—but he remarked, that the Oxford arts were a bad finish for a religious man's education. (p. 159)

Here, as is not infrequently the case, Hogg's tongue is firmly in his cheek. The culturally dominant narrative of 'the journey north' suggests that in travelling south to the world of metropolitan Imperial culture (Oxford, London), one moves towards modernity, rationality, normality, and civilised values. But in Hogg's novel Oxford becomes, teasingly, the home of 'the *black arts*'. A few pages later Robert finds an opportunity for insight and salvation, not at sophisticated, academic, and Imperial Oxford but in the Scottish Borders, in the modest home of 'a poor hind' or farm labourer 'who could only accommodate me with a bed of rushes at his fire-side' (p. 162). Here again, as so often in Hogg's writings, we have an elegant, playful, teasing, unobtrusive, understated and impassioned suggestion that value and significance may be encountered in subaltern Scotland as well as in the Imperial elite, and that the Imperial elite may sometimes be more flawed and foolish than is entirely comfortable for its *amour propre*.

In the present post-Imperial age, there can appear to be something prescient about Hogg's approach. However, *Mador of the Moor*, *The Three Perils of Woman* and *The Private Memoirs and Confessions of a Justified Sinner* were not well received on their first publication, and were undeservedly neglected until the second half of the twentieth century. *Waverley*, on the other hand, deservedly became one of the nineteenth century's most influential and most widely read novels.

Rob Roy and Nicol Jarvie

It is worth remembering, however, that Hogg was not the only novelist to question and modify aspects of *Waverley*'s story: indeed, Scott arguably does this himself in *Rob*

Roy (1817). In this novel, as in *Waverley*, a young Englishman travels north from a modern and civilised England into the wild northern regions of the island of Great Britain; again as in *Waverley*, this young Englishman becomes embroiled in plans for a Jacobite rising; and again as in *Waverley* the rising is defeated, and the hero obtains a bride from the Jacobite past with whom he can enter the prosperous future of Hanoverian Britain. At first sight, then, it would appear that *Rob Roy* is simply a re-hash of its predecessor—but, as we shall see, this novel is in some ways somewhat darker, more complex, and more assertively Scottish than *Waverley* in its support for the Union and for the Hanoverian status quo.

Unlike *Waverley*, *Rob Roy* has a first-person narrator. Frank Osbaldistone, the young Englishman who travels north in the later novel, tells his own story as he looks back on the adventures of his youth from the perspective of old age—and the novel's account of events has at times an air of confusion and uncertainty very different from the confident all-seeing authority exuded by Waverley's narrator. Frank's journey north is prompted when he is sent by his father to Osbaldistone Hall, the ancestral family mansion in the North of England, and the home of Frank's uncle. This northern mansion, when Frank arrives there, proves to be 'a large and antiquated edifice, peeping out from a Druidical grove of huge oaks'.[21] The oak was a Jacobite emblem, but there is a further resonance here. In a Scott text, 'Druidical' oaks tend to suggest an archaic and primitive stage of social development. We have seen that, in *The Lady of the Lake*, the influence of the Druidical holy man provided an indication of the Highland clan's backwardness. Similarly, in his novel *Kenilworth* Scott describes a masque, presented in the presence of Queen Elizabeth of England, which represents 'the various nations by which England had at different times been occupied'. These nations are the 'aboriginal Britons', the Romans, the Saxons, and the Normans. The 'aboriginal Britons' are, of course, the most primitive of these groups; and the Britons are 'ushered in by two ancient Druids, whose hoary hair was crowned with a chaplet of oak'.[22]

Rob Roy, like *Waverley*, is concerned with what Scott presents as a Jacobite attempt to put back the clock—and when Frank arrives at Osbaldistone Hall it becomes apparent that he has in effect moved far backwards in time from the modern world of Hanoverian Britain in which his father successfully operates, and has arrived in the midst of a disturbingly archaic Jacobite world. Feasting in the old manner is carried on in the Stone Hall at the heart of the ancient edifice. Frank remarks:

> This venerable apartment, which had witnessed the feasts of several generations of the Osbaldistone family, bore also evidence of their success in field-sports. Huge antlers of deer, which might have been trophies of the hunting of Chevy Chace, were ranged around the walls, interspersed with the stuffed skins of badgers, otters, martins, and other animals of the chase. Amidst some remnants of old armour, which had, perhaps, served against the Scotch, hung the more valued weapons of silvan war,

cross-bows, guns of various device and construction, nets, fishing-rods, otter-spears, hunting-poles, with many other singular devices and engines for taking or killing game. (p. 107)

Frank, in coming to the home of his uncle and cousins, has entered a nest of Jacobites. Frank finds several Jacobite cousins at Osbaldistone Hall, including the beautiful and lively Die Vernon, an ardent supporter of the Stuart cause. Another cousin, Rashleigh Osbaldistone, proves to be a mainspring of plots that are about to set in motion the Jacobite rising of 1715. Rashleigh's machinations threaten not only to restore the Jacobites to power, but also to bring Frank's Hanoverian father to bankruptcy. Here we have a significant difference from the *Waverley* pattern. The core of the archaic old world, the heart of the Jacobite plot, is no longer located in Highland Scotland, as in *Waverley*. In *Rob Roy* it is located in Northern England. This is a significant and assertively Scottish alteration to the *Waverley* pattern, and this alteration helps Scott to enhance and deepen the positive aspects of the Highlanders of *Rob Roy*, in comparison with the Highlanders of *Waverley*.

Frank has to travel into Scotland in an attempt to thwart Rashleigh's plotting, and in due course he meets two Scotsmen who, although kinsmen, sum up marked differences between contrasting strands in the fabric of Scottish life. One of these is Bailie Nicol Jarvie, a Lowlander and a Glasgow merchant, and the Scottish equivalent of Frank's father. A staunch Hanoverian, Jarvie is an eloquent supporter of the recent Union, which (he argues) has promoted Scottish prosperity by opening the way for Glasgow merchants to trade with England's (now Britain's) American colonies. Jarvie says:

> There's naething sae gude on this side o' time but it might hae been better, and that may be said o' the Union. Nane were keener against it than the Glasgow folk, wi' their rabblings and their risings, and their mobs, as they ca' them now-a-days. But it's an ill wind blaws naebody gude—Let ilka ane roose the ford as they find it—I say, Let Glasgow flourish! whilk is judiciously and elegantly putten round the town's arms, by way of by-word.—Now, since St Mungo catched herrings in the Clyde, what was ever like to gar us flourish like the sugar and tobacco-trade? Will ony body tell me that, and grumble at the treaty that opened us a road west-awa' yonder?   (p. 312)

Jarvie is part of the new and prosperous post-Union commercial world of the British Empire, the world of 'the sugar and tobacco-trade' with North America. Even the limes for his brandy-punch, Jarvie tells Frank, '"were from his own little farm yonder-awa," (indicating the West Indies with a knowing shrug of his shoulders)' (p. 295). However, Jarvie's cousin, the Highland outlaw Rob Roy, is a man from a very different world, the old world of a pre-North-British Scotland. Aspects of the view taken by

Scott's text of that old world find expression when Rob Roy, as clan chieftain, is about to be greeted by Dougal, one of his clansmen, who is described as follows:

> He was a wild shock-headed looking animal, whose profusion of red hair covered and obscured his features, which were otherwise only characterised by the extravagant joy that affected him at the sight of my guide [Rob Roy]. In my experience I have met nothing so absolutely resembling my idea of a very uncouth, wild, and ugly savage, adoring the idol of his tribe. He grinned, he shivered, he laughed, he was near crying, if he did not actually cry. He had a 'Where shall I go?—What can I do for you?' expression of face; the complete, surrendered, and anxious subservience and devotion of which it is difficult to describe, otherwise than by the awkward combination which I have attempted. The fellow's voice seemed choking in his ecstasy, and only could express itself in such interjections as 'Oigh, oigh—Ay, ay—it's lang since she's seen ye!' and other exclamations equally brief, expressed in the same unknown tongue in which he had communicated with my conductor while we were on the outside of the jail door. (p. 258)

We have here a less attractive and more primitive but equally striking version of Evan Dhu's loyalty to his chief. Rob's clansman, like Sawney in the Boghouse, can be read as an embodiment of an eighteenth-century Londoner's nightmares about primitive sub-human Highlanders. There is something reminiscent of an orang-utan in the description of this 'wild shock-headed looking animal', with his 'profusion of red hair'—and it may well be that there is an oblique reference here to Dr Johnson's famous and robust dismissal of the Scottish Enlightenment writer Lord Monboddo's pre-Darwinian theory that orang-utans are wild men, members of a human sub-species capable of being taught language. At all events, the wild shock-headed looking clansman is presented as a disturbing throwback, as a survival from an earlier stage of human development. Indeed Rob Roy ('Red Robert') himself seems to be another wild man, whose limbs are likewise 'covered with a fell of thick, short, red hair, especially around his knees' (p. 374). Furthermore, elsewhere in the novel Frank (as narrator) describes Rob as having arms

> so very long as to be rather a deformity. I afterwards heard that this length of arm was a circumstance on which he prided himself; that when he wore his native Highland garb, he could tie the garters of his hose without stooping; [...] it gave something wild, irregular, and, as it were, unearthly, to his appearance, and reminded me involuntarily, of the tales which Mabel used to tell of the old Picts who ravaged Northumberland in ancient times, who, according to her tradition, were a sort of half-goblin half-human beings, distinguished, like this man, for courage, cunning, ferocity, the length of their arms, and the squareness of their shoulders. (p. 273)

In all this, we have a reference to the old notion of the Highlander-as-monkey who gibbers forth his gross conceptions in incomprehensible Gaelic. Scott, however, does not leave Rob-as-wild-man at that point, and this Highlander does not emerge from the novel as a sub-human figure. On the contrary, Rob Roy is resourceful, adaptable, a man of impressive energy. Frank brings the novel to a conclusion by describing Rob as 'the Robin Hood of Scotland, the dread of the wealthy, but the friend of the poor, and possessed of many qualities, both of head and heart, which would have graced a less equivocal profession than that to which his fate condemned him' (p. 452).

What, then, lies behind Scott's complex portrait of Rob Roy? In the Introduction he wrote for the 1828 'Magnum Opus' edition of this novel, Scott writes about the historical Rob Roy as follows:

> He owed his fame in a great measure to his residing on the very verge of the Highlands, and playing such pranks in the beginning of the 18th century, as are usually ascribed to Robin Hood in the middle ages,—and that within forty miles of Glasgow, a great commercial city, the seat of a learned university. Thus a character like his, blending the wild virtues, the subtle policy, and unrestrained license of an American Indian, was flourishing in Scotland during the Augustan age of Queen Anne and George I. Addison, it is probable, or Pope, would have been considerably surprised if they had known that there existed in the same island with them a personage of Rob Roy's peculiar habits and profession. It is this strong contrast betwixt the civilised and cultivated mode of life on the one side of the Highland line, and the wild and lawless adventures which were habitually undertaken and achieved by one who dwelt on the opposite side of that ideal boundary, which creates the interest attached to his name. (p. 5)

The heart of the matter with regard to *Rob Roy* is connected with this contrast between the civilised and cultivated southern world of Queen Anne and George I, and Rob Roy's northern world of 'wild and lawless adventures'. Although lawless and unrestrained, Rob's world has its 'wild virtues' and offers a primeval, liberating energy that has the potential to energise the somewhat etiolated Augustan refinement of the British Imperial centre, as embodied by Addison or Pope. Rob is a Highlander who may be primitive, but who is not sub-human. The most prominent sub-humans in Scott's novel are Frank's gang of Neanderthal male cousins at Osbaldistone Hall, who are aptly dismissed by Die Vernon as 'the Ourang-Outangs' (p. 152). These English Jacobites are locked in the past. Indeed, they become extinct: at the end of the novel they die out with a rapidity that is apt as well as comical and convenient, thus leaving Frank to inherit the ancestral Osbaldistone Hall, and the future.

Apart from the potentially useful quality of loyalty to his chief, Rob Roy's devoted red-haired clansman Dougal is presented as being as outmoded as Frank's Neanderthal

Osbaldistone cousins. However, Rob himself is another kind of primitive, a much more positive kind of orang-utan. As Ian Duncan puts it in the Introduction of his edition of the novel, 'in Rob Roy's case the primitive signifies a rugged vitality and cultural integrity ("honour"), quite the opposite of a destiny of extinction—he is quintessentially a survivor, triumphant over the proscription of his clan' (p. xxv). Taken together, the Scottish cousins Rob Roy and Nicol Jarvie (Highlander and Lowlander) demonstrate the qualities that Scotland is able to bring to the Imperial cause. At the end of the novel, Jarvie finds himself in a position to confirm and extend his lucrative co-operation with the powerful London mercantile house of Frank's father: the Imperial centre, it is clear, will find in Jarvie a very useful junior partner. Highland resourcefulness, honour, loyalty, and primitive energy (as embodied in Rob) likewise will have much to offer, as the Empire fights its way to world dominance at Waterloo and elsewhere. In short, Rob demonstrates even more powerfully than *Waverley*'s Evan Dhu the potential of Highlanders (once properly re-educated) to serve the purposes of the Imperial centre.

Perhaps the enhanced view of Highlanders as exemplified by Rob has something to do with the sterling service in the British cause famously performed by Highland soldiers at Waterloo, which was fought during the interval between the publication of *Waverley* in 1814 and the writing of *Rob Roy* in 1817. Interestingly, an uncharacteristically positive reference to a Scot in *Vanity Fair* relates to the behaviour of Highland troops immediately before Waterloo. Thackeray's narrator comments:

> This flat, flourishing, easy country never could have looked more rich and prosperous, than in that opening summer of 1815, when its green fields and quiet cities were enlivened by multiplied red-coats; when its wide *chaussées* swarmed with brilliant English equipages; when its great canal-boats, gliding by rich pastures and pleasant quaint old villages, by old châteaux lying amongst old trees, were all crowded with well-to-do English travellers: when the soldier who drank at the village inn, not only drank, but paid his score; and Donald, the Highlander, billeted in the Flemish farm-house, rocked the baby's cradle, while Jean and Jeanette were out getting in the hay. As our painters are bent on military subjects just now, I throw out this as a good subject for the pencil, to illustrate the principle of an honest English war. (p. 336)

If not quite an English gentleman as yet, by 1815 Sawney nevertheless appears to have left the boghouse behind, and to have evolved into a person fit to be employed in fighting an honest English war. The erstwhile orang-utan is becoming a hero of Empire, and the wild music of his bagpipes is becoming 'the pibroch of Europe', civilised music that in due course will be heard with profound relief in the darkest days of the Indian Mutiny.

Rob Roy and Later Fictions

> For why? Because the good old rule
>   Sufficeth them; the simple plan,
> That they should take who have the power,
>   And they should keep who can.
>   Wordsworth, 'Rob Roy's Grave'

At the conclusion of *Rob Roy*, Rashleigh's nefarious Jacobite schemes come to nothing, and Frank regains Osbaldistone Hall for Hanoverian Britain, as the true heir. Frank likewise marries his cousin Die Vernon, bringing her out of her Jacobite darkness (she had been destined for life in a French Catholic convent, a horrible fate in British Protestant eyes) into the bright new world of the civilised modernity and commercial wealth of Imperial Britain. Much of this, of course, is entirely in tune with the *Waverley* narrative pattern, but in *Rob Roy* the triumph of modernity, which ought to be embodied and confirmed by the marriage of Frank and Die, is complicated by the fact that the central couple do not live happily ever after. As he writes of his youthful adventures Frank has outlived Die, and the conclusion of this lonely widower's narrative leaves an impression, not of triumph and fulfilment, but of deprivation and emptiness. The novel ends on a note of mourning for a lost vitality.

Many classic Westerns (*Shane*, for example, or *The Man Who Shot Liberty Valance*), follow Scott's *Rob Roy* in focusing on a time when an old world of 'wild and lawless adventures' is giving way to a 'civilised and cultivated' new world of commerce and the rule of law. At the end of *Shane*, the heroic gunfighter rides off into the sunset, his time over, as we hear a haunting, lamenting cry of 'Shane, Shane'. In *Rob Roy* the death of the (all too aptly-named) Jacobite heroine 'Die' has a similar resonance. Like these Westerns, Scott's novel deeply regrets the passing of the old world of 'wild and lawless adventures', while accepting the inevitability (and ultimate desirability) of the advance of modernity. Although the wild Highland virtues embodied by Rob Roy will find renewed expression in the sterling deeds of the Highland regiments of the British Army at Waterloo and elsewhere, Rob's own world, like Shane's, is rapidly passing away. Rob manages to operate in the old ways until the end of his long life, but that way of life is not a possibility for his sons. And this is a cause for regret. The coming of modernity brings many benefits, but also involves a loss of liberty, freedom, romance, heroism.

In *Waverley* and *Rob Roy* the British north has many of the features later associated with the American West, and both Edward Waverley and Frank Osbaldistone make a journey north to a place that is dangerous but potentially liberating, anarchic but potentially heroic. The Brontë sisters, like many people of their generation, were avid admirers of Scott's novels—and in *Wuthering Heights* Emily Brontë adapts the narrative pattern of *Rob Roy* for her own purposes, as she sets up a contrast between the orderly modern world of Thrushcross Grange (secure in its cultivated valley), and the liberating, dangerous, primeval world of Wuthering Heights and the moors. Like Frank Osbaldistone, Mr Lockwood (the first-person narrator of *Wuthering Heights*) leaves a modern and civilised southern world behind, and journeys north into wilder, older, more lawless, but potentially liberating territory. Lockwood's arrival at Wuthering Heights seems to echo Frank's arrival at Osbaldistone Hall. Each house is a manifestation of the ways of the old, uncivilised northern world, and each house has a room at its heart that gives expression to the life and culture of the inhabitants of this archaic territory. We have already considered Frank's description of the Stone Hall in Scott's novel. Lockwood's description of the equivalent room at Wuthering Heights reads as follows:

> One end, indeed, reflected splendidly both light and heat from ranks of immense pewter dishes, interspersed with silver jugs and tankards, towering row after row, in a vast oak dresser, to the very roof. The latter had never been underdrawn: its entire anatomy lay bare to an inquiring eye, except where a frame of wood laden with oatcakes, and clusters of legs of beef, mutton and ham, concealed it. Above the chimney were sundry villanous old guns, and a couple of horse-pistols, and, by way of ornament, three gaudily painted canisters disposed along its ledge. The floor was of smooth, white stone: the chairs, high-backed, primitive structures, painted green: one or two heavy black ones lurking in the shade. In an arch under the dresser, reposed a huge, liver-coloured bitch pointer, surrounded by a swarm of squealing puppies, and other dogs haunted other recesses.[23]

This is a place of feasting, of old weapons, of trophies—a place teeming with the primeval life of the huge pointer bitch and her swarm of squealing puppies. Arrival here is a crucial stage in Lockwood's journey to a disturbingly wild north, just as arrival in the Stone Hall marks a crucial stage of Frank's journey north into a dangerous encounter with an old world of Jacobitism. The house at Wuthering Heights, like the surrounding landscape of the moors, embodies a world startlingly different from the cultivated and elegant world from which Lockwood comes—a world embodied in the novel by the civilised comforts of Thrushcross Grange.

Like the first-person narrator of *Rob Roy*, the first-person narrator of *Wuthering Heights* has a good opinion of himself. Lockwood assumes that his polished manners are likely to win the heart of young Catherine, the Wuthering Heights equivalent of Osbaldistone Hall's Die Vernon. Catherine is not exactly galvanised by Lockwood's elegance, however: her future partner will be someone very different, the boorish and apparently irredeemable Hareton, who at this stage is an example of uncivilised northern barbarity at its least attractive.

Lockwood attempts to narrate a Waverley novel after the manner of *Rob Roy*, with himself in the role of Frank Osbaldistone, but this pattern is soon disrupted. In the first three chapters of the novel a series of disconcerting and even terrifying experiences open out for Lockwood when he visits Wuthering Heights, the home of Heathcliff, his landlord, from whom he is renting Thrushcross Grange. After his return to Thrushcross Grange, Lockwood contrives to find out more about the mysterious situation at Wuthering Heights by inviting his servant Nelly Dean to tell him about the Wuthering Heights family (whom she has served for most of her life). A responsive Nelly launches into a fireside oral narrative, the first of a series; and the story Nelly tells to Lockwood—her fireside winter evening tale, as it were—forms much of the text of *Wuthering Heights*.

Nelly's fireside winter evening tale suggests an approach towards Hogg's territory—and Christine Alexander, Winifred Gérin and others have shown that, in the 1820s, the young Brontës were avid readers of Hogg.[24] It may be, then, that in *Wuthering Heights* a Waverley novel in the making is subverted and displaced by an orally-based narrative of the kind to be found in Hogg's *Shepherd's Calendar* and *Winter Evening Tales*. Disruption of a Scott-style narrative by an oral narrative is repeated in the final chapters of Emily Brontë's novel. After a period of absence, Lockwood returns to the north, where he finds a radically changed situation—and the events that have brought about the change are elucidated by an oral narrative from Nelly Dean. It appears, then, that Lockwood, like the Editor of the *Justified Sinner*, sets out to offer a narrative in the Scott manner—but, as is also the case with the Editor, Lockwood's narrative is modified and subverted when it is displaced by another narrative. If the narrative pattern of *Rob Roy* is present in *Wuthering Heights*, so too (in a different way) is the narrative pattern of Hogg's *Justified Sinner*.

It may be, then, that in *Wuthering* Heights Emily Brontë creates her own distinctive vision while drawing heavily on the energising, creative debate between Scott and Hogg about the significance of the journey north. Likewise, it seems possible that the pervasive imagery of *Wuthering Heights* (1847) echoes a passage in *Queen Hynde* (1824), a passage in which Hogg writes with real feeling about the nature of his own poetry. The Ettrick Shepherd (that man of a primitive old world) here claims a place for himself as a poetic child of Nature: he is as it were another Donnchadh Bàn Mac an t-Saoir, one whose lack of formal education is more than compensated by natural genius and native energy. Hogg concludes the first Book of his epic with the following invitation to his reader, the 'Maid of Dunedin':

> Let those who list, the garden chuse,
> Where flowers are regular and profuse;
> Come thou to dell and lonely lea,
> And cull the mountain gems with me;
> And sweeter blooms may be thine own,
> By nature's hand at random sown;

And sweeter strains may touch thy heart
Than are producible by art.
The nightingale may give delight,
A while, 'mid silence of the night,
But th' lark lost in the heavens blue,
O her wild strain is ever new![25]

These lines became fairly well known in the 1820s, and may well have been familiar to Hogg's enthusiastic admirers at that time, the young Brontës. Clearly, it is possible to see in them something of the contrast in Emily Brontë's novel between Thrushcross Grange and Wuthering Heights. Likewise, it is interesting to note that *Wuthering Heights* follows *The Three Perils of Woman* in that both novels end (somewhat unusually) in contemplation of a triple grave shared by a young woman, her husband, and her lover. Scott's importance for later novelists has long been justly recognised, but it may be that, as the revival of Hogg's reputation continues to make an increasingly wide range of his texts readily available, hitherto unobserved strands of connection and reference will become visible in the nineteenth-century fiction of Britain and America.

Notes

1   Alfred Tennyson, *Ballads and Other Poems* (London: Kegan Paul, 1880), pp. 99–111 (pp. 104–05, 110–11).

2   *Sawney in the Boghouse* (London: 1745), reproduced from the copy in The British Museum.

3   Chinua Achebe, 'An Image of Africa: Racism is Conrad's *Heart of Darkness*', in Joseph Conrad, *Heart of Darkness*, Norton Critical Editions, 3rd edn (New York: Norton, 1988), pp. 251–62 (p. 257).

4   Achebe, 'An Image of Africa', p. 258.

5   *An Lasair: Anthology of 18th Century Scottish Gaelic Verse*, ed. by Ronald Black (Edinburgh: Birlinn, 2001), pp. 472–73.

6   *The Poetry of Scotland: Gaelic, Scots and English 1380–1980*, ed. by Roderick Watson (Edinburgh: Edinburgh University Press, 1995), p. 263.

7   James Macpherson, *The Poems of Ossian and Related Works*, ed. by Howard Gaskell with an Introduction by Fiona Stafford (Edinburgh: Edinburgh University Press, 1996), pp. ix–x.

8   *The Poems of Ossian*, pp. xiii–xiv.

9   James Boswell, *Life of Johnson*, ed. by R. W. Chapman (Oxford: Oxford University Press, 1970), pp. 304–05.

10   Samuel Johnson and James Boswell, *Journey to the Hebrides: A Journey to the Western Islands of Scotland; and, The Journal of a Tour to the Hebrides with Samuel Johnson,*

ed. by Ian McGowan, Canongate Classics, 68 (Edinburgh: Canongate, 1996), p. 101.

11   Johnson and Boswell, *Journey to the Hebrides*, p. 22.

12   R. F. Foster, *Modern Ireland 1600–1972* (London: Penguin, 1989), p. 101.

13   Johnson and Boswell, *Journey to the Hebrides*, pp. 29–30.

14   From the passage by the historian Michael Lynch quoted in Chapter 1: see Lynch, *Scotland: A New History* (London: Pimlico, 1992), pp. 338–39.

15   *The Poems of Ossian*, p. xv.

16   Walter Scott, *The Lady of the Lake* (Edinburgh: Ballantyne; London: Longman, 1810), Canto ii stanza 14.

17   James Hogg, *Mador of the Moor*, ed. by James E. Barcus, Stirling / South Carolina Research Edition of the Collected Works of James Hogg (Edinburgh: Edinburgh University Press, 2005), p. 12.

18   For a discussion of this, see James Hogg, *Queen Hynde*, ed. by Suzanne Gilbert and Douglas S. Mack, Stirling / South Carolina Research Edition of the Collected Works of James Hogg (Edinburgh: Edinburgh University Press, 1998), p. xxxvii.

19   Here Hogg uses a long-established literary convention for presenting the High-land-English of native Gaelic speakers. 'Examples of such pseudo-Highland speech are to be found throughout Scottish literature from as early as 1450, and though some of its features do have some basis in fact, most are merely a literary convention: for instance, the de-voicing of the voiced consonant [b] to [p] [...] is an accurate reflection of Gaelic usage; *ta* for *the* is not authentic; nor is the use of *she*, most commonly substituted for *I*, but sometimes also used for *you* [...] or *he*, *it* [...]. This purely literary pseudo-Highland occurs, for example, in the works of Smollett, Scott, Galt, George Macdonald and Stevenson.' (Mairi Robinson, 'Modern Literary Scots: Fergusson and After', in *Lowland Scots*, ed. by A. J. Aitken (Edinburgh: ASLS, 1973), pp. 38–55 (p. 39).) Other features of conventional Highland-English include the substitution of *c* for *g*, and *t* for *d*: thus *god* becomes *cot*.

20   For a discussion of the significance of references to angels in Hogg's writings, see Douglas S. Mack, 'Hogg and Angels', *Studies in Hogg and his World*, 15 (2004), 90–98.

21   Scott, *Rob Roy*, ed. by Ian Duncan, World's Classics (Oxford: Oxford University Press, 1998), p. 100. Future page references are to this edition, and are given in the text.

22   Scott, *Kenilworth: A Romance*, ed. by J. H. Alexander, Edinburgh Edition of the Waverley Novels (Edinburgh: Edinburgh University Press, 1993), p. 349.

23   Emily Brontë, *Wuthering Heights*, ed. by Ian Jack, World's Classics (Oxford: Oxford University Press, 1981), p. 3.

24   See Christine Alexander, 'Readers and Writers: *Blackwood's* and the Brontës', *The Gaskell Society Journal*, 8 (1994), 54–69; and Winifred Gérin, *Emily Brontë: A Biography* (Oxford: Clarendon Press, 1971), p. 16.

25   See Hogg, *Queen Hynde*, ed. Gilbert and Mack, p. 31.

Telling Lowland Scotland's Story

'We too might have a story to tell.' (Achebe)

A New Commercial World of Britishness and Empire

In the eighteenth century there were marked cultural differences between Highland Scotland and Lowland Scotland—and, as we have seen, these differences were memorably portrayed by Scott through the contrasting characters of the Highland outlaw Rob Roy and his Lowland cousin, the merchant Nicol Jarvie. This chapter will focus on Lowland Scotland's long process of adjustment to the realities of involvement in the British Empire during the century or so that followed Union with England in 1707. Particular attention will be paid to the ways in which that process of adjustment shaped, and was shaped by, the telling of stories.

The second half of the eighteenth century saw the American and French Revolutions, and the radical, democratic political ideals widely current at that time made themselves felt in Lowland Scotland, as elsewhere. In Lowland Scotland, however, these ideals took a particular form that was deeply influenced by memories of the Covenanters. These subaltern Presbyterians had defied what they saw as despotic and arbitrary royal authority when, in 1666 and again in 1679, they rose in armed rebellion against attempts by Charles II to change the egalitarian and democratic ethos of the Church of Scotland by the imposition of Episcopalian (in effect, Anglican) forms of liturgy and church government. Persecution of the Covenanters intensified in the 'Killing Times' of the mid-1680s, during the reign of James VII and II, Charles II's brother and successor. In the Protestant and Presbyterian popular culture that was especially strong among the subaltern people of the western Lowlands, the Killing Times came to be remembered with reverence as a defining moment, as a period of heroic struggle that had secured the civil and religious liberties of the people by paving the way for the deposition of James VII and II in the 'Glorious Revolution' of 1688–89. For eighteenth-century Scottish Radicals like the poet Robert Burns, the struggles of the Covenanters provided a deeply encouraging example of ultimately successful popular opposition to an unjust and tyrannical aristocratic regime.[1]

The eighteenth century was also the time of the Scottish Enlightenment, that remarkable period when writers like David Hume and Adam Smith made Edinburgh one of the most influential intellectual and cultural centres of Europe. Furthermore, the political and intellectual ferment in eighteenth-century Lowland Scotland interacted with the profound economic and social changes that began to flow from the Union of 1707. This potent mix was to produce much memorable writing in the later decades of the eighteenth century, and in the first decades of the nineteenth century.

The new post-Union economic developments were particularly spectacular in Glasgow and the western Lowlands, the area which had been the heartland of the Covenanters. *Rob Roy* is set in 1715, and, as we have seen, Scott's novel presents Nicol Jarvie as an embodiment of the thriving commercial world that established itself in Glasgow and other parts of the western Lowlands after England's colonies in North America were converted, post-1707, into British colonies to which Scotland had full trading access. Nicol Jarvie's succinct defence of the Treaty of Union has already been quoted:

> I say, Let Glasgow flourish! whilk is judiciously and elegantly putten round the town's arms, by way of by-word.—Now, since St Mungo catched herrings in the Clyde, what was ever like to gar us flourish like the sugar and tobacco-trade? Will ony body tell me that, and grumble at the treaty that opened us a road west-awa' yonder? (p. 312)

In the new situation created by the 'Glorious Revolution' and the Union, the focus in the western Lowlands began to move away from the old impassioned struggle of the Covenanters for civil and religious liberty. Instead, the succulent opportunities offered by the sugar and tobacco-trade with British North America began to move towards centre-stage.

Glasgow and its river the Clyde had the geographical advantage of ready access to the trade-routes of the North Atlantic, and the great eighteenth-century prosperity of Glasgow and Greenock (the major commercial centres of the Clyde) was firmly based on trade in tobacco from Virginia and in sugar from the West Indies. During the period between the Treaty of Union of 1707 and the American War of Independence in the 1770s, Glasgow's tobacco trade enjoyed spectacular success. The historian T. M. Devine writes:

> The tobacco trade transformed the social and cultural world of Glasgow. A new breed of merchants came on the scene. Their wealth and commercial power were unprecedented in the city's history, so much so that they were dubbed 'tobacco lords' as an acknowledgement of their pre-eminence. They were said to promenade the streets of

Glasgow clad in scarlet cloaks, satin suits and cocked hats, with gold-tipped canes in hand and an aloof air. This new aristocracy built splendid mansions, founded banks and industries, and dominated the political and cultural life of the city.[2]

The amiable Nicol Jarvie is not at all 'aloof ', but nevertheless he is Scott's portrait of a highly successful merchant of the eighteenth-century Glasgow of the tobacco lords. Scott paints a notably sympathetic and unthreatening portrait of Jarvie, a portrait designed to strengthen acceptance in England of Lowland Scotland's significant post-Union role in the Empire's highly profitable commercial activity. When he describes Jarvie, however, Scott manages to avoid direct engagement with some potentially difficult areas. For example, the methods of the tobacco lords were not always above reproach, and their success tended to provoke resentment in England. Devine writes as follows:

> English mercantile interests complained vociferously that the Scots were taking their business away because of systematic fraud practised on a massive scale. [...] Investigations made by the Scottish customs in the early 1720s confirmed that a high level of fraud existed and that the principal abuse in the Scottish trade involved conspiracies between merchants and officers to under-weigh incoming cargoes on a very large scale. In the years from 1715 to 1717, smuggled imports were estimated at 62 per cent of legal imports; at 47 per cent between 1720 and 1721; at 26 per cent between 1722 and 1731, and still as high as 22 per cent in the period from 1739 to 1748.[3]

There were, in addition, still more problematic features of Glasgow's eighteenth-century 'sugar and tobacco-trade'. The cultivation of tobacco in mainland North America depended upon the use of slave labour, and an even more brutal regime of slavery underpinned the production of sugar in the West Indies. In *Rob Roy*, however, the reader is not made particularly aware of this aspect of West Indian life. Nicol Jarvie, while entertaining Frank Osbaldistone in Glasgow, remarks that the limes for their brandy-punch '"were from his own little farm yonder-awa," (indicating the West Indies with a knowing shrug of his shoulders)' (p. 295). Scott, however, avoids any suggestion that Jarvie's 'little farm' would have been a less than idyllic place.

In the British and Imperial context, the 'sugar and tobacco-trade' provided opportunities of various kinds at all levels of Lowland society. There was a potential for rich pickings: huge fortunes could be made by the owners of West Indian plantations (one remembers Miss Swartz in *Vanity Fair*), and even the employees of such plantations could pick up substantial wealth in a short time if they were fortunate enough to survive the ever-present threat of fatal disease. Scots were heavily involved in Imperial commercial activity in the West Indies in the eighteenth century,[4] and in 1786 Robert Burns (at a particularly complex crisis in his relationships with Jean Armour and Mary

Campbell, and in an effort to escape from the grinding poverty of life as a Lowland peasant-farmer) seriously considered accepting employment as a book-keeper on a Scottish-owned sugar plantation in Jamaica. However, when he was about to embark at Greenock to become 'a poor Negro-driver' (as he put it in a letter),[5] the success of the Kilmarnock edition of his poems (and the death of Mary Campbell) gave him the opportunity to abandon his Caribbean project, and to decide (no doubt with some relief) to remain in Scotland.

Economic and other pressures almost drove Burns to Jamaica, but it seems clear that his political ideals would have made an uncomfortable fit with life on a Caribbean sugar plantation—even although he would have been there as a book-keeper rather than literally as a 'Negro-driver', whip in hand. Burns had strongly radical and egalitarian political views that had been shaped by the Presbyterian popular culture of his native western Lowlands, the country of the Covenanters. Discussing this, Liam McIlvanney writes:

> It remains unfortunate that Burns's run-ins with the kirk have obscured the extent to which his own political philosophy is grounded in his religious inheritance. His politics are shaped by two complementary strands of Presbyterian thought: on the one hand, the New Light, with its subjection of all forms of authority to the tribunal of the individual reason; on the other, the traditional contractarian political theory long associated with Presbyterianism. These influences are evident in Burns's repeated avowal of 'revolution principles', in his support for the American Revolution, and, above all, in his satirical attacks on political corruption. The whole framework of assumption on which Burns's political satires rest recalls the contractarian principles of Presbyterian thought: that authority ascends from below; that government is a contract, and political power a trust; and that even the humblest members of society are competent to censure their governors. That Burns deplored certain aspects of Calvinism—its harsh soteriology, its emphasis on faith over works—should not blind us to his sincere identification with the Presbyterian political inheritance.[6]

Like many subaltern Scottish Lowlanders in the eighteenth century, Burns inherited strongly-held radical and egalitarian attitudes from a pre-Union Presbyterian popular culture that took for granted the right of the people to depose the tyrannical James VII in the 'Glorious Revolution'. However, like many other eighteenth-century Lowland Scots, Burns had to reconcile these inherited attitudes with the realities, pressures, and potential financial rewards of a post-Union Imperial economy enriched by the slavery-based 'sugar and tobacco-trade'. In this situation, comfortable and easy solutions were not always readily available. As we shall see in the remainder of this chapter, attempts to reconcile the revered principles of the Covenanters and the 'Glorious Revolution' with post-Union Imperial reality and with the insights of the Enlightenment preoccupied not only Burns, but also the major Scottish writers of the next generation, the generation of Scott and Hogg. The elite and subaltern perspectives on these questions could be very different, and these differences energised a debate carried on during the 1810s and 1820s in a remarkable group of technically innovative and politically charged Scottish fictions. One of the most significant and most innovative of these was Hogg's *The Brownie of Bodsbeck*, a short novel that seems to have been first planned in the early 1810s as part of a projected series of 'rural and traditionary tales' designed to give voice to the insights, the history, and the concerns of the subaltern people of Hogg's native Ettrick Forest. Scott's *Waverley* (1814) is rightly seen as the book that inaugurated the historical novel, one of the dominant literary genres of the nineteenth century. However, even before the publication of *Waverley* Hogg seems to have been using his 'rural and traditionary tales' in order to feel his way towards the creation of his own kind of historical fiction—and in this project Hogg wished, like Achebe a century and a half later, to say on behalf of his own people that 'we too might have a story to tell'.

'Rural and Traditionary Tales'

Even although the success of the Kilmarnock edition allowed Burns to avoid embarkation for Jamaica at Greenock in 1786, he never fully escaped from poverty—perhaps because his radical political views and his lowly social background placed a glass ceiling on his progress in the class-dominated world of Imperial-era Scotland. However, Burns continued to place great value on the deeply-rooted cultural traditions of his native community, and until his death in 1796 his poems continued to speak eloquently from and for subaltern post-Union Lowland Scotland. In his final years Burns devoted much time and energy to collecting and re-creating the traditional songs of the people of the Lowlands, and the spirit in which he approached this task can be sensed in lines from 'The Answer'. In this poem he looks back on his poetic ambitions while still 'beardless, young and blate':

> Ev'n then a wish (I mind its power)
> A wish, that to my latest hour
>   Shall strongly heave my breast;
> That I for poor old Scotland's sake
> Some useful plan, or book could make,
>   Or sing a sang at least.[7]

At first glance, Walter Scott's *Minstrelsy of the Scottish Border*, a collection of traditional ballads (1802–03), appears to be a project very similar to Burns's work on the Scottish song tradition a decade earlier. There are significant differences, however, as well as resemblances. Scott concludes his Introduction to the *Minstrelsy* by saying that he has attempted to create a record of 'popular superstitions, and legendary history, which, if not now collected, must soon have been totally forgotten'. He goes on:

> By such efforts, feeble as they are, I may contribute somewhat to the history of my native country; the peculiar features of whose manners and character are daily melting and dissolving into those of her sister and ally. And, trivial as may appear such an offering, to the manes of a kingdom, once proud and independent, I hang it upon her altar with a mixture of feelings, which I shall not attempt to describe.[8]

Clearly, Scott's project (like Burns's) was driven by a deep commitment to traditional Scottish culture. However, where Scott regarded himself as gathering up the remnants of a dying tradition, Burns regarded himself as collecting and refurbishing the traditional songs of an oral tradition still vigorously alive among the people of subaltern Lowland Scotland. Furthermore, Scott tended to see the best of the ballads he collected as relics of an ancient and now-dead aristocratic tradition, fortuitously preserved in the popular folk-memory. For example, in his long narrative poem *The Lay of the Last Minstrel* (1805), Scott makes it clear that the Lay sung by the last of the old Minstrels of the Scottish Border 'was not framed for village churles, | But for high dames and mighty earls'.[9]

James Hogg had given assistance to Scott during the collection of material for *Minstrelsy of the Scottish Border*. However, Hogg seems to have felt that he had grown up within what was still at that time a living tradition of old oral ballads and songs that had been produced by 'village churles' like himself. For Hogg, these old ballads and songs were none the worse for not belonging to the world of 'high dames and mighty earls', and this view emerges strongly in his own poetry, most notably in *The Mountain Bard* (1807), *The Queen's Wake* (first version 1813, final revised version 1819), and *Mador of the Moor* (written 1813, published 1816). It also lies behind *The Forest Minstrel* (1810), a volume that can be regarded (in one of its aspects) as an attempt by Hogg to carry on Burns's project for the refurbishing of the living song tradition of subaltern Lowland Scotland.

In the early 1810s, as part of an attempt to establish himself as a professional writer based in Edinburgh, Hogg began to explore the possibility of embarking on a project that would operate in parallel with *The Forest Minstrel*. This new venture was to have far-reaching consequences. For it, he would write prose tales based on the kind of traditional oral story-telling with which he had grown up in his native Ettrick, and this marked the beginning of his career as a writer of prose fiction. Furthermore, Hogg's 'rural and traditionary tales' led him into innovations in narrative technique that were to prove fruitful not only in his own writings, but also in the writings of others.

The first products of the new project were short stories published in his own periodical *The Spy* (1810–1811). After *The Spy* closed in financial difficulties in August 1811,

Hogg had an unexpected popular success when his book-length poem *The Queen's Wake* appeared in January 1813. No doubt encouraged by this success, he wrote to Scott on 3 April 1813 about his new plan for a series of rural and traditionary tales:

> I would fain publish 2 vol^s 8vo. close print of *Scottish Rural tales* anonymous in prose I have one will make about 200 pages alone some of the others you have seen in the Spy &c. Some people say they are original and interesting. I mention all these for your advice when I come.[10]

Ian Duncan has argued convincingly that the story that would 'make about 200 pages' was probably 'The Bridal of Polmood', which in the event was not published until it appeared in Hogg's *Winter Evening Tales* in 1820.[11] At all events, Scott's 'advice' about the new project seems to have been distinctly encouraging. In a letter to Bernard Barton of 5 July 1813, Hogg reports:

> Mr Wal^r Scott says in a letter "If I may judge from my own feelings and the interest I took in them the tales are superior at least in the management to any I have read: the stile of them is likewise quite new."[12]

This is not unqualified praise: 'at least in the management' carries a hint of a chill. Nevertheless Hogg must have been delighted by Scott's reaction, which clearly signals a positive response to his innovative attempts to re-create on paper the manner and the content of Ettrick's vigorous tradition of oral story-telling. Thus encouraged, Hogg duly offered his projected collection to the publisher Archibald Constable in a letter of 20 May 1813:

> I have for many years been collecting the rural and traditionary tales of Scotland and I have of late been writing them over again and new-modelling them, and have the vanity to suppose they will form a most interesting work. They will fill two large vols 8vo price £1 or 4 vols 12mo price the same.[13]

This offer was declined, in spite of Hogg's recent popular success with *The Queen's Wake*: as Ian Duncan remarks, 'Fiction was not in Constable's line—until the following year, when he consented to publish a novel called *Waverley*'.[14] As a result of Constable's refusal the rural and traditionary tales seem to have gone on the back burner for a time, and during the next couple of years Hogg's projects included his play *The Hunting of Badlewe* and his long poems *Mador of the Moor* and *Pilgrims of the Sun*.

In December 1814, about a year and a half after failing to place his rural and traditionary tales with Constable, Hogg had business dealings for the first time with the rising Edinburgh publisher William Blackwood—and in due course this gave him the opportunity to offer his rural tales to Blackwood. In his edition of Hogg's *Winter Evening Tales*, Ian Duncan has summarised what seems to have happened next:

> In his 'Memoir' Hogg says he showed Blackwood the manuscript of 'two tales I wished to publish', 'The Bridal of Polmood' and 'The Brownie of Bodsbeck'. Blackwood accepted 'The Brownie' but 'would have nothing to do' with 'The Bridal of Polmood'. Hogg replaced it with 'The Wool-gatherer', revised from *The Spy* (where it had appeared as 'The Country Laird', February 1811), and a new tale, 'The Hunt of Eildon', to make up a two-volume set.[15] If the set sold well, another two volumes would follow. In December [1817] Hogg wrote to Mrs Izet: 'My Cottage tales in prose will be published in the spring two or four volumes as my friends shall advise after they have seen the first two[.]'[16] In the New Year he sent Blackwood the text of an advertisement:
>
> > In the press and speedily will be published Vol's 1 and 2 of Mr Hogg's *Cottage Tales* containing *The Brownie of Bodsbeck* and *The Wool-Gatherer*. These tales have been selected by him among the Shepherds and peasantry of Scotland and are arranged so as to delineate the manners and superstitions of that class in ancient and modern times &c &c.[17]

In May 1818 Blackwood duly published *The Brownie of Bodsbeck and Other Tales* as a two-volume set, and *Winter Evening Tales* (published in two well-filled volumes by Oliver & Boyd in 1820) finally carried Hogg's sequence of 'rural and traditionary tales' to its projected length of four volumes.

In the draft advertising material just quoted, Hogg stresses that his '*Cottage Tales*' belong to his native community: they have been '*selected* by him *among* the Shepherds and peasantry of Scotland' (emphasis added). In short, these rural and traditional tales set out to extend Burns's work on traditional song into another genre, and they form part of Hogg's long-term and sustained attempt to tell stories that will allow the voice of subaltern Scotland to be heard. In particular, subaltern Ettrick has a story to tell— and Hogg is going to try to tell it.

But how is narrative authority to be given to the voice of subaltern Ettrick? As we shall see, Hogg tackles this problem with some ingenuity in the frame narrative provided in the opening chapter of *The Bridal of Polmood*. It is therefore not particularly surprising that, when consulted in April 1813 about *The Bridal of Polmood* and Hogg's other rural and traditionary tales, Scott seems to have been especially impressed by their 'management' and by their innovative 'stile'.

It will be remembered that Hogg's draft advertising material (quoted above) indicates that his tales will deal with 'ancient and modern times'. *The Bridal of Polmood* is set during the reign of James IV in pre-Reformation Scotland, and it may be that, in Hogg's original conception of his collection of rural and traditionary tales, this 'ancient' story would have been placed at the beginning of the series. If so, the frame narrative of the *Bridal* would have served to introduce not merely that particular story, but also the collection as a whole. The frame narrative begins:

> Last autumn, on my return from the Lakes of Cumberland to Edinburgh, I fell in with an old gentleman at the village of Moffat, whose manners and conversation deeply interested me. He was cheerful, unaffected, and loquacious, to a degree which I have not often witnessed; but his loquacity was divested of egotism—his good humour communicated itself to all present, and his narratives were fraught with traditionary knowledge, the information to which, of all others, my heart is most fondly attached.[18]

Following this meeting the loquacious old gentleman joins the 'I' of the frame narrative on a journey to Edinburgh:

> We breakfasted at a good inn by the side of the river, and, on proceeding a little farther, I observed on the opposite bank, an old decayed house standing in a small wood of stately trees, and asked my intelligent companion how it was named? (p. 260)

The house turns out to be Polmood, and this is the cue for 'my intelligent companion' to tell one of his narratives 'fraught with traditionary knowledge'. We read: 'As soon as I reached Edinburgh I wrote it down; and waiting upon the narrator, who is now one of my most intimate friends, I read it over to him, correcting and enlarging it, according to his directions' (p. 261).

In *The Bridal of Polmood*, then, the 'I' of the frame narrative and his 'intelligent companion' join forces to produce a narrative voice that can speak from within the traditional oral culture of Lowland Scotland, without being contained or restricted by that culture. Significantly in this context, it was Hogg's original intention to publish his rural and traditionary tales under a pseudonym. In the letter of 20 May 1813 in which he offered the collection to Constable, Hogg writes:

> But as I think the Ettrick Shepherd is rather become a hackneyed name, and imagine that having gained a character as a bard is perhaps no commendation to a writer of prose tales I am determined to publish them under a fictitious title The title page will consequently be to this purpose. *The Rural and Traditionary Tales of Scotland* by J. H. Craig of Douglas Esq.[19]

It may be, however, that Hogg's real reason for proposing to use a pseudonym had to do with the question of narrative authority. The second edition of *The Queen's Wake* was published in June 1813, and in it George Goldie added an Advertisement to the effect that this remarkable poem was *'really and truly the production of* JAMES HOGG, *a common shepherd'*: some readers of the first edition (January 1813) had apparently been refusing to believe that it was possible for a common shepherd to be capable of such an achievement. Reactions of this kind must have made Hogg acutely aware of the difficulty of investing the voice of subaltern Ettrick with full narrative authority, and presumably he hoped to circumvent this problem by making the narrator of his rural and traditionary tales a combination of an 'old gentleman' full of 'traditionary knowledge', and 'J. H. Craig of Douglas Esq'. That 'Esq' is an unmistakable indication that J. H. Craig is (like his informant) a gentleman, not a mere farm labourer. Perhaps Hogg hoped that the knee-jerk reaction of his readers to the voice of 'a common shepherd' could be avoided if the narrative voice for his rural and traditionary tales were to be that of a gentleman with full access to the people's rich stores of 'traditionary knowledge'.

That is not the whole story, however. It is worth noting that 'Craig of Douglas' is the name of a farm situated at the confluence of the Douglas Burn and Yarrow Water. Hogg had worked as a shepherd in the immediate vicinity of Craig of Douglas while employed at Blackhouse farm in the 1790s, and in the early 1810s his elderly parents were living in a cottage there. Furthermore, the confluence of the Douglas Burn and Yarrow Water (both famous in traditional ballads) is clearly a site redolent of the riches of the traditional oral culture of Ettrick Forrest. Elaine Petrie has suggested, intriguingly and convincingly, that Hogg's proposed pseudonym can be decoded as J[ames] H[ogg] [writing from] Craig of Douglas.[20] Hogg is thus able to give a coded signal confirming that the compound narrative voice of his rural and traditionary tales is firmly anchored within the traditional oral culture of the subaltern people of Ettrick Forest. Furthermore, having collected stories 'fraught with traditionary knowledge', 'J. H. Craig of Douglas Esq' writes them down on reaching Edinburgh, then corrects and enlarges the resulting text 'according to the directions' of his traditional informant. As a result of this process, the compound narrative voice established in the frame narrative allows Hogg's rural and traditionary tales to speak from and for the traditional oral culture of subaltern Lowland Scotland with all the authority of a native insider (such as James Hogg, an Ettrick shepherd), while also allowing them to speak with all the authority of a man of the sophisticated literary world of post-Enlightenment Edinburgh (such as James Hogg, the Edinburgh-based professional writer). The ingenuity of this device may lie behind Scott's reported response in April 1813 (already quoted) to Hogg's as-yet-unpublished rural collection: 'If I may judge from my own feelings and the interest I took in them the tales are superior at least in the management to any I have read: the stile of them is likewise quite new'.

The Bridal of Polmood is a picture of life in Ettrick Forest when the district was still one of the hunting-grounds of the Scottish royal family. The story is set in the time of James IV, who reigned from 1488 till 1513, and it gives a subaltern's-eye-view of the inadequacies of the Scottish royal court during the period leading up to the catastrophic Scottish defeat at the battle of Flodden in 1513, a battle at which James (having invaded England) was out-generalled and killed. Flodden had particularly disastrous consequences for Ettrick. The men of the royal Forest fought in the immediate vicinity of their king, and most of them died as they attempted to defend him. Even now, many centuries later, Flodden can still evoke powerful emotions among the people of Ettrick Forest, as anyone who has had the privilege of being present at the annual Selkirk Common Riding can testify. It is natural, then, that *The Bridal of Polmood* should be one of the cornerstones of the collection of rural and traditionary tales through which Hogg hoped to give voice to the story of his own native subaltern community. *The Brownie of Bodsbeck* was another such story.

The Brownie of Bodsbeck

> The Solemn League and Covenant
>   Now brings a smile, now brings a tear.
> But sacred Freedom, too, was theirs;
>   If thou 'rt a slave, indulge thy sneer.
>   (Robert Burns, 'The Solemn League and Covenant')

Alongside Flodden, the other major disaster lodged in the folk memory of Hogg's Ettrick was the 'Killing Times' of the late seventeenth century, the period of ferocious royalist persecution of those much-revered subaltern heroes, the Covenanters. Hogg's novel *The Brownie of Bodsbeck* is set during the Killing Times, and, as Ian Duncan points out, it is clear that 'Hogg had always thought of *The Brownie* as belonging to the series that he variously called "Rural and Traditionary Tales", "Cottage Winter Nights" and "Winter Evening Tales".'[21] Indeed, *The Brownie of Bodsbeck* and *The Bridal of Polmood* can be regarded as matched cornerstones of Hogg's projected four-volume 'rural and traditionary' collection. Each runs to the length of a short novel; each puts a particular focus on the area around Megget-dale and Loch Skeen; each involves a severe implied criticism of the King of Scots reigning at the time of the story's events; and each connects with a particularly traumatic period of the history of Ettrick Forest.

The narrative voice of *The Brownie*, like that of *The Bridal*, is located both inside and outside the traditional oral culture of the Ettrick community. In *The Brownie*, however, Hogg pushes on even further with his attempts to find ways to allow the voice of the subaltern oral tradition to achieve narrative authority in a modern print publication. *The Brownie* has a third-person narrator who clearly has access to Ettrick traditions and insights, but who is nevertheless able to maintain a certain objectivity and distance from them: it may be useful to think of him as manifestation not only of 'J. H. Craig of Douglas Esq.', but also of James Hogg.

However, in *The Brownie* this third-person narrator does not remain in sole control of the narrative. Instead, this text finds ways to allow a good deal of its story to be told directly through the voices of its Ettrick characters. Appropriately, the first words of the novel form part of a fireside conversation in an Ettrick farmhouse:

> "It will be a bloody night in Gemsop this," said Walter of Chapelhope, as he sat one evening by the side of his little parlour fire, and wrung the rim of his wet bonnet into the grate. His wife sat by his side, airing a pair of clean hosen for her husband, to replace his wet ones.[22]

The opening chapter is devoted to a conversation between Walter and his wife Maron, with minimal comment by the narrator. Then, after a brief second chapter in which the narrator unobtrusively provides some explanatory background information, the third chapter begins as follows:

> Things were precisely in this state, when the goodman of Chapelhope, taking his plaid and staff, went out to the heights one misty day in autumn to drive off a neighbour's flock from his pasture; but, as Walter was wont to relate the story himself, when any stranger came there on a winter evening, as long as he lived, it may haply be acceptable to the curious, and the lovers of rustic simplicity, to read it in his own words, although he drew it out to an inordinate length, and perhaps kept his own personal feelings and prowess too much in view for the fastidious or critical reader to approve.
>
> "It was on a mirk misty day in September," said Walter, "I mind it weel, that I took my plaid about me, and a bit gay steeve aik stick in my hand, and away I sets to turn aff the Winterhopeburn sheep. [...]   (p. 18)

Here the third-person narrator gives way to an oral, Ettrick voice telling a fireside tale of the kind traditionally told in rural cottages in the long dark winter evenings when farm work was impossible. From time to time throughout this novel various Ettrick voices likewise take command of the story-telling—and this innovation in narrative technique greatly assists Hogg's 'rural and traditionary tales' to achieve their objective of gaining a hearing for subaltern Ettrick's story. In *The Modern Scottish Novel*, Cairns Craig points to Lewis Grassic Gibbon's *A Scots Quair* and Irvine Welsh's *Trainspotting* as twentieth-century novels that centre on 'a community's self-narration in dialect'.[23] Arguably, these novels follow a trail that had been blazed by Hogg in *The Brownie of Bodsbeck*.

Walter Laidlaw's winter evening tale in Chapter 3 of *The Brownie of Bodsbeck* turns out to be a compelling *tour-de-force* of oral narration in the indigenous language of the country. It will be remembered that Colonel Talbot, in *Waverley*, dismisses Gaelic as 'gibberish' and adds that 'even the Lowlanders talk a kind of English little better than the negroes in Jamaica'. However, here and elsewhere in Hogg's novel, Walter's narrative voice does not live down to linguistic prejudices of this kind: his fireside tales prove to be concise, articulate, and graphic. Ettrick voices are heard in another way when royalist forces arrive at Walter's farm of Chapelhope under the command of John Graham of Claverhouse, the murderous, aristocratic demon-figure 'Clavers' of the folk-memory of Hogg's people about the Killing Times. The Ettrick community has been set on edge by the royalist regime's imposition of an Episcopalian curate, and Clavers suspects that fugitive rebel Covenanters are being given shelter on the moorland hills of Chapelhope, in defiance of the government. These suspicions are well-founded: Walter and his daughter Kate (although themselves royalists) are secretly providing food to separate bands of starving Covenanters.

Having arrived at Chapelhope, Clavers examines John of the Muchrah, one of Walter's shepherds, in an attempt to gain information. Most of Chapter 7 of the novel is devoted to this examination, in which the aristocratic Clavers cuts a less than impressive figure. The exchange between the two men is given without the interruption of either comment or speech attribution, and it continues over several pages. In this interrogation, as is often the case in Hogg's writings, a Scots-speaking subaltern voice engages in a contest with an English-speaking elite voice.

> "How did it appear to you that they had been slain? were they cut with swords, or pierced with bullets?"
> "I canna say, but they were sair hashed."
> "How do you mean when you say they were hashed?"
> "Champit like—a' broozled and jermummled, as it war."
> "Do you mean that they were cut, or cloven, or minced?"
> "Na, na—no that ava—But they had gotten some sair doofs—They had been terribly paikit and daddit wi' something."
> "I do not in the least conceive what you mean."   (p. 61)

In his discussion of *A Scots Quair* and *Trainspotting* in *The Modern Scottish Novel*, Cairns Craig comments:

> Novels committed to the use of dialect necessarily involve themselves not only in dialogue—the speech of the demotic—and in the dialogic—in Bakhtin's sense of multiple voices within a text—but also in dialectic, because the existence of two or more distinct linguistic contexts within the text presumes the existence of alternative value systems which those linguistic contexts express, and therefore of a dialectical process of debate and argument between those values.[24]

In *The Brownie of Bodsbeck* there is debate and argument between the subaltern values of the Ettrick people and the values represented by the more aristocratic figure of

Claverhouse. This is more complex than a simple debate between Covenanters and royalists, however. Indeed, like the other Chapelhope people, John of the Muchrah is not a Covenanter but is loyal to the royalist cause. He answers honestly during his interrogation, and what he says tends to indicate that Walter, in his family worship, uses the Prayer Book approved by the royalist regime rather than the extempore prayer employed by the Covenanters.[25] In spite of all this John's evidence is wilfully misinterpreted by his inquisitors, and at the end of the interrogation Clavers issues orders which are promptly obeyed 'without any mitigation':

> "Take the old ignorant animal away—Burn him on the cheek, cut off his ears, and do not part with him till he pay you down a fine of two hundred merks, or value to that amount. [...]" (p. 66)

This is a truly appalling outcome, in no way justified by what John has said during his examination. Clearly, *The Brownie of Bodsbeck* is driven by the folk-tradition's anger about the atrocities perpetrated by royalists during the Killing Times. In spite of its strong pro-subaltern sympathies, however, Hogg's novel does not present an uncomplicated pattern of binary oppositions in which the Covenanters behave well in all circumstances, while aristocratic royalists are all alike perpetrators of vile atrocities. The narrator writes as follows about Hay of Drumelzier, Walter Laidlaw's royalist landlord:

> Drumelzier was a bold and determined loyalist—was, indeed, in high trust with the Privy-council, and had it in his power to have harassed the country as much, and more, than the greater part of those who did so; but, fortunately for that south-east division of Scotland, he was a gentleman of high honour, benevolence, and suavity of manners, and detested any act of injustice or oppression. He by these means contributed materially to the keeping of a large division of Scotland (though as whiggishly inclined as any part of it, Ayrshire perhaps excepted) in perfect peace. (pp. 101–02)

Drumelzier's royalist politics are very similar to those of Claverhouse; but Drumelzier, unlike Claverhouse, 'detested any act of injustice or oppression'. Indeed, in *The Brownie of Bodsbeck* Hogg once again seems to be writing in accordance with the 'message' which, as we saw in Chapter 3, George Orwell finds in Dickens: 'If men would behave decently the world would be decent'. Hogg's novel can be read as an attack on *all* acts of injustice or oppression, and *The Brownie of Bodsbeck* is willing to recognise that such acts were committed by downtrodden Covenanters as well as by aristocratic royalists. For example, some of the novel's more extreme Covenanters are responsible for the deplorable murder of a priest (p. 25).

The Brownie of Bodsbeck celebrates the values of practical compassion exhibited by members of the Ettrick community as they help the persecuted Covenanters, the values of 'the late worthy Mr Brydon, of Crosslee'—and it focuses on a debate between those values and the more fanatical, cause-driven values of the Covenanters and their royalist persecutors. In doing so, Hogg's novel draws on oral tradition in order to give voice, in a modern print publication, to the experiences of the Ettrick community during a particularly trying period of that community's history. In *Things Fall Apart*, Achebe gives the Igbo side of the story with regard to the arrival of Empire in Africa. In *The Brownie of Bodsbeck* Hogg likewise gives subaltern Ettrick's side of the story with regard to the Killing Times.

How, then, does subaltern Ettrick emerge from Hogg's novel? In *Things Fall Apart* Achebe is prepared to recognise flaws in the pre-Imperial Igbo society that he values. Likewise, Hogg values subaltern Ettrick but is nevertheless willing to see its flaws and limitations. For example, in *The Brownie* the traditional culture of Ettrick does not emerge at all well from its treatment of Walter Laidlaw's daughter Kate. In the early chapters of the novel the Ettrick community blames Kate for being in league with the Brownie of Bodsbeck, a supernatural being thought to haunt Chapelhope. It eventually turns out, however, that she has actually been secretly helping a group of extreme Covenanters led by John Brown of Caldwell, who had been disfigured a few years earlier by wounds received at Bothwell Bridge in battle with the royalists during the rising of the Covenanters in 1679. In short, the Ettrick community's rejection of Kate for much of the novel is based on ignorance, superstitious credulity, and prejudice. In *The Brownie of Bodsbeck* the Ettrick community is capable of acts of heroic generosity in assisting the fugitive Covenanters, but it is also capable of absurdity, small-mindedness, and lack of perception.

In his own Ettrick youth Hogg had encountered problems not unlike Kate's. He had been a member of a 'literary society' of radical young shepherds during the post-French-Revolution political unrest of the early 1790s, and it so happened that one of the society's meetings (at Entertrony, far up the Ettrick valley) took place on the night of a violent and destructive snow-storm. It seems to have been assumed by older members of the Ettrick community that the 'literary society', like many other working-class societies of the early 1790s, had a deep interest in radical politics. At all events the Ettrick community (including Hogg's much-loved mother) jumped to the conclusion that dark supernatural forces had been at work at the meeting, and that the impious and radical young shepherds had provoked God's judgement in the form of the storm. Hogg tells the story in *The Shepherd's Calendar*, in an essay entitled 'Storms':

The storm was altogether an unusual convulsion of nature. Nothing like it had ever been seen, or heard of in Britain before; and it was enough of itself to arouse every spark of superstition that lingered among these mountains—It did so—It was universally viewed as a judgement sent by God for the punishment of some heineous offence, but what that offence was, could not for a while be ascertained: but when it came out, that so many men had been assembled, in a lone unfrequented place, and busily engaged in some mysterious work at the very instant that the blast came on, no doubts were entertained that all had not been right there, and that some horrible rite, or correspondence with the powers of darkness had been going on. It so happened too, that this sheiling of Entertrony was situated in the very vortex of the storm; the devastations made by it extended all around that, to a certain extent; and no farther in any one quarter than another. This was easily and soon remarked, and upon the whole the first view of the matter had rather an equivocal appearance to those around who had suffered so severely by it. But still as the rumour grew the certainty of the event gained ground—new corroborative circumstances were every day divulged, till the whole district was in an uproar, and several of the members began to meditate a speedy retreat from the country; some of them I know would have fled, if it had not been for the advice of the late worthy and judicious Mr Bryden of Crosslee.[26]

The late worthy and judicious Mr Bryden of Crosslee is of course the same man who had saved the young James Hogg's family from destitution: a man whose practical compassion on that occasion is paralleled by the behaviour of Walter and Kate Laidlaw in *The Brownie of Bodsbeck*. In Hogg's novel, as in his personal reminiscences in 'Storms', there are things in Ettrick from which it would no doubt be good to escape to the intellectual excitements of the rational and Enlightened world of the Edinburgh of the North British elite. Nevertheless, in the resonant decency of Walter and Kate, and in the resonant decency of the late worthy and judicious Mr Bryden of Crosslee, subaltern Ettrick at its best embodies Hogg's core values. In *The Brownie of Bodsbeck* Hogg does indeed manage (in a clear-eyed, unsentimental way) to give subaltern Ettrick's side of the story with regard to the Killing Times—just as Achebe in *Things Fall Apart* contrives (in a clear-eyed, unsentimental way) to give the Igbo side of the story with regard to the sequence of events that the Empire chose to regard as 'the pacification of the primitive tribes of the Lower Niger'. In short, both Hogg and Achebe succeed powerfully in their own modern versions of the traditional bardic role, as they draw on oral tradition in order to give voice to the experiences of their native communities during particularly traumatic periods. However, the Imperial elites of North and South Britain did not turn out to be wildly enthused by *The Brownie of Bodsbeck* when Hogg's novel was eventually published in March 1818.

The Empire Strikes Back

In his *Familiar Anecdotes of Sir Walter Scott*, Hogg gives an account of a highly-charged conversation that he had with Scott on the day after the publication of *The Brownie of Bodsbeck*:

His shaggy eyebrows were hanging very sore down, a bad prelude, which I knew too well.

"I have read through your new work Mr Hogg" said he "and must tell you downright and plainly as I always do that I like it very ill—very ill indeed."

"What for Mr Scott?"

"Because it is a false and unfair picture of the times and the existing characters altogether An exhaggerated and unfair picture!"

"I dinna ken Mr Scott. It is the picture I hae been bred up in the belief o' sin' ever I was born and I had it frae them whom I was most bound to honour and believe. An' mair nor that there is not one single incident in the tale—not one—which I cannot prove from history to be literally and positively true. I was obliged sometimes to change the situations to make one part coalesce with another but in no one instance have I related a story of a cruelty or a murder which is not literally true. An' that's a great deal mair than you can say for your tale o' Auld Mortality."

"You are over shooting the mark now Mr Hogg. I wish it were my tale. But it is *not* with regard to that, that I find fault with your tale at all but merely because it is an unfair and partial picture of the age in which it is laid."

"Na I shouldna hae said it was *your* tale for ye hae said to your best friends that it was not an' there I was wrang. Ye may hinder a man to speak but ye canna hinder him to think an' I can yerk at the thinking. But whoever wrote Auld Mortality kenning what I ken an' what ye ken I wadna wonder at you being ill-pleased with my tale if ye thought it written as a counter-poise to that but ye ken weel it was written lang afore the other was heard of."

"Yes I know that a part of it was in M.S. last year but I suspect it has been greatly exhaggerated since."

"As I am an honest man Sir there has not been a line altered or added that I remember of. The original copy was printed. Mr Blackwood was the only man beside yourself who saw it. He read it painfully which I now know you did not and I appeal to him."

"Well well. As to its running counter to Old Mortality I have nothing to say. Nothing in the world: I only tell you that with the exception of Old Nanny the crop-eared Covenanter who is by far the best character you ever drew in your life I dislike the tale exceedingly and assure you it is a distorted a prejudiced and untrue picture of the Royal party."

"It is a devilish deal truer than your's though; and on that ground I make my appeal to my country." And with that I rose and was going off in a great huff.

"No no! stop" cried he "You are not to go and leave me again in bad humour. You ought not to be offended at me for telling you my mind freely."

"Why to be sure it is the greatest folly in the world for me to be sae. But ane's beuks are like his bairns he disna like to hear them spoken ill o' especially when he is concious that they dinna deserve it."

Sir Walter then after his customary short good humoured laugh repeated a proverb about the Gordons which was exceedingly *apropos* to my feelings at the time but all that I can do I cannot remember it though I generally remembered every [word] that he said of any import.[27]

Hogg here makes the claim that, although *The Brownie of Bodsbeck* was not published until 1818, a substantial part of it 'was written lang afore' the publication in December 1816 of *Old Mortality*, Scott's famous novel of the Covenanters. This has been disputed, but the relevant evidence does seem to support the main thrust of Hogg's claim.[28] However, it would appear that the surprising vehemence of Scott's response to *The Brownie* does not derive from a dispute about the date of writing of Hogg's novel. Instead, Scott's deeply hostile reaction seems to have its roots in perceived connections between the legacy of the Covenanters and political tensions current during the later 1810s. What, then, was the nature of these perceived connections?

In considering this question it will be useful to return to Burns's political radicalism, which, as we have seen, was deeply rooted in the Presbyterian political tradition of subaltern Lowland Scotland. For Burns's radical contemporaries in late eighteenth-century France, the church was firmly associated with elite power. Consequently, the Jacobins were secular and anti-clerical. However, in late eighteenth-century Scotland those who sympathised with the Jacobins were apt to hero-worship the Covenanters, and tended to see defence of the religion of the people as a defiant radical virtue. Such attitudes continued to prevail in the Scotland of the late 1810s

Like Burns, Hogg was profoundly influenced by the Presbyterian tradition in which they both grew up, and *The Brownie of Bodsbeck* reflects the egalitarian assumptions of that tradition as it attempts to tell the story of the experiences of the people of Ettrick during the Killing Times. Clearly, Scott regarded the powerfully-expressed subaltern's-eye-view of *The Brownie* as dangerously subversive in the fraught political atmosphere of 1818. Describing the political situation in the second half of the 1810s, T. M. Devine records that 'insurrectionary cells bent on achieving the overthrow of government by physical force' developed on a significant scale in the western Lowlands at that time. Related discontent in England formed the background to the notorious Peterloo Massacre of August 1819, and the so-called 'Radical War' followed in Scotland in 1820. The Radical War was a potentially formidable affair, and for a time the government had reason to feel seriously threatened. Devine comments:

The middle classes, terrified by fear of revolution and the danger to property, closed ranks behind the government and, as they had done in the 1790s, filled the ranks of the yeomanry and volunteer regiments established to police potentially seditious communities.[29]

The early 1790s had seen fears (or hopes, depending on one's view of the matter) that Republican France would manage to export the principles of the French Revolution to the rest of Europe, including Britain—and in the later 1810s there were hopes (for some) or fears (for others) that Revolution was once again a distinct possibility within the home base of Imperial Britain. In this highly-charged political atmosphere the well-remembered subaltern armed rebellions of the Covenanters had an obvious relevance to current debates. In December 1816 Scott had given his own deeply-felt and elite-based perspective on these matters in his 'tale o' Auld Mortality'—and after its publication his novel had been vigorously criticised by supporters of the Covenanters, the most notable of whom was Dr Thomas McCrie, a distinguished Presbyterian clergyman and the biographer of John Knox.[30]

Various points were at issue in the debate over *Old Mortality*, but the most important questions were starkly straightforward and immediate. Had the Covenanters (like our modern Radicals) been heroic defenders of the liberties of the people, in the face of brutal aristocratic and royal oppression? Or had the Covenanters been dangerous fanatics, akin to the deplorable Radicals who were now seeking to undermine the sacred rights of property and the very fabric of society? And—crucially—who was going to shape the general understanding of Scotland's past and of Scotland's present by telling the definitive story about the Covenanters?

The Tale of Old Mortality

> To the Lords of Convention 'twas Claver'se who spoke,
> "Ere the King's crown shall fall there are crowns to be broke;
> So let each Cavalier who loves honour and me,
> Come follow the bonnet of Bonny Dundee."
>
> (Scott, from *The Doom of Devorgoil*)

Waverley, Scott's first novel, was published anonymously in 1814 as the long years of the Napoleonic Wars approached their end. The book achieved an immediate and lasting popular success, and in the process did much to ensure that the novel would become the dominant literary genre in post-war Britain, replacing the wartime genre of the verse romance. After *Waverley* appeared there was much excited speculation about the identity of 'the Great Unknown', the mysterious new novelist who had become the latest literary sensation, putting old favourites like the poet Walter Scott into the shade. Two other novels by 'the Author of Waverley' quickly appeared: *Guy Mannering* (1815) and *The Antiquary* (1816). These new publications repeated the success of their predecessor. Revelling in the widespread speculation about the identity of 'the Great Unknown', Scott decided to make an unexpected move. *The Antiquary* was not to be followed by a fourth novel by 'the Author of *Waverley*'. Instead, a new rival for the Unknown would be invented—and by becoming his own rival, Scott would be able to strike out into a new path, into a new kind of fiction. The newly-invented rival to the

Author of *Waverley* would produce narratives constructed from the raw materials provided by oral tales told by a variety of speakers in a fictional country inn.

This audacious and spirited plan bore its first fruits in *Tales of my Landlord*. When he began work on this project in the autumn of 1816, Scott proposed to write four separate tales, each occupying one volume. Each tale was to be devoted to a different province of Scotland: the Borders, the Highlands, the western Lowlands, and Fife.[31] The four corners of the country would thus be portrayed in a series of tales that would combine to form a complex portrait of the life and manners of Scotland. These tales were to be presented as having been told by various travellers, the customers of 'my landlord' at the Wallace Inn in the village of Gandercleuch (that is to say, 'Goose Hollow': here as elsewhere, Scott offers his fictions with a tone of detached irony).

Appropriately, the Wallace Inn of *Tales of my Landlord* is named after Scotland's national hero, Sir William Wallace (1272?–1305); and, equally appropriately, it is situated at a crossroads at the very heart of the country, at a place where, as it were, all the paths of Scotland converge. The new rival to 'the Author of *Waverley*' is Peter Pattieson, the young assistant schoolmaster of Gandercleuch, who is struggling with an illness that will bring him to an early grave. Pattieson's role is to listen to the travellers at the Wallace Inn (one such traveller being 'Old Mortality', an elderly man who has devoted his latter years to travelling round Scotland cleaning and repairing the gravestones of his heroes the Covenanters). Having heard various oral tales at the inn, Pattieson recasts them into a series of written narratives. Publication of these *Tales of my Landlord* turns out to be posthumous, however. After his early and expected death, Pattieson's narratives are prepared for the press from his surviving papers by his patron Jedidiah Cleishbotham (that is to say, 'Solomon Smackbottom'),[32] the local schoolmaster and Session Clerk.

It will be remembered that, in a letter to Bernard Barton of 5 July 1813, Hogg reports that Scott, when consulted in April 1813 about his as yet unpublished rural and traditional tales, had commented: 'If I may judge from my own feelings and the interest I took in them the tales are superior at least in the management to any I have read: the stile of them is likewise quite new'. In adopting an orally-based narrative strategy for *Tales of my Landlord* in the autumn of 1816, Scott was perhaps setting out to explore the possibilities that had been opened out by Hogg's recent innovations in narrative technique. As we have seen, in his rural and traditional tales Hogg had tried to give narrative authority to the tales of oral tradition by devising a compound narrative voice, derived from a loquacious old gentleman with large stores of 'traditionary knowledge' who tells a story at an inn to J. H. Craig of Douglas Esq. Likewise, Scott's combined Pattieson / Cleishbotham narrative voice is used as a vehicle for conveying the riches of oral material, as encountered in the stories told by travellers at an inn.

To suggest that the frame narrative of *Tales of my Landlord* owes a possible debt to Hogg is not to imply that Scott was guilty of something in some way underhand. In his biography *The Life of Walter Scott*, John Sutherland has asserted that, in *The Lay of the Last Minstrel* (1805), Scott had been guilty of 'plagiarism' in making use of the metrical innovations of Coleridge's as yet unpublished 'Christabel'.[33] Here, as is frequently the case in *The Life of Walter Scott*, Sutherland contrives to steer well clear of any danger of erring on the side of generosity in his assessment of Scott's motives and conduct. An author who becomes aware of a breakthrough in literary technique is fully entitled to experiment with that breakthrough for his or her own purposes.

If Scott did indeed draw on the 'management' of Hogg's rural and traditionary tales in *Tales of my Landlord*, he nevertheless adapted Hogg's narrative strategy to his own purposes. If Hogg had been re-telling the oral tale of Old Mortality, his objective would have been to allow that particular subaltern voice to be heard. In *Tales of my Landlord*, however, Scott is careful to give his own take on the oral tales of his subaltern story-tellers by filtering their utterances through the sensibility of the university-educated and Enlightenment-influenced Peter Pattieson, a man who shares his own attitudes and assumptions. Crucially, Pattieson sets out to evaluate the stories he hears at the inn against his own objective assessment of the evidence. In the preliminary frame narrative that introduces *The Tale of Old Mortality* Pattieson writes:

> My readers will of course understand, that, in embodying into one compressed narrative many of the anecdotes which I had the advantage of deriving from Old Mortality, I have been far from adopting either his style, his opinions, or even his facts, so far as they appear to have been distorted by party prejudice. I have endeavoured to correct or verify them from the most authentic sources of tradition, afforded by the representatives of either party.[34]

This stands in marked contrast to the way in which, as we have seen, Hogg's third-person narrator introduces the first of Walter Laidlaw's winter evening tales in *The Brownie of Bodsbeck*:

> as Walter was wont to relate the story himself, when any stranger came there on a winter evening, as long as he lived, it may haply be acceptable to the curious, and the lovers of rustic simplicity, to read it in his own words, although he drew it out to an inordinate length, and perhaps kept his own personal feelings and prowess too much in view for the fastidious or critical reader to approve. (p. 18)

Indeed, Hogg's narrator goes further when introducing another of Walter's winter evening tales later in the novel: 'such scenes, and such adventures are not worth a farthing, unless described and related in the language of the country to which they are peculiar' (p. 146).

Scott's original plan for a tale from each of the four corners of Scotland was somewhat modified in *Tales of my Landlord* as published. The framing narrative of Pattieson and Cleishbotham remains intact; and, as planned, the first volume of the 1816 *Tales* is devoted to the projected tale of the Borders. This tale, *The Black Dwarf*, is followed by *Old Mortality*, the tale of the west. According to the original plan, *Old Mortality* ought, like *The Black Dwarf*, to have been confined to a single volume. As it took shape, however, this particular story so powerfully caught hold of Scott's imagination that it expanded to fill the remaining three volumes of the first series of *Tales of my Landlord*. It is not difficult to find a reason for the expansion of *Old Mortality*. Scott was strongly committed to the political status quo that had been established by the 'Glorious Revolution' and the Union, and this novel connects powerfully with his deeply-felt fears about the potential threat posed to that status quo by the possibility of popular revolution. Such fears came naturally to people of Scott's class and generation, who as young adults had watched the French Revolution of 1789 and its aftermath with a fascinated, appalled interest and concern.

Most of the events of *The Tale of Old Mortality* (as the novel is called in Scott's manuscript) take place in the space of a few weeks in 1679 during a popular insurrection by the Covenanters of the west of Scotland against the regime of Charles II. The novel then concludes with an account of events that take place in 1689, in the aftermath of the deposition of James VII and the 'Glorious Revolution'. The action of *The Tale of Old Mortality* is focused on the area around Hamilton and Bothwell in the western Lowlands, that is to say in an area near the confluence of the rivers Avon (or Evan) and Clyde. This part of the west of Scotland was the home base of the Dukes of Hamilton, and the Duke of Scott's novel proves to be singularly ineffectual in keeping rebellion in check in his own territory. This incompetent Duke provides one of many links between *The Tale of Old Mortality* and the political concerns of Scott's own day.

In 1819, some three years after the publication of *The Tale of Old Mortality*, Scott wrote *The Visionary*. This political squib appeared in the *Edinburgh Weekly Journal* under the pseudonym 'Somnambulus', and it was quickly reprinted as a pamphlet. It contains an attack on the tenth Duke of Hamilton, a man whom Scott had known for many years, and who had recently enraged Scott and other Tories in the aftermath of the Peterloo massacre by publicly donating £50 'in aid of those who have suffered in Manchester'.[35] Somnambulus has a dream in the Duke's park: 'The rocks, the sky, the rivers of Evan and of Clyde were the same, but every vestige of beauty and plenty, once the distinctive marks of the landscape, were vanished and gone'. The dreamer learns that he is in 'the Land of Radicals' and he is confronted by a 'half naked ruffian', who carries a huge club:

> He was unshaved and uncombed; the matted locks of his hair and his beard obscuring a physiognomy, which, from the unbridled indulgence of every passion as it awaked in its turn, was rather brutal than human.[36]

This ruffian (like 'the Wild Boar of the Ardennes', discussed in Chapter 2) is an embodiment of Scott's vision of the potentially disastrous consequences of radical politics. In the 'Land of Radicals' the fabric of society has disintegrated, leaving famine and desolation to inherit the ruins. The tenth Duke of Hamilton had supported the radicals of Peterloo; and, as Peter Garside points out, *The Visionary* is clearly intended as 'a warning against erratic behaviour such as Hamilton's in high circles'. Garside further suggests that Scott regarded his own kinsman the Duke of Buccleuch as a model aristocrat, who successfully undertook the aristocrat's task of binding together and sustaining his local community. In contrast to the admirable example of Buccleuch, Garside argues, 'Scott apparently saw an obverse in the Duke of Hamilton'.[37]

Habakkuk Meiklewrath, one of the prominent Covenanters in *Old Mortality*, has much in common with the 'half naked ruffian' who presides over 'the Land of Radicals' in *The Visionary*. The rebellion of the Covenanters in *Old Mortality* begins with victory over Government forces under John Grahame of Claverhouse at Loudoun-hill; and Meiklewrath is described as follows, as he addresses the victorious Covenanters after this battle:

> The rags of a dress which had once been black, added to the tattered fragments of a shepherd's plaid, composed a covering scarce fit for the purposes of decency, much less for those of warmth or comfort. A long beard, as white as snow, hung down on his bosom, and mingled with bushy, uncombed, grizzled hair, which hung in elf-locks around his wild and staring visage. The features seemed to be extenuated by penury and famine, until they hardly retained the likeness of a human aspect. The eyes, grey, wild, and wandering, evidently betokened a bewildered imagination. He held in his hand a rusty sword, clotted with blood, as were his long lean hands, which were garnished at the extremity with nails like eagle's claws. (p. 180)

In Scott's novel the moderate Covenanter Henry Morton is 'surprised, shocked, and even startled' at the appearance of Meiklewrath, as well he might be. Nevertheless, Meiklewrath has the support of the extreme wing of the Covenanters, who believe that 'he speaketh of the spirit', and who believe that they 'fructify by his pouring forth' (p. 181). Meiklewrath duly proceeds to pour forth; and, with the approval of the extreme Covenanters, he makes the following proposal for dealing with Lady Margaret Bellenden and her family, the inhabitants of the local royalist stronghold of Tillietudlem:

> "Who talks of peace and safe-conduct? who speaks of mercy to the bloody house of the malignants? I say, take the infants and dash them against the stones; take the daughters and the mothers of the house and hurl them from the battlements of their trust, that the dogs may fatten on their blood as they did on that of Jezebel the spouse

of Ahab, and that their carcases may be dung to the face of the field even in the portion of their fathers!" (p. 181)

In 1789, the year of the French Revolution, Scott had been in his late teens. When, in his forties, he was writing *The Tale of Old Mortality*, fear of revolution at home was one of his liveliest concerns. A novel on the rebellion of the Covenanters in the west of Scotland in 1679 made it possible for Scott to confront nightmarish visions of the chaos and horror engendered by civil war and violent revolution, and in *The Tale of Old Mortality* extreme Covenanters like Meiklewrath and Balfour of Burley are radical revolutionaries capable of releasing atrocities as terrible as anything thrown up by the French Revolution. By facing up to these disturbing possibilities, *The Tale of Old Mortality* articulates some of the most troubling fears of the gentlemanly elite of Scott's generation; fears which also animate the dream of Somnambulus about the conversion of the Duke of Hamilton's prosperous and well-ordered park into the desolation and famine of 'the Land of Radicals'.

This is not to suggest that *The Tale of Old Mortality* takes a wholly negative view of the Covenanters. For example, the young preacher Macbriar endures torture with an admirable fortitude and loyalty, when on trial for rebellion after Bothwell Bridge:

> "Will you yet say," repeated the Duke of Lauderdale, "where and when you last parted from Balfour of Burley?"
>
> "You have my answer," said the sufferer resolutely, and the second blow fell. The third and fourth succeeded, but at the fifth, when a larger wedge was introduced, the prisoner set up a scream of agony. (p. 281)

In *The Tale of Old Mortality*, Macbriar is a prominent figure on the extreme wing of the Covenanters; and here, in spite of excruciating torture, he heroically refuses to betray either his principles or his friend. A few pages earlier in this complex and subtle novel, however, Macbriar had joined forces with Meiklewrath in a decision to kill the moderate Covenanter Henry Morton in cold blood. For Macbriar and Meiklewrath, Morton's tolerant moderation amounts to a betrayal of the cause of the Covenant. Macbriar says:

> His blood be on his head, the deceiver,—let him go down to Tophet with the ill-mumbled mass which he calls a prayer-book in his right hand. (pp. 264–65)

Meiklewrath then prepares for the immediate killing of Morton, so that 'the wicked may be taken away from among the people, and the Covenant established in its purity'. It is clear that Macbriar has loyalty and heroism; but in spite of this it appears that he also has something in common with the guilt of his own royalist persecutor, the Duke of Lauderdale.

Fear of the instability generated by rebellion runs powerfully through *Old Mortality*. Men of Scott's generation and class tended to see themselves as pivotal figures in the task of defending society against such dangers. On this view, each land-owning gentleman had the task of binding society together in his own district; and it fell to the King to undertake this task on a national scale, thus establishing the orderly organisation of society as a whole. Such arrangements meant that everyone knew his or her place; but people of Scott's circle feared that this satisfactory and safe state of affairs was threatened by the Radicals, with their newfangled and dangerous desire to experiment with the mob rule of democracy. Such fears are given powerful expression in *Old Mortality*.

Extreme Covenanters are not the only dangerous people in *Old Mortality*, however. In keeping with Scott's approval of the 'Glorious Revolution', there are dangerous royalists too—and one of these is John Grahame of Claverhouse. Nevertheless, the Claverhouse of Scott's novel is very different from the demonic figure of popular tradition recorded in *The Brownie of Bodsbeck*. In *Old Mortality* Claverhouse emerges as one of Scott's complex Jacobites, a man of heroic but flawed loyalty to an outdated cause.

As a loyal follower, first of Charles II and later of James VII, the Claverhouse of *The Tale of Old Mortality* exhibits both the virtues and the flaws which the novel suggests were characteristic of the rule of the Stuarts. This Claverhouse is a cultivated gentleman, elegant and civilised; but he is also despotic and arbitrary, with a frightening disregard for the rights of the King's subjects. The rule of law has little meaning for him: the King's will is what matters. At one point Henry Morton, being unjustly held captive by Claverhouse's troops, demands to be taken before a civil magistrate. Claverhouse, however, replies 'coolly' that Morton

> is one of those scrupulous gentlemen, who, like the madman in the play, will not tie his cravat without the warrant of Mr Justice Overdo; but I will let him see, before we part, that my shoulder-knot is as legal a badge of authority as the mace of the Justiciary. (p. 114)

Scott's support for the 'Glorious Revolution' rested on deeply-felt fears about the arbitrary abuse of royal power. Such fears find expression in *Old Mortality* when Milnewood, the home of Henry Morton's uncle, is invaded by a party of royal troops led by Serjeant Bothwell. In this scene Bothwell represents Charles II partly because he is a soldier in the King's army, and partly because he is a close blood relation. Bothwell, it appears, is the great-grandson of an illegitimate child of James V— and Charles II was the great-grandson of James V's legitimate daughter, Mary Queen of Scots. In spite of his royal blood, however, Bothwell does not prove to be a welcome guest at Milnewood.

> "What is your pleasure here, gentlemen?" said Milnewood, humbling himself before the satellites of power.

"We come in behalf of the king," answered Bothwell; "why the devil did you keep us so long standing at the door?" (p. 63)

The miserly old laird reluctantly tries to placate the troopers by offering a drink; and the offer is accepted with alacrity.

"Brandy, ale, and wine, sack, and claret,—we'll try them all," said Bothwell, "and stick to that which is best. There's good sense in that, if the damn'dest whig in Scotland had said it." (p. 63)

And so Bothwell and his men begin, in effect, to loot the house, taking young Henry Morton of Milnewood prisoner in the process. This outrage forces Henry into open rebellion against the government; and it thus gives concrete expression to the reasons why the arbitrary exercise of royal power will prove to be unsustainable in the long term, and will in due course precipitate the 'Glorious Revolution'. Scott's novel takes the view that political stability requires that able gentlemen like Henry Morton should support the political status quo. Such men have an essential role in binding society together. If and when they turn to rebellion, the old order's days are numbered.

In taking this line, *The Tale of Old Mortality* reflects the assumptions and concerns of property-owning gentlemen of Scott's generation. Clearly, such people would feel more secure if their continued possession of their wealth depended, not on the whims of arbitrary royal power, but on due legal process; and for this reason they would be likely to regard the limitation of royal power that had been imposed at the 'Glorious Revolution' as a benign development. After the Revolution and the Union of 1707, real power in Britain came to lie with Parliament rather than the Monarch; and the owners of property were the only people who could vote at British Parliamentary elections. So long as that situation could be maintained, neither the mob rule of democracy nor the arbitrary rule of the Monarch could seriously threaten the position of property-owning gentlemen. Both the royalist looting of Milnewood and the radical revolutionary horrors embodied in Meiklewrath give expression, in their different ways, to the deep fears of the North British elite about the dangers of departing from this satisfactory situation by returning to the bad old days before the Union and the 'Glorious Revolution'.

In *The Tale of Old Mortality*, characters like Lady Margaret Bellenden, or Mause Headrigg, or Ephraim Macbriar seem completely at home in the world of late-seventeenth-century Scotland. Unlike these characters, however, Henry Morton seems to have entered the novel's world from another period. He emerges from the page as someone who lives by the gentlemanly values of the Britain of the 1810s, the Britain of the Regency period. No doubt Henry exhibits the Covenanters' cardinal virtue, the brave defence of freedom, as he energetically opposes the differing but equally dangerous threats to freedom under the law offered by Claverhouse on the one hand and

Meiklewrath on the other. Nevertheless, Morton can be seen as Scott's novel's idealised embodiment of the virtues of the British officer class, who, a few months before the writing and publication of *Old Mortality*, had faced down the tyrant Napoleon at Waterloo. Morton, in Scott's novel, is a man who represents the future—and the future is British and Imperial. Morton acts on behalf of the forces that will move Scotland from a dark past of despotic violence into a happy, law-abiding, fertile, and domestic world; the world, that is to say, of the Britain of Scott's own Regency period. As the man who embodies this future, Morton wins a bride from the defeated side, a bride through whom something of value is rescued from the dark old dying world of the Jacobite past. Morton's bride is Edith Bellenden; and, like Rose Bradwardine in *Waverley*, Edith is a Jacobite bride who is docile, quiet, unthreatening. These meek women represent a Jacobitism tamed and made acceptable for a new world of domesticity.

The British political settlement ushered in by the 'Glorious Revolution' of 1688 and the Union of 1707 remained in place in all its essentials when Scott was writing *The Tale of Old Mortality* in the final weeks of 1816. Indeed, it remained in place until the Reform Bill of 1832 introduced major changes by extending the right to vote; and Scott, by then sinking into illness and old age, bitterly opposed these changes. It is possible to read Scott's novel of the Covenanters as an eloquent defence of the political status quo of the Scotland of his own day, a status quo to which he was deeply committed. This novel, that is to say, celebrates the 'Glorious Revolution' and the Union as the precursors of a rational, stable British settlement that secured the rights of men of property by establishing freedom, under the law, from arbitrary power.

The virtues of the new order inherited by Scott's North Britain are given expression in the concluding chapters of *The Tale of Old Mortality*. These chapters are set in 1689, and mark the decisive step by which the new order of the 'Glorious Revolution' replaced the old order of the Stuarts: they mark the opening out of 'a new æra', as the narrator of *The Tale of Old Mortality* puts it (p. 286). Significantly, many of the events of these chapters take place in the immediate vicinity of Bothwell Bridge, the place where the pressures that would help to create the new world had so memorably manifested themselves in the major battle of 1679 that forms a centrepiece of Scott's novel.

The new post-Revolution world has dawned over Bothwell Bridge, as Henry Morton, in 1689, returns from exile to seek Edith Bellenden as his bride.

> The opposite field, once the scene of slaughter and conflict, now lay as placid and quiet as the surface of a summer lake. The trees and bushes, which grew around in romantic variety of shade, were hardly seen to stir under the influence of the evening breeze. The very murmur of the river seemed to soften itself into unison with the stillness of the scene around. The path, through which the traveller descended, was occasionally shaded by detached trees of great size, and elsewhere by the hedges and boughs of flourishing orchards, now loaden with summer fruit. (p. 288)

All, it appears, is peace, plenty, and fertility in the post-Revolution world. In fact, after the Revolution Scotland was faced with a series of failed harvests and serious famine during the 'seven ill years' of the 1690s, while food shortages had been rare in the period between 1660 and 1690.[38] However, the peace and plenty depicted in Scott's novel can be taken as representing, not the literal truth about Scotland in the immediate post-Revolution reign of King William, but Scott's vision of the future prosperity that (in his view) the Revolution (and the Union which followed) would ultimately usher in as the eighteenth century advanced. This vision of post-Revolution fertility and prosperity is likewise reflected in the fate of the major characters, both male and female, who are in tune with the new world order. Marriage, happiness, and many children await them; but death is the fate of those characters who remain enmeshed in the ways of the old world. Here again, as in *Waverley*, we have a text that operates on Enlightenment-influenced assumptions about Progress. On these assumptions, the world was moving from the darkness of barbarity into the light of civilisation. In North and South Britain alike, power now lay in the hands of an Enlightened property-owning male elite, and it was felt to be right and proper that these Enlightened gentlemen should keep a firm hold of the reins of power. This would allow them to maintain stability and order, and to advance the cause of Enlightenment and civilisation, by holding the line against the dangerous forces represented on the one hand by the old-fashioned monarchical tyranny of the Stuarts, and on the other by the unbridled anarchy of the mob rule of democracy. It was the duty of the Enlightened elite to secure the pacification of the lower orders at home, just as it was the Empire's task to secure the pacification of the primitive tribes of the Lower Niger abroad.

As we have seen, in Scott's novel Peter Pattieson asserts that his own 'unbiassed' picture differs significantly from Old Mortality's strongly biased pro-Covenanter account. Scott's novel is careful to stress that Pattieson's conclusions are balanced and even-handed, and these conclusions duly find important things to admire in the legacy of the Covenanters. For example, Pattieson writes movingly of the reverence felt by 'the peasantry' for the tombs of Covenanters who died during the Killing Times:

> The peasantry continue to attach to the tombs of these victims of prelacy an honour which they do not render to more splendid mausoleums; and, when they point them out to their sons, and narrate the fate of the sufferers, usually conclude, by exhorting them to be ready, should times call for it, to resist to the death in the cause of civil and religious liberty, like their brave forefathers. (p. 7)

In Scott's novel, extreme Covenanters like Burley, Macbriar, and Meiklewrath release the nightmarish energies of revolutionary Radicalism. The moderate Covenanter Henry Morton, in contrast, is a man who helps create a better future by being ready to resist to the death in the cause of civil and religious liberty, when the times do indeed call for it.

The Tale of Old Mortality, then, is a text that celebrates the legacy of the moderate Covenanters and of the 'Glorious Revolution'; and it is also a text that warns of the horrors that await if revolutionary Radicals, heirs of the extreme Covenanters, are allowed to rise up and overthrow the benign political settlement established by the 'Glorious Revolution'. This is not a novel that challenges the class hierarchy of society, as quickly becomes clear. After Pattieson's preliminary frame narrative, the novel proper begins with a description of a traditional 'wappen-schaw' held under 'the reign of the last Stuarts'. The festivities include a shooting contest, in which Henry Morton establishes his credentials as the novel's hero by defeating Lord Evandale, the moderate royalist who is his rival in love. Third place in the contest is taken by the ploughman Cuddie Headrigg, who acquits himself well but whose final shot goes past the suspended target 'so nearly' that 'it was seen to shiver' (p. 21). Cuddie cannot in the end match the skill of the two gentlemen, Morton and Evandale, and one feels that, in Scott's fictional world, the laws of physics are such that it is simply impossible for a ploughman to emerge as victor in such a contest. Cuddie's fate, rather, is to become a devoted Gurth to Henry Morton's Ivanhoe.

Scott's view that revolutionary Radicals posed a dangerous threat to the stability of society was not universally shared in the Scotland of his day. Indeed, many people outside the gentlemanly elite hoped for precisely the developments that Scott dreaded. A few months before Scott began to write *The Tale of Old Mortality*, thousands of 'democrats' (mainly textile workers from the west of Scotland) assembled on the battlefield of Loudoun-hill to celebrate the escape of Napoleon from Elba; and also to celebrate the victory at Loudoun-hill in 1679 of their ancestors the Covenanters against the established government of the day.[39] Clearly, subaltern Scotland and the North British elite did not necessarily have the same agenda with regard to the legacy of the Covenanters.

The folk-memory of events like the battle at Loudoun-hill remained a potent force in the Scotland of the 1810s and the 1820s, precisely because the Covenanters symbolised the possibility of a heroic, principled, and ultimately successful armed defence of the rights of the people against an unjust aristocratic government. This potentially dangerous folk-memory was the tiger that *Old Mortality* sought to tame, by demonstrating not only what Scott perceived to be valuable, but also what Scott perceived to be dangerous, in the legacy of those revered national heroes the Covenanters.

John Galt, the Covenanters, and the Tobacco Lords

For the love of money is the root of all evil: which while some coveted after, they have erred from the faith, and pierced themselves through with many sorrows.

(1 Timothy 6. 10)

We have seen that Hogg felt that his portrayal, in *The Brownie of Bodsbeck*, of the conflict between royalists and Covenanters was 'a devilish deal truer' than that of Scott in *Old*

Mortality. The novelist John Galt (1779–1839) likewise felt that *Old Mortality* had been both unfair and inaccurate in presenting some Covenanters as deranged, absurd, but dangerous fanatics. Galt, like Burns, was born in Ayrshire in the western Lowlands, and, like Burns, he was deeply influenced by Ayrshire's strong tradition of radical Presbyterianism. Addressing this issue, John MacQueen has aptly remarked that, while Scott's natural haunts were in the eastern Lowlands among 'the monuments and antiquities of Edinburgh and Tweeddale', Galt had his roots in 'the commercial and radical west, which formed the scene of many of his novels, and usually served for the rest as ultimate background'.[40]

When Galt was ten years old his father, a sea-captain, became the owner of a ship trading to the West Indies, and the family moved to Greenock in the neighbouring county of Renfrewshire. However, this mercantile family background did not distance Galt from the west of Scotland's popular tradition of radical Presbyterianism. Writing about Burns's cultural context, Liam McIlvanney comments:

> Whereas Lutheranism and Anglicanism tended to develop through the sponsorship of princes, and so remained politically quiescent and deferential to the civil power, Calvinism developed in open conflict with hostile Catholic courts in Scotland as in France, and produced more radical theories of resistance. Repudiating the right of the king to intervene in matters of spiritual moment, Calvinism stood for limited government in an age of monarchical absolutism. Moreover, Calvinism drew its support from social classes—merchants, artisans, peasants—which were excluded from existing power structures. It gave these groups a share in ecclesiastical power by adopting a partially democratic system of government by church courts (Presbyterianism). And increasingly, given its hostile relationship with the crown, Scottish Calvinism asserted not only the religious but also the civil and political competence of the people, their right to resist bad government.[41]

The Presbyterianism of the western Lowlands, that is to say, drew its support not only from people of a peasant background such as Burns and Hogg, but also from merchant-class people such as Galt's father—and it was this Presbyterian merchant class that produced the tobacco lords, Glasgow's new eighteenth-century aristocracy. Galt never became a tobacco lord (although in the later 1820s he did play a significant part in organising British settlement in Canada).[42] However, he wrote about the Presbyterian culture of the western Lowlands as an insider, as a member of a community whose story he wished to tell. As we shall see, part of his project was to explore tensions between the inherited Presbyterian values of his community, and the realities of its involvement in the new Imperial 'sugar and tobacco-trade'.

Galt's radical Presbyterian roots are strongly present in his major three-volume novel *Ringan Gilhaize* (1823), of which he writes in his *Literary Life*:

> The book itself was certainly suggested by Sir Walter Scott's Old Mortality, in which I thought he treated the defenders of the Presbyterian Church with too much levity, and not according to my impressions derived from the history of that time. Indeed, to tell the truth, I was hugely provoked that he [...] should have been so forgetful of what was due to the spirit of that epoch, as to throw it in to what I felt was ridicule.[43]

Old Mortality is a story that articulates Scott's fears about potential revolution, but Galt in *Ringan Gilhaize* constructs a competing egalitarian story about liberty, in which the Covenanters are seen as defenders of the rights of the people as well as 'defenders of the Presbyterian Church'. Indeed, in his 'Postscript' to *Ringan* Galt writes about the particular 'character of liberty' among the Scots, and goes on to print a translation of the fourteenth-century Declaration of Arbroath, an address to the Pope which asserts the determination of the Scottish people to resist conquest by England, and which also asserts the willingness of the Scottish people to depose their heroic and much-loved king, Robert the Bruce, should he turn against this cause at some future date. Galt sees the Declaration of Arbroath as a Scottish equivalent of England's Magna Carta: these documents are fundamental statements about human rights and about liberty, and as such are 'the two most important public documents extant'. The Declaration of Arbroath, Galt adds, is not widely known, and therefore 'a translation is subjoined, of the time of Ringan Gilhaize—the sacred original is in the Register Office'.[44]

Galt's view is that the particular 'character of liberty' among the Scots, as articulated in the Declaration of Arbroath and elsewhere, is based on the contractarian assumption that authority ascends from below, and that it is therefore entirely right and proper to resist and depose a ruler who, by abuse of power, breaks his or her contract with the people. Liam McIlvanney gives a concise account of Presbyterian contractarian theory:

> The theory of justified resistance was developed by Presbyterian thinkers in a series of polemical works, often written in times of armed rebellion: George Buchanan's *De jure regni apud Scotos* (1579), written after the deposition of Mary; Samuel Rutherford's *Lex Rex: The Law and the Prince* (1644), written during the Presbyterian resistance to Charles I; and Alexander Shields's *A Hind Let Loose* (1687), written during the later Covenanting struggles. In these seminal works, the right to resist is put forward as part of a contractarian theory of government, in which sovereignty is seen to be vested in the people as a whole.[45]

In *De jure regni*, George Buchanan provided a theoretical basis for the deposition of Mary, Queen of Scots—and a little more than a century later, Buchanan's book helped to provide an intellectual framework for those who sought the deposition of James VII and II in the 'Glorious Revolution'. However, the Presbyterian tradition which Buchanan articulated was not against monarchical rule as such. For example, those signing the National Covenant of 1638 asserted that they were upholding *legitimate* royal power, as well as true religion and the liberties of the country: the King's power should only be opposed if he broke his contract with the people through tyrannical and arbitrary acts. This is part of the context in which Scott, like other early-nineteenth-century Scottish Tories, warmed to Buchanan as a pillar of the 'Glorious Revolution', the event that had done so much to establish the political status quo which he wished to defend. However, Scott also saw clearly that Buchanan's Presbyterian theory of justified resistance had the potential to lend support to the radical challenges that were making themselves felt during the second half of the 1810s—and he framed *Old Mortality* accordingly, praising the moderate Covenanter Henry Morton as an embodiment of the virtues of the 'Glorious Revolution', while deploring the excesses of extreme Covenanters like Meiklewrath and Balfour of Burley. Responding to Scott's powerful anti-radical novel, Galt sets out in *Ringan Gilhaize* to construct a competing story that will speak from and for the people of the Presbyterian tradition of the western Lowlands, the territory of the Covenanters: 'we too might have a story to tell'. To this end, *Ringan Gilhaize* tells the story of the resistance offered to corrupt monarchs by three generations of the subaltern Gilhaize family, from the time of the Scottish Reformation in the sixteenth century (the period of George Buchanan and Mary, Queen of Scots) until the time of the later Covenanters towards the end of the seventeenth century (the period of the 'Glorious Revolution'). In Galt's novel the Gilhaize family endures much suffering, but their cause is finally seen to triumph in 1689 when Ringan Gilhaize, at the battle of Killiecrankie, is able to defuse a potentially potent rising in support of the recently-deposed James VII and II. Ringan achieves this by killing Claverhouse, the leader of the rising.

We have seen that Hogg, in his 'rural and traditionary tales', devised ways of locating narrative authority within the Ettrick community. Likewise, in attempting to tell a story that would speak for and from a particular community, Galt in *Ringan Gilhaize* had to contrive to gain narrative authority for a voice that speaks from and for the subaltern Presbyterian people of the western Lowlands. He achieves this by making the seventeenth-century Covenanter Ringan Gilhaize the novel's first-person narrator—and the necessary historical reach is achieved because Ringan, before giving an account of his own experiences, tells the story of the adventures of his grandfather Michael Gilhaize in the days of Mary, Queen of Scots. The result is a *tour-de-force* of narrative technique, in the course of which Galt convincingly conveys a Covenanter's-eye-view of a century and a half of Scottish history. As we shall see, however, this is not necessarily to suggest that Galt's own view of events is identical in every way with Ringan's.[46]

Ringan emerges from Galt's novel as a representative Covenanter, as a man whose personal experiences and personal emotional development reflect those of the movement as a whole. For example, this novel's view of the persecution of the Covenanters by the royalist regime is conveyed when Ringan, returning home to his farm of

Quharist, finds that his wife and daughters have been murdered by royalist soldiers (pp. 365–66). Traumatised, Ringan descends into madness for a while, but he has at least partly recovered by 1689, the year which (as in *Old Mortality*) provides the setting for the novel's final events.

In 1689, shortly after the 'Glorious Revolution', John Graham of Claverhouse led a Jacobite rising in support of the deposed James VII and II and won a notable victory at Killiecrankie. In *Old Mortality* Claverhouse's rising takes place off-stage. In Galt's novel, however, Ringan is at the battle, and sees Claverhouse's victory with dismay:

> I ran to and fro on the brow of the hill—and I stampt with my feet—and I beat my breast—and I rubbed my hands with the frenzy of despair—and I threw myself on the ground—and all the sufferings of which I have written returned upon me—and I started up and I cried aloud the blasphemy of the fool, 'There is no God.'
>
> But scarcely had the dreadful words escaped my profane lips, when I heard, as it were, thunders in the heavens, and the voice of an oracle crying in the ears of my soul, 'The victory of this day is given into thy hands!' and strange wonder and awe fell upon me, and a mighty spirit entered into mine, and I felt as if I was in that moment clothed with the armour of divine might. (pp. 445–46)

Seeing Claverhouse approaching, Ringan takes up his position behind a low wall. He fires twice, but to no effect: 'the oppressor' is 'still proudly on his war-horse'.

> Then I remembered that I had not implored the help of Heaven, and I prepared for the third time, and when all was ready, and Claverhouse was coming forward, I took off my bonnet, and kneeling with the gun in my hand, cried, 'Lord, remember David and all his afflictions;' and having so prayed, I took aim as I knelt, and Claverhouse raising his arm in command, I fired. In the same moment I looked up, and there was a vision in the air as if all the angels of brightness, and the martyrs in their vestments of glory, were assembled on the walls and battlements of heaven to witness the event,—and I started up and cried, 'I have delivered my native land!' But in the same instant I remembered to whom the glory was due, and falling again on my knees, I raised my hands and bowed my head as I said, 'Not mine, O Lord, but thine is the victory!' (pp. 446–47)

How are we to understand this? We can see clearly enough how Ringan interprets the killing of Claverhouse. However, while Ringan remains a sympathetic figure throughout Galt's novel, the reader does not necessarily see things exactly as Ringan sees them. Galt is careful to show that Ringan has been damaged mentally and emotionally by the murder of his family, and in this novel, as in Galt's other 'fictional autobiographies' (such as *Annals of the Parish*, published in 1821), narrative devices such as the arrangement and juxtaposition of incidents allow the reader not only to see events through the eyes of the first-person narrator, but also to gain a wider perspective. Like Achebe in *Things Fall Apart* and Hogg in *The Brownie of Bodsbeck*, Galt in *Ringan Gilhaize* is willing and able to confront problematic aspects of the society on whose behalf the story is being told. For this reason, in a reader's response to the concluding pages of Galt's novel, compassion for Ringan's partial and stress-induced madness may well combine with uneasiness about the killing of Claverhouse in cold blood. Nevertheless, while Ringan's killing of this cruel tyrant can be seen to be problematic, it can also be interpreted as an apt conclusion to a narrative that eloquently speaks for and from the Presbyterian tradition. *Ringan Gilhaize* asserts the validity of that tradition's claim to the right of justified resistance, and that claim is part of the context for the killing of Claverhouse.

Ringan Gilhaize (1823) is a companion-piece to another three-volume by Galt, *The Entail; or, The Lairds of Grippy* (published at the end of 1822, but with 1823 on the titlepage). In *Ringan*, the history of Lowland Scotland from the Reformation in the 1560s until the 'Glorious Revolution' of the late 1680s is traced through the telling of the story of the Gilhaize family. Correspondingly, *The Entail* tells the story of the west of Scotland Walkinshaw family, in order to trace the history of Lowlands from the 1690s until the onset of the Napoleonic Wars a century later. Taken together, then, these two novels survey the history of Lowland Scotland over two and a half centuries, from the time of the Reformation until the time of Galt's own youth. And in *The Entail* Galt explores the damaging consequences of the eighteenth-century change of focus in the western Lowlands from the aspirations of the Covenanters to the avid pursuit of wealth through the Imperial 'sugar and tobacco-trade'.

As with the story of the Gilhaize family, the story of the Walkinshaws of Kittlestonheugh broadly reflects the story of their community as a whole. In *The Entail*, the Walkinshaws lose their wealth and estates in the 1690s as a result of that national disaster for Scotland, the failure of the Darien Expedition. In the opening paragraph of Galt's novel we learn that Claud Walkinshaw, the family's 'sole surviving male heir', 'was scarcely a year old when his father sailed' towards death on the 'Mosquito shore' of Darien.[47] The opening chapters of *The Entail* go on to focus on Claud's obsessive efforts to restore the family fortunes. The impoverished and dispossessed heir begins a career in trade as a lowly pedlar, but is so adept at earning and hoarding money that he is eventually able to establish himself profitably in a shop in Glasgow. Although he never manages to gain wealth on the scale of the Glasgow tobacco lords, Claud does manage to prosper substantially. However, the 'sordid avidity' (p. 54) of his love of money produces many troubles for himself and his family.

Having gained wealth, Claud marries the daughter of the laird of the Ayrshire estate of Plealands, and he also acquires the farm known as the Grippy, part of his lost ancestral estate. Three sons and a daughter are born to the marriage, the mentally-retarded second son (Walter, his mother's favourite) being heir by entail of the maternal estate of Plealands. The eldest son and prospective heir of Grippy, Charles, is at first the apple of Claud's eye. However, Charles displeases his father by marrying Isabella (to whom he is engaged), even although her father has unexpectedly lost all his money through the collapse of the Ayr Bank—thus rendering the match much less attractive to Claud. Tempted to combine his own estate with that of Plealands, and being unable to disinherit Walter because of the entail, Claud disinherits Charles and, by means of a new entail, leaves his own estate to Walter and to Walter's male heirs.

Walter marries, but his wife dies in childbirth. Her child is a daughter, thus dashing Claud's hopes. In due course Walter inherits the combined estates on his father's death, but his younger brother, George (who has inherited their father's intense love of money) now moves centre-stage. In his youth, we are told, George had been

> placed in the counting-house of one of the most eminent West Indian merchants at that period in Glasgow. This incident was in no other respect important in the history of the Lairds of Grippy, than as serving to open a career to George, that would lead him into a higher class of acquaintance than his elder brothers: for it was about this time that the general merchants of the royal city began to arrogate to themselves that aristocratic superiority over the shopkeepers, which they have since established into an oligarchy, as proud and sacred, in what respects the reciprocities of society, as the famous Seignories of Venice and of Genoa. (p. 109)

As his career advances, George becomes a prominent figure in the Glasgow of the tobacco lords, highly respected among his peers in 'that stately class who, though entirely devoted to the pursuit of lucre, still held their heads high as ancestral gentry' (p. 209). The now-eminent George contrives to become the next Laird of Grippy by having Walter declared legally insane.

So far, their intense pursuit of wealth has involved the Walkinshaws in various morally questionable actions, and has brought much unhappiness to the family. However, as the novel approaches its end a healing process begins to operate after George dies in a somewhat melodramatic shipwreck. Claud's widow is able to ensure that her grandson James (son of the disinherited and long-dead Charles) is eventually restored to the family estates in preference to George's only child (a grasping and selfish daughter, Robina). The process of restoration and healing continues when James marries into an old Highland Jacobite family, plays a heroic part in the Napoleonic Wars, and finally, after Waterloo, settles with his wife and children at the ancient Walkinshaw estate of Kittlestonheugh 'with all his blushing honours thick upon him' (p. 363).

The story of the Walkinshaws seems designed to suggest that, in the eighteenth century, the western Lowlands drifted away from the values of the Covenanters and into an obsessive and destructive 'pursuit of lucre', before regaining contact with ancestral values by wholeheartedly joining Britain's struggle against that latter-day tyrant, the

Emperor Napoleon. Galt's novel, it would appear, is in conscious debate with Scott's *Rob Roy* about the lucrative but slavery-based 'sugar and tobacco-trade' which allowed Glasgow to flourish in the eighteenth century. Indeed, Galt seems to go out of his way to remind readers that he is telling an alternative story about the world of Scott's Bailie Nicol Jarvie. This emerges, for example, in an incident connected with the marriage of Charles and Isabella.

When Charles's prospective father-in-law loses his money, Claud's first move is to persuade Charles and Isabella to postpone their marriage for a year. Isabella's father arranges for her to go to Glasgow to assist 'Miss Mally Trimmings, a celebrated mantua-maker of that time'. Once in Glasgow, however, Isabella has a particularly bruising encounter with one of Miss Mally's customers, 'Mrs Jarvie, the wife of the far-famed Bailie Nicol, the same Matty who lighted the worthy magistrate to the Tolbooth, on that memorable night when he, the son of the deacon, found his kins-man Rob Roy there' (pp. 43–44, 45–46). Matty, like her husband the Bailie, is an ami-able character in *Rob Roy*. However, in *The Entail* she responds with venomous fury when she finds that an expensive gown brought to her by Isabella is too small. It is Isabella's acute distress over this incident that prompts the young couple of Galt's novel to proceed with their marriage without further delay, in spite of Claud's opposi-tion. The memorable display of ill-nature by Mrs Jarvie thus plays a significant part in the process that leads to Claud's decision to disinherit his eldest son. Clearly, Galt's picture of the Glasgow of the 'sugar and tobacco-trade' is designed to be noticeably less favourable than Scott's.

In *The Entail*, Claud's obsession with money serves to illuminate the real and avari-cious nature of the Glasgow of the Imperial 'sugar and tobacco-trade', and to demon-strate the departure of that world from the values of the Covenanters. This is made plain at many points in Galt's novel. For example, in Volume II Chapter 8 a shaken and (for the time being) deeply penitent Claud, soon after the death of his disinherited son Charles, has a revealing and painfully honest conversation with the excellent Presbyte-rian clergyman Dr Denholm, who is an embodiment of all that was best about the Covenanters. Claud says:

> when I was but a bairn, I kent na what it was to hae the innocence o' a young heart. I used to hide the sma' presents of siller I got frae my frien's, even when Maudge Dobbie, the auld kind creature that brought me up, could na earn a sufficiency for our scrimpit meals; I did na gang near her when I kent she was in poortith and bedrid, for fear my heart would relent, and gar me gie her something out o' the gathering I was making for the redemption o' this vile yird that is mair grateful than me, for it repays with its fruits the care o' the tiller. I stiffled the very sense o' loving kindness within me; and in furtherance of my wicked avarice, I married a woman—Heaven may forgie the aversion I had to her; but my own nature never can. (p. 150)

Dr Denholm speaks to Claud about what he believes to be truly valuable: 'when ye behold nothing in your goods and gear but trash and splendid dirt, then may ye be sure that ye hae gotten better than silver or gold' (p. 151). Towards the end of the chapter the clergyman's eloquence has (for a time) re-connected Claud with the values of the Covenanters, and at this point

> a distant strain of wild and holy music, rising from a hundred voices, drew their atten-
> tion towards a shaggy bank of natural birch and hazel, where, on the sloping ground in
> front, they saw a number of Cameronians from Glasgow, and the neighbouring vil-
> lages, assembled to commemorate in worship the persecutions which their forefathers
> had suffered there for righteousness sake. (pp. 151–52)

Cameronians were particularly strict and austere Presbyterians, regarding themselves as the most faithful of the heirs of the Covenanters; and the geography of the novel suggests that the Cameronians are meeting to commemorate the Battle of Bothwell Bridge.

The story of the Walkinshaws also connects with the larger story of their society in other ways, and some passages in *The Entail* seem designed to prompt readers to pon-der possible parallels between the plight of Charles Walkinshaw and the situation of another eighteenth-century disinherited heir, Prince Charles Edward Stuart. For exam-ple, at a point in the novel before he has lost his father's favour, 'Charlie' Walkinshaw is described by his mother as Claud's 'darling chevalier' (p. 65). This is an unmistakable reference to the most famous of all Jacobite songs, 'Charlie is my Darling', in which the disinherited Prince is called 'the young chevalier'. Furthermore, Charles Walkinshaw's children are called James and Mary. There were no fewer than seven Stuart Kings of Scots called James—eight if one counts 'the Old Pretender', father of Bonny Prince Charlie. And, of course, the most famous of all Stuart queens was Mary, Queen of Scots. Even the name 'Walkinshaw' recalls Clementina Walkinshaw (1726?–1802), mis-tress of Prince Charles Edward and mother of his child.

These Jacobite resonances may seem strange in a novel by a nineteenth-century Pres-byterian writer such as Galt. However, as we have seen, even seventeenth-century Cov-enanters regarded themselves as supporters of *legitimate* royal power. That seminal six-teenth-century Presbyterian work, Buchanan's *De jure regni*, was written to justify the deposition of Mary, Queen of Scots. However, when Queen Mary was deposed for breaking her contract with the people, it was taken for granted by Presbyterians that the natural consequence was her replacement by her infant son and heir, James VI. Like-wise, when James VII and II was deposed he was succeeded first by his Protestant daughter Mary (and her husband William of Orange); and after their deaths the succes-sion passed to James's Protestant daughter Anne. However, a potentially more dis-turbing disruption of the natural succession came after Queen Anne's death in 1714, when the claims of the Old Pretender (James VII and II's Catholic son James) were passed over in favour of his very distant Protestant relative the Elector of Hanover (who duly came to the throne as George I).

The Presbyterian doctrine of the right of resistance, as elucidated by George Buchanan, provides a justification for deposing a tyrannical and unjust monarch—and James VII and II was seen in that light at the time of the 'Glorious Revolution'. Arguably, however, under Buchanan's doctrine the Old Pretender deserved his chance, and ought not to have been excluded from the throne until he had proved himself to be a tyrant like his father. No doubt the succession of the various Hanoverian and Protestant King Georges of the eighteenth century helped to advance the interests of the Protestant and Imperial British state under which Glasgow's 'sugar and tobacco-trade' flourished so spectacularly in the post-Union period. *The Entail,* however, tends to raise questions about an arrangement that (it suggests) may have owed more to perceived commercial advantage than to natural justice. At all events it is interesting to remember that Claud's ruthlessly successful third son George shares a name with the Hanoverian kings of the time.

As it tells the story of the western Lowlands in the eighteenth century, *The Entail* is prepared to confront problematic aspects of the interaction between the values of the Covenanters and the values of the tobacco lords. However, like Hogg in *The Brownie of Bodsbeck*, Galt in *The Entail* is seeking to gain a hearing for the story of his own community—and, like Hogg in *The Brownie of Bodsbeck*, Galt finds ways to give narrative authority to the voice of that community. In part, this is achieved by a particularly full use in the dialogue of *The Entail* of the rich resources of the Scots speech of the western Lowlands. However, Galt is also careful to indicate that the third-person narrator of *The Entail* is himself part of the Lowland Scottish world about which he is writing. There is a contrast here with Scott's approach. For example, the third-person narrator of *Waverley* adopts the tone of a detached and objective observer as he describes the Scottish society of the mid-1740s. Frank Osbaldistone (the Englishman who is the first-person narrator of *Rob Roy*) likewise views the Scottish society of the mid-1710s from the perspective of an outsider. In contrast, Galt's third-person narrator has an insider's perspective, being (it would appear) a native inhabitant of the western Lowlands himself. Thus when he happens 'to be walking alone' past the scene of Walter's wedding festivities on 'a calm and beautiful evening', he is duly invited to become one of the wedding guests (p. 99).

Oddly, in view of their links with the potentially radical subaltern / Presbyterian tradition, Hogg and Galt were both associated with the Tory *Blackwood's Edinburgh Magazine*. The subaltern / Presbyterian tradition, although radical and egalitarian in politics, was nevertheless sympathetic to aspects of religious culture; culturally nationalist; and enthusiastic about reviving and maintaining the pre-Union cultural traditions of subaltern Scotland. Aspects of these concerns overlap with aspects of the British and Unionist Tory cultural nationalism of the *Blackwood's* project, and this helped to open the pages of the magazine to Hogg and Galt. *Blackwood's* shared Scott's desire to re-shape Scottish national feeling in ways that would serve the purposes of the British and Unionist Tory political agenda. In the magazine, therefore, John Wilson tends to present Hogg (and Burns) as writers about pious and loyal peasants—as writers about Gurth-figures who keep up the good old traditions of the good old days. For example, in line with the view that Burns and Hogg depict peasants who are the salt of the earth and the backbone of Britain, Wilson particularly praised Burns's 'The Cotter's Saturday Night'—and that poem, read in that way, duly became a particular favourite in Victorian Scotland. However, an egalitarian and radical reading of 'The Cotter's Saturday Night' is also possible, in which the poem can be seen to assert that real worth and value lie with the Cotter's family, and that the respect conventionally given to decadent aristocrats is wholly undeserved.[48]

In spite of areas of overlap, the subaltern Presbyterian tradition did not fit entirely comfortably with the *Blackwood's* project. This can be seen, for example, with regard to cultural nationalism. A parallel with New Zealand's experience may be useful here. In *Still Being Punished* (Wellington: Huia, 1999), Rachael Selby writes that 'four of the stories told in this book are from men and women who went to native schools', and who suffered corporal punishment 'when they accidentally spoke in their own language inside the school gate' (p. 4). It was of course in the Empire's interest to ensure that Maori people learned to speak what was called 'the King's English', and abandoned use of their own language. This policy had its parallels in Scottish schools until the middle of the twentieth century, as many monoglot Scots- or Gaelic-speaking Scottish children painfully learned when they first passed through the gates of the schools of Imperial Britain. If one said in effect 'I'm going to go on speaking Maori (or Scots) anyway, because that's who I am, and these people aren't going to make me into someone I'm not', then one became a Maori (or Scottish) cultural nationalist. Subaltern cultural assertiveness of this kind was very much in tune with the egalitarian assertiveness of the Presbyterian tradition, and provides the energy which drives the extensive use of Scots in the writings of Burns, Hogg, and Galt. However, the Unionist and Tory cultural nationalism of *Blackwood's* had different objects in mind as it sought to modify and re-focus the Scottish Presbyterian tradition, in order to incorporate its energies within the project of the Imperial British state.

Unsurprisingly, given this situation, Galt and Hogg both experienced persistent strains and tensions in their dealings with William Blackwood as a publisher. Ian Gordon has shown that Blackwood, dissatisfied with the tone of *The Entail*, urged 'his author to fill out the third volume with the kind of incident he called "striking"' (one thinks of the shipwreck in which George dies). Ian Gordon argues that Blackwood's interference produced 'an abrupt change of tone' towards the end of the novel, resulting in the insertion of 'considerable material alien to the run of the earlier narrative'. These were the circumstances in which Galt changed to another publisher, Oliver & Boyd, for *Ringan Gilhaize*, his next novel.[49]

Some particularly perceptive comments by Susan Manning on Hogg's cultural position provide a useful parallel here. Freed from Wilsonian spin, and seen in relationship to a subaltern / Presbyterian / radical tradition, Hogg no longer seems to be a satellite of what Manning has called 'a world of lairds, lawyers and aristocrats, the visible face of Scotland's official literary landscape in the Regency period, where Scott, Jeffrey, Mackenzie and Wilson were the legislators and Hogg would always, as an outsider, be an easy target'. Instead, he emerges as a writer who speaks from and for what Manning describes as the 'fascinating, dense alternative if not counter culture' in which Hogg's periodical *The Spy* (1810–11) was rooted. This culture was to be encountered in non-elite Edinburgh, and its members included 'printers, schoolteachers, physicians, working farmers', and women as writers as well as readers.[50] It had strongly radical and egalitarian elements inherited from the subaltern Presbyterian tradition, and it forms a particularly significant part of the context from which Hogg's writings emerged.

We have seen that *The Brownie of Bodsbeck* is not best understood as a pro-Presbyterian response to Scott's *Old Mortality*, but that Galt in *Ringan Gilhaize* did produce such a response to Scott's novel. However, a year after the publication of *Ringan*, in 1824, Hogg was to produce a book that was in effect a reply to both *Ringan Gilhaize* and *Old Mortality*. The book in question was *The Private Memoirs and Confessions of a Justified Sinner*.

The Private Memoirs and Confessions of a Justified Sinner

In Chapter 3 we saw that, in Hogg's most famous novel, 'The Editor's Narrative' seems designed to echo and reflect *Old Mortality*'s perspective on the Covenanters. The second main narrative in the *Justified Sinner* consists of Robert Wringhim's 'Private Memoirs and Confessions', and this document proves to be an intense and subjective first-person narrative somewhat reminiscent of *Ringan Gilhaize*. Hogg does not often set his fiction in the west of Scotland, but in the *Justified Sinner* the opening of each main narrative is firmly rooted in the vicinity of Glasgow—thus, arguably, signalling a connection with those other tales of the west, *Old Mortality* and *Ringan Gilhaize*. Significantly, both main narratives of the *Justified Sinner* contain a reported piece of oral story-telling. In these 'oral' passages Hogg is as it were in his own story-telling territory, and through these passages he articulates his critique of the competing stories told by Scott and Galt about the Covenanters of the west of Scotland.

The Scott-like nature of 'The Editor's Narrative' can be traced in its opening pages, which give an account of the wedding night of Robert Wringhim's mother. This account, at first sight plausible and convincing, makes plain where this narrator's sympathies lie. According to the Editor, the gentlemanly bridegroom (the Laird of Dalcastle) 'was what his country neighbours called "a droll, careless chap," with a very limited pro-portion of the fear of God in his heart, and very nearly as little of the fear of man' (pp. 3–4). But the bride, a Roundhead to the Laird's Cavalier, is an upholder of the views of the Covenanters, and 'the most severe and gloomy of all bigots to the principles of the Reformation' (p. 4). The Editor gives a hilarious account of the wedding night of this ill-matched couple. In the privacy of their bedroom, the bride invites the groom to pray before retiring to bed; but the groom, tired after much dancing and brandy, tells her to get on with the praying herself, if prayers there must be. The Editor's tone is detached, ironic, Scott-like:

> The meek mind of Lady Dalcastle was somewhat disarranged by this sudden evolu-tion. She felt that she was left rather in an awkward situation. However, to show her unconscionable spouse that she was resolved to hold fast her integrity, she kneeled down and prayed in terms so potent, that she deemed she was sure of making an im-pression on him. She did so; for in a short time the laird began to utter a response so fervent, that she was utterly astounded, and fairly driven from the chain of her ori-sons. He began, in truth, to sound a nasal bugle of no ordinary calibre,—the notes being little inferior to those of a military trumpet. (p. 6)

When the laird eventually wakes up early next morning, his bride has left the wed-ding chamber. Searching through the house, he enters the hall, scene of the wedding festivities; and, 'as he opened the various window-boards, loving couples flew off like hares surprised too late in the morning among the early braird' (p. 7). There is sexual fulfilment everywhere at this wedding feast, it seems, except for the newly-married cou-ple. The laird, determined to put matters right, manages to find his wife; and then 'he rolled her in a blanket, and bore her triumphantly away to his chamber, taking care to keep a fold or two of the blanket always rather near to her mouth, in case of any outra-geous forthcoming of noise' (p. 8). This action clearly has the approval of the Editor, and it is decisive enough to lead to the birth of a son, George Colwan junior, the laird's namesake and the hero of the Editor's Narrative.

The possibility of an alternative perspective begins to emerge towards the end of the Editor's Narrative, however, when the prostitute Bell Calvert gives an oral account of what she saw on the night of young George's death. Her story is told out of the bitter experience of someone on the margins of society, of one of the outcast and the despised, of someone who has been reduced 'to utter destitution and shame' (p. 49). She explains the circumstances, as she begins her tale.

> I had been abandoned in York, by an artful and consummate fiend; found guilty of being art and part concerned in the most heinous atrocities, and, in his place, suffered what I yet shudder to think of. I was banished the county—begged my way with my

poor outcast child up to Edinburgh, and was there obliged, for the second time in my life, to betake myself to the most degrading of all means to support two wretched lives. I hired a dress, and betook me, shivering, to the High Street, too well aware that my form and appearance would soon draw me suitors enow at that throng and intemperate time of the parliament. On my very first stepping out to the street, a party of young gentlemen was passing. I heard by the noise they made, and the tenor of their speech, that they were more than mellow, and so I resolved to keep near them, in order, if possible, to make some of them my prey. But just as one of them began to eye me, I was rudely thrust into a narrow close by one of the guardsmen. I had heard to what house the party was bound, for the men were talking exceedingly loud, and making no secret of it: so I hasted down the close, and round below to the one where their rendezvous was to be. (pp. 49–50)

Bell's oral tale has much in common with the oral testimonies of *The Brownie of Bodsbeck*, and as she continues with it the appalling nature of her situation becomes more and more clear: 'I was perishing with famine, and was like to fall down' (p. 50). It also becomes clear that Bell's 'party of young gentlemen' includes young George, and that we are hearing a re-telling of an incident already narrated by the Editor. In the Editor's version, George, as host, is to meet for a jovial evening with his Jacobite friends; friends, it emerges, who are willing to hint at their loyalty to the exiled Old Pretender in defiance of the claims of the reigning monarch, Queen Anne.

The day arrived—the party of young noblemen and gentlemen met, and were as happy and jovial as men could be. George was never seen so brilliant, or so full of spirits; and exulting to see so many gallant young chiefs and gentlemen about him, who all gloried in the same principles of loyalty, (perhaps this word should have been written *disloyalty,*) he made speeches, gave toasts, and sung songs, all leaning slily to the same side, until a very late hour. By that time he had pushed the bottle so long and so freely, that its fumes had taken possession of every brain to such a degree, that they held Dame Reason rather at the staff's end, overbearing all her counsels and expostulations; and it was imprudently proposed by a wild inebriated spark, and carried by a majority of voices, that the whole party should adjourn to a bagnio for the remainder of the night. (p. 36)

The Editor's elite's-eye-view presents a 'happy and jovial' group of 'gallant young chiefs and gentlemen', who are holding 'Dame Reason rather at the staff's end' as they conclude their revels, while the oral tale's subaltern's-eye-view presents a group of noisy drunks, eyeing up Bell, who is 'perishing with famine' as she resorts to 'the most degrading of all means to support two wretched lives'. The contrast is disturbing, and invites the reader to reconsider the Editor's account of other events. And when we begin to distrust the Editor's hilarious account of the wedding night, a very different picture emerges.

If the reader breaks free from the Editor's view, and considers matters from the point of view of the Presbyterian bride, the events of the wedding night begin to seem to be far from hilarious. A new interpretation begins to open out, in which the young, devout, and presumably virginal Rabina, having sought refuge in marriage from what is clearly an uncongenial parental home, finds herself trapped in the bedroom of a drunken old husband. Seeking comfort in 'the writings of the Evangelists', she

> turned away her head, and spoke of the follies of aged men, and something of the broad way that leadeth to destruction. The laird did not thoroughly comprehend this allusion; but being considerably flustered by drinking, and disposed to take all in good part, he only remarked, as he took off his shoes and stockings, "that whether the way was broad or narrow, it was time that they were in their bed." (p. 5)

There is a reference here to Matthew 7. 13–14, a crucial passage from Christ's Sermon on the Mount which asserts that 'strait *is* the gate, and narrow *is* the way, which leadeth unto life', but that 'wide *is* the gate, and broad *is* the way, that leadeth to destruction'. In the Dalcastle wedding-chamber, the laird entangles Christ's words with sexual innuendo. Still worse is to follow for the unfortunate Rabina. After the laird wakes up from his drunken sleep and carries her off in a blanket, it would appear that he rapes her violently (although naturally the Editor does not spell this out in quite those terms).

> The next day at breakfast the bride was long in making her appearance. Her maid asked to see her; but George did not choose that any body should see her but himself: he paid her several visits, and always turned the key as he came out. At length breakfast was served; and during the time of refreshment the laird tried to break several jokes; but it was remarked, that they wanted their accustomed brilliancy, and that his nose was particularly red at the top. (p. 8)

Bell Calvert's oral tale alerts the reader to the need to distrust and question the Editor, and it thus helps us to read the Editor's Narrative more deeply and more perceptively. In short, it becomes clear that the story of the Covenanters as told by Edinburgh's literary elite is neither the whole story nor the only story.

As we shall see, Robert Wringhim's Private Memoirs and Confessions are likewise questioned by the telling of an oral story. However, Robert (like the Editor) begins his narrative confident that he knows the meaning of the story he is about to tell. The opening words of his Private Memoirs are as follows:

My life has been a life of trouble and turmoil; of change and vicissitude; of anger and exultation; of sorrow and of vengeance. My sorrows have all been for a slighted gospel, and my vengeance has been wreaked on its adversaries. Therefore, in the might of heaven I will sit down and write. (p. 67)

Robert presents himself as God's champion, a heroic figure whose task is to kill God's enemies, 'the wicked of this world' (p. 67). There is, perhaps, more than a hint in this of the killing of Claverhouse at the end of *Ringan Gilhaize*—a point which seems to be supported by the fact that, in the dialogue of the Editor's Narrative, the Wringhims are referred to as 'the Ringans, or some sic name' (p. 47). Writing of *Ringan Gilhaize*, John MacQueen remarks on

the "purification" which was central to the Protestant Reformation in its more extreme forms. A significant phrase which occurs almost at the end of the book, is "The godly people of Edinburgh … rose, as it were with one accord … and purified the chapel, even to desolation" (III. xxviii)—that is, they reduced it to ruins. Gilhaize purifies his life in an almost identical way.[51]

In Hogg's novel, Robert's desire to cleanse the world by killing God's enemies exhibits this urge for 'purification' in a particularly extreme form.

Worries about Robert's project are confirmed towards the end of his Private Memoirs when his servant Samuel Scrape tells him what 'the auld wives o' the clachan' have been saying:

"Oo, I trow it's a' stuff;—folk shouldna heed what's said by auld crazy kimmers. But there are some o' them weel kend for witches too; an' they say—lord have a care o' us!—they say the deil's often seen gaun sidie for sidie w'ye, whiles in ae shape, an' whiles in another. An' they say that he whiles takes your ain shape, or else enters into you, and then you turn a deil yoursel." (p. 135)

Samuel goes on to repeat an oral story told by Lucky Shaw, one of the auld wives, about the tricks of the Devil among the pious people of Auchtermuchty.

Gin it hadna been an auld carl, Robin Ruthven, Auchtermuchty wad at that time hae been ruined and lost for ever. But Robin was a cunning man, an' had rather mae wits than his ain, for he had been in the hands o' the fairies when he was young, an' a' kinds o' spirits were visible to his een, an' their language as familiar to him as his ain mother tongue. (p. 137)

Robin is the only person able to recognise the Devil in the great preacher who delights the town, and Auchtermuchty is saved when Robin lifts the preacher's gown, thus revealing 'a pair o' cloven feet' for all to see (p. 139). Samuel concludes his re-telling of Lucky Shaw's story as follows:

> " 'Now, this is a true story, my man,' quo the auld wife; 'an' whenever you are doubtfu' of a man, take auld Robin Ruthven's plan, an' look for the cloven foot, for it's a thing that winna weel hide; an' it appears whiles where ane wadna think o't. It will keek out frae aneath the parson's gown, the lawyer's wig, and the Cameronian's blue bannet; but still there is a gouden rule whereby to detect it, an' that never, never fails.' (p. 140)

The 'gouden rule' is the famous Golden Rule of Christ's Sermon on the Mount:

> Therefore all things whatsoever ye would that men should do to you, do ye even so to them: for this is the law and the prophets. (Matthew 7. 12)

Robert is deeply disturbed by Samuel's comments:

> I then went to try my works by the Saviour's golden rule, as my servant had put it into my head to do; and, behold, not one of them would stand the test. I had shed blood on a ground on which I could not admit that any man had a right to shed mine; and I began to doubt the motives of my adviser once more, not that they were intentionally bad, but that his was some great mind led astray by enthusiasm, or some overpowering passion. (p. 140)

Lucky Shaw's oral tale makes it abundantly clear that Robert's Private Memoirs and Confessions do not (as he hopes) tell the story of a purification of the world through the slaughter of the wicked. Instead, the oral tale suggests that Robert's 'adviser' Gil-Martin is the Devil, and that Robert himself is a deluded fool, ensnared and entrapped by dangerous and evil forces that he can neither understand nor control. Obviously, Robert's murderous career does not make him an ideal advert for the Presbyterian tra-dition of the Covenanters. Nevertheless, it is difficult to avoid feeling sympathy with this incompetent and lonely killer as his Private Memoirs and Confessions show his devious 'adviser' sardonically ushering him towards the gaping mouth of Hell.

As we have seen, Old Mortality's publication at the end of 1816 had provoked a strongly hostile reaction from Scottish Presbyterian opinion. In the Justified Sinner, the Editor makes what appears to be a veiled reference to this controversy over Old Mortal-ity, when he introduces Robert's Private Memoirs and Confessions with these words: 'We have heard much of the rage of fanaticism in former days, but nothing to this' (p. 64). There seems to be a suggestion here that Hogg's novel presents an example of 'the rage of fanaticism in former days' even more appalling than anything to be found in *Old Mortality*; and indeed it is hard to imagine anything much more extreme than Robert's story, which involves a progression from murder to fratricide and matricide.

This does not mean, however, that Hogg's project is to show that the Covenanters were even worse than *Old Mortality* suggests. The embedded oral tales hint at another possibility: that Hogg's project may in fact be to outflank Scott's disdainful hostility towards Covenanting fanaticism by demonstrating that the Editor's Scott-like account of Robert is inadequate. We may be dealing with as bad a case of deranged Covenanting fanaticism as can easily be imagined; but if the reader comes to some kind of sympathetic understanding of Robert's plight—if the reader is moved to say 'there but for the grace of God go I'—then Scott's disdainful hostility has been shown to be an inadequate response to 'the rage of fanaticism in former days'. Likewise, Hogg's novel remains sympathetic to the egalitarian tradition of the Covenanters even as it responds to *Ringan Gilhaize* by articulating powerful reservations about purification by murder.

In the *Justified Sinner* the two main narrators seem to be very different: that urbane and rational man of the Enlightenment, the Editor, lives by a set of assumptions far removed from those of Robert. Likewise, their respective attempts to tell Robert's story are far from identical. Nevertheless the two narrators and their two narratives have more in common than appears to be the case at first. The Editor and Robert both begin their narratives convinced that they have a firm hold of the truth—and yet by the end of the book the certainty of both has been severely shaken. Likewise, both see themselves as part of an elite: while Robert sees himself as one of the Elect, the Editor sees himself as one of the Enlightened. Early in his narrative Robert records that, on being made aware that he is 'a justified person, adopted among the number of God's children', he feels himself to be 'as an eagle among the children of men, soaring on high, and looking down with pity and contempt on the grovelling creatures below' (pp. 79–80). The Editor is not so very different. In *his* narrative he describes how young George Colwan, climbing a hill early in the morning, sees 'a bright halo in the cloud of haze'. Ever a man of the Enlightenment, the Editor provides a rational explanation of 'the lovely vision':

> [George] soon perceived the cause of the phenomenon, and that it proceeded from the rays of the sun from a pure unclouded morning sky striking upon this dense vapour which refracted them. But the better the works of nature are understood, the more they will be ever admired. That was a scene that would have entranced the man of science with delight, but which the uninitiated and sordid man would have regarded less than the mole rearing up his hill in silence and in darkness. (p. 29)

As he responds to *Old Mortality* and to *Ringan Gilhaize*, Hogg rejects the elitism of the Enlightened and the elitism of the Elect, and asserts the potential worth and value of 'the uninitiated and sordid man' and of 'the grovelling creatures below'. His deeply egalitarian novel sees value (as well as blind spots) in the urbane Editor, and it evokes a deep sympathy with the plight of the doomed and deluded murderer, Robert. But it also suggests that neither the Enlightened nor the Elect have a monopoly of wisdom, and it powerfully asserts that attention must be paid to the story of the prostitute Bell Calvert and to the story told by the servant Samuel Scrape. Indeed, the most morally impressive character in the *Justified Sinner* is a 'poor hind'. This farm servant is another Mr Bryden of Crosslee. His actions can comfortably sustain the scrutiny of Christ's Golden Rule as his 'humble cot' provides an outcast and haunted Robert with desperately-needed sanctuary and succour (p. 162).

In the strongly class-conscious Britain of the late 1810s and the early 1820s, the assertive egalitarianism of *The Brownie of Bodsbeck* and *The Private Memoirs and Confessions of a Justified Sinner* did not help these remarkable novels to find a wide audience. *Ringan Gilhaize* and *The Entail* were Galt's most ambitious novels, but their assertive defence of the subaltern Presbyterian tradition likewise proved less attractive to the British reading public of the time than Scott's nuanced and lively defence of the political status quo in *Old Mortality* and *Rob Roy*. All these technically-innovative novels were first published during the ten years that followed the Battle of Waterloo, and their eloquent and deeply-engaged debates about the Covenanters and about 'the sugar and tobacco-trade' provide a remarkable insight into the elite / subaltern tensions that existed in a Scotland that was soon to take a prominent, profitable, and troubling role in the Victorian high noon of the British Empire.

Notes

1   For a valuable discussion of this topic see '"First Principles in Religion and Politics": Discourses of Radicalism in Late Eighteenth-Century Scotland', the first chapter of Liam McIlvanney, *Burns the Radical: Poetry and Politics in Late Eighteenth-Century Scotland* (East Linton: Tuckwell Press, 2002), pp. 15–37.

2   T. M. Devine, *Scotland's Empire 1600–1815* (London: Allen Lane, 2003), p. 73.

3   Devine, *Scotland's Empire*, p. 75.

4   See Devine, *Scotland's Empire*, pp. 221–49.

5   See Burns's letter to Dr John Moore of 2 August 1787, J. De Lancey Ferguson, *The Letters of Robert Burns*, 2nd edn, rev. by G. Ross Roy, 2 vols (Oxford: Clarendon Press, 1985), I, 133–46 (p. 144); and Devine, *Scotland's Empire*, pp. 230, 244. For a discussion of Burns's complex situation at this period, see David Daiches, *Robert Burns* (London: Bell, 1952), pp. 89–104.

6   McIlvanney, *Burns the Radical*, p. 7.

7   See *The Poems and Songs of Robert Burns*, ed. by James Kinsley, 3 vols (Oxford: Clarendon Press, 1968), I, 326 (Kinsley 147B).

8   *Minstrelsy of the Scottish Border*, 2 vols (Kelso: James Ballantyne for Cadell and Davies,

London, 1802), I, cix–cx. A third volume was added to the second edition (Edinburgh: James Ballantyne for Longman and Rees, London, 1803).

9   Walter Scott, *The Lay of the Last Minstrel* (London: Longman; Edinburgh: Constable, 1805), p. 7.

10 See *The Collected Letters of James Hogg*, ed. by Gillian Hughes, The Stirling / South Carolina Research Edition of the Collected Works of James Hogg (Edinburgh: Edinburgh University Press, 2004–   ), I, 1800–1819 (2004), p. 136.

11 See Hogg, *Winter Evening Tales*, ed. by Ian Duncan, The Stirling / South Carolina Research Edition of the Collected Works of James Hogg (Edinburgh: Edinburgh University Press, 2002: paperback reprint 2004), p. xiv.

12 Hogg, *Collected Letters*, ed. Hughes, I, 151. Like many letters written to Hogg at this unsettled period of his life, Scott's letter does not seem to have survived.

13 Hogg, *Collected Letters*, ed. Hughes, I, 145.

14 See Hogg, *Winter Evening Tales*, ed. Ian Duncan, p. xvi.

15 'See *Memoir*, p. 45, where Hogg says that both the substitutions were newly written' [Ian Duncan's footnote: for *Memoir*, see James Hogg, *Memoir of the Author's Life* and *Familiar Anecdotes of Sir Walter Scott*, ed. by Douglas S. Mack (Edinburgh: Scottish Academic Press, 1972)].

16 To E. [Eliza Izet], 14 December 1817, in the James Hogg Collection, Beinecke Rare Book and Manuscript Library, Yale University: General MSS 61, Box 1, Folder 38 [Ian Duncan's footnote].

17 'Letter dated 13 January 1818, in NLS MS 4003, fol. 86' [Ian Duncan's footnote]. The passage by Ian Duncan quoted here can be found in *Winter Evening Tales*, ed. Duncan, pp. xvi–xvii.

18 *Winter Evening Tales*, ed. Duncan, p. 259. Subsequent page references are to this edition, and are given in the text.

19 Hogg, *Collected Letters*, ed. Hughes, I, 145.

20 See *Winter Evening Tales*, ed. Duncan, p. xxiii.

21 *Winter Evening Tales*, ed. Duncan, p. xx.

22 Hogg, *The Brownie of Bodsbeck*, ed. by Douglas S. Mack (Edinburgh: Scottish Academic Press, 1976), p. 3. Subsequent page references are to this edition, and are given in the text.

23 Cairns Craig, *The Modern Scottish Novel: Narrative and the National Imagination* (Edinburgh: Edinburgh University Press, 1999), p. 97.

24 Craig, *The Modern Scottish Novel*, p. 98.

25 See Hogg, *The Brownie of Bodsbeck*, ed. Mack, p. 65.

26 Hogg, *The Shepherd's Calendar*, ed. by Douglas S. Mack, The Stirling / South Carolina Research Edition of the Collected Works of James Hogg (Edinburgh: Edinburgh University Press, 1995: paperback reprint 2002), pp. 15–16.

27 Hogg, *Anecdotes of Scott*, ed. by Jill Rubenstein, The Stirling / South Carolina Research Edition of the Collected Works of James Hogg (Edinburgh: Edinburgh University Press, 1999: paperback reprint 2004), pp. 50–52.

28 The relevant evidence is discussed in Hogg, *The Brownie of Bodsbeck*, ed. Mack, pp. xvi–xvii. As this discussion shows, the 'original copy' was revised before printing, contrary to what Hogg says in his *Anecdotes of Scott*. Nevertheless, the evidence does seem to confirm that a substantial section of the novel existed in manuscript 'lang afore' *Old Mortality* was 'heard of '.

29 T. M. Devine, *The Scottish Nation 1700–2000* (London: Allen Lane, 1999), pp. 226–27.

30 For a discussion of McCrie's attack on *Old Mortality* see John Sutherland, *The Life of Walter Scott: A Critical Biography* (Oxford: Blackwell, 1995), p. 220.

31 For a detailed account of the original plans for *Tales of my Landlord*, see Scott, *The Black Dwarf*, ed. by P. D. Garside, The Edinburgh Edition of the Waverley Novels (Edinburgh: Edinburgh University Press, 1993), pp. 125, 128–30.

32 For 'Jedidiah' as an equivalent of 'Solomon', see II Samuel 12. 24–25.

33 See Sutherland, *The Life of Walter Scott*, pp. 100–02.

34 See Scott, *The Tale of Old Mortality*, ed. by Douglas S. Mack, The Edinburgh Edition of the Waverley Novels (Edinburgh: Edinburgh University Press, 1993), p. 13. Subsequent page references are to this edition, and are given in the text.

35 Scott, *The Visionary*, ed. by Peter Garside, Regency Reprints, 1 (Cardiff: University College Cardiff Press, 1984), p. vii.

36 *The Visionary*, ed. Garside, p. 33.

37 *The Visionary*, ed. Garside, p. viii.

38 See Michael Lynch, *Scotland: A New History* (London: Pimlico, 1992), p. 309.

39 This incident is discussed in David Stevenson, *The Covenanters: The National Covenant and Scotland* (Edinburgh: Saltire Society, 1988), pp. 76–77.

40 John MacQueen, *The Rise of the Historical Novel* (Edinburgh: Scottish Academic Press, 1989), p. 110.

41 McIlvanney, *Burns the Radical*, p. 18.

42 See Ian A. Gordon, *John Galt: The Life of a Writer* (Edinburgh: Oliver & Boyd, 1972), pp. 85–89.

43 John Galt, *The Literary Life and Miscellanies*, 3 vols (Edinburgh: Blackwood; London: Cadell, 1834), I, 254.

44 John Galt, *Ringan Gilhaize; or, The Covenanters*, ed. by Patricia J. Wilson, Canongate Classics, 64 (Edinburgh: Canongate, 1995), p. 450. Subsequent page references are to this edition, and are given in the text.

45 McIlvanney, *Burns the Radical*, p. 18.

46 Galt discusses his narrative strategy in *Ringan Gilhaize* in *The Autobiography of John Galt*, 2 vols (London: Cochrane and M'Crone, 1833), I, 220–21.

47 John Galt, *The Entail; or, The Lairds of Grippy*, ed. by Ian A. Gordon, World's Classics (Oxford: Oxford University Press, 1984), p. 3. Subsequent page references are to this edition, and are given in the text.

48 For a discussion of the reception of 'The Cotter's Saturday Night', see Andrew Nash, 'The Cotter's Kailyard', in *Robert Burns and Cultural Authority*, ed. by Robert Crawford (Edinburgh: Edinburgh University Press, 1997), pp. 180–97.

49 Gordon, *John Galt*, p. 57; see also pp. 62–63.

50 See Susan Manning's review of the Stirling / South Carolina edition of Hogg's *The Spy*, ed. by Gillian Hughes (Edinburgh: Edinburgh University Press, 2000), in *Studies in Hogg and his World*, 11 (2000), 134–37 (p. 135).

51 MacQueen, *The Rise of the Historical Novel*, p. 136. The quotation MacQueen gives from Volume III Chapter 28 of *Ringan Gilhaize* appears on p. 424 of Patricia J. Wilson's Canongate Classics edition of the novel (1995).

SIX

South Africa and the South Seas:
Scottish Fiction and the Zenith of Empire

The Disruption and the Imperial Mission

'Dr Livingstone, I presume?'

David Livingstone (1813–73) was a truly extraordinary product of the deeply-rooted and egalitarian Presbyterian tradition of subaltern Scotland. This Victorian explorer, missionary, and hero of the British Empire was a native of Blantyre, a village situated on the Clyde a few miles upstream from Glasgow. As it happens, in *The Entail* Galt places the ancestral territory of the Walkinshaws in the vicinity of this village: for example, we have seen that the novel's narrator becomes involved in Walter's wedding festivities when 'walking alone towards Blantyre' (p. 99). It may be that, in deciding on the location of the Walkinshaw lands, Galt was mindful of the fact that Blantyre lies on the opposite bank of the river from the neighbouring village of Bothwell, and is thus not far from the site of that defining moment in the history of the Covenanters, the Battle of Bothwell Bridge—the historical event around which the narrative of *Old Mortality* centres. At all events, when David Livingstone was born in Blantyre in 1813 he came into a west of Scotland world whose past was soon to be depicted and debated in *Old Mortality* (1816), *Rob Roy* (1818), *The Entail* (1822), *Ringan Gilhaize* (1823), and *The Private Memoirs and Confessions of a Justified Sinner* (1824). Crucially, the values Livingstone inherited from his deeply religious parents were much closer to the austere, steely, and uncompromising idealism of the Covenanter Ringan Gilhaize than to the more worldly values of the tobacco lords.

The final events of *The Entail* are set towards the end of the Napoleonic Wars, that is to say around the time of Livingstone's birth. By this period the west of Scotland was beginning to feel the effects of the Industrial Revolution, and the young David's childhood was dominated by work in a cotton mill. In the *Oxford Dictionary of National Biography* (*ODNB*), A. D. Roberts records that Livingstone was employed from the age of ten in the cotton mill at Blantyre 'as a "piecer", tying up broken threads on spinning jennies for twelve hours a day'. Nevertheless, 'David and a few other children still had the energy and will-power after work to put in two hours at the village school'.[1] A steely determination to continue his studies enabled Livingstone in due course to obtain the educational qualifications required for employment as a medical missionary, and in December 1840 (by now in his late twenties) he set out for Southern Africa. Most of the rest of his life was spent in Africa, and by the time of his death in 1873 he had experienced various failures (for example in the Zambesi expedition of 1858–64), as well as notable successes. A streak of harsh austerity in his character could combine with tactlessness to mar some of his personal relationships, but nevertheless he continues to command respect as an implacable opponent of the slave trade which in his day still disfigured Africa. His endeavours as missionary and explorer had a commercial aspect, in that he believed that what he called 'legitimate trade' would not only undermine the slave trade, but would also promote the interests of the Christian gospel and the interests of Africans. As A. D. Roberts aptly puts it in the *ODNB* (XXXIV, 81), Livingstone 'became a symbol of what the British—and other Europeans—wished to believe about their motives as they took over tropical Africa in the late nineteenth century'.

Roberts goes on to observe that Livingstone was strikingly free from the racial prejudice prevalent among the British—and other Europeans—of the day, as well as being a committed advocate of what he called 'native agency'. This aspect of the great explorer's personality is confirmed by Hubert F. Wilson (Livingstone's grandson), who writes of having discussed his grandfather with 'an African from Northern Rhodesia', who said that Africans 'liked and trusted' Livingstone

> '[…] because he did not come to the gates of our village stockades demanding admission—he always asked if he might enter and then he sat down among us and talked to us as if he was one of ourselves.'[2]

Behaviour of this kind can be seen as a natural enough outcome of the egalitarian assumptions of Scottish Presbyterianism. However, Livingstone's advocacy of giving responsibility to Africans did not make much headway within the power-structures of the British Empire, and he does not seem to have allowed himself to become fully aware of the extent to which the Imperial project was driven by a love of money worthy of the tobacco lords, as opposed to an altruistic concern for the advancement of 'native' people.

Neil Livingstone, David's father, brought his children up in the Church of Scotland. However, in 1832 both Neil and David left the Church of Scotland to become members of the Congregational Church, a denomination in which the power of decision-making lies entirely with the members of each local congregation. The decision of the Livingstones to become Congregationalists can be seen as a manifestation of a widespread subaltern dissatisfaction with aspects of the functioning of the national Church. This dissatisfaction had rumbled on through much of the eighteenth century, and it came to a head in the Disruption of 1843, when over a third of the clergy gave up their secure Church of Scotland manses and their endowed stipends, and joined with almost half of the Kirk's laity in setting up, from scratch, the Free Church of Scotland.[3]

The dispute that led to the Disruption was at root about the same question that had caused dissension between Covenanters and royalists in the seventeenth century: with whom did power ultimately lie in the affairs of the church? In the eighteenth and nineteenth centuries, the immediate focus for this question was over 'patronage'. During the seventeenth century, the right to appoint a clergyman to a particular parish had been claimed (with the support of the Crown) by local nobles and lairds, as 'patrons'. However, patronage was vigorously opposed by the Covenanters, who believed that each congregation had the right to appoint its own minister. In 1690, after the 'Glorious Revolution', the Scottish Parliament abolished patronage in what was now a firmly Presbyterian Church of Scotland, and this arrangement was confirmed when the Treaty of Union of 1707 provided guarantees that the current religious settlement in Scotland would be preserved. However, in 1712 the new British Parliament restored lay patronage within the Church of Scotland, in spite of the Church's vigorously-expressed objections.

As the eighteenth century advanced, the patronage question provoked increasing tensions as the civil authorities imposed implementation of the legal rights of patrons. This was seen by many as a violation of the fundamental rights of a free people, and as an insult to the memory of the Covenanters. Feelings ran high, and, as Stewart. J. Brown records in his article on the Disruption in *The Oxford Companion to Scottish History*, 'from the 1730s onwards, parishioners often rioted against the settlement of patrons' candidates, with confrontations between troops and parishioners resulting in injuries and deaths'.[4] There were major secessions from the Church of Scotland over the patronage issue in 1733 (to form the Secession Church) and in 1752 (to form the Relief Church), and by 1766 adherents of the Secession and Relief churches represented nearly 10 per cent of Scotland's population.

Meantime, two parties had developed within the Church of Scotland: the Moderates, who tended to identify with the gentry, and who were broadly in sympathy with the ideas of the Scottish Enlightenment; and the Evangelicals, who tended to identify with the people, and who regarded themselves as the guardians of the traditions of the Covenanters. The major secessions of 1733 and 1752 weakened the Evangelical party within the Church of Scotland itself, and Moderate dominance increased in the

1790s as members of the elite exerted themselves to counter the threat to their interests posed by the French Revolution. However, after the end of the Napoleonic Wars a revived Evangelical party emerged within the Church of Scotland, and became particularly active among the industrial working classes. From the mid-1820s the Evangelicals began to press once again for the abolition of patronage, but the legal rights of patrons were upheld by the civil courts. Intense conflict over this matter led directly to the Disruption of 1843 and to the establishment of the Free Church of Scotland.

The Church of Scotland and the majority of the Free Church came together again in the Union of 1929, but the Disruption was a defining moment for Victorian Scotland. Starting without buildings and without funds, the Free Church had to overcome many problems. In rural areas its adherents often faced persecution from landowners who regarded it as a threat to the traditional social order. Likewise, the Free Church was often refused permission to erect places of worship on land owned by lairds. But it refused to be intimidated. The historian T. M. Devine writes:

> The greatest single collective act of defiance of landlordism was probably the emergence of the Free Church in 1843, which drew many communities in the western Highlands and Islands from the established Church of Scotland. [...] The Disruption of 1843 was not an overtly political movement in the Highlands; it was about Christian belief rather than an explicit attack on landlordism. Nevertheless, the sheer size of the exodus from the Established Church in the teeth of landlord opposition was deeply significant.[5]

Showing a determination and commitment worthy of the Covenanters, the Free Church quickly established itself in Highlands and Lowlands alike as a vibrant national institution. Sometimes in danger of being narrowly puritanical and excessively austere, it was nevertheless prodigal in the selfless expenditure of money and energy, and during the second half of the nineteenth century it was vigorously active in mission work at home (not least among the slums of the industrial working class) and abroad (not least in Africa). It also became a rich source of political support for Gladstone's Liberal party. A popular rhyme of the time compared it tellingly with its rival, the established Church of Scotland:

> The wee kirk, the free kirk
> The kirk without the steeple;
> The auld kirk, the cauld kirk
> The kirk without the people.

Deeply-felt idealistic commitment produced the Disruption and created the Free Kirk. A similar commitment likewise helped to propel David Livingstone to Africa, and we shall see that this kind of idealism also played a part in shaping the complex attitudes to Empire of two writers who grew up in families dominated by the ethos of the Presbyterianism of Victorian Scotland. The writers in question were Robert Louis Stevenson and John Buchan.

Robert Louis Stevenson and the Auld Kirk

In the Victorian era the established Church of Scotland was weakened, not only by the Disruption, by also by the allegiance of many Scottish aristocrats and landowners to the Scottish Episcopal Church. Being strongly Jacobite in sympathy, the Scottish Episcopal Church had been subject to penal laws for much of the eighteenth century, but these laws were relaxed after the death of Prince Charles Edward ('the Young Pretender') in 1788. Thereafter the Episcopal Church strengthened its links with the Church of England, and as a result came to be the church of choice for a Scottish aristocracy that was in the process of becoming integrated into a unified and culturally Anglican British aristocracy. In the second half of the nineteenth century, the Church of Scotland had to compete with an Episcopal Church bolstered by aristocratic support and energised by the Oxford Movement, and it also had to contend with the idealistic vigour of the recently-formed Free Kirk. However, the Auld Kirk did not by any means wither away. For example, it retained the active allegiance of many members of Scotland's professional elite—and it was into a family of devout Auld Kirk professionals that Robert Louis Stevenson was born in 1850.

On his father's side, Stevenson was the great-grandson of Alan Stevenson (1752–74), a West India merchant who died of fever in St Kitts. Alan's only child was Robert Stevenson (1772–1850), who became a distinguished civil engineer and the celebrated builder of the Bell Rock lighthouse. Robert's son Thomas (1818–87, the father of Robert Louis) was, like his father, a distinguished civil engineer and lighthouse builder; and Thomas, like his father before him, was a devoted member of the Church of Scotland.[6] Furthermore, Robert Louis Stevenson's mother Margaret (1829–97) was the daughter of Lewis Balfour (a Church of Scotland minister), while her maternal grandfather was James Balfour of Pilrig (Professor of Moral Philosophy at Edinburgh University, and a philosophical opponent of the scepticism of David Hume). Stevenson was thus born into a solidly Auld Kirk family which operated at the heart of the North British professional elite, while having a connection with minor landowners through the lairds of Pilrig.

Being successful Scottish engineers, the Stevensons belonged to a section of the North British elite that was not particularly close to the really significant levers of Imperial power. Equally, this somewhat stern and austere Auld Kirk Presbyterian family did not by any means share all the prevailing attitudes and cultural assumptions of the elite of South Britain. It is likewise worth remembering that Robert Louis Stevenson's

Auld Kirk childhood was enlivened by a more popular form of Presbyterian piety. This was encountered by way of his devoted nurse 'Cummy' (Alison Cunningham), from whom he heard many stories of the heroism and sufferings of the Covenanters. Indeed, Stevenson's first published work, *The Pentland Rising* (1866), is a sympathetic account of one of the Covenanters' most important attempts to assert the rights of the people by force of arms. Unquestionably, a Bohemian streak in Robert Louis Stevenson's character produced a reaction against the austerity of his Auld Kirk up-bringing, and generated painful conflicts with his father. Nevertheless, the legacy of the Covenanters and of Presbyterian contractarian theory worked alongside Bohemian rebelliousness in the shaping of a man who turned out to be entirely ready in his final years to question aspects of the operation of Imperial power.

Earlier in the nineteenth century, Walter Scott (the son of a Presbyterian lawyer) had grown up, like Stevenson, within the Church of Scotland and within the North British professional elite. In later life, however, an empathy with aristocracy led Scott to friendship with the Duke of Buccleuch, to the building up of his own landed estate at Abbotsford, and to an inclination towards Episcopal rather than Presbyterian forms of worship. Like Scott, Stevenson did not become in adult life an actively committed member of the Church of Scotland. Unlike Scott, however, Stevenson did not drift towards Episcopalianism. Rather, as a man fully in tune with the intellectual currents of the later nineteenth century (such as Darwinism), he no doubt felt the force of the pressures towards loss of faith articulated, for example, in Matthew Arnold's 'Dover Beach'. Nevertheless, and in spite of his Bohemian streak, there is a sense in which Stevenson always remained culturally a Presbyterian, a man on whom an indelible mark had been left by Cummy's tales of the heroic sufferings endured by Covenanters as they resisted an evil royalist regime. Some of the assumptions that lie behind *Dr Jekyll and Mr Hyde* (1886) have to do with Darwinian and pre-Freudian ideas about the ape within humanity, about the subconscious, and about the Id; but Stevenson's famous novella is also haunted by Cummy's ancestral Calvinist visions of the ways in which a malignant evil seeks, in a Fallen world, to overcome what is still good and what is still virtuous in Fallen human nature.

An Auld Kirk *Waverley*

> Then Samuel took the horn of oil and anointed him in the midst of his brethren: and the Spirit of the LORD came upon David from that day forward.   (1 Samuel 16. 13)

As Barry Menikoff has demonstrated in exact detail, Stevenson's active and scholarly interest in Scottish history bore fruit in his two 'David Balfour' novels.[7] The first of these, *Kidnapped*, was published in 1886, while that novel's sequel *Catriona* (published in America under its author's original and preferred title *David Balfour*) appeared in 1893, having been written in the South Seas after Stevenson moved there in the late 1880s. For Scots of Stevenson's generation, Sir Walter Scott remained the revered and definitive interpreter of the nation's past, and the two David Balfour novels, taken together, can be seen as Stevenson's re-working and re-focusing of the *Waverley* narrative pattern. In the Balfour books, as in *Waverley*, a Hanoverian outsider (in this case David Balfour) finds himself in the exotic, dangerous, but potentially liberating territory of the Scottish Highlands. Once there, he has a life-changing encounter with the flawed heroism of the outmoded forces of Jacobitism, before marrying a Jacobite bride with whom he settles down to enjoy a life of genteel domesticity in a prosperous and modern Hanoverian world.

However, Stevenson's version of this basic story differs significantly and interestingly from Scott's. In *Waverley* the main concern is with events of 1745–46, as Scott sets out to defend the political status quo of Hanoverian Britain by focusing on the nature of the Jacobite rising and the reasons for its failure. Stevenson, on the other hand, sets the main events of his narrative in the early 1750s, and this allows him to focus on the situation of quasi-Imperial conquest that existed in the Highlands after the Hanoverian victory at Culloden in 1746.

Stevenson's first-person narrator is David Balfour, who finds himself in the Highlands in 1751 after being kidnapped on the orders of his uncle, who has cheated him of his rightful inheritance. Only the chance of being shipwrecked off the Isle of Mull saves David from a future devoted to 'slaving alongside of negroes in the tobacco fields' of the Carolinas. As he travels on foot through the Highlands after the shipwreck, he encounters a dispossessed and conquered society. On the small ferry on which he eventually leaves Mull, he is puzzled to see a large ship:

> not only her decks, but the sea-beach also, were quite black with people, and skiffs were continually plying to and fro between them. Yet nearer, and there began to come to our ears a great sound of mourning, the people on board and those on shore crying and lamenting to one another so as to pierce the heart.
>
> Then I understood this was an emigrant ship bound for the American colonies.[8]

It is worth remembering that, in these middle years of the eighteenth century (the period leading up to the American Revolution), British North America's voracious need for labour was met not only by the kidnapping and importation of Africans as slaves, but also by an 'indenture' system under which (as T. M. Devine puts it) European

> men and women at the bottom of the social ladder [...] virtually sold themselves to ships' captains in return for passage and were in turn auctioned in the colonies to the highest bidder. Jacobite prisoners, prostitutes and vagrants also came into this category. They were bound by law to do their master's bidding for the period of the

indenture, could be sold against their wishes, forced to remain unmarried during their contract and required to remain within a specified area of their master's home.[9]

Many of the Scots who arrived in Britain's American colonies at this period did so under the indenture system.

It is likewise worth remembering that the period of unrest and conflict in the Highlands known as 'the Crofters' War' was at its height around the time that *Kidnapped* was being written and published. As we saw in Chapter 1, Edward Said asserts in *Culture and Imperialism* that 'the main battle in imperialism is over land'. During the 1880s and 1890s this battle was in progress in many parts of the world: Joseph Conrad encountered aspects of it as he journeyed up the Congo in 1890, and 1890 also saw a cruelly decisive setback for the Native American cause at the massacre at Wounded Knee. Land rights were likewise fiercely contested in Highland Scotland during the Crofters' War. As T. M. Devine puts it in *The Scottish Nation 1700–2000*, 'the people did eventually mount a successful challenge to landlordism in the 1880s', in spite of the ever-present fear of eviction.[10]

The protest began in 1882 in the district of Skye known as Braes, when a petition for the restoration of traditional grazing rights led to a violent confrontation with police that is now remembered as the 'Battle of the Braes'. More widespread acts of resistance to landlords followed, and the support of the Highland Land Law Association (a body analogous to the Irish Land League) helped to secure the passage of the Crofters Holdings (Scotland) Act, which enhanced the position of the crofters in many ways, not least by guaranteeing their security of tenure. T. M. Devine records that by 1886 (the year of publication of *Kidnapped*), 'the balance of power between landlords and small tenants had been irrevocably altered'.[11] According to Derick Thomson, the songs of Màiri Mhór nan Oran (Mary Macpherson, 1821–1898)

> contributed significantly to the victory of the popular land-law reform candidates in the Highlands in 1885 and 1886, and she was indeed the bard of that movement. Her song *"Brosnachadh nan Gaidheal"* ("Incitement of the Gaels") was composed for the 1885 elections. Her *"Oran Beinn-Li"* ("Song of Ben Lee") recalls the Skye land-reform fighters in glowing terms, and it is clear that she took an independent and fearless stand on this issue.[12]

The Crofters' War is one of the relevant contexts for Stevenson's depiction of the Highlands in *Kidnapped*. Writing of his experiences of Highlanders while still on Mull, David Balfour comments:

> I met plenty of people, grubbing in little miserable fields that would not keep a cat, or herding little kine about the bigness of asses. The Highland dress being forbidden by

law since the rebellion, and the people condemned to the Lowland habit, which they much disliked, it was strange to see the variety of their array. Some went bare, only for a hanging cloak or great-coat, and carried their trousers on their backs like a useless burthen; some had made an imitation of the tartan with little parti-coloured stripes patched together like an old wife's quilt; others, again, still wore the Highland philabeg, but by putting a few stitches between the legs, transformed it into a pair of trousers like a Dutchman's. All those makeshifts were condemned and punished, for the law was harshly applied, in hopes to break up the clan spirit; but in that out-the-way, sea-bound isle, there were few to make remarks and fewer to tell tales. (pp. 92–93)

As Barry Menikoff has shown, Stevenson follows his historical sources very closely in this and in similar passages which depict the condition of the recently-conquered Highlands in the early 1750s.[13]

Stevenson's discussion of the post-Culloden law against the wearing of Highland dress serves as a reminder that an urge to make conquered peoples wear proper clothes seems to have been characteristic of European imperial expansion. As we saw in Chapter 1, feisty opposition to the post-Culloden laws against the Highland dress finds lively expression in the Gaelic poetry of the time.[14] However, to repeat Fiona Stafford's words (quoted in Chapter 4), the years following Culloden were a period of 'systematic cultural destruction' in the Highlands, as the victorious British state sought to impose its own cultural traditions, language, and values on a defeated native population. In the century and a half after Culloden such experiences were to be the lot of many peoples in many parts of the world, as the great European Empires expanded. Among European intellectuals a sense of unease about these matters was beginning to emerge as the nineteenth century approached its end—and it may be that this played a part in Stevenson's decision to set his reworking of the *Waverley* story in the early 1750s, rather than in 1745–46.

We shall go on to explore the ways in which the David Balfour books challenge some aspects of the post-Union British state. Nevertheless, these books continue to share some of the assumptions that underpin Scott's pioneering pro-Union and pro-British novel. For example, the gallant Jacobite loyalty of Evan Dhu, depicted so memorably in *Waverley*, finds various echoes in Stevenson's Balfour books, not least in the personality of David's friend Allan Breck Stewart. Likewise, Stevenson follows Scott in taking it for granted that Jacobite Highlanders (despite the admirable qualities that some of them sometimes display) are products of an atavistic and backward society. For example, the Inveraray scenes of *Catriona* vividly support the view that even apparently civilised Highlanders are disturbingly close to being savages. However, the Inveraray scenes in this complex novel also point to a crucial difference between Stevenson and Scott, in that these scenes present a powerful case for supposing that there was something rotten at the core of the modern Hanoverian Britain celebrated in *Waverley.*

What, then, happens at Inveraray in *Catriona?* In Stevenson's novel, David Balfour is determined to give evidence in favour of James Stewart (known as James of the Glens), a Highland Jacobite falsely accused of the murder of Colin Campbell, 'the King's agent', who is known as the Red Fox (p. 103). The clan Campbell was consistently loyal to the Hanoverian cause, and Stevenson's novel reflects historical events when the Red Fox is assassinated while on his way to implement government policy by forcibly evicting tenants in the Jacobite territory of Appin. Stevenson's novel again accurately reflects the historical record when it indicates that the cards are stacked against James of the Glens because his trial takes place at Inveraray, the main town of the Campbells, with no less a person than the Duke of Argyll, chief of the clan Campbell, presiding on the bench.

In short, the government was determined to secure a conviction, and Stevenson's novel shows David being kidnapped by agents of the government, in order to silence his evidence by keeping him away from Inveraray. However, with great perseverance, fortitude, and ingenuity, David contrives to get to Inveraray before the end of the trial. On his arrival there, James Stewart's lawyer (another Stewart) rejoices vehemently: 'The oak shall go over the myrtle yet; we'll ding the Campbells yet in their own town. Praise God that I should see the day!' (p. 346). The oak is the clan badge of the Stewarts, and the myrtle is the clan badge of the Campbells.[15] Reflecting on these things, and on his ultimate failure to save James, David remarks:

> it was forced home upon my mind how this, that had the externals of a sober process of law, was in its essence a clan battle between savage clans. I thought my friend the Writer [i.e., Stewart the Lawyer] none of the least savage. Who, that had only seen him at a counsel's back before the Lord Ordinary or following a golf ball and laying down his clubs on Bruntsfield links, could have recognised for the same person this voluble and violent clansman? (p. 346)

The apparently civilised lawyer turns out to be a Highlander who is atavistic and flawed. Seen from one perspective, he thus has much in common with *Waverley*'s clan chief, Fergus MacIvor. A complementary late-Victorian perspective is also possible, however. *Kidnapped* was published in 1886, *Catriona* in 1893. In Kipling's story 'On the City Wall' (1888), Wali Dad is an apparently Europeanised 'young Mohammedan' who is 'suffering acutely from education of the English variety'. However, Wali Dad is presented as reverting to savagery during a night of communal violence in Lahore:

> His nostrils were distended, his eyes were fixed, and he was smiting himself softly on the breast. The crowd poured by with renewed riot—a gang of Mussulmans hard

pressed by some hundred Hindu fanatics. Wali Dad left my side with an oath, and shouting: 'Ya Hasan! Ya Hussain!' plunged into the thick of the fight, where I lost sight of him.[16]

'On the City Wall' and Stevenson's David Balfour books take it for granted that a conquered native people remains close to savagery. To that extent, Stevenson remains trapped in the assumptions of his period. However, as we shall see, he is much more willing than Kipling to challenge the operations of the British Imperial state.

In 'On the City Wall', Kipling describes what was often called 'the white man's burden', as he asserts that the Imperial 'Supreme Government' operates benevolently in the interest of the people of India:

Year by year England sends out fresh drafts for the first fighting-line, which is officially called the Indian Civil Service. These die, or kill themselves by overwork, or are worried to death, or broken in health and hope in order that the land may be protected from death and sickness, famine and war, and may eventually become capable of standing alone. It will never stand alone, but the idea is a pretty one, and men are willing to die for it, and yearly the work of pushing and coaxing and scolding and petting the country into good living goes forward. If an advance be made all credit is given to the native, while the Englishmen stand back and wipe their foreheads. If a failure occurs the Englishmen step forward and take the blame. (p. 223)

In the David Balfour books, in contrast, it is repeatedly made clear that the British government is exploiting the conquered Highlands in an unprincipled way. Furthermore, corruption is seen to lie at the very heart of the government's activities—a situation embodied by the Lord Advocate Prestongrange, the complex, in some ways decent and kindly, but devious and worldly man who is the mainspring and representative of the post-Culloden British / Hanoverian government in Scotland. Above all, Prestongrange masterminds the trial at Inveraray of James of the Glens, a trial that results in the hanging of an innocent man. Reflecting on this, David comments that James of the Glens

had been hanged by fraud and violence, and the world wagged along, and there was not a pennyweight of difference; and the villains of that horrid plot were decent, kind, respectable fathers of families, who went to kirk and took the sacrament!

But I had had my view of that detestable business they call politics—I had seen it from behind, where it is all bones and blackness; and I was cured for life of any temptations to take part in it again. A plain, quiet, private path was that which I was ambitious to walk in, when I might keep my head out of the way of dangers and my conscience out of the road of temptation. (pp. 382–83)

In writing of the 'bones and blackness' behind the comely facade of the workings of the British state, David is echoing Christ's rebuke to the leaders of Israel: 'Woe unto you, scribes and Pharisees, hypocrites! for ye are like unto whited sepulchres, which indeed appear beautiful outward, but are within full of dead *men's* bones, and of all uncleanness' (Matthew 23. 27). Here, in his clear support for David's line of thought, Stevenson differs not only from Kipling, but also from Scott. In *Waverley*, Scott extracts his central character from the Jacobite rising before Culloden, and thus avoids the need to confront directly the 'bones and blackness' of the post-Culloden atrocities.

Although *Waverley* and the David Balfour books tell fundamentally the same story, important differences of emphasis allow Stevenson to use the story to serve his own distinctive ends. For example, Edward Waverley's political allegiance wavers between the Hanoverian Whigs and the Jacobite Tories before he finally chooses (albeit with an element of real regret), the 'correct' side, the side of the modern Hanoverian and British world, the side seen by Scott as embodying progress and the future. David Balfour, Stevenson's corresponding character, performs a different function in Stevenson's version of the *Waverley* story. David's loyalty to Whig values and principles remains rock-solid throughout, and this allows his integrity to provide an eloquent contrast to the 'bones and blackness' of a Whig regime that is manifestly failing to live up to its own declared principles.

At this point it is important to remember that, in a Scottish context, 'Whig values' suggests 'the values of the Covenanters'. As *The Scottish National Dictionary* (*SND*) points out (under WHIG, *n.*³, *v.*⁴), the word was first used as 'a nickname for an adherent of the National Covenant of 1638 and hence of Presbyterianism', and was later applied to 'the Covenanters of S.W. Scotland who rose in arms in the reigns of Charles II and James [VII and] II'. Continuing, the *SND* points out that *Whig* was adopted in England in the late seventeenth century as the name of the party who 'opposed the succession of James, as being a Roman Catholic'. Hence, after 'the Revolution of 1688', use of the word *Whig*

> was extended to the anti-Jacobite party, the word *Tory* being applied to their opponents, both parties retaining these names until the middle of the 19th c. when *Liberal* was substituted for *Whig* and *Conservative*, except in partisan usage, for *Tory*.

Embodying Whig values and principles as he does, David Balfour can be seen as a representative of the austere Presbyterian principles and values which the older generations of Stevenson's family had inherited from the Covenanters. This is confirmed by the many hints in the Balfour books that David is, as it were, an embodiment of the author's family. The decision to call his central character by his mother's maiden name was clearly a conscious one on Stevenson's part, and the family connection is underlined in *Catriona* when David has occasion to call on the help of his kinsman Balfour of Pilrig. Furthermore, the major traits of the fictional David Balfour's character seem to be modelled on Robert Stevenson, Robert Louis Stevenson's paternal grandfather. In his article on Robert Stevenson in the *ODNB*, Roland Paxton comments (LII, p. 596):

> Prominent points of Stevenson's character noted by his sons were sagacity, fortitude, perseverance, unselfishness, generosity, a high sense of duty, and extensive and unwearied exertions in forwarding the progress of young professional men. He was a member of the Church of Scotland and an elder, first at St Mary's, Edinburgh, from 1828–43 and afterwards at Greenside parish church. He died at his home, 1 Baxter's Place, Edinburgh, on 12 July 1850 and was buried in the new Calton cemetery. An affectionate portrait is given by his grandson [Robert Louis, in *Records of a Family of Engineers* (1912)].

Robert Stevenson's 'high sense of duty', for example, finds an echo in David Balfour's determination to risk his own life in order to give evidence at the trial of James of the Glens. In *Kidnapped* and *Catriona* David finds himself in a series of difficult and morally testing situations. However, throughout his many trials and tribulations he manages to maintain his integrity, exhibiting in the process qualities such as 'sagacity, fortitude, perseverance, unselfishness, generosity', while also displaying a certain austere cack-handedness and an endearingly cumbersome lack of tact. He is, in short, an admirable and worthy embodiment of the Whig values of the Stevenson family, the values reputed to underpin the 'Glorious Revolution' and the Hanoverian post-Union British state.

However, in the David Balfour books the British state falls very far short of living up to the values embodied by David: and David's integrity makes the state's lack of integrity (not least in the judicial murder of James of the Glens) all the more glaringly obvious. Scott and Stevenson both wrote from a position within the North British elite, but in the David Balfour books, Stevenson demonstrated a willingness to investigate some very dark places at the heart of the activities of the 'Supreme Government' of post-Culloden Britain.

Stevenson in the South Seas

A couple of years after the publication of *Kidnapped* in 1886, Stevenson set out from America for the South Seas, and as things turned out he was to remain in the South Seas until his death in 1893. In part, this move was undertaken for health reasons: Stevenson was plagued by ill-health throughout his life, and it was felt that the climate of the South Seas would assist him. However, he was no doubt also attracted by the exotic appeal of the 'primitive'. An interest in the exotic and the primitive, it will be remembered, also took Paul Gaugin to the South Seas around this time.

In the eighteenth century it had not been unusual to draw parallels between the traditional clan-based culture of Highland Scotland, and the cultures of the tribal societies encountered by the Empire. In *Narrating Scotland: The Imagination of Robert Louis Stevenson*, Barry Menikoff remarks that 'for English readers in the 1750s (and even later) the customs and manners of the Highlanders were, to use a recurrent analogy from the magazine literature of the time, as alien and exotic as "those of the wild barbarians in the heart of Africa"'.[17] Such attitudes to 'wild barbarians' were still commonplace in nineteenth-century Britain. However, when Stevenson went to the South Seas in the 1880s, perceived parallels with Highland Scotland tended to encourage an instinctive sympathy with Polynesian culture.

During his South Seas years in the 1880s and 1890s, Stevenson came into direct contact with the harsh realities of the coal-face of Empire, and his resulting anger at the exploitation of Polynesians prompted him to go further than before in his questioning of the elite / Imperial position. At this time Samoa was under the joint control of Germany, Britain, and the United States, with Germany being in the dominant position. Jenni Calder writes:

> Stevenson was outraged by the political manoeuvrings and manipulations of all three powers, none of which showed much regard for the needs and traditions of the Samoans. His indignation was sharply expressed in a series of letters to *The Times* which rehearsed, with an ironic wit that surely owed something to his Edinburgh legal training, a tale of imperialist treachery and doublethink. Once in Samoa Stevenson openly allied himself with the chief Mataafa, a man for whom he had great personal regard and political respect. Mataafa was the main rival to the German-backed puppet chief Malietoa. The British, while recognising privately Mataafa's claims, disliked him because he was a Catholic, and were anyway reluctant to disturb a situation that suited them quite well. [...] Stevenson produced his own account of the situation and the background to the conflict in a book which he called *A Footnote to History*. [18]

In short, Stevenson's active and sympathetic interest in Polynesian political causes drew him towards defending the oppressed against the impositions of the powerful. Here again, perhaps, the influence of Cummy's stories of the Covenanters can be detected.

Concerns of these kinds emerge in various texts written during Stevenson's South Seas period, including *Catriona*, *The Beach of Falesá*, *The Ebb Tide*, and *Weir of Hermiston*. These texts of the 1890s can be approached by way of that earlier landmark of Victorian fiction, Thackeray's *Vanity Fair* (1847–48). Like *Weir of Hermiston*, Thackeray's novel is set in the Britain of the 1810s;[19] and, like *The Beach of Falesá*, it is much concerned with Imperial themes. *Vanity Fair*'s engagement with Empire emerges in that novel's central focus on the British Imperial triumph at Waterloo, and, as we saw in Chapter 3, an Imperial dimension can also be detected in Thackeray's unsympathetic depiction of the rich young West Indian heiress, Miss Swartz.

Like Miss Swartz, the children of Wiltshire and Uma in *The Beach of Falesá* are of mixed-race parentage, and here is what Wiltshire has to say about his 'half caste' children in the final paragraph of Stevenson's novella:

> My public house? Not a bit of it, nor ever likely; I'm stuck here, I fancy; I don't like to leave the kids, you see; and there's no use talking—they're better here than what they would be in a white man's country. Though Ben took the eldest up to Auckland, where he's being schooled with the best. But what bothers me is the girls. They're only half castes of course; I know that as well as you do, and there's nobody thinks less of half castes than I do; but they're mine, and about all I've got; I can't reconcile my mind to their taking up with kanakas, and I'd like to know where I'm to find them whites? [20]

Wiltshire is a rough-and-ready English trader who operates in the South Seas at the coal-face of Empire—and in this passage Stevenson uses Wiltshire's voice to raise some disturbing questions about racial issues. We have seen that *Vanity Fair*'s presentation of Miss Swartz likewise offers an insight into the deeply unpleasant attitudes to 'half castes' that prevailed in Imperial-era Britain. Nevertheless, a distinction can be drawn between the presentation of Miss Swartz's dilemma in *Vanity Fair* (a text of the 1840s) and the presentation of the dilemma of Wiltshire's daughters in *The Beach of Falesá* (a text of the 1890s). As we saw in Chapter 3, we are invited in *Vanity Fair* to regard Miss Swartz as less than fully human as she sits at her piano: she is only able to play two pieces, she only knows three songs, and, in short, she has nothing whatsoever to commend her other than her simple-minded good nature and her two hundred thousand pounds. In inviting its readers to deplore the willingness of old Osborne and McMull to marry this 'Hottentot Venus' for her money, Thackeray's novel seems to take it for granted that the 'half caste' Miss Swartz cannot possibly be admired for anything other than her wealth. *The Beach of Falesá* is not entirely free from such attitudes, but Stevenson's text does not allow crass Imperial assumptions to remain unquestioned. This emerges, for example, in Wiltshire's account of his mock wedding with Uma:

> She was dressed and scented; her kilt was of fine tapa, looking richer in the folds than any silk; her bust, which was of the colour of dark honey, she wore bare only for some half a dozen necklaces of seeds and flowers; and behind her ears and in her hair, she had the scarlet flowers of the hybiscus. She showed the best bearing for a bride conceivable, serious and still; and I thought shame to stand up with her in that mean house and before that grinning negro. I thought shame I say; for the mountebank was dressed with a big paper collar, the book he made believe to read from was an odd volume of a novel, and the words of his service not fit to be set down. (p. 123)

The phrase about 'that grinning negro' is jarring, but at least Uma is being taken seri-ously. At all events Wiltshire goes through with the ceremony, and he goes on to de-scribe how Uma is given a marriage certificate which reads:

This is to certify that *Uma* daughter of *Faavao* of Falesá island of _____ ,
is illegally married to *Mr John Wiltshire* for one night, and Mr John Wiltshire is at
liberty to send her to hell next morning.

John Blackamoor
Chaplain to the Hulks.

Extracted from the register
by William T. Randall
Master Mariner.

That was a nice paper to put in a girl's hand and see her hide away like gold. A man
might easily feel cheap for less. But it was the practise in these parts, and (as I told
myself) not the least the fault of us White Men but of the missionaries. If they had
let the natives be, I had never needed this deception, but taken all the wives I wished,
and left them when I pleased, with a clear conscience. (p. 124)

Here Wiltshire reveals more than he realises, and in the description of the mock wed-ding Stevenson provides a devastating image of the relationship of European traders to Polynesians in the South Seas. Clearly, this is a relationship based on deception and exploitation.

Jenni Calder has suggested that it is helpful to compare Stevenson's South Seas fic-tion of the 1890s with Conrad's *Heart of Darkness* (1902). She writes:

Literary convention associates one great novelist in particular with the exploration
and exposure of the tensions and conflicts inherent not just in the confrontation be-tween imperialist powers and native populations, but in the sensations of the repre-sentatives of imperialism. This writer is Joseph Conrad, and his *Heart of Darkness* has
become an emblem of the rotten core of exploitation. But a parallel and a companion
to Conrad's great novella can be found in the earlier and equally impressive story by
Stevenson, *The Beach of Falesá*. [21]

Famously, Henry Morton Stanley had travelled into the interior of Africa in 1871 to find Livingstone, and had come back with a story about a heroic, saintly figure, the embodiment and vindication of the Imperial project of bringing Light to the Dark Continent. In Conrad's novel, Marlow travels into the interior of Africa in order to find the celebrated and enlightened Kurtz, but, unlike Stanley, Marlow comes back with a story that utterly undermines the Imperial Grand Narrative's assertions and assumptions. However, as we saw in Chapter 3, Chinua Achebe has argued that racist Imperial assumptions are present, both in Conrad himself and in *Heart of Darkness*. For Achebe, the attack on Imperialism in *Heart of Darkness* co-exists with a damaging failure to recognise the value of pre-Imperial African civilisation, and the full humanity of Africans. Arguably, Stevenson not only anticipates aspects of Conrad's critique of Imperialism in *The Beach of Falesá*, but he actually goes beyond *Heart of Darkness* in some ways, not least in his openness to the possibility that there was real value in the pre-Imperial cultures of peoples that the European Empires tended to dismiss as 'savages'.

However, while Stevenson's pro-Polynesian instincts are real and admirable, it remains possible to question the extent to which a genuine subaltern Polynesian voice can be heard to speak in *The Beach of Falesá*. At this point, let us consider *Weir of Hermiston* (1896) another text of Stevenson's Samoan years. *Weir* is about Scotland, of course—but it may be that Stevenson, having encountered the elite / subaltern problem in its severe South Seas manifestation, turns in *Weir* (and in *Catriona*) to an exploration of that problem in its Scottish manifestation.

In *Weir*, there are many representatives of Scotland's intellectual, legal, and social elite: people such as Adam Weir (the Lord Justice Clerk), and the judge Lord Glenalmond, who are well able to operate comfortably within the power structures of the Imperial Britain of the 1810s. However, Stevenson's novel also finds a place for the Elliotts of Cauldstaneslap, representatives of a subaltern Scotland whose roots lie in the old oral culture of the ballads. Like the Polynesians of *The Beach of Falesá* (who are likewise products of an old oral culture), the Elliotts are presented in *Weir* with a sympathy that is very real as far as it goes. This sympathy emerges, for example, when we learn that the dark-haired brothers of the Elliott family (the four Black Brothers) have avenged the death of their father in a heroic exploit that seems to belong to a former age: 'Some century earlier the last of the minstrels might have fashioned the last of the ballads out of that Homeric fight and chase' (p. 136).

The Elliotts are introduced in detail in 'A Border Family', one of the sections of the chapter in *Weir* entitled 'Winter on the Moors'. We learn that this subaltern family has become moderately prosperous, but nevertheless the narrator stresses that 'scarce the breadth of a hair divided them from the peasantry' (p. 142). Revealingly, it appears that marriage between elite and subaltern has the potential to be problematic, not only in the South Seas of *The Beach of Falesá*, but also in the Scotland of *Weir of Hermiston*. Exiled to the moorland estate of Hermiston because of his rebellion against his father, Archie Weir falls in love with Christina Elliott of Cauldstaneslap. Problems arise, however, for a relationship between the son of the Lord Justice Clerk and a young subaltern woman scathingly described as a 'milkmaid' by the fashionable young lawyer, Frank Innes. Indeed, Innes puts the problem to Archie with a brutal clarity:

There are two horns to your dilemma, and I must say for myself I should look mighty ruefully on either. Do you see yourself explaining to the four Black Brothers? or do you see yourself presenting the milkmaid to papa as the future lady of Hermiston? Do you? I tell you plainly, I don't! (p. 181)

Dand Elliott, one the four Black Brothers, has various traits that call James Hogg to mind. Dand is a poet who is also a Border shepherd, and Stevenson echoes well-known passages about dogs and storms in Hogg's *The Shepherd's Calendar* when he tells us that 'nobody could train a dog like Dandie; nobody, through the peril of great storms in the winter time, could do more gallantly' (p. 140). Like Hogg, Dand makes Robert Burns 'his hero and model'; and (again like Hogg) he helps Walter Scott collect old ballads for publication in *Minstrelsy of the Scottish Border* (p.140). Indeed, Dand and Hogg know each other: 'The Ettrick Shepherd was his sworn crony; they would meet, drink to excess, roar out their lyrics in each other's faces, and quarrel and make it up again till bedtime' (pp. 140–41).

In *Weir of Hermiston*, Dand and Hogg belong to the same world, and they have a good deal in common as they operate in the potentially 'Homeric' context of the oral culture of the old Border ballads. However, Stevenson makes it very clear indeed that Dandie is no Homer. The damningly faint praise is: 'No question but he had a certain accomplishment in minor verse' (p. 140). It seems that Dand's talent, while real, is strictly limited: after all, he is only a shepherd.

Stevenson's sense of the possible range of Hogg's achievement as an author is interesting in this context. In 'Robert Louis Stevenson and *The Private Memoirs and Confessions of a Justified Sinner*', Eric Massie has argued cogently that *The Master of Ballantrae* owes a significant debt to Hogg's novel.[22] As part of his argument Massie points to a letter written by Stevenson to George Saintsbury on 17 May 1891. In this letter Stevenson comments on Saintsbury's recently-published *Essays in English Literature 1780–1860*, a book in which the suggestion is floated that the Oxford-educated John Gibson Lockhart may have collaborated with Hogg in writing the *Justified Sinner*.[23] Stevenson's comment is as follows:

I particularly like your Hogg, and your admirable quotations from the unequal fellow. Your theory about the *Justified Sinner* interests and (I think I may say) convinces me; the book since I read it, in black, pouring weather on Tweedside, has always haunted and puzzled me. One felt it *could not* be Hogg. I had heard Lockhart mentioned, and much as I admire *Adam Blair*, it seemed beyond the reach of Lockhart. But with the two together, it is possible.[24]

'One felt it *could not* be Hogg'. By the 1890s, Hogg had come to be generally regarded as a rather boorish 'peasant poet' who no doubt had (like Dand Elliott) 'a certain accomplishment in minor verse', but who certainly did not deserve to be taken entirely seriously. At this period people like Stevenson and Saintsbury had the intelligence to perceive the value of the then little-known *Justified Sinner*. This placed them in a dilemma, however, because they assumed that Hogg was a boorish peasant whose real but decidedly limited talent did not—indeed, *could not*—go beyond 'a certain accomplishment in minor verse'. The Ettrick Shepherd, wrapped in his plaid while herding his sheep, might well have been able to dream up some pretty lyrics, but obviously such a man *could not*, unaided, have produced a novel as complex and sophisticated as the *Justified Sinner*. Stevenson and Saintsbury therefore cheerfully assumed (without any supporting evidence) that the peasant poet must have had the assistance of a gentleman (Lockhart, for example) in creating that remarkable work. This subaltern shepherd-poet might to some extent be able to speak, but clearly there were limits to what such a man could say if unaided by one of his betters.

In 'Father and Son', the second chapter of *Weir of Hermiston*, Lord Glenalmond speaks to Archie:

'[...] Yet I would like it very ill if my young friend were to misjudge his father. He has all the Roman virtues: Cato and Brutus were such; I think a son's heart might well be proud of such an ancestry of one.'

'And I would sooner he were a plaided herd,' cried Archie, with sudden bitterness.

'And that is neither very wise, nor I believe entirely true,' returned Glenalmond. 'Before you are done you will find some of these expressions rise on you like a remorse. [...]' (p. 100)

It does not seem very likely that Archie is being rebuked here (either by Glenalmond or by Stevenson) for his manifest unfairness to 'plaided herds': on the contrary, Glenalmond's rebuke is concerned with Archie's unfairness to the Lord Justice Clerk. In *Weir*, such subaltern figures as Dand Elliott and the Ettrick Shepherd may be admirable in their way: they may indeed have 'a certain accomplishment in minor verse', and they may even rise to involvement in Homeric adventures. However, it is clear that, in the world of Edinburgh's elite, one would not wish one's father to be such a person; and one would not wish one's daughter to marry one. Such attitudes are not very far removed from Wiltshire's views (already quoted) about the marriage prospects of his 'half caste' daughters: 'I can't reconcile my mind to their taking up with kanakas, and I'd like to know where I'm to find them whites?'.

Perhaps Stevenson's inability to accept Hogg as the author of the *Justified Sinner* connects with a rigid and inflexible application of the elite / subaltern distinction. On such a view a plaided herd is a plaided herd, and a South Sea islander is a South Sea islander—and while such people may be admirable in their own ways, they must necessarily operate within the limitations of their subaltern status and nature: they do not—

indeed, *cannot*—operate at the same level of sophistication as a university-educated nineteenth-century gentleman. In this context, when an author like Stevenson tries to speak from within the elite on behalf of the subaltern, what readers tend to hear is the voice of an elite ventriloquist, rather than a genuine subaltern voice.

It is clear that Stevenson was in sympathy with the Scottish subaltern world of Dand and the other Elliotts in *Weir of Hermiston*: that sympathy can be seen very strongly in (for example) the account of the conversation between Archie and the older Kirsty in the chapter entitled 'A Nocturnal Visit'. There were limits to that sympathy, however. Wonderfully, the portrait of Uma in *The Beach of Falesá* is much more perceptive and sympathetic than the portrait of Miss Swartz in *Vanity Fair*—but nevertheless one cannot imagine Uma, any more than Dand Elliott, rising to authorship of a complex and sophisticated novel such as *The Private Memoirs and Confessions of a Justified Sinner*. In short, Stevenson to some extent remained enmeshed in the Imperial assumptions of his time about 'native' peoples and their 'primitive' cultures: as Jenni Calder has observed, he was a man of his time, someone who 'seems to have shared the belief held by even the most enlightened investigators that tribal societies represented a primitive stage in human evolution which would inevitably give way to "civilisation"'.[25]

We return to the words of Edward Said, quoted in Chapter 1:

> Stories are at the heart of what explorers and novelists say about strange regions of the world; they also become the method colonized people use to assert their own identity and the existence of their own history. The main battle in imperialism is over land, of course; but when it came to who owned the land, who had the right to settle and work on it, who kept it going, who won it back, and who now plans its future—these issues were reflected, contested, and even for a time decided in narrative.

The Beach of Falesá and *Heart of Darkness* take part in this battle of the stories from an interesting perspective. These are not stories (like Achebe's *Things Fall Apart*, say, or Hogg's *The Brownie of Bodsbeck*) through which a colonised or subaltern people find their voice and 'assert their own identity and the existence of their own history'. The colonised subaltern does not fully find a voice in *The Beach of Falesá*, and is still less able to speak in *Heart of Darkness*. Instead, these novellas by Stevenson and Conrad do something else, and something of great value: they draw on direct and disturbing personal experience to question the Imperial story from a position within the Imperial project. These two texts emerged at a pivotal moment when the European elites were beginning to lose the self-confidence, the certainty, and the moral blinkers that had helped to sustain the great European Empires in earlier years. As a devastating critique of Empire, *The Beach of Falesá* takes its place alongside *Heart of Darkness* among the most powerful and significant stories of the past century and a half.

A Son of the Free Kirk Manse

While Robert Louis Stevenson (1850–93) grew up in the post-Disruption Auld Kirk, John Buchan (1875–1940) grew up in the post-Disruption Free Kirk. Indeed, Buchan (in the old Scottish phrase) was a son of the manse: his father, the Rev. John Buchan (1847–1911) was a minister of the Free Church. In his autobiographical book *Memory Hold-the-Door* Buchan writes:

> When a few months old I was brought by my parents to a little grey manse on the Fife coast. It was a square, stone house standing in a big garden, with a railway behind it, and in front, across a muddy by-road, a linoleum factory, a coal-pit and a rope-walk, with a bleaching-works somewhere in the rear.

Some twelve years later, in 1888, the Rev. John Buchan left this 'little grey manse' at Pathhead near Kirkcaldy, and moved with his family to the John Knox Church in the Gorbals district of Glasgow.

Buchan records that his father died in his early sixties, 'his strong physique [...] worn out by unceasing toil in a slum parish, an endless round of sermons and addresses, and visits at all hours to the sick and sorrowful'. To his son, the Rev. John Buchan had an 'air of gentle, wondering cheerfulness' and a 'benign, surprised enjoyment of the mere fact of living'. A 'voracious reader', the father (according to his son) saw the past as

> a design in snow and ink, one long contest between villains of admitted villainy and honest men. His dividing line was oddly drawn. In the eighteenth century the Jacobites were for him the children of light; in the seventeenth the Covenanters. For the latter indeed he cherished a fervent private cult, admitting no flaw in their perfection. [...] Beginning life as a Liberal he lost his confidence in Mr. Gladstone after Gordon's death in Khartoum, and the Home Rule question drove him to the Unionist side. He detected in Ulster some kinship with his beloved Covenanters.[26]

Charles George Gordon, a somewhat puritanical man, was a hero of popular British imperialist sentiment, and when he was killed in 1885 during the siege of Khartoum in the Sudan, Gladstone's Liberal government was widely blamed for being tardy in sending succour. As for the Covenanters, their arch-enemy was the Catholic James VII and II, and the Rev. John Buchan was not the only Presbyterian of his time for whom an admiration of the Covenanters went hand in hand with a deep dislike and distrust of Catholicism. Such a man was unlikely to warm to Gladstone's policy of Home Rule for Ireland.

John Buchan's mother was an indomitable, energetic, and formidable woman in the Free Kirk tradition. Her son writes:

> My mother was married at seventeen, and had at once to take charge of a kirk and a
> manse, to which was soon added a family. [...] Her world was the Church, or rather a
> little section of the Church. Her ambitions were narrowly ecclesiastical. A popular
> preacher, a famous theologian seemed to her the height of human greatness—a view
> which was not shared by her family. [...] She must have had a remarkable talent for
> administration to make a tiny income go so far, and to steer my father among the
> pitfalls of his profession. (pp. 249, 250, 251)

The 'tiny income' of a Free Kirk minister was the family's only resource: the Rev. John
Buchan's father, yet another John Buchan, was a successful lawyer who had lost his
money in the 1878 crash of the City of Glasgow Bank.

All this might be taken to indicate that the future novelist had to grow up in a stifled
and repressed atmosphere, but the reality of life in the Free Kirk manses of the Buchan
family seems to have been happier and more interesting than the stereotype would
suggest. For example, John's sister Anna, in her family memoir *Unforgettable, Unforgotten*, writes of the social life of the Buchan manse in Glasgow:

> We had the church people, to whom we were deeply attached, and all the kind hospi-
> table Glasgow people who lived round us. There were, too, the University professors
> and their wives, and life was greatly enriched for me when we got to know many of
> the Glasgow artists. [...] Perhaps the most enjoyable parties we attended were at the
> Camerons' house. Everyone knows D. Y. Cameron's pictures, and the exquisite water-
> colours of his sister Katharine, but all the members of that large family were gifted.[27]

Nevertheless, the family's 'tiny income' meant that the Rev. John Buchan's children had
to make their own way in the world, and they tended to do so with notable success: for
example Anna (1877–1948) became well known as a novelist writing under the name
of O. Douglas. Likewise William (1880–1912) passed the exacting examinations for
entry to the Indian Civil Service, but (in a manner that calls to mind Kipling's words in
'On the City Wall', quoted above) illness and early death cut short his distinguished
career in India.

John, the oldest child and future novelist, was the most successful of all. He worked
ferociously during his Glasgow youth with a view to gaining academic distinction, first
as a schoolboy and later at the city's University. The winning of a bursary eased the
Glasgow student's financial situation, and thereafter the winning of a scholarship
opened the way to life as an Oxford undergraduate from 1895 until 1899. At Oxford,
money was tight at first. In *Unforgettable, Unforgotten* Anna quotes from a letter to
William written by John during his first term at Brasenose College, Oxford:

> My college bills for the week come only to 17s. You see I have been so much out at

meals. I find that at the end of term we have certain payments to make: this has completely stumped me! [...] I am going a long walk this afternoon and then I shall write an article for the *Glasgow Herald*. I must make money. (p. 77)

Buchan did not have the graceful indifference towards money sometimes exhibited by the children of rich parents, but on the other hand he does not seem to have regarded the making of money as an end in itself. Anna comments that her brother's writing was very soon 'bringing in a good income, so he had money to do things and could make the most of his time at Oxford' (p. 77).

John did not take to Oxford at first. In *Memory Hold-the-Door* he writes:

My first impressions of Oxford were unhappy. The soft autumn air did not suit my health; the lectures which I attended seemed jejune and platitudinous, and the regime slack, after the strenuous life of Glasgow; I played no game well enough to acquire an absorbing interest in it. Above all, being a year older than my contemporaries, I felt that I had been pitchforked into a kindergarten. The revels of alcoholic children offended me, and, having an unfortunate gift of plain speech, I did not make myself popular among those emancipated schoolboys. I must have been at that time an intolerable prig. (pp. 47–48)

In *John Buchan: A Memoir* (1982), Buchan's son William writes about this passage:

The young freshmen of BNC [Brasenose College], freed from the restrictions of home and school, and with money of their own to spend, were busy making their first experiments in drinking. JB, reared in a totally abstaining household—partly because a manse, in those days, could scarcely be otherwise; partly because, in a poor parish, the heartbreaking effects of drunkenness were a daily spectacle—was not inclined to be tolerant of inebriated adolescents. 'Paper-faced babies,' he once told me, still scornfully, 'puking all over the chapel steps.' One night, in the old Presbyterian tradition of 'testifying', he waded into a crowd of those infant pukers, who were demonstrating against the College Principal, Dr Heberden, whom JB liked and admired, and made them a speech not unworthy of John Knox at his most trenchant. Nobody attacked him. Nobody seems to have told him to go away and mind his own business. The crowd, half-stunned by alcohol, was further stunned to silence by a torrent of Scottish eloquence. From being a totally obscure young man, John Buchan became the talk of the university.[28]

Nevertheless, Oxford came to cast its powerful spell on this son of a Free Kirk Manse, and friendships made at Oxford were important for his future direction. In the *Oxford DNB*, H. C. G. Matthew writes: 'It was during his time at Brasenose that

Buchan met the public-school set whose ethos and patois his best-known novels were to record' (VIII, 450). Likewise, in *Memory Hold-the-Door* Buchan himself writes of his Oxford friends: 'In the world of action we were ripe for any venture; in the things of the mind we were critical and decorous, chary of enthusiasm—*revenants* from the Augustan age' (p. 54).

As H. C. G. Matthew records, 'Oxford gave Buchan easy access to London society, and he chose to establish himself there rather than return to Scotland'. This son of the manse knew that high achievement was expected of him by his family, and he also knew that he would have to make his own way in the world without any of the advantages of inherited wealth. Buchan was well aware of the glittering prizes available in London at the end of the 1890s for a talented young man just down from Oxford: so to London he went. A London society marriage followed in due course. H. C. G. Matthew writes:

> on 15 July 1907 at St George's, Hanover Square, London, in a great society wedding, he married Susan Charlotte Grosvenor (1882–1977), daughter of Norman de l'Aigle Grosvenor (1845–1898), son of Lord Robert Grosvenor (1801–1893), and his wife, Caroline Susan Theodora, *née* Stuart-Wortley (*d.* 1940). Susan Grosvenor was very well connected but not rich. (*ODNB*, VIII, 450, 451).

And, culturally, Susan Grosvenor was very aristocratic, very English, and very Anglican: not all of which were necessarily qualities to commend her to her formidable Free Kirk mother-in-law. Writing about his paternal grandmother in *John Buchan: A Memoir*, William Buchan recalls 'all that business about going to church', as well as 'edifying stories of the general brilliance and exceptional virtue of my father and his family at my age'. 'It was all rather tiring', he writes, adding that he was 'faced with statements and questions and propositions quite different from any that I ever heard at home' (p. 72). He comments (p. 69) on his grandmother's deep involvement in 'the, to her, immensely important world of the Free Church', and one senses that he does not share her view of the importance of that world. In its preliminaries, *John Buchan: A Memoir* offers a 'Family Tree of John Buchan' in which (rather oddly) the first person named is Robert Grosvenor, Lord Edbury (grandfather of John Buchan's wife). This oddity, however, is helpful for the reader, who cannot fail to notice the important fact that the author of *John Buchan: A Memoir* is the great-grandson of a Lord. It seems that William Buchan's siblings (all great-grandchildren of a Lord) shared his view of their paternal grandmother. He writes (p. 73): 'Of Gran, my sister Alice wrote, in *A Scrap Screen*: "My grandmother's personality affected me like a piece of grit in the eye"'. While still in her teens, Mrs Buchan had been a wife and a mother, very much in charge of her husband's Free Kirk manse. This capable, confident, and lively woman was not at all likely to submit meekly to being patronised by her aristocratic grandchildren, and her vigorous but futile efforts to lick them into a proper Free Kirk shape must indeed have been irksome to these inhabitants of a very different world. In a sense, Mrs Buchan's relationship with her grandchildren sums up a dilemma that faced the North British elite during the Imperial era: if one is to achieve one's longed-for success among the glittering prizes on offer in Oxford and London, can one only do so by becoming a different person, by ceasing to be oneself? And if so, is the game worth the candle? As we shall see in Chapter 7, Buchan explores questions of this kind in *Sick Heart River* (1941), written during his last illness.

In the course of John Buchan's career, the idealism, ambition, and sense of duty of a son of the Free Kirk manse combined with the attitudes of an Oxford *revenant* from the Augustan age to produce an active and devoted servant of the British Imperial cause. The call to serve this cause in a practical way came in 1901, when the young Buchan, not long out of Oxford, was invited by Lord Milner to go to South Africa for two years, to assist in the reconstruction of the country after the Second South African War. '"I am to be paid £1,200 a year—out of which I suppose I could save £600," he told his mother' (*John Buchan: A Memoir*, p. 103).

In *Memory Hold-the-Door* Buchan records that in South Africa he came in contact for the first time with the British army, and with 'the men of the Dominions—South Africans of the various irregular corps, Canadians, Australians and New Zealanders'. These men, Buchan writes,

> combined a passionate devotion to their own countries with the vision of a great brotherhood based on race and a common culture, a vision none the less real because they rarely tried to put it into words. I began to see that the Empire, which had hitherto been only a phrase to me, might be a potent and beneficent force in the world. (pp. 111–12)

A few pages later Buchan continues:

> I learned a good deal in South Africa […].
>
> Above all I ceased to be an individualist and became a citizen. I acquired a political faith. Those were the days when a vision of what the Empire might be made dawned upon certain minds with almost the force of a revelation. To-day [1940] the word is sadly tarnished. Its mislikers have managed to identify it with uglinesses like corrugated-iron roofs and raw townships, or, worse still, with a callous racial arrogance. Its dreams, once so bright, have been so pawed by unctuous hands that their glory has departed. Phrases which held a world of idealism and poetry have been spoilt by their use in bad verse and in after-dinner perorations. […]
>
> I dreamed of a world-wide brotherhood with the background of a common race and creed, consecrated to the service of peace; Britain enriching the rest out of her

culture and traditions, and the spirit of the Dominions like a strong wind freshening the stuffiness of the old lands. I saw in the Empire a means of giving to the congested masses at home open country instead of a blind alley. I saw hope for a new afflatus in art and literature and thought. Our creed was not based on antagonism to any other people. It was humanitarian and international; we believed that we were laying the basis of a federation of the world. As for the native races under our rule, we had a high conscientiousness; Milner and Rhodes had a far-sighted native policy. The "white man's burden" is now an almost meaningless phrase; then it involved a new philosophy of politics, and an ethical standard, serious and surely not ignoble. (pp. 124–25)

It is not necessary to agree with such views in order to sense that Buchan held them sincerely, and it is possible to see in them something of a secular equivalent of the deeply-held convictions that had driven David Livingstone and many another Victorian Scottish missionary to undertake a share of what they believed to be the supremely important task of bringing the light of Christ to Africa, 'the Dark Continent'. At all events, and as we shall see, Buchan's deeply-felt Imperial convictions helped to shape his widely-enjoyed story-telling.

Waverley in South Africa

> You think that a wall as solid as the earth separates civilisation from Barbarism. I tell you the division is a thread, a sheet of glass.
>
> (John Buchan, *The Power House*)

After his time in South Africa, and while still based in London, John Buchan began to earn a substantial income by working for Thomas Nelson and Sons, a large and successful Edinburgh publishing firm which had an important London office. Nelsons was owned by the family of his Oxford friend Tommie Nelson, and was noted for the cheap publication of high-quality fiction. Work as a publisher sat well with Buchan's own literary activities, and in *Memory Hold-the-Door* he writes:

> In my undergraduate days I had tried my hand at historical novels, and had then some ambition to write fiction in the grand manner, by interpreting and clarifying a large piece of life. This ambition waned and, apart from a few short stories, I let fiction alone until 1910, when, being appalled as a publisher by the dullness of most boys' books, I thought I would attempt one of my own, based on my African experience. The result was *Prester John*, which has since become a school-reader in many languages. (p. 194)

As it happens, the present writer first encountered *Prester John* as a child, when given it as a school-reader in the early 1950s. Although little read now, *Prester John* enjoyed a long run during the final decades of the British Empire.

An adventure story for boys is not necessarily innocent of political significance, as George Orwell argues in his essay 'Boys' Weeklies', written in 1939:

> It is probable that many people who could consider themselves extremely sophisticated and "advanced" are actually carrying through life an imaginative background which they acquired in childhood from (for instance) Sapper and Ian Hay. If that is so, the boys' twopenny weeklies are of the deepest importance. Here is the stuff that is read somewhere between the ages of twelve and eighteen by a very large proportion, perhaps an actual majority, of English boys, including many who will never read anything else except newspapers; and along with it they are absorbing a set of beliefs which would be regarded as hopelessly out of date in the Central Office of the Conservative Party. All the better because it is done indirectly, there is being pumped into them the conviction that the major problems of our time do not exist, that there is nothing wrong with *laissez-faire* capitalism, that foreigners are unimportant comics and that the British Empire is a sort of charity-concern which will last for ever. Considering who owns these papers, it is difficult to believe that this is unintentional. [...] if you feel the need of a fantasy-life in which you travel to Mars and fight lions barehanded (and what boy doesn't?) you can only have it by delivering yourself over, mentally, to people like Lord Camrose. For there is no competition.[29]

As many boy-readers no doubt excitedly told each other in 1910, *Prester John* is a rattling good yarn. David Crawfurd, its first-person narrator, is a son of the Auld Kirk manse of 'Kirkcaple' on the coast of Fife. Being a son of the manse, David is one 'of the genteel in Kirkcaple', and he and his friends are natural enemies of 'the town roughs': indeed, their 'greatest exploit' is 'a fight with the roughs at the Dyve tanwork'.[30] In due course David becomes a student at Edinburgh University, but he has to abandon his studies when his father dies unexpectedly, and a post as a rural storekeeper is found for him in South Africa. Striking adventures of a fighting-lions-barehanded nature follow rapidly, during which David plays a decisive part in foiling a dangerous uprising of 'natives'. In the course of his adventures, David also obtains for himself a vast hoard of jewels: Buchan was always well aware of the material rewards the Empire could supply.

However, *Prester John* is more than a rattling good yarn: Buchan's adventure story for boys can be seen as a deeply-felt (and in some important ways deeply disturbing) attempt to further the cause of Empire by re-telling the *Waverley* story in the context of British Imperial Africa. Scott's Jacobite novel tells of the return of an exiled Prince, who attempts to defy the inexorable march of Progress by leading a romantic and noble (but nevertheless doomed and flawed) attempt to revive a lost past by reclaiming a lost throne. *Prester John* imagines a similar venture in Africa.

In the fifth chapter of Buchan's novel the schoolmaster Mr Wardlaw predicts the possibility of a 'native' rising that 'would be a second and bloodier Indian Mutiny'. David Crawfurd responds:

> "But they would never find a leader. If there was some exiled prince of Chaka's blood, who came back like Prince Charlie to free his people, there might be danger; but their royalties are fat men with top hats and old frock coats, who live in dirty locations." (pp. 95, 96)

However, it later emerges that the Africans do indeed have a leader in the Rev. John Laputa, who places himself at the head of an African equivalent of the '45 by inspiring a 'native' rising. Laputa's objective is to overthrow the Empire by reclaiming the throne of Prester John, the Priest-King of African legend.

All this still lies in the future when Laputa makes his appearance in the first chapter of the novel, 'On the Kirkcaple Shore'. The young David Crawfurd is playing truant from the evening service on Communion Sunday at his father's church, and makes his way to the shore with two friends, one of whom, Tam Dyke, is 'of the Free Church persuasion'. Tam tells the other boys that

> notable events had happened that day in his church. A black man, the Rev. John Something-or-other, had been preaching. Tam was full of the portent. "A nigger," he said, "a great black chap as big as your father, Archie." He seemed to have banged the bookboard with some effect, and had kept Tam, for once in his life, awake. He had preached about the heathen in Africa, and how a black man was as good as a white man in the sight of God, and he had forecast a day when the negroes would have something to teach the British in the way of civilization. So at any rate ran the account of Tam Dyke, who did not share the preacher's views. "It's all nonsense, Davie. The Bible says that the children of Ham were to be our servants. If I were the minister I wouldn't let a nigger into the pulpit, I wouldn't let him farther than the Sabbath school." (pp. 11–12)

In Genesis 9, Ham ('the father of Canaan'), is one of the three sons of Noah, and thus one of the three male ancestors of the various races of humanity after the Flood. Ham sees his father's drunken nakedness: 'And Noah awoke from his wine [...]. And he said, Cursed *be* Canaan; a servant of servants shall he be unto his brethren'. This biblical passage was widely used (not least in South Africa) to bolster attempts to justify the subjugation of the non-white races. One would like to think that *Prester John* invites its readers to dismiss Tam Dyke's racist attitude as the folly of a bigoted child, but it is difficult to find evidence of any such invitation in Buchan's novel. At all events, the boys conceal themselves and look on as the black minister, 'invoking strange gods in the moonlight' (p. 37), performs heathen rituals on the shore. He discovers them, and they only escape after a thrilling pursuit up the Kirkcaple cliffs.

In due course we learn that the minister's name is the Rev. John Laputa. In Book III of Swift's *Gulliver's Travels*, 'Laputa' is a land in which the leaders are immersed in absurdly impractical theories. Clearly, the naming of the minister is intended to provide a comment on Laputa's project, and on the whole notion that 'a black man was as good as a white man in the sight of God'. Manifestly, Buchan's vision of the future of South Africa did not foresee the Presidency of Nelson Mandela.

Nevertheless, it is made clear throughout the novel that John Laputa is a complex figure, someone who is worthy of respect—but only up to a point. This is made explicit by Captain Arcoll, a notable example of the British officer class, and a man whose business it is 'to act as chief Intelligence officer among the natives' (p. 131). As was the case with Tam Dyke, *Prester John* does not seem to reject Arcoll's racist views: indeed, this novel seems calculated to reinforce such views. At all events, Arcoll tells David Crawfurd that Laputa is about to lead a rebellion, and David remarks: 'You say he is an educated man. He must know he has no chance in the long run'. Arcoll responds:

> "I said he was an educated man, but he is also a Kaffir. He can see the first stage of a thing, and maybe the second, but no more. That is the native mind. If it was not like that our chance would be the worse." (p. 137)

For Arcoll, the 'native mind' *cannot* match the white man's mind: and he assumes that Laputa, as a 'Kaffir', has severe limitations. However, Arcoll goes on to praise the African leader:

> I tell you, in my opinion he is a great genius. If he had been white he might have been a second Napoleon. He is a born leader of men, and as brave as a lion. There is no villainy he would not do if necessary, and yet I should hesitate to call him a blackguard. Ay, you may look surprised at me, you two pragmatical Scotsmen; but I have, so to speak, lived with the man for months, and there's fineness and nobility in him. He would be a terrible enemy, but a just one. He has the heart of a poet and a king, and it is God's curse that he has been born among the children of Ham. I hope to shoot him like a dog in a day or two, but I am glad to bear testimony to his greatness. (p. 138)

When he meets Prince Charles in Scott's novel, Edward Waverley (an officer in King George's British army) is seduced by the romance of the situation: he allows his heart to rule his head for a time, and, carried away by emotion, he joins the Prince's Jacobite army. David Crawfurd is likewise tempted to go over to the enemy when, in disguise, he hears Laputa accept the proffered leadership of the African people. The scene is an impressive one: indeed, it is reminiscent 'of Samuel ordaining Saul as king of Israel' (p. 181). David, Laputa's eventual conqueror, records that the new African king speaks to his people with great eloquence:

he told tales of white infamy, lands snatched from their rightful possessors, unjust laws which forced the Ethiopian to the bondage of a despised caste, the
finger of scorn everywhere, and the mocking word. [...] By rights, I suppose,
my blood should have been boiling at this treason. I am ashamed to confess
that it did nothing of the sort. My mind was mesmerized by this amazing man.
I could not refrain from shouting with the rest. Indeed I was a convert, if there
can be conversion when the emotions are dominant and there is no assent from
the brain. I had a mad desire to be of Laputa's party. Or rather, I longed for a
leader who should master me and make my soul his own, as this man mastered
his followers. (pp. 190–92)

Would David's longing have been answered in the Germany of the 1930s, perhaps? At
all events, in this novel written before the First World War by a firm supporter of Britain's Imperial project, it is the young David's manifest destiny to quell 'native' rebellion, not to join it. He recoils from his moment of madness, and remains Laputa's
enemy.

Buchan was a well-read and intellectually sophisticated man, and when writing
Prester John in 1910 he would undoubtedly have been aware of the intellectual climate
of the time. Conrad's *Heart of Darkness* had made its first appearance a decade earlier
(in the pages of *Blackwood's Magazine*), and it is presumably no accident that David
Crawfurd (as he recalls the ceremony at which Laputa accepts his kingly role) speaks of
having 'looked into the heart of darkness' (p. 200). Buchan would likewise have been
well aware of the subversive import of (for example) Stevenson's South Seas fiction of
the early 1890s, and *Prester John* can be seen as a vigorous rallying-call on behalf of the
Imperial cause, written at a time when novels of real significance and stature had already
begun to question and subvert that cause.

What, then, is the basis of the pro-Imperial case that *Prester John* seeks to make?
Buchan makes this explicit in the novel's penultimate chapter, 'A Great Peril and a Great
Salvation'. Throughout *Prester John* the 'natives' are represented as living on the plains,
while the white population is located on the plateau of the high veld. The symbolism
here is obvious enough, and is given dramatic expression in the novel in the half-
dozen or so enthralling climbs to safety undertaken by David Crawfurd—a number of
which directly involve an escape from Laputa. Again, the symbolism is clear: the text
invites its readers to see David's escapes as being in some sense climbs out of the dangers of Barbarism, towards the safety of Civilisation. In the first paragraph of the
penultimate chapter, Crawfurd writes that a formal history of Laputa's 'great Rising'
would 'show how the Plains found at all points the Plateau guarded, how wits over-
came numbers, and at every pass which the natives tried the great guns spoke and the
tide rolled back' (p. 352). In short, this novel tells a story of 'native' Barbarism being
overcome by Civilisation (as embodied in the Empire). We see, that is to say, some-

thing akin to the pacification of the primitive tribes of the Lower Niger.

Nevertheless, Laputa's rising has indeed been a 'Great Peril': after it, 'white Africa drew breath again with certain grave reflections left in her head' (p. 353). As the narrative of *Prester John* approaches its conclusion, Buchan takes care to ensure that the romance of Laputa's project is not over-played, and there are hints of an instructive parallel with the 'Indian Mutiny':

> There was no leader left when Laputa had gone. There were months of guerrilla fighting, and then months of reprisals, when chief after chief was hunted down and brought to trial. [...] Romance died with "the heir of John," and the crusade became a sorry mutiny. (pp. 352–53)

However, Buchan's rallying-call to the Imperial cause focuses not only on a 'Great Peril', but also on a 'Great Salvation'. The Empire, chastened by the Rising, is presented as turning with renewed energy to the noble task of carrying 'the white man's burden'. In 'A Great Peril and a Great Salvation', the penultimate paragraph gives an account of 'the white man's duty':

> He has to take all risks, recking nothing of his life or his fortunes, and well content to find his reward in the fulfilment of his task. That is the difference between white and black, the gift of responsibility, the power of being in a little way a king; and so long as we know this and practise it, we will rule not in Africa alone but wherever there are dark men who live only for the day and their own bellies. (p. 365)

Buchan's novel then goes on to offer, in its final chapter, a vision of South Africa prospering under the benign influence of a firm British Imperialism in which various Scots are notably, prominently, and prosperously active.

Manifestly, *Prester John* is deeply and offensively racist in many of its assumptions: the comment about 'dark men who live only for the day and their own bellies' is only one example of the many truly appalling things of a like nature in the novel. It is also all too clear that Buchan enthusiastically approved of the kind of opportunity for acquiring wealth that, in *Prester John*, the Empire offers to David Crawfurd and his various Scottish friends. All this is true, and needs to be said, and needs to be deplored. Nevertheless, it also seems clear that Buchan was entirely sincere in his belief that, selflessly, 'the white man' had a duty 'to take all risks, recking nothing of his life or his fortunes', and to be 'well content to find his reward in the fulfilment of his task'. In spite of his sometimes utterly deplorable attitudes on matters of race, this son of the Free Kirk manse also had something of David Livingstone's impulse towards a life of self-sacrificing service to a cause that he believed to be noble.

A Dangerous Fallen Angel

> As when a Gryphon through the wilderness
> With wingéd step, o'er hill and moory dale
> Pursues the Arimaspian.   (Milton, *Paradise Lost*)

Four years after the publication of *Prester John*, during the first months of the First World War, Buchan was ill and confined to bed. Partly to pass the time, and partly (once more) with a view to issuing a rallying-call to Britain's cause, he began work on another novel of striking adventure, this time with an adult audience in mind. The book in question, *The Thirty-Nine Steps*, became an enormous popular success on its publication in 1915.

The story opens with its first-person narrator, Richard Hannay, feeling bored in the pre-war London of May 1914. Hannay is a South African mining engineer of Scottish parentage who has made his pile ('not one of the big ones, but good enough for me'),[31] and he has come to settle in the Imperial capital with a view to enjoying his money. Suddenly, however, his world is turned upside down, and he becomes a murder suspect, on the run not only from the police, but also from a gang of German spies whose activities are aimed towards the destruction of Britain's navy on the eve of the war destined to begin later in the year. Various adventures follow at breakneck pace, and (in a bow to the 'Flight in the Heather' chapters in Stevenson's *Kidnapped*) Buchan depicts Hannay as a fugitive in the moors and hills of southern Scotland. Having evaded his pursuers, however, Hannay returns to London to clear his name and save the navy.

Chapter 4, 'The Adventure of the Radical Candidate', finds Hannay in southern Scotland passing himself off as an Australian called Twisdon. Unfortunately, events conspire to make it necessary for Twisdon to make a speech at a political meeting in support of Sir Harry, a would-be Liberal politician. This decent but deluded young man is a Cambridge graduate and well-connected, but his brain has been addled by too much reading of 'the *Progressive Magazine*' (p. 45). Sir Harry (the Radical Candidate) is the first speaker to address the meeting:

> It was the most appalling rot, too. He talked about the 'German menace', and said it was all a Tory invention to cheat the poor of their rights and keep back the great flood of social reform, but that 'organised labour' realised this and laughed the Tories to scorn. He was all for reducing our Navy as a proof of our good faith, and then sending Germany an ultimatum telling her to do the same or we would knock her into a cocked hat. (p. 44)

In character as Twisdon, Hannay speaks next:

> I simply told them all I could remember about Australia, praying there should be no

Australian there [...] and I woke them up a bit when I started in to tell them the kind of glorious business I thought could be made out of the Empire if we really put our backs into it. (p. 44)

Like *Prester John*, *The Thirty-Nine Steps* is an adventure yarn with a political agenda.

Part of that agenda concerns the need to make acceptable sense of war with Germany. The clear implication of the Imperial Grand Narrative was that the nation that had produced Goethe, Schiller, and Beethoven ought to be Britain's partner in the noble work of bringing the light of civilisation to the dark places of the earth. However, the real driving forces behind Empire were a desire for power and a desire for wealth, and Germany was therefore Britain's rival rather than its partner. Buchan's belief in the ultimate nobility of the Imperial cause did not allow him to face this squarely. So how could he explain, to himself and to others, the need for war? In *The Thirty-Nine Steps* he provides an answer by presenting Germany as a fallen angel.

This solution is offered, cryptically, in Chapter 3 ('The Adventure of the Literary Innkeeper'). Hannay at this point is being pursued by the German spy ring across the moorland of southern Scotland, when he finds refuge with a literary innkeeper.

He was smoking a long clay pipe and studying the water with spectacled eyes. In his left hand was a small book with a finger marking the place. Slowly he repeated—

> As when a Gryphon through the wilderness
> With wingéd step, o'er hill and moory dale
> Pursues the Arimaspian. (p. 31)

Here Hannay can be identified with the Arimaspian of Book Two of *Paradise Lost*, while the Gryphon (that is to say, Lucifer) can be identified with the fallen angel of Germany—a noble civilisation gone to the bad, which now must be confronted and overcome if a universal lapse into barbarity is to be avoided.[32]

Although written in the first months of the First World War, *The Thirty-Nine Steps* can perhaps be seen as a final flourish from the old pre-war world of Britain's Imperial high noon. However, when Buchan was writing this novel in 1914, that old world's days were already numbered. Hannay's feats of derring-do notwithstanding, the First World War was destined to change everything, including John Buchan's fiction. Buchan's post-war fiction will be discussed in the chapter which follows, after that chapter has considered the ways in which the post-war situation helped to generate a new literary movement that came to be known as 'the Scottish Renaissance'.

Notes

1   *Oxford Dictionary of National Biography*, ed. by H. C. G. Matthew and Brian Harrison, 60 vols (Oxford: Oxford University Press, 2004), xxxiv, 73–82 (p. 73). The *Oxford Dictionary of National Biography* is hereafter quoted (as *ODNB*), within the text.

2   See Wilson's Introduction to James I. MacNair, *Livingstone the Liberator: A Study of a Dynamic Personality* (London: Collins, 1940; repr. 1960), p. 5.

3   Stewart J. Brown has contributed a valuable discussion of the Disruption to *The Oxford Companion to Scottish History*, ed. by Michael Lynch (Oxford: Oxford University Press, 2001), pp. 170–72.

4   *Oxford Companion*, p. 171.

5   T. M. Devine, *The Scottish Nation 1700–2000* (London: Allen Lane, 1999), p. 426.

6   Details of Stevenson's family background are conveniently available in his own *ODNB* article, and in the *ODNB* articles on his grandfather (Robert Stevenson, 1772–1855) and father (Thomas Stevenson, 1818–87).

7   See Barry Menikoff, *Narrating Scotland: The Imagination of Robert Louis Stevenson* (Columbia, SC: University of South Carolina Press, 2005).

8   Robert Louis Stevenson, *Kidnapped* and *Catriona*, ed. by Emma Letley (Oxford: Oxford University Press, 1986), pp. 48, 99. Future references to Stevenson's two David Balfour novels are to this edition, and are given in the text.

9   T. M. Devine, *Scotland's Empire 1600–1815* (London: Allen Lane, 2003), p. 102.

10   Devine, *The Scottish Nation 1700–2000*, p. 427.

11   See Devine, *The Scottish Nation 1700–2000*, pp. 430–31.

12   Derick Thomson, *An Introduction to Gaelic Poetry* (Edinburgh: Edinburgh University Press, 1990), pp. 245–46.

13   See Menikoff, *Narrating Scotland*, pp. 38–39.

14   See *The Poetry of Scotland*, ed. by Roderick Watson (Edinburgh: Edinburgh University Press, 1995), pp. 262–333.

15   See Sir Thomas Innes of Learney, *The Tartans of the Clans and Families of Scotland*, 7th ed. (Edinburgh: Johnston & Bacon, 1964), pp. 88, 284.

16   Rudyard Kipling, *The Man who would be King and Other Stories*, ed. by Louis L. Cornell, World's Classics (Oxford: Oxford University Press, 1987), pp. 222, 238. Subsequent page references are to this edition, and are given in the text.

17   Menikoff, *Narrating Scotland*, p. 29. Menikoff's quotation is from the *Gentleman's Magazine*, 24 (1754), p. 342.

18   Robert Louis Stevenson, *Tales of the South Seas*, ed. by Jenni Calder, Canongate Classics, 72 (Edinburgh: Canongate, 1996), pp. ix–xx.

19   We are told that, at Hermiston, Archie Weir 'stirred the maidens of the county with the charm of Byronism when Byronism was new': Stevenson, *The Strange Case of Dr Jekyll and Mr Hyde* and *Weir of Hermiston*, ed. by Emma Letley, World's Classics (Oxford: Oxford University Press, 1987), p. 128. Subsequent page references to *Weir of Hermiston* are to this edition, and are given in the text.

20   Barry Menikoff, *Robert Louis Stevenson and 'The Beach of Falesá': A Study in Victorian Publishing, with the Original Text* (Edinburgh: Edinburgh University Press, 1984), p. 186. Subsequent page references are to this edition, and are given in the text.

21   Stevenson, *Tales of the South Seas*, ed. Calder, p. xvii.

22   Eric Massie, 'Robert Louis Stevenson and *The Private Memoirs and Confessions of a Justified Sinner*', *Studies in Hogg and his World*, 10 (1999), 73–77.

23 Massie, p. 73.

24 *The Letters of Robert Louis Stevenson*, ed. by Bradford Booth and Ernest Mehew, 8 vols (New Haven: Yale University Press, 1994–95), VII, 125–6.

25 Stevenson, *Tales of the South Seas*, ed. Calder, pp. xiv–xv.

26 John Buchan, *Memory Hold-the-Door* (London: Hodder and Stoughton, 1940), pp. 13, 245, 246, 248. Future page references are to this edition, and are given in the text.

27 Anna Buchan, *Unforgettable, Unforgotten* (London: Hodder & Stoughton, 1945), pp. 84–85. Future page references are to this edition, and are given in the text.

28 William Buchan, *John Buchan: A Memoir* (London: Buchan & Enright, 1982), pp. 87–88. Future page references are to this edition, and are given in the text.

29 *The Collected Essays, Journalism and Letters of George Orwell*, ed. by Sonia Orwell and Ian Angus, 4 vols (London: Secker & Warburg, 1968), I, 482–83.

30 John Buchan, *Prester John* (London: Nelson, 1910), pp. 10, 9. Future page references are to this edition, and are given in the text.

31 John Buchan, *The Thirty-Nine Steps*, ed. by Christopher Harvie, Oxford World's Classics (Oxford: Oxford University Press, 1999), p. 7. Future page references are to this edition, and are given in the text.

32 For discussions of this crucial passage in *The Thirty-Nine Steps* see David Daniell, 'At the Foot of the Thirty-Ninth Step', *John Buchan Journal*, 10 (1991), 15–28; and the Introduction of *The Thirty-Nine Steps*, ed. Harvie, pp. xviii–xix.

SEVEN

Imperial Decline and Fall

The Post-War World and the Scottish Renaissance

> Things fall apart; the centre cannot hold;
> Mere anarchy is loosed upon the world,
> The blood-dimmed tide is loosed, and everywhere
> The ceremony of innocence is drowned;
> W. B. Yeats, 'The Second Coming' (*written in 1919*)

The experience of the unspeakable horror of the trench warfare of the First World War was in itself enough to ensure that the post-1918 world would be very different from the pre-1914 world. After the war, it was felt by many that the secure and established foundations of civilisation had been shaken. T. S. Eliot's *The Waste Land* (first published in 1922) surveys a desolate world: 'On Margate Sands. | I can connect | Nothing with nothing'. Peter Ackroyd writes that 'Eliot's distress was not caused by private matters alone':

> The year in which *The Waste Land* was written [1921] was one of intense political and economic discontent: the post-war 'boom' had collapsed, there were two million unemployed and the economic chaos was exacerbated by the indecisiveness of the coalition government.[1]

Nevertheless, there were people for whom the upheavals of the post-war world seemed to hold out hope for new beginnings and for revolutionary change—and that spirit animated the writers of the post-war literary movement that came to be known as 'the Scottish Renaissance'. As they set out to re-connect with the pre-British culture of Scotland, these socialist writers of the 1920s and 1930s were in sympathy with various major developments that had taken place since the second half of the 1910s.

One such development, the Easter Rising of 1916, took place in Ireland. The Rising was quickly crushed by British forces and its leaders were executed. However, these executions proved to be counter-productive in that they served to harden and intensify support for the cause of Irish Independence. In his poem 'Easter 1916' W. B. Yeats gave memorable expression to this post-Rising mood in Ireland: 'All changed, changed utterly: | A terrible beauty is born'.

Not only a terrible beauty, but also a terrible conflict. The Irish Republican Army continued the violent resistance to British rule that had manifested itself in the Rising, and its bloody activities were met with ruthless reprisals. A resolution of sorts was made available by the British Parliament's Government of Ireland Act (1920), which provided for the partition of Ireland between a new Irish Free State and the six counties of Northern Ireland (which would remain with Britain). The Irish Free State duly came into being in January 1922, but this happened on terms that were repugnant to Irish Republican opinion: oaths of loyalty to the British monarch were required, for example. These terms had only been accepted by Irish Republican leaders because Lloyd George, the British Prime Minister, had threatened war on Ireland if they had been rejected. In the event their acceptance provoked civil war in the Irish Free State during the 1920s. Indeed, troubles continued on the island of Ireland long after the 1920s, and it was not until 2005 that the IRA declared that its war with Britain was finally over.

The Russian Revolutions of 1917 were of even greater significance than the Easter Rising. By 1917, catastrophic defeats of the Imperial Russian army by German forces during the First World War had created conditions that opened the way for the rule of the Tsars to be overthrown in the February Revolution, and for the rule of the Bolsheviks (under Lenin) to be established by the October Revolution. As a result of these developments the Union of Soviet Socialist Republics was established in 1923—an important step in the process by which the old Russian Empire was transformed into a new and potent force dedicated to the world-wide spread of socialism. The British Empire, weakened by the war, was now confronted by a disturbingly influential and powerful rival in the USSR. Furthermore, the USA, having made a decisive intervention in the final stages of the First World War, was beginning to flex its muscles as a major world power. Indeed, later in the twentieth century a titanic struggle for dominance developed between the USSR and the USA, with Britain being relegated to a subordinate role on the sidelines.

Another event of seismic importance for the future of the British Empire was Mahatma Gandhi's decision in 1919 to become actively involved in Indian politics as an advocate of Independence. Gandhi (1869–1948) was, as it happens, an almost exact contemporary of John Buchan (1875–1940). Following a childhood spent in India, Gandhi went to England to study law in 1888, and then lived and worked in South Africa from 1893 until 1914. After returning to India he became politically active in 1919, and emerged as the leader of the Indian National Congress, the movement which by the late 1940s had secured Independence, and the ending of British Imperial rule in India.

Gandhi was shocked at the extent of the racial discrimination in South Africa, and while living there he undertook a series of challenges to the government. Buchan, it will be remembered, worked for Lord Milner in South Africa from 1901 till 1903, that is to say during Gandhi's time there. Indeed, Gandhi was still in South Africa when Buchan, now back in London, was writing the confidently pro-Imperial *Prester John* (1910).

After the First World War, an exhausted and impoverished Imperial Britain was faced with potent and troublesome new opponents: the USSR, the IRA, and the Indian National Congress (to name but three). Furthermore, those in charge of the British Imperial project began to find it more difficult to believe wholeheartedly in the rightness of their cause. When faced with the reality of opponents like Gandhi, it was not easy to continue to assume that it truly was 'the white man's duty' to take over and run the countries of 'dark men who live only for the day and their own bellies', as Buchan puts it in *Prester John* (p. 365). In this situation the British Empire began to run out of conviction, and it also began to run out of energy.

MacDiarmid, Gibbon, and the Scottish Renaissance

> crystals gleaming like precious stones
> In the light reflected from the snow; and behind them
> The eternal lightning of Lenin's bones.
> Hugh MacDiarmid,
> 'The Skeleton of the Future (At Lenin's Tomb)'

In 1922 (the year of the first publication of Eliot's *The Waste Land* and Joyce's *Ulysses*) a new periodical called *The Scottish Chapbook* made its debut. Edited by Christopher Murray Grieve and containing contributions by Grieve's alter ego Hugh MacDiarmid, the new periodical inaugurated the literary movement that came to be known as the Scottish Renaissance. Strongly socialist in its sympathies, this movement was in tune with the ideals of Russia's October Revolution—and, as it advocated Independence for Scotland and a revival of the Scots and Gaelic languages, it was also in tune with current nationalist developments in India and in Ireland. There was thus some potential for tension between communist and nationalist strands within the movement. Rather splendidly, Hugh MacDiarmid was not only expelled in 1933 from the National Party of Scotland (a forerunner of the modern SNP) because of his communist sympathies, but was also expelled in 1936 from the Communist Party of Great Britain because of his 'nationalist deviationism'.[2]

The Scottish Renaissance produced some poetry of outstanding quality, particularly notable examples being MacDiarmid's *A Drunk Man Looks at the Thistle* (in Scots) and

Sorley MacLean's poem-sequence *Dàin do Eimhir* (in Gaelic). The movement also produced some excellent novels, several of which focus on a particular individual growing up within a subaltern community. Such novels set out to give voice to the story of the community as well as to the story of the individual, and subaltern concerns are powerfully articulated in (for example) Nan Shepherd's *The Quarry Wood* (1928), Neil Gunn's *Highland River* (1937), and Jessie Kesson's *The White Bird Passes* (1958). There is a widely-held view, however, that the most remarkable of all the novels of the Scottish Renaissance is *Sunset Song* (1932), which was written by (James) Leslie Mitchell under the pseudonym Lewis Grassic Gibbon. This novel forms the first part of Gibbon's remarkable trilogy *A Scots Quair* (1932–34).

Like Burns and Hogg before him, Leslie Mitchell (1901–35) was born to parents whose families had deep and long-established roots in the Scottish peasantry. Leslie's father was James Mitchell, a hard-working but strict and severe tenant-farmer, while his mother Lilias (*née* Gibbon) was the daughter of George Gibbon (a farm servant) and Lilias Gibbon (*née* Grassick). James Mitchell was farming at Hillhead of Seggat in Aberdeenshire at the time of Leslie's birth, but in 1909 the family moved to a farm in the parish of Arbuthnott, which lies in the Kincardineshire district known as the Howe of the Mearns.

The new farm was a poor one, and the family had a hard struggle to scrape a living from it. Leslie helped with the work of the farm in moods that included a resentful reluctance, and he found an escape from the drudgery of farm routines in the books of writers such as Rider Haggard, Darwin, and H. G. Wells. In 1917 (when he was sixteen) the family expectation was that Leslie would get a job as a farm labourer, but he was determined to be a writer, and by his own efforts he got himself a job in Aberdeen as a junior reporter on the *Aberdeen Journal*. Enthusiasm for the Russian Revolution of 1917 confirmed the young journalist in the socialist beliefs that had been shaped by his early reading, and it was as a convinced communist that he moved to Glasgow in the first half of 1919 to take up a post on the *Scottish Farmer*. It is worth remembering that Glasgow at this time was in the midst of its 'Red Clydeside' period, in which a prominent part was played by the revolutionary socialist leader John Maclean (1879–1923), whose parents had come to Glasgow as a result of the Highland Clearances. Terry Brotherstone writes in *The Oxford Companion to Scottish History*:

> In 1918 John Maclean—appointed a consul for Russia's Bolshevik government—received the longest of his several prison sentences for seditious activities. But five years became little more than six months when the end of the war, fears for Maclean's health, and working-class pressure, led to his release. Early in 1919 the west of Scotland was at the centre of the post-war labour unrest. The 40 hours' strike resulted in a riot which the Scottish Secretary told the cabinet was a 'Bolshevist rising' and in a low-level military occupation of central Glasgow.[3]

The shock and anger with which Leslie Mitchell observed the slums of Glasgow in 1919 lends energy to a later essay on that city, written in the 1930s under his pen-name 'Lewis Grassic Gibbon'. This essay appeared in *Scottish Scene; or, The Intelligent Man's Guide to Albyn* (London: Jarrolds, 1934), a book consisting of contributions by Gibbon and Hugh MacDiarmid. Gibbon's 'Glasgow' (pp. 136–47) opens with characteristic vigour:

> Glasgow is one of the few places in Scotland which defy personification. To imagine Edinburgh as a disappointed spinster, with a hare-lip and inhibitions, is at least to approximate as closely to the truth as to imagine the Prime Mover as a Levantine Semite. So with Dundee, a frowsy fisher-wife addicted to gin and infanticide, Aberdeen a thin-lipped peasant-woman who has borne eleven and buried nine. (p. 136)

For Gibbon, however, the slums of Glasgow are simply too horrific for such personification to be appropriate. He goes on to write of the conditions in which life 'festers in the courts and wynds and alleys of Camlachie, Govan, the Gorbals'. In Glasgow slum districts such as these

> there are over a hundred and fifty thousand human beings living in such conditions as the most bitterly pressed primitive in Tierra del Fuego never visioned. [...] The hundred and fifty thousand eat and sleep and copulate and conceive and crawl into childhood in those waste jungles of stench and disease and hopelessness, sub-humans as definitely as the Morlocks of Wells—and without even the consolation of feeding on their oppressors' flesh. (pp. 137–38).

It is interesting to remember that John Buchan's father had been minister of the John Knox Church in the Gorbals from 1888 until his retirement in 1909, and that Buchan himself had been a Glasgow schoolboy and undergraduate as a son of the John Knox manse.

In Glasgow in 1919, Leslie Mitchell became politically active. He also, as Douglas F. Young puts it, 'lost his job as a journalist, apparently for fiddling his expenses to fund his politics'.[4] It may well be that 'fiddling his expenses' did not strike this idealistic and angry young communist as an act of petty dishonesty, but rather as a small blow struck at a deeply corrupt capitalism in the cause of the coming Revolution. At all events loss of his job in this way ended his career in journalism, and placed him in a fairly desperate situation. *Faute de mieux*, Mitchell joined the Royal Army Service Corps, in which he served from 1919 until 1923 before enlisting as a clerk in the Royal Air Force, in which he served from 1923 until 1929. Army life did not suit Mitchell. However, it brought him the compensation of postings in various interesting parts of the Middle East, and he made use of his experiences in these exotic locations when, during his RAF years, he began serious work as a writer. During this RAF period he married Rebecca

('Ray') Middleton, whom he had known since childhood in Arbuthnott.

Courageously, Mitchell gave up the young couple's only reliable source of income in 1929 when he left the RAF with a view to becoming a full-time writer. An impoverished period in London followed, but by 1931 he had prospered sufficiently to be able to move to Welwyn Garden City, a new town a little to the north of London that had been established in 1920 as part of the 'Garden City' movement. This was an environment of a kind that did not appeal to John Buchan, who in *Mr Standfast* (1919) describes with some distaste the 'gimcrack little "arty" houses' and the pacifist and socialist sympathies of 'the Garden City of Biggleswick'.[5] However, it was in Welwyn Garden City, in the few years that remained to him before his early death in 1935, that Leslie Mitchell wrote his best work.

Sunset Song and *A Scots Quair*

Like James Hogg, Leslie Mitchell was born into a peasant society which, in some moods, he found restricting, and beyond which he was determined to move into a wider world rich with the promise of intellectual excitements. Many of Mitchell's novels were written in his own name, and these books tend to focus on exotic locations and situations, far from his childhood home in Arbuthnott. Among the Mitchell novels, *Spartacus* (1933) is especially notable, and grows out of a socialist's natural interest in the slave revolt led by Spartacus in the days of the Roman Empire. However, Mitchell was also like Hogg in that he had a deep emotional involvement with his native community, and it was to the world of Arbuthnott that he turned in *Sunset Song* (1932). It was for this new focusing on the territory of his childhood that he first adopted the pen-name of Lewis Grassic Gibbon.

We have seen that the Scottish Renaissance movement combined a commitment to socialism with a commitment to cultural nationalism. For Gibbon, the commitment to socialism was what really mattered: the achievement of power for the proletariat was much more important than the revival of the Gaelic language and similar concerns. Nevertheless, an affirmation of the value of the traditional culture of his native community forms part of the structure of Gibbon's trilogy, 'A Scots Quair'. *Sunset Song*, the first novel of the trilogy, celebrates the world of the old Scottish peasantry—a world which it regards as having been brought to an end by the cataclysm of the First World War. *Cloud Howe* (1933), the second novel, moves its focus to a small town and presents the well-intentioned Christianity of Robert Colquohoun as being, in the end, a set of cloudy dreams, inadequate as a response to the troubles and demands of the post-war world. Finally, in *Grey Granite* (1934; dedicated to Hugh MacDiarmid), the focus moves to a city and the struggle for revolution, a struggle that will finally be won by human qualities symbolised by the sparkling hardness of grey granite. Gandhi could sit at his spinning wheel to symbolise the need to overthrow British rule, and the need to re-connect India's future with its past. For Gibbon, the old ways were worthy of celebration, but they were in the past, and had to remain in the past. The path to the future lay elsewhere.

Sunset Song is in some ways strongly autobiographical: for example, like the Mitchells, the novel's Guthrie family moves from Aberdeenshire to the Howe of the Mearns a few years before the outbreak of the First World War. However, the central concern of Gibbon's narrative is with a Mearns farming community as a whole, rather than with his own personal experiences as a boy growing up in the Mearns—and *Sunset Song* achieves a fruitful combination of detachment and personal involvement by making its central character, Chris, a daughter rather than a son of the Guthrie family.

In part, *Sunset Song* focuses on the farming community of Kinraddie through scenes in which the community comes together for one purpose or another: the communal attempt to put out the fire at Chae Strachan's farm, the communal celebration of Chris's wedding, and so on. There is another aspect to this, however. As we saw in Chapter 5, Gibbon's novel (like Hogg's *The Brownie of Bodsbeck*) centres, in Cairns Craig's phrase, on 'a community's self-narration in dialect'. This project involved practical problems for Gibbon. For commercial reasons, making the 'dialect' of *Sunset Song* a full rendition of the Scots speech of the Mearns was not a practical possibility in the 1930s for a professional writer working for a London publisher. Nevertheless, it was clear that the community of the Mearns could not achieve a convincing or authentic 'self-narration' through the medium of standard English; and it was also clear that, in order to achieve a community's self-narration in dialect, it would be necessary to find a way to locate narrative authority within the community itself, rather than confining narrative authority to an external observer.

Gibbon overcomes these problems with great skill. The narrative voice of *Sunset Song* modulates unobtrusively between three registers: comment from an authorial perspective; an articulation of the shared consciousness of the community—'the speak of the Mearns'; and an articulation of the consciousness of Chris Guthrie. With regard to dialect, Gibbon outlines his strategy in a 'Note' at the beginning of the novel:

> If the great Dutch language disappeared from literary usage and a Dutchman wrote in German a story of the Lekside peasants, one may hazard he would ask and receive a certain latitude and forbearance in his usage of German. He might import into his pages some score or so untranslatable words and idioms—untranslatable except in their context and setting; he might mould in some fashion his German to the rhythms and cadence of the kindred speech that his peasants speak. Beyond that, in fairness to his hosts, he hardly could go: to seek effect by a spray of apostrophes would be both impertinence and mis-translation.
>
> The courtesy that the hypothetical Dutchman might receive from German a Scot may invoke from the great English tongue.[6]

Just over a century earlier, Galt had adopted a similar strategy for the narrative voice of 'fictional autobiographies' such as *The Provost* and *Ringan Gilhaize*—and Gibbon, like Galt, is able to create a narrative voice that speaks convincingly for and from the author's native community.

As we saw in Chapter 5, Cairns Craig argues that novels committed to the use of dialect

> necessarily involve themselves not only in dialogue—the speech of the demotic—
> and in the dialogic—in Bakhtin's sense of multiple voices within a text—but also
> in dialectic, because the existence of two or more distinct linguistic contexts within
> the text presumes the existence of alternative value systems which those linguistic
> contexts express, and therefore of a dialectical process of debate and argument be-
> tween those values.[7]

In *Sunset Song*, this dialectic exists within Chris herself. Like a Maori-speaking child educated in one of the Empire's English-language schools, Chris finds herself divided between the value-system of her native speech and community, and the value-system of her formal education:

> So that was Chris and her reading and schooling, two Chrisses there were that
> fought for her heart and tormented her. You hated the land and the coarse speak
> of the folk and learning was brave and fine one day; and the next you'd waken
> with the peewits crying across the hills, deep and deep, crying in the heart of you
> and the smell of the earth in your face, almost you'd cry for that, the beauty of it
> and the sweetness of the Scottish land and skies. You saw their faces in the fire-
> light, father's and mother's and the neighbours', before the lamps lit up, tired
> and kind, faces dear and close to you, you wanted the words they'd known and
> used, forgotten in the far-off youngness of their lives, Scots words to tell to
> your heart how they wrung it and held it, the toil of their days and unendingly
> their fight. And the next minute that passed from you, you were English, back
> to the English words so sharp and clean and true—for a while, for a while, till
> they slid so smooth from your throat you knew they could never say anything
> that was worth saying at all. (p. 32)

Like Achebe in *Things Fall Apart*, Gibbon paints a warts-and-all picture of the ances-tral world of his native community, even as he asserts the worth of that world and asserts that it, too, has a story to tell. For example, early in *Sunset Song* John Guthrie strikes his son Will for using the word 'Jehovah':

> Chris had cried and hidden her face but now she looked again, Will was sitting up

slowly, the blood on his face, and John Guthrie speaking to him, not looking at him, grooming Bess.

And mind, my mannie, if I ever hear you again take your Maker's name in vain, if I ever hear you use that word again, I'll libb you. Mind that. Libb you like a lamb. (p. 30)

To *libb* is to castrate. The dark side of the Scottish Presbyterian tradition includes a potential for fierce, fanatical violence—and that dark potential emerges in John Guthrie, here and elsewhere. The novel's portrait of Guthrie is not wholly negative, however: for example, his fierce and Covenanter-like refusal to cow-tow to 'gentry' is consistently presented as admirable.

For Gibbon, John Guthrie is a figure from the past: the future lies elsewhere, with socialism. Guthrie is a Liberal in politics (p. 95), and with his socialist neighbours Chae Strachan and Long Rob of the Mill he forcefully supports a Liberal against a Tory at an election meeting (pp. 96–97). Chae is a socialist who retains a religious belief; Rob, more advanced on the path towards a socialist future, is an atheist. At the election meeting, the Tory candidate (whose uncle is a Lord) is given a hard time by the audience. Heckling him, Chae declares:

there was a greater Lord who heard when the Tories took the name of poor folk in vain. The God of old Scotland there was, aye fighting on the side of the people since the days of old John Knox, and He would yet bring to an end the day of wealth and wastry throughout the world, liberty and equality and fraternity were coming though all the damned lordies in the House of Lords should pawn their bit coronets and throw their whores back in the streets and raise private armies to fight the common folk with their savings. (pp. 96–97)

In a passage from *The Thirty-Nine Steps* discussed in Chapter 6, Richard Hannay speaks to a pre-First-World-War election meeting about 'the kind of glorious business I thought could be made out of the Empire if we really put our backs into it'. Chae's views have a rather different emphasis at *Sunset Song*'s pre-First-World-War election meeting.

John Guthrie is a figure representative of the people in their struggles 'since the days of old John Knox', and his significance in this context is emphasised later in the novel. On the day when their love begins to deepen, Chris and her future husband (the farm worker Ewan Tavendale) visit Dunottar Castle, where many Covenanters had been imprisoned in the seventeenth century. Chris thinks of the Covenanters and remembers her now-dead father:

down below, in the dungeons, were the mouldering clefts where a prisoner's hands were nailed while they put him to torment. There the Covenanting folk had screamed and died while the gentry dined and danced in their lithe, warm halls, Chris stared at the places, sick and angry and sad for those folk she never could help now, that hatred of rulers and gentry a flame in her heart, John Guthrie's hate. Her folk and his they had been. (p. 125)

Sunset Song, the first novel of Gibbon's trilogy, ends with the unveiling of Kinraddie's War Memorial in a ceremony organised by the community's new minister, Robert Colquohoun. There are four names on the War Memorial, with 'James Leslie' being added to those of Chae, Rob, and Ewan (p. 255). Interestingly, James Leslie is not mentioned elsewhere in the novel. Here, it seems, the author James Leslie Mitchell is making a cameo appearance, in order to identify himself with the pre-First-World-War peasant-farming community in which he grew up.

In *Things Fall Apart*, Achebe celebrates the traditional world of pre-Imperial Igbo society, providing a warts-and-all portrait of a now-destroyed society deeply worthy of respect: 'we, too, might have a story to tell'. Like Achebe, Gibbon sets out to tell the story of the past of his own people. At the unveiling of the War Memorial in *Sunset Song*, Robert Colquohoun makes explicit what the whole novel has declared, as he speaks eloquently and movingly of 'those four who died in France':

> *With them we may say there died a thing older than themselves, these were the Last of the Peasants, the last of the Old Scots folk. A new generation comes up that will know them not, except as a memory in a song, they pass with the things that seemed good to them, with loves and desires that grow dim and alien in the days to be. It was the old Scotland that perished then, and we may believe that never again will the old speech and the old songs, the old curses and the old benedictions, rise but with alien effort to our lips. The last of the peasants, those four that you knew, took that with them to the darkness and the quietness of the places where they sleep.* (p. 256: Gibbon's italics)

John Buchan Between the Wars

In *Sunset Song*, Long Rob of the Mill is deeply opposed to the First World War, and he puts up a long and heroic resistance to being conscripted into the wartime army. Rob's attitude would have been anathema to John Buchan's war hero Richard Hannay, and it is interesting to imagine a conversation on this subject between Rob and Hannay. For his part, Buchan himself worked as an intelligence officer during the First World War, and in 1918 he became Director of the Department of Information, a position in which he was directly responsible to the Prime Minister. After the war was over, in 1919 he bought Elsfield Manor (situated a few miles from Oxford) as a family home. Life in a manor-house was expensive, but Buchan generated a substantial income through his continuing work in the Nelson's publishing house, and by becoming first a director and then deputy chairman of the press agency Reuters. He also continued with his writing, and his extensive output included a sympathetic and well-received biography of Sir Walter Scott (1932). Buchan had political ambitions, and in 1927 he entered Parliament as a Tory M.P., representing the Scottish Universities. To his disappointment, cabinet office eluded him, but various other honours came his way. After the Free Kirk and the Auld Kirk had re-united in 1929, he represented the Monarch as Lord High Commissioner to the General Assembly of the Church of Scotland in 1933 and again in 1934. Then, in 1935, as Lord Tweedsmuir of Elsfield, he was appointed Governor-General of Canada. As Governor-General he signed Canada's declaration of war on Germany in 1939, and he died in office in February 1940.

Buchan's *Huntingtower* (like Eliot's *The Waste Land* and Joyce's *Ulysses* in this, if in nothing else) was first published in 1922. Manifestly designed as a riposte to the Bolsheviks and the Russian Revolution, this particular Buchan thriller opens in January 1916 at a ball in the Nirski Palace in Russia. The young, beautiful, and ardent Saskia is about 'to begin nursing at the Alexander Hospital', secure in her belief that Russia will be victorious in the war. Quentin, recently wounded on the Volhynian front, is not so confident. He takes three small ivory figures (a priest, a soldier, and a draught-ox), and on them he balances a heavy casket of 'dark green imperial jade'. He comments:

> Look, Saskia! If you were living inside that box you would think it very secure. You would note the thickness of the walls and the hardness of the stone, and you would dream away in a peaceful green dusk. But all the time it would be held up by trifles—brittle trifles.[8]

Two of the supports slip after Saskia moves away, but Quentin manages 'to prevent the jade casket from crashing to the floor'. The opening chapter of *Huntingtower* ends as follows:

> He replaced the thing on its proper table and stood silent for a moment.
> "The priest and the soldier gone, and only the beast of burden left. . . . If I were inclined to be superstitious, I should call that a dashed bad omen." (p. 14)

In 1922, the first readers of *Huntingtower* would have had no difficulty in interpreting the significance of this dashed bad omen. Buchan's image suggests that the world of Imperial Russia is destined to be overturned in 1917 because the common people (represented by 'the beast of burden') have disturbingly remained standing, while the church and the army have collapsed. However, it seems that there remains a chance that the casket of 'dark green imperial jade' can still be caught in time, and restored unscathed to 'its proper table'.

The remainder of Buchan's thriller is set in post-war Scotland, where Saskia is in hiding from the Bolsheviks as she attempts to conceal the rich hoard of jewels that she holds in trust for Russians still loyal to the old regime. We discover that Saskia's family is 'among the greatest in Russia, the very greatest after the throne' (p. 102); and we also discover that the dastardly Bolsheviks are hot on her trail. This 'Princess', however, is destined to be saved by Dickson McCunn, a rich and recently-retired Glasgow grocer who is a descendant, we are told on p. v, of the Bailie Nicol Jarvie of Scott's *Rob Roy*. Like his remarkable ancestor, this unlikely and somewhat comical rescuer of a princess embodies the solid worth of middle-class values and commercial success. Nevertheless we are told that, 'like the Bailie', Dickson 'can count kin, should he wish, with Rob Roy himself' (p. vi). A dash of outlaw blood will stand Buchan's grocer-hero in good stead during the headlong adventures of *Huntingtower*.

Dickson has allies. John Heritage, a socialist poet educated at Harrow and Cambridge, comes to see the error of his ways and helps to rescue the Princess. Buchan's post-war thrillers tend to return to the figure of the socialist intellectual who is a good chap really, in spite of his socialism: the Oxford-educated Launcelot Wake in *Mr Standfast* is another example. Reassuring both himself and his readers, Buchan stresses that these people can be relied upon to do the decent thing when it comes to the crunch.

Crucial assistance in the rescue of the Princess is also provided by 'the Gorbals Die-Hards',

> a kind of unauthorized and unofficial Boy Scouts, who, without uniform or badge or any kind of paraphernalia, followed the banner of Sir Robert Baden-Powell and subjected themselves to a rude discipline. They were far too poor to join an orthodox troop, but they faithfully copied what they believed to be the practices of more fortunate boys. (p. 25)

Anna Buchan records that, when her brother John was an undergraduate at Glasgow University, he taught 'a Sunday School class of eight very bad small boys' at the Rev. John Buchan's John Knox Free Kirk in the Gorbals. Her brother, Anna writes,

> delighted in them, and there is no doubt that they were the originals of the Gorbals Die-hards in *Huntingtower*. It is probable that he learned more from them than they learned from him. When he spoke to them on the lesson for the day they were often reminded by it of some experience of their own. They nodded their heads over the story of the sick man let down through the roof, and said they had seen a sailor in merry mood dancing on a bakehouse, and *he* went down through the roof. When the lesson was over John told them a story, which caused great excitement and went on serially from Sunday to Sunday. The hero was a missionary, which was supposed to make it suitable for Sunday School.[9]

In the novel, Dougal (the leader of the Die-Hards) at one point sings 'a strange ditty' that has been learned by his friend Wee Jaikie at 'a Socialist Sunday School':

> Class-conscious we are, and class-conscious wull be
> Till our fit's on the neck o' the Boorjoyzee. (pp. 200, 199)

In the happy ending that concludes the adventures of *Huntingtower*, the rich and quint-essentially bourgeois Dickson McCunn promises to take the Gorbals Die-Hards under his wing:

> You're fine laddies, and I'm going to see that you turn into fine men. There's the stuff in you to make Generals and Provosts—ay, and Prime Ministers, and Dod! it'll not be my blame if it doesn't get out. (p. 318)

For Buchan, the future does not lie with socialist revolution, but with giving the children of the slums the opportunity to turn themselves into Richard Hannay or Bailie Nicol Jarvie.

Huntingtower was a popular success, and, intriguingly, a film version was made in 1925 with Harry Lauder (no less) in the role of Dickson McCunn.[10] However, Buchan produced a darker response to the troubles of the post-war world in *The Three Hostages* (1924). In this novel Richard Hannay is now a contented family man, and after an extremely distinguished record of service in the war General Hannay has settled in a manor-house near Oxford. However, his rural idyll is disturbed when (as in honour bound) he responds to the call of duty, and attempts to resolve a particularly distressing situation: the children of three VIPs are being held hostage. The hostage-taking is no mere vulgar attempt to extort money, but turns out to be a manifestation of a disturbing large-scale plot masterminded by the much-admired and apparently respectable Dominic Medina—a plot which seeks to subvert all civilised values. At the core of *The Three Hostages* is a contest to the death between Richard Hannay (for Buchan, an embodiment of the traditional civilised and civilising values of the British Empire) and Dominic Medina (for Buchan, an embodiment of all the jejune fanaticisms that threaten, in the angst of the post-war world, to destroy civilisation).

What Hannay represents can be glimpsed when he and his friend Sandy Arbuthnot meet for breakfast at a Cotswold inn, as they try to devise ways to defeat Medina.

> The sounds of the morning were beginning to rise from the little village far away in the bottom, the jolt of a wagon, the 'clink-clenk' from the smithy, the babble of children at play. In a fortnight the may-fly would be here, and every laburnum and guelder rose in bloom. Sandy, who had been away from England for years, did not speak for a long time, but drank in the sweet-scented peace of it.[11]

Throughout Buchan's Hannay books, Sandy Arbuthnot (Lord Clanroyden) is presented as a thoroughly admirable character, whose views are eminently worthy of respect. In *The Three Hostages*, Sandy forcefully sets out his reasons for thinking that Imperial Britain's foreign policy has gone badly off the rails since the war:

> I loathe our new manners in foreign policy. The old English way was to regard all
> foreigners as slightly childish and rather idiotic and ourselves as the only grown-ups in
> a kindergarten world. That meant that we had a cool detached view and did even-
> handed unsympathetic justice. But now we have got into the nursery ourselves and are
> bear-fighting on the floor. We take violent sides, and make pets, and of course, if you
> are *–phil* something or other you have got to be *–phobe* something else. It is all wrong.
> (p. 712)

That certainly puts Johnny Foreigner firmly in his kindergarten place; and, for better or for worse, that is the kind of view that Hannay and his friends embody on behalf of their creator.

What Medina represents can be glimpsed in a scene very different from the epiphany at the Cotswold inn. Hannay, as he seeks to free the three hostages, finds himself at a night-club which later turns out to be a cover for aspects of Medina's operation. Emphatically, Hannay does not enjoy the show:

> It seemed to me a wholly rotten and funereal business. A nigger band, looking like
> monkeys in uniform, pounded out some kind of barbarous jingle, and sad-faced mari-
> onettes moved to it. There was no gaiety or devil in the dancing, only a kind of bored
> perfection. Thin young men with rabbit heads and hair brushed straight back from
> their brows, who I suppose were professional dancing partners, held close to their
> breasts women of every shape and age, but all alike in having dead eyes and masks for
> faces, and the *macabre* procession moved like automata to the niggers' rhythm.   (pp.
> 747–48)

The racism that is all too painfully evident here can also be seen in the novel's repeated insistence on the shape of Medina's head. Hannay remarks: 'The way he brushed his hair front and back made it look square, but I saw that it was really round, the roundest head I have ever seen except in a Kaffir' (p. 703). At a later point, when he again sees that Medina's head is 'round as a football', Hannay asks himself: 'What did a head like that portend? I had a vague remembrance that I had heard somewhere that it meant madness—at any rate degeneracy' (p. 757). Clearly, the apparently respectable Medina is not all that he seems: he is more 'primitive', more dangerous.

Arguably, *The Three Hostages* is Buchan's equivalent of Bram Stoker's *Dracula* (1897). Stoker's novel draws on fears regarding the Darwinian ape within humanity as it confronts the possibility that dark atavistic forces, having been released in 'primitive' parts of the world, might threaten civilised Europe. A process of reverse colonisation is envisaged, as Dracula plans to penetrate and to conquer London from his ancient Transylvanian fastness. In *The Three Hostages*, Medina has contrived (in spite of his round 'Kaffir' head) to establish himself as an admired and well-liked figure in the powerful world of London's clubland. This is the world that Buchan himself had entered, after Oxford: but Medina, another Dracula, has entered London's citadel in order to destroy what it stands for. As Sandy Arbuthnot puts it, Medina 'aims at conquering the very heart, the very soundest part of our society' (p. 783).

Buchan's Dracula is partly Irish, and (inspired by his mother) his cause is in part the cause of the Easter Rising. At one point in the novel Hannay observes Medina conversing with his mother in Irish Gaelic (which Hannay himself does not understand), and imagines her 'spinning beside a peat fire, nursing ancient hate and madness, and crooning forgotten poetry'. Hannay continues:

> I wished to Heaven I knew what they were saying. Sluicing out malice about my country, no doubt, or planning the ruin of our civilization for the sake of a neurotic dream. (p. 757)

However, as his name suggests, Buchan's Dracula also has links with the East: after Mecca, Medina is Islam's most holy city. Indeed, *The Three Hostages* presents its villain as an embodiment of all the neurotic fanaticisms that, for this novel, lie behind the 'stark craziness that the War has left in the world' (p. 666). Apparently articulating Buchan's view of the matter, Sandy Arbuthnot identifies Gandhi and Lenin as examples of that dangerous post-war phenomenon, 'the rational fanatic':

> In ordinary times he will not be heard, because, as I say, his world is not our world. But let there come a time of great suffering or discontent, when the mind of the ordinary man is in desperation, and the rational fanatic will come by his own. When he appeals to the sane and the sane respond, revolutions begin. (pp. 712–13)

Like Gandhi and Lenin, it seems, Medina is a 'rational fanatic' who poses a profound threat to the sound and civilised values of the British Empire.

Inevitably (for this is a Buchan novel) Hannay plays a crucial role in securing the release of the three hostages. He then finally overcomes Medina in a thrilling final sequence, as they stalk each other in the Scottish Highland deer forest of Machray. Deerstalking in the Highlands is, of course, a quintessentially Buchanesque activity: after the Clearances came the sheep, and when sheep-farming ceased to be profitable it was replaced in its turn by the aristocratic sport of deerstalking. We are told in *The Three Hostages* that Kennedy, one of Hannay's people on the Machray estate, 'was of Lowland stock; his father had come to the North from Galloway in the days of the boom in sheep, and had remained as a keeper when sheep prices fell' (p. 903). This might fairly be described as a somewhat bland and indirect reference to the troubles experienced by the people of the Highlands during the Clearances. However, as we shall see, the troubles of an indigenous people do loom large in *Sick Heart River*—Buchan's last novel (and, perhaps, his best).

Last Things

> For whosoever will save his life shall lose it: but whosoever will
> lose his life for my sake, the same shall save it. (Luke 9. 24)

> '*Car celui qui voudra sauver sa vie la perdra; et celui qui perdra sa vie*
> *pour l'amour de moi, la retrouvera.*' (John Buchan, *Sick Heart River*)

Written in illness by the Governor-General of Canada during the deeply troubled time around the outbreak of the Second World War, *Sick Heart River* (published posthumously in 1941) is a re-examination—and, ultimately, a re-affirmation—of John Buchan's core values. Set in 1939 and 1940, *Sick Heart River* focuses on the predicament of Francis Galliard, a French-Canadian who has become an important player in the world of New York high finance, but who has now vanished into the Canadian North after having experienced a crisis of identity, a crisis of the soul. As his name suggests, Galliard is a man of spirit and energy, a man likely to make a mark in a significant world. He has indeed done so in New York, but he has now absented himself without explanation.

Sir Edward Leithen is the man chosen for the task of finding Galliard, and restoring him to his proper place in society. An impressive figure from various earlier Buchan novels, Leithen is a Scot who is a major player in the British political establishment and in London's clubland. Leithen finds Galliard in the Canadian Arctic, and in due course a point comes when Galliard explains why he has abandoned his successful life in New York. Buchan's narrator summarises:

> He had been brought up a strict Catholic, but since he left home he had let his religion fall from him. He had never been to mass. Felicity was an Episcopalian who took her creed lightly, and they had been married in a fashionable New York church. Now all the fears and repressions of his youth came back to him. He had forgotten something of desperate importance, his eternal welfare. He had never thought much about religion, but had simply taken it for granted till he began to neglect it, so he had no sceptical apparatus to support him. His conduct had not been the result of enlightenment, but flat treason.
>
> 'I came to realise that I had forgotten God,' he said simply.
>
> The breaking-point came because of his love for Felicity. The further he moved

away from her and her world, the dearer she became. The one thing he was resolved should not happen was a slow decline in their affection. Either he would recover what he had lost and harmonise it with what he had gained, or a clean cut would be made, with no raw edges to fester ... So on a spring morning, with a breaking heart, he walked out of Felicity's life ...[12]

Buchan, the son of the Free Kirk manse, was very far from being a Catholic, nor did he at any time walk out of the life of his own well-connected Anglican wife, after their marriage in a fashionable London church. Nevertheless, it seems clear that in *Sick Heart River* he is using Galliard's predicament to explore his own departure from the world of his Free Kirk upbringing. In Chapter 6 we saw the tragi-comic failures of under-standing that existed between Buchan's aristocratic children and their forceful Free Kirk grandmother. Like Galliard, Buchan in his youth left his ancestral northern world in order to win the glittering prizes available in the powerful neighbouring country to the south. In *Sick Heart River* Buchan faces up to the loss involved in his departure from his ancestral world, and asks whether it is possible to 'recover what he had lost and harmonise it with what he had gained'. Leithen expresses the dilemma succinctly (p. 137): is Galliard, in making a new life for himself in New York, a man who has 'sold his birthright'? Or is it 'possible to keep your birthright and live in a new world'? In short, *Sick Heart River* asks whether Lord Tweedsmuir of Elsfield Manor has sold out on the Free Kirk's noble ideals of sacrificial service—the ideals for which the Rev. John Buchan (shortening his own life in the process) had worked long and hard in the slums of the Gorbals. Lord Tweedsmuir's last novel also asks whether these ancestral Free Kirk ideals can in fact be harmonised with a successful life in the powerful and glamorous world of London's elite.

In *Sick Heart River* Sir Edward Leithen is a Scot who has prospered nobly among the glittering prizes of London's clubland, and he is clearly in some sense another repre-sentative within the fiction of Buchan himself. Leithen (like Buchan)

had been brought up in a Calvinistic household and the atmosphere still clung to him, though in the ordinary way he was not a religious man. For example, he had always had an acute sense of sin, which had made him something of a Puritan in his way of life. He had believed firmly in God, a Being of ineffable purity and power, and conse-quently had had no undue reverence for man. He had always felt his own insignifi-cance and imperfections and was not inclined to cavil at fate. (p. 12)

Leithen believes himself to be a dying man as he journeys to the Canadian North in the summer of 1939. His lungs are suffering from the after-effects of gas poisoning during the First World War, and the best medical advice indicates that he has only a year to live. The journey to the wild and potentially liberating (but dangerous and potentially destructive) arctic North involves both Leithen and Galliard in a deepening relationship with ultimate realities, and with God. After a very close approach to death at Sick Heart River, Leithen's lungs begin to improve under the influence of the pure arctic air. A welcome new lease of life seems to be opening out for the man who had been dying, but he chooses to turn away from a course of action that would lead to restored health, in order to take over the leadership of a group of ill and demoralised Hare Indians, natives of the northern wilderness. In choosing this course, Leithen feels that he is making his own contribution to the struggle for the forces of Life against the forces of Death, a struggle that is also manifesting itself in the war that has recently broken out in Europe (p. 182). Leithen duly succeeds in saving the Hares, but (as he had foreseen) he loses his own life in the process.

This course of heroic self-sacrifice is not chosen out of any particular admiration for the Hares. When the appeal to help them first comes, Leithen feels no urge to respond:

> He had more urgent things to think about than the future of a few hundred degenerate Indians who mattered not at all in his scheme of things. His business was with Galliard, who mattered a good deal. (p. 150)

Leithen is aware that he seems to be winning his battle against illness, but 'now he was being asked to stake all his winnings on a trivial cause—the *malaise* of human kites and crows roosting at the ends of the earth' (p. 151).

There is a contempt here for the Hares that makes one wince, as does the arrogance in Buchan's assumption that, while the Hares cannot save themselves, Leithen (the White Man) can save them. But then again, there is no getting away from the point that Leithen is willing, in the end, to sacrifice his own life in order to save the Hares.

In making this sacrifice, Leithen also helps Galliard to 'recover what he had lost and harmonise it with what he had gained': the way of a God known during a northern youth can also be followed by a successful man of a larger, richer, more powerful world which lies to the south. The basis for Buchan's belief in this can be traced in the disturbing words from *Prester John* quoted in Chapter 6, according to which 'the white man's duty' is

> to take all risks, recking nothing of his life or his fortunes, and well content to find his reward in the fulfilment of his task. That is the difference between white and black, the gift of responsibility, the power of being in a little way a king; and so long as we know this and practise it, we will rule not in Africa alone but wherever there are dark men who live only for the day and their own bellies. (p. 365)

Sick Heart River presents Leithen as being 'in a little way a king', as being a servant of God and of the forces of Life during his self-sacrificial saving of the Hares. Likewise, at the end of the novel Galliard (having been saved by Leithen) is preparing to go off to do his duty in the Second World War.

In *Memory Hold-the-Door* (written about the same time as *Sick Heart River*) Buchan looks back on his time in South Africa before the First World War:

> As for the native races under our rule, we had a high conscientiousness; Milner and Rhodes had a far-sighted native policy. The "white man's burden" is now an almost meaningless phrase; then it involved a new philosophy of politics, and an ethical standard, serious and surely not ignoble. (p. 125)

In one of its least attractive aspects, the Scottish Presbyterian tradition spawned a sectarian antagonism against Roman Catholicism that found (and sometimes still finds) an outlet in violent hostility to Irish Catholic immigrants and their descendants. That hostility flourished (and still flourishes) under the banner of the pro-British and pro-Unionist politics of the Orange Order. Edwin Morgan's poem 'King Billy' reflects on the funeral in Glasgow in the 1960s of a violent Orange working-class gang leader of the 1930s.

> Bareheaded, in dark suits, with flutes
> and drums, they brought him here, in procession
> seriously, King Billy of Brigton, dead,
> from Bridgeton Cross: [...]
> So a thousand people stopped the traffic
> for the hearse of a folk hero and the flutes
> threw 'Onward Christian Soldiers' to the winds
> from unironic lips, the mourners kept
> in step, and there were some who wept.[13]

As we saw at the beginning of Chapter 1, Ranajit Guha has suggested that during the British raj the indigenous portion of the dominant Indian elite could include people belonging to 'hierarchically inferior' social strata, who nevertheless acted in the interests of the elite *'and not in conformity to interests corresponding truly to their own social being'* [Guha's italics]. Arguably, many members of the Orange Order have traditionally occupied a similar position, not only in Scotland but also in Northern Ireland. At all events, in Edwin Morgan's poem the dead King Billy of Brigton was 'a quiet man at last, dying | alone in Bridgeton in a box bed'. In King Billy of Brigton we encounter someone very different from John Buchan's clubland heroes, albeit someone who lived and died not very far from the Rev. John Buchan's John Knox Kirk: Bridgeton is close to the Gorbals. Like Buchan's clubland heroes, this violent Glasgow Orangeman aspired in his way to be a servant of the cause of Imperial Britain. Edwin Morgan's poem concludes with lines that may serve not only as an epitaph for King Billy of Brigton, but also as an epitaph for John Buchan and the British Empire:

> Go from the grave. The shrill flutes
> are silent, the march dispersed.
> Deplore what is to be deplored,
> and then find out the rest.

Notes

1 Peter Ackroyd, *T. S. Eliot* (London: Hamish Hamilton, 1984), p. 109.

2 See Alan Bold, *MacDiarmid: Christopher Murray Grieve, A Critical Biography* (London: John Murray, 1988), pp. 289, 343.

3 Terry Brotherstone, 'Red Clydeside', in *The Oxford Companion to Scottish History*, ed. by Michael Lynch (Oxford: Oxford University Press, 2001), 499–500 (p. 500).

4 Quoted from Douglas F. Young's excellent article on [James] Leslie Mitchell in the *Oxford Dictionary of National Biography*.

5 John Buchan, *The Complete Richard Hannay: The Thirty-Nine Steps; Greenmantle; Mr Standfast; The Three Hostages; The Island of Sheep* (London: Penguin, 1992), pp. 367, 369.

6 Lewis Grassic Gibbon, *A Scots Quair: Sunset Song; Cloud Howe; Grey Granite*, ed. by Tom Crawford, Canongate Classics, 59 (Edinburgh: Canongate, 1995), p. xiii. Subsequent references are to this edition, and are given in the text.

7 Cairns Craig, *The Modern Scottish Novel: Narrative and the National Imagination* (Edinburgh: Edinburgh University Press, 1999), p. 98.

8 John Buchan, *Huntingtower* (London: Nelson, 1924; 1st edn Nelson, 1922), pp. 10, 12–13. Subsequent references are to the 1924 edition, and are given in the text.

9 Anna Buchan, *Unforgettable, Unforgotten* (London: Hodder & Stoughton, 1945), p. 71. For 'the story of the sick man let down through the roof', see Mark 2. 1–5.

10 See Janet Adam Smith, *John Buchan: A Biography* (Oxford: Oxford University Press, 1985), p. 300. Harry Lauder was an early-twentieth-century music hall star, whose act depended on an exaggerated comic portrayal of Scottish stereotypes.

11 John Buchan, *The Complete Richard Hannay: The Thirty-Nine Steps; Greenmantle; Mr Standfast; The Three Hostages; The Island of Sheep* (London: Penguin, 1992), pp. 781–82. Future references to *The Three Hostages* are to this edition, and are given in the text.

12 *Sick Heart River*, in John Buchan, *The Leithen Stories*, introduced by Christopher Harvie (Edinburgh: Canongate, 2000), p. 142. Future references to *Sick Heart River* are to this edition, and are given in the text.

13 'King Billy' appears in Edwin Morgan, *The Second Life* (Edinburgh: Edinburgh University Press, 1968), pp. 35–36.

EIGHT

Postscript: After the Empire

Post-Imperial Champions of Empire

The British Empire did not long survive the Second World War. India had achieved Independence by the end of the 1940s, while in the 1950s and 1960s Harold Macmillan's 'wind of change' brought to a close the British Imperial era in Africa. As the twenty-first century opens, we are half a century on from the end of Empire. Nevertheless, the legacy of Empire remains active in all sorts of ways, and the Scott / Buchan and Hogg / Gibbon traditions of the Imperial era have continued to have an impact on recent and current Scottish writing.

Notably, the writings of the distinguished Scottish novelist Allan Massie owe much to Sir Walter Scott and the Waverley Novels. Admittedly, Massie's historical novels tend to focus on events outside Scotland: for example, *Augustus* (1986) is set in Imperial Rome, while *A Question of Loyalties* (1989) examines the predicament of France during and after the Second World War. The reasons for this choice of non-Scottish settings can be readily understood in the light of a review, written by Massie in 1979, of Francis R. Hart's *The Scottish Novel.* For Massie, as a result of 'our century's centripetal force', Scotland has ceased to be a distinctive society where interesting and important things happen: in the twentieth century, Scotland no longer has a significant story to tell. Developing his point, Massie writes that Eric Linklater's 'consciousness of himself as a "Scottish novelist" rather than just a novelist, *tout court*, somehow got in the way of his talent'. Massie continues:

> The suggestion is reinforced by reading James Kennaway and Muriel Spark, both of whom refused to be held in the trap, though in *Household Ghosts* and *The Prime of Miss Jean Brodie* respectively they painted penetrating and illuminating pictures of Scotch society. But they neither of them worked in Scottish settings as a rule, both preferring

to see themselves as writers whose loyalty was to their age rather than to any geographical expression. So they turned to where the significant action was, wherever
they found it.[1]

Nevertheless, the debt owed by Massie's historical novels to Sir Walter Scott is evident and acknowledged. Discussing the 'profound influence' of the Waverley Novels
on the ways in which Massie constructs 'non-Scottish histories', Cairns Craig makes the
point that Massie's narrators

> are almost always people caught unawares between competing historical forces, just as
> Scott's protagonists are: the narrators may reflect on the action rather than participat-
> ing urgently in it, but they replicate Scott's deliberately banal heroes in their passive
> ability to see both sides of a conflict. In *A Question of Loyalties*, for instance, the issue
> of France's complicity with Nazism during the Second World War is narrated by
> Etienne de Balafré, son of one of those who participated in the Vichy government.
> Etienne stands between the generation of his father, caught up in vast historical
> events, and the generation of his daughter, student activists who 'believe that words
> can cause movement'. Etienne, however, himself resides in Switzerland—an intellec-
> tual neutral in the battles of history, a waverer like Scott's Waverley, who contrasts the
> 'clear imperatives of the Trojan War' with the 'hesitating morality by which I lived
> myself '.[2]

Massie's interest in Scott also emerges in *The Ragged Lion* (1994). This historical novel
(which, exceptionally for Massie, *is* set in Scotland) is a sympathetically-imagined and
factually-based account of Scott's life.

The Scottish historian Niall Ferguson's widely-discussed and influential book *Empire: How Britain Made the Modern World* (2003) can likewise be seen as a recent work that
is comfortably in tune with the Scott / Buchan tradition. In the 'Introduction' of *Empire*, Ferguson records that in 1966 his own father, 'having completed his medical studies in Glasgow', took 'his wife and two infant children to Kenya, where he worked for
two years teaching and practising medicine in Nairobi'. Ferguson continues:

> Thus, thanks to the British Empire, my earliest childhood memories are of colonial
> Africa; for although Kenya had been independent for three years, and the radio con-
> stantly played Jomo Kenyatta's signature tune 'Harambe, Harambe' ('Let's all pull to-
> gether'), scarcely anything had changed since the days of White Mischief. We had our
> bungalow, our maid, our smattering of Swahili—and our sense of unshakeable secu-
> rity. It was a magical time, which indelibly impressed on my consciousness the sight of
> the hunting cheetah, the sound of Kikuyu women singing, the smell of the first rains
> and the taste of ripe mango. I suspect my mother was never happier. And although we
> finally came back to the grey skies and the winter slush of Glasgow, our house was

always filled with Kenyan memorabilia. There was the antelope skin on the sofa; the Masai warrior's portrait on the wall; the crudely carved but exquisitely decorated footstool that my sister and I liked to perch on.[3]

These souvenirs of Empire perhaps qualify Niall Ferguson to be regarded as a member of the last generation to have had direct personal experience of the long and deep Scottish involvement in Britain's African empire. However, in the 'Conclusion' of his book on *Empire*, Ferguson does not see imperial politics as being locked irretrievably in the past. On the contrary, he argues that in some sense the imperial torch has now been passed on to the United States. He writes:

In 1899 Rudyard Kipling, the Empire's greatest poet, addressed a powerful appeal to the United States to shoulder its imperial responsibilities:

> Take up the White Man's Burden—
> Send forth the best ye breed—
> Go bind your sons in exile
> To serve your captives' need;
> To wait in heavy harness
> On fluttered folk and wild—
> Your new-caught, sullen peoples,
> Half devil and half child.
>
> Take up the White Man's Burden
> And reap his old reward:
> The blame of those ye better,
> The hate of those ye guard …

No one would dare use such politically incorrect language today. The reality is nevertheless that the United States has—whether it admits it or not—taken up some kind of global burden, just as Kipling urged. It considers itself responsible not just for waging a war against terrorism and rogue states, but also for spreading the benefits of capitalism and democracy overseas. And just like the British Empire before it, the American Empire unfailingly acts in the name of liberty, even when its own self-interest is manifestly uppermost. That was the point made by John Buchan, looking back on the heyday of Milner's imperialist kindergarten from the dark vantage point of 1940.

Ferguson then gives the following abbreviated version of a passage from *Memory Hold-the Door* that has already been quoted in Chapter 6:

I dreamed of a world-wide brotherhood with the background of a common race and creed, consecrated to the service of peace; Britain enriching the rest out of her culture and traditions, and the spirit of the Dominions like a strong wind freshening the stuffiness of the old lands . . . We believed that we were laying the basis of a federation of the world . . . The 'white man's burden' is now an almost meaningless phrase; then it involved a new philosophy of politics, and an ethical standard, serious and surely not ignoble.[4]

Among other things, Ferguson omits from this passage Buchan's praise of the 'far-sighted' policy of Milner and Rhodes towards 'the native races under our rule'.

In the first decade of the twenty-first century, it appears that the United States has indeed taken up the 'white man's burden' in Iraq: with what ultimate success, time will no doubt tell.

'All that Kelman, Gray stuff'

The Scott / Buchan tradition continues to flourish. However, recent Scottish writing (for example in the fiction of Alasdair Gray and James Kelman) has likewise been energised by the continuing vitality of the non-elite Hogg / Gibbon tradition. In an interview published in 2004 Irvine Welsh (author of *Trainspotting*) was asked whether Hogg's *Justified Sinner* had made an impact on his own writing. He replied:

Oh yeah, definitely. That Hogg's *Confessions of a Justified Sinner* is one of the best, most brilliant books ever written. In a way, that's where it all fucking starts from—all that Kelman, Gray stuff—that's where it starts from.[5]

In Gray's landmark novel *Lanark* (1981), the protagonist Duncan Thaw is a working-class Glasgow artist whose background has a good deal in common with that of Alasdair Gray himself—and in its Thaw / Lanark doublings and in its imaginative scope *Lanark* likewise has features in common with Hogg's *Confessions of a Justified Sinner*. The present writer has pleasant memories of a lunchtime conversation in Stirling in the 1990s, during which Alasdair Gray demonstrated a detailed knowledge of, and a great admiration for, Hogg's writings.

In his essay 'The Importance of Glasgow in my Work' (1992), Gray's friend James Kelman has given a summary of what he describes as his own Glasgow 'working-class background'.

Born and bred in Govan and Drumchapel, inner city tenement to the housing scheme homeland on the outer reaches of the city. Four brothers, my mother a full-time parent, my father in the picture framemaking and gilding trade, trying to operate a one-man business. And I left school at 15 etc. etc. [...] For one reason or another, by the age of 21/22 I decided to write stories. The stories I wanted to write would derive from my own background, my own socio-cultural experience. I wanted to write as one of my own people, I wanted to write and remain a member of my own community.[6]

Clearly, the ambition that Kelman articulates here has a good deal in common with (for example) Hogg's project in *The Brownie of Bodsbeck* and Gibbon's project in *Sunset Song*. Perhaps not coincidentally, Kelman is an admirer of Hogg's work, and, in his collection of essays *"And the Judges Said ... "* (2002), he writes perceptively and persuasively about 'the latter pages' of *The Private Memoirs and Confessions of a Justified Sinner*, pages in which 'real-life members of the contemporary literati of Edinburgh are suddenly introduced into the tale'. Kelman continues:

> The literati being portrayed by Hogg were in the main contemptuous of his inferior social standing. As well as being a famous poet he had spent much of his life as a shepherd and he spoke in the language of his own cultural background (until his late teens he was close to illiterate). There was a tendency amongst his peers to patronise the poetry while failing to appreciate the prose. Hogg's novel is written in the ordinary standard English literary form of the period. When he brings the literati into the story he has them speak in that same standard form.
>
>   But then he introduces himself into the story and this 'self' is the man who is employed at wheeling and dealing in ewes, lambs and rams at country markets; not the 'self' as writer. He has this shepherd 'self' speak in the phoneticised language of someone who, by English literary standards, is a certain social inferior. The irony works on different levels but the most hair-raising one of the lot is that which is structured on the premise that somebody who speaks in a 'culturally debased' linguistic form could not conceivably create this prose masterpiece in the imperial language of English.[7]

Like Hogg, Kelman dismisses the 'preposterous élitism' of that premise; and Kelman's novels (like those of Hogg and Gibbon) demonstrate that a subaltern Scottish writer is not necessarily focusing on the trivial, the insignificant, and the merely local when seeking 'to write as one of my own people'. Writing as one of his own people, Kelman in his novels explores existential themes with Kafkaesque depth and subtlety.

Kelman's example has been a fruitful one. As Cairns Craig puts it:

> The style of Welsh's *Trainspotting*, like the style of much new Scottish writing in the early 1990s, owes a substantial debt to the work of James Kelman and to Kelman's radical renewal, with the publication of *The Busconductor Hines* in 1984, of the potentialities of both working-class fiction and the dialect novel.[8]

Scottish writers for whom the work of Kelman and Gray has helped to blaze a benign and helpful trail include Iain Banks, Janice Galloway, Jackie Kay, A. L. Kennedy, and Liz Lochhead, as well as Irvine Welsh.

For some of these writers, and notably for Kelman and Welsh, the question of language is a significant one: when Kelman writes (as he puts it) 'as one of my own people', he uses (as is natural) the urban demotic language of his own people. This aspect of his writing caused much unfavourable comment in sections of the press when he won the Booker Prize in October 1994 with *How late it was, how late*.[9] Like Kelman, the poet Tom Leonard often writes in the present-day urban demotic language of Glasgow—and in a well-known and much-anthologised passage from 'Ghostie Men' (1984) Leonard provides a witty and forceful defence of the value of this allegedly debased language:

> right inuff
> ma language is disgraceful
>
> ma maw tellt mi
> ma teacher tellt mi
> thi doactir tellt mi
> thi priest tellt mi
>
> ma boss tellt mi
> ma landlady in carrington street tellt mi
> the lassie ah tried tay get aff way in 1969 tellt mi
> sum wee smout thit thoat ah hudny read chomsky tellt mi
> a calvinistic communist thit thoat ah wuz revisionist tellt mi

The list continues, and we are tellt (for example) that 'ma wife tellt mi jist-tay-get-inty-this-poem tellt mi'. To crown all, 'even thi introduction tay thi Scottish National Dictionary tellt mi'. But after the list comes a concluding note of assertive defiance:

> ach well
> all livin language is sacred
> fuck thi lohta thim [10]

Like Kelman, Leonard is a socialist who writes in the language of his own people as he asserts the validity of working-class experience. Operating from a class-based rather than a national perspective, these socialist writers are not concerned with attempting to revive the cultural traditions associated with Lowland Scots, the language recorded in *The Scottish National Dictionary* : rather, they are concerned with using the real language actually spoken by their own people, now.

However, 'all livin language is sacred', and this applies to (for example) the Maori language as well as to the modern urban demotic language of Glasgow. Let us, then, consider the implications of the possibility that, for a Maori, the desire to 'write as one of my own people' might involve a decision to write in Maori rather than English, the language of Imperial power.

After the British Empire established itself in Aotearoa (the islands which newly-arrived seventeenth-century Europeans decided to call 'New Zealand'), the indigenous Maori language and culture began to go into decline. In order to encourage this decline, Maori children were routinely subjected to corporal punishment for speaking Maori rather than English in the 'native schools' set up under British rule. Similar things happened in Scottish schools during the Imperial period, and one such scene forms part of the childhood experience of Conn Docherty in William McIlvanney's novel *Docherty* (1975). When asked by his school teacher what has happened to his face, Conn replies in his native Scots:

> 'Skint ma nose, sur.'
>
> 'How?'
>
> 'Ah fell an' bumped ma heid in the sheuch, sur.'
>
> 'I beg your pardon?'
>
> 'Ah fell an' bumped ma heid in the sheuch, sur.'
>
> 'I beg your pardon?'
>
> In the pause Conn understands the nature of the choice, tremblingly, compulsively, makes it.
>
> 'Ah fell an' bumped ma heid in the sheuch, sur.'
>
> The blow is instant. His ear seems to enlarge, is muffed in numbness. But it's only the dread of tears that hurts. Mr Pirrie distends on a lozenge of light which mustn't be allowed to break. It doesn't. Conn hasn't cried.
>
> 'That, Docherty, is impertinence. You will translate, please, into the mother-tongue.'
>
> The blow is a mistake, Conn knows. If he tells his father, he will come up to the school. 'Ye'll take whit ye get wi' the strap an' like it. But if onybody takes their hauns tae ye, ye'll let me ken.' He thinks about it. But the problem is his own. It frightens him more to imagine his father coming up.
>
> 'I'm waiting, Docherty. What happened?'
>
> 'I bumped my head, sir.'
>
> 'Where? Where did you bump it, Docherty?'
>
> 'In the gutter, sir.'
>
> 'Not an inappropriate setting for you, if I may say so.' [11]

Similar incidents are recorded in 'Don's Story', one of the accounts of real-life Maori childhood experiences recorded in Rachael Selby's *Still Being Punished*:

> I would go home and say, 'We were whacked today for speaking Maori.' I can still see
> the pain on my father's face. But he never did anything, the teacher was sacrosanct. I
> think our parents accepted it because they thought what the teacher was doing was
> good for us. We had to become brown Pakeha. It was the right thing at that time. I
> remember once I told my father the teacher had whacked me for speaking Maori and I
> think out of sheer frustration he hit me too.[12]

'Pakeha' are white New Zealanders.

'We had to become brown Pakeha'. The suppression of the Maori language continued in New Zealand schools from the 1860s until the 1960s, and was part of a policy
to impose the Imperial language, English, on the Maori people. However, the post-
Imperial period has seen a strong revival of the Maori language, a revival that began to
gather force in the 1980s.

The story of the Maori people in nineteenth- and twentieth-century New Zealand
can be interpreted in economic and class terms: the Empire converted the Maori into a
downtrodden, exploited class. However, to see their plight *exclusively* in economic and
class terms would be to underplay the significance of the cultural aspects of the process
of Imperial conquest: 'We had to become brown Pakeha'. The recent revival in the use
of the Maori language represents resistance to a process of cultural imperialism, and
has something in common with Kelman's desire to 'write as one of my own people':
to speak Maori is to speak 'as one of my own people', and not as a 'brown Pakeha'.
The post-Imperial Maori ambition to be Maori rather than 'brown Pakeha' does not
grow out of an impossible desire to turn back the clock in order to revert to a lost pre-
Imperial past. Rather, it reflects a desire (not particularly shared by Kelman in a Scottish
context, but certainly shared by MacDiarmid) to re-connect in a post-Imperial world
with the pre-Imperial culture of one's own people.

Gaelic, like Maori, was firmly discouraged in the schools of Imperial Britain: as we
saw in Chapter 2, when Sorley MacLean started school in his native Raasay he had perforce to master English, the language of the schoolroom. However, as we also saw in
Chapter 2, when MacLean wrote 'Hallaig' he wrote it in his native Gaelic—'as one of
my own people', in Kelman's phrase. He could do no other. Like *The Busconductor
Hines* and 'Ghostie Men', 'Hallaig' speaks for 'my own people' in the language of 'my
own people'. 'Hallaig' is one of the outstanding European poems of the twentieth
century. But the firm discouragement of Gaelic in the Highland schools of the Imperial era had a devastating effect on the language, and in spite of a Maori-style post-
Imperial revival, only a few thousand people now speak Gaelic. 'Hallaig' is a major
poem that could only have been written in Gaelic, but it is therefore written in a language that very few people can now read.

The British Empire is no longer with us, but its legacy lingers in all sorts of ways. One thinks, to take a pleasant and benign example, of the Indian sub-continent's continuing obsession with cricket. The immense and expanding power and dominance of English as an international language is also in many ways a benign and useful legacy of Empire, but that particular legacy perhaps involves loss as well as gain.

The Scottish Diaspora: Alice Munro

Another legacy of Empire is the Scottish Diaspora, and in the first decade of the twenty-first century two Canadians of Scottish descent (Alice Munro and Alistair MacLeod) may be numbered among the most interesting and impressive writers of fiction currently active anywhere in the world. As it happens, Alice Munro (*née* Laidlaw) is descended from James Hogg's maternal grandfather Will Laidlaw of Phaup (a connection of which she is well aware);[13] and, as it also happens, Alice Munro's short stories tend to operate in tune with some of the themes and concerns of the Hogg / Gibbon tradition in Scottish writing. In particular, her stories are capable of revealing the potential for profound significance to be found in apparently unremarkable lives that are lived out in apparently humdrum places, far away from the obviously significant action.

In 'A Wilderness Station', which appears in Munro's collection *Open Secrets* (1994), connections with Hogg are particularly near the surface. Like many of Munro's stories, in *Open Secrets* and in other collections, 'A Wilderness Station' is set in 'Alice Munro country': the quiet (and, to the unsympathetic and superficial observer, rather dull) area of south-western Ontario where she grew up and where she has spent much of her life. This particular story begins with a letter written in the 1850s and ends with a letter written in the 1950s. There is no third-person narrator. 'A Wilderness Station' proceeds by presenting various documents, through which we hear the voices of various people. From these documents, a story emerges which traces the evolution of twentieth-century small-town Ontario from its roots in the days of the area's original nineteenth-century European settlers (many of whom were Scots).

'A Wilderness Station' is a sombre and disturbing story. One of its letter-writers from the 1850s is 'the Reverend Walter McBain, Minister of the Free Presbyterian Church of North Huron'. McBain writes:

> I came to this area in November of last year, being the first minister of any kind to venture. My parish is as yet mostly bush, and there is nowhere for me to lodge but at the Carstairs Inn. I was born in the west of Scotland and came to this country under the auspices of the Glasgow Mission. After applying to know God's will, I was directed by Him to go to preach wherever was most need of a minister.[14]

'A Wilderness Station' gets its name from words by Thomas Boston quoted by the dying Walter McBain at the end of his final letter: '*This world is a wilderness, in which we may indeed get our station changed, but the move will be out of one wilderness station unto another*'.[15] Thomas Boston (a theologian of great and enduring reputation) was minister of James Hogg's native Ettrick from 1707 until 1732. He is discussed by Hogg in *The Shepherd's Calendar*.[16]

Arguably, 'A Wilderness Station' offers a dark alternative to one of the best-known and most widely-read narratives of nineteenth-century Canadian life, L. M. Montgomery's *Anne of Green Gables* (1925). In Montgomery's novel, Anne is a child from an orphanage who is taken into the family of Matthew and Marilla Cuthbert, an elderly brother and sister of Scottish extraction who live on a farm in Prince Edward Island. The feisty, intelligent, red-haired, and imaginative Anne comes into the rather staid Presbyterian world of the Cuthberts as a breath of fresh air, and she transforms the life of the old couple for the better. Nevertheless, Anne's story has its darker moments. For example, she tells Marilla:

> Then Mrs Hammond from up the river came down and said she'd take me, seeing I was handy with children, and I went up the river to live with her in a little clearing among the stumps. It was a very lonesome place. [...] Mrs Hammond had eight children. She had twins three times. I like babies in moderation, but twins three times in succession is *too much*. I told Mrs Hammond so firmly, when the last pair came. I used to get so dreadfully tired carrying them about.[17]

Such hints of the possibility of desolation 'among the stumps' of the newly-cleared bush are extended and deepened in 'A Wilderness Station'. Here, the girl from the orphanage is called Annie McKillop. A young man of Scottish extraction, Simon Herron, is setting out with his brother George to clear a farm from the bush of south-western Ontario. Simon wants a wife, and Annie is duly sent to him from the orphanage. The Herron home is within the ambit of the Rev. Walter McBain's congregation, but it decidedly lacks the love and warmth of that other Presbyterian home, Green Gables. Indeed, the various letters and documents that make up 'A Wilderness Station' make it clear that Simon is a brutally violent man who comes to a brutally violent end. But was his death the result of a tree-felling accident (the officially-accepted version)? Or was he murdered by his brother George? Or was he murdered by his wife Annie, supplied by the orphanage and subsequently abused? Like Hogg's *Confessions of a Justified Sinner*, 'A Wilderness Station' offers a range of flawed and unreliable narrators as it gives its dark account of a mysterious and violent death in a Calvinist world. And like Hogg's novel, Munro's story offers disturbing questions rather than comforting answers.

The Scottish Diaspora: Alistair MacLeod

> 'MacDonalds?' he says. 'Are you the guys who make the hamburgers?'
> 'No,' says Calum, 'we're not the guys who make the hamburgers.'
>
> Alistair MacLeod, *No Great Mischief* [18]

Alistair MacLeod's novel *No Great Mischief* (1999) contains two distinct time-frames. On one level the book is set in the late twentieth century, and tells the story of a visit by the first-person narrator, Alexander MacDonald, to his older brother Calum. Interwoven with this story, however, is the story of the brothers' family history over several generations. The family story is about exile from post-Culloden Highland Scotland, and about the family's subsequent life in Cape Breton Island in the Canadian Maritimes. Finally, during the adult lives of the present generation of the family, there is dispersal from Cape Breton to different parts of Canada. In *No Great Mischief*, Alistair MacLeod is writing as one of his own people, in order to tell the story of his own people: he himself grew up in Cape Breton Island, the descendant of Scottish Highlanders. Alexander MacDonald, as first-person narrator of *No Great Mischief*, is likewise telling the story of *his* own people. Significantly, Alexander MacDonald is a namesake of the great eighteenth-century Gaelic poet Alasdair MacMhaighstir Alasdair, whose name in English (it will be remembered) was Alexander (or 'Sawney') MacDonald. Taken together, all these circumstances ensure that Alistair MacLeod (like Hogg, Galt, Gibbon, and Kelman) is able to locate narrative authority and the narrative voice within the subaltern community whose story is being told.

On the opening page of the novel the first-person narrator, en route to visit his brother, is driving through the extravagantly fruitful September fields and orchards of south-western Ontario. 'Pick your own', the signs say, and many prosperous Canadian families are doing so. Alexander MacDonald continues:

> On some of the larger farms much of the picking is done by imported workers: they too, often, in family groups. They do not 'pick your own' but pick instead for wages to take with them when they leave. This land is not their own. Many of them are from the Caribbean and some are Mennonites from Mexico and some are French Canadians from New Brunswick and Quebec. (p. 1)

This image of the contrasting groups of fruit-pickers will recur from time to time later in the novel, and it can be read as a modern Canadian version of the elite / subaltern contrast. Still on the first page of the novel, the implications of the image begin to be developed. Alexander MacDonald writes: 'on the land that has already been picked over, the farmers' tractors move across the darkening fields, ploughing down the old crops while preparing for the new'. This triggers a memory:

Once, outside of Leamington, my grandmother, who was visiting at the time, burst into tears at the sight of the rejected and overripe tomatoes which were being ploughed under. She wept for what she called 'an awful waste' and had almost to be restrained from running into the fields to save the tomatoes from their fate in the approaching furrows. She was fifteen hundred miles from her preserving kettle, and had spent decades of summers and autumns nurturing her few precious plants in rocky soil and in shortened growing seasons. In the fall she would take her few surviving green tomatoes and place and turn them on the windowsills, hoping they might ripen in the weakened sun which slanted through her windowpanes. To her they were precious and rare and hard to come by. (pp. 1–2)

The very different tomatoes of Leamington and Cape Breton provide powerfully contrasting images of an excessive and wasteful superabundance on the one hand, and of a hard and testing underabundance on the other. These images point to the appalling contrast, in the early twenty-first century, between the superabundant wealth of the First World and the poverty of the Third World. That contrast provides a significant context for *No Great Mischief*.

Likewise, the tomatoes of the novel's opening pages locate the earlier generations of Alexander MacDonald's family firmly among the Have Nots rather than the Haves of the world. Furthermore, we discover later in Chapter 1 that Alexander's older brother Calum, who is living in squalor in Toronto's slums, is still very much one of the Have Nots. It thus quickly becomes clear that the family story of the MacDonalds will be a story of the subaltern, not a story of the elite.

Chapter 1 of *No Great Mischief* opens the story of the visit, and Chapter 2 opens the story of the family. It appears that *Calum Ruadh* ('red-haired Calum'), the narrator's great-great-great-grandfather, came with his family from the Scottish Highlands to Cape Breton in 1779, some thirty-three years after Culloden, and some six years after the tour of Johnson and Boswell to the Highlands and the Hebrides. 'Anyone who knows the history of Scotland, particularly that of the Highlands and the Western Isles in the period around 1779, is not hard-pressed to understand the reasons for their leaving' (pp. 17–80). Narrating *No Great Mischief*, Alexander MacDonald comments that, in leaving Scotland in 1779, his great-great-great-grandfather was

unaware that the French Revolution was coming and that a boy named Napoleon was but ten, and had not yet set out to conquer the world. Although he was not surprised, later, at the number of his own relatives who died before and during Waterloo, still shouting Gaelic war cries while fighting for the British against the resistant French. General James Wolfe, whom he perhaps did not remember from the Forty-Five, was already dead twenty years, dying with the Highlanders on the Plains of Abraham—the same Highlanders he had tried to exterminate some fourteen years before. (p. 19)

Wolfe had fought on the Hanoverian side at Culloden in 1746, and in 1759 he died in battle in Quebec when his British army defeated the French at the Plains of Abraham, thus securing Canada for the British Empire. In that battle, Wolfe had deliberately placed his Highland soldiers in the front line, having earlier explained that they were 'a secret enemy' and that it would be 'no great mischief if they fall' (see *No Great Mischief*, pp. 217, 219).

Calum Ruadh's family were of course Gaelic-speaking when they left Scotland in 1779; but English was the predominant language in Canada, and as the generations pass the speech of the family increasingly moves away from Gaelic towards English. In Alexander MacDonald's generation, the members of the family speak English, but with a strong smattering of Gaelic (and the language of the novel reflects this). Indeed, as narrator of *No Great Mischief*, Alexander MacDonald recalls that in his pre-school days he was always called within the family *gille beag ruadh* ('the little red-haired boy'). He thus thought of this as his name. At the roll-call on his first day at primary school, he therefore does not recognise himself when his name is called as 'Alexander MacDonald':

> Thankfully, however, we were of the generation who were no longer beaten because we uttered Gaelic, 'beaten for your own good,' as the phrase seemed to go, 'so you will learn English and become good Canadian citizens'. Instead she [the teacher] merely asked, 'Is your name Alexander?'
>
> 'Yes,' I said, having regained some shreds of composure.
>
> 'In the future, please answer when your name is called from the roll,' she said.
>
> 'I will,' I said to myself, making a sharp mental note to be on the lookout for the foreign sound in the future. (pp. 16–17)

However, in focusing on the North American experiences of exiled Scottish Highlanders, *No Great Mischief* points to parallels with other experiences and other struggles. At a point in the family story when Alexander is working as a miner with his brother Calum, the two discuss the Vietnam War, then currently being fought. A parallel is drawn between events in Vietnam and events in Scotland in the eighteenth century:

> 'From what I understand of this war, ' he continued, 'those people are only fighting for their own country and their own way of being. It's hard to say they should be killed for that.'
>
> 'I know,' I said. 'Wars touch all of us in different ways. I suppose we have been influenced by lots of wars ourselves. We are probably what we are because of the '45. We are, ourselves, directly or indirectly the children of Culloden Moor, and what happened in its aftermath.' (p. 192)

And there are other parallels. In the penultimate chapter of the novel, travelling home in the gathering darkness after his visit to Calum, Alexander MacDonald thinks again of the subaltern fruit-pickers he had observed on his outward journey. He goes on to think of the 'native peoples' on the East Coast, who 'move across the land, harvesting':

> Tomorrow they will cross back and forth across the borders, following the potato harvest and the blueberries, passing from New Brunswick into Maine and then back again. They are older than the borders and the boundaries between countries and they pay them little mind.
>
> In Kenya, at the base of Mount Kilimanjaro, the tall and arrogant Masai follow their herds. For strength they drink the blood of their cattle. They follow the cycle of the seasons and pay no heed to the boundaries of the parks and the game preserves. They were there first, they reason. Unlike the Zulus, they have not yet been confined to certain 'homelands' which are really not their homes at all. Perhaps the Masai do not know that others are planning 'to do something' with them. 'Soon', perhaps.   (pp. 253–54)

As first-person narrator of *No Great Mischief*, Alexander MacDonald tells how, when he was about eleven years old and making kindling with his grandfather, he learned more about the arrival in North America of their ancestor Calum Ruadh:

> 'After they landed on the shores of Pictou,' he said '*Calum Ruadh* broke down and wept and he cried for two whole days and I guess they were all around him, including the dog, and no one knew what to do.'
>
> 'Cried?' I said incredulously. Because even by then I was conditioned by movies where the people all broke into applause when they saw the Statue of Liberty which their ship was approaching. Always they seemed to hug and dance and be *happy* at landing in the New World. And also the idea of a fifty-five-year-old man crying was a bit more than I was ready for. 'Cried?' I said. 'What in the world would he cry for?'
>
> I remember the way my grandfather drove the axe into the chopping block—with such violent force that it became so deeply embedded he had difficulty in getting it out later—and he looked at me with such temporary anger in his eyes that I thought he would snatch me by my jacket front and shake me. His eyes said that he could not believe I was so stupid, but they said so only for a moment. (p. 21)

After gaining control of himself, the narrator's grandfather explains:

> 'He was,' he said, composing himself and after a thoughtful moment, 'crying for his history. He had left his country and lost his wife and spoke a foreign language. He had left as a husband and arrived as a widower and a grandfather, and he was responsible

for all those people clustered around him. He was,' he said, looking up to the sky, 'like the goose who points the V, and he temporarily wavered and lost his courage.

'Anyway,' he went on, 'they waited there for two weeks, trying to get a shallop to take them across the water and here to Cape Breton. And then, I guess, he got better and "set his teeth", as they say, and resolved to carry on. It's a good thing for us that he did.' (p. 22)

An important and resonant story is told in the movies in which the people all break into applause when their ship approaches the Statue of Liberty. Such movies tell a story that articulates America's sense of itself, and the Grand Narrative about the liberation offered by the New World to the Old World's huddled masses is a story that richly deserves a hearing. But it is neither the whole story nor the only story. The story of the arrival in the New World of Europe's huddled masses takes on darker shades when seen from an African or a Native American perspective. Toni Morrison's *Beloved* (1987), for example, tells a powerful alternative story about the African-American experience of America. Likewise, *No Great Mischief* tells a powerful alternative story that focuses on the connections between modern North America and the traumas of post-Culloden Highland Scotland—and this story, in confronting the desolating, dislocating pain of exile, is able to extend and complicate the resonant Grand Narrative in which the immigrants dance as their ship approaches the Statue of Liberty. Like Achebe's *Things Fall Apart* and Morrison's *Beloved*, MacLeod's *No Great Mischief* declares that 'we too might have a story to tell'. And all three novels tell a story that is well worth telling.

Notes

1 Allan Massie, 'Tartan Armies', *London Magazine*, n.s. 19.7 (October 1979), 92–96 (pp. 94, 96).

2 Craig, *The Modern Scottish Novel*, p. 136.

3 Niall Ferguson, *Empire: How Britain Made the Modern World* (London: Penguin, 2004), pp. xiv–xv.

4 Ferguson, *Empire*, pp. 380–81.

5 'Irvine Welsh: In Conversation with Aaron Kelly', *Edinburgh Review*, 113 (2004), 7–17 (p. 9).

6 James Kelman, *Some Recent Attacks: Essays Cultural and Political* (Stirling: AK Press, 1992), p. 81.

7 James Kelman, 'A Reading from the Work of Noam Chomsky and the Scottish Tradition in the Philosophy of Commonn Sense', in *"And the Judges Said …": Essays* (London: Secker & Warburg, 2002), pp. 140–86 (pp. 177–78).

8 Craig, *The Modern Scottish Novel*, p. 99.

9 For a discussion of this, see James Wood, 'In Defence of Kelman', *Guardian*, 25 October 1994.

10 Quoted from *The Poetry of Scotland: Gaelic, Scots and English 1380–1980*, ed. by Roderick Watson (Edinburgh: Edinburgh University Press, 1995), p. 704.

11 William McIlvanney, *Docherty* (London: Allen & Unwin, 1975), p. 109.

12 Rachael Selby, *Still Being Punished* (Wellington: Huia, 1999), p. 23.

13 For Alice Munro's family connection to Hogg, see 'The Scottish Ancestor: A Conversation with Alice Munro', *Scotlands*, 2 (1994), 83–96; see also Sheila Munro, *Lives of Mothers & Daughters: Growing Up with Alice Munro*, (Toronto: McClelland & Stewart, 2001), pp. 175–77. For Hogg's cousin James Laidlaw (ancestor pf Alice Munro) see *The Collected Letters of James Hogg*, ed. by Gillian Hughes, The Stirling / South Carolina Research Edition of the Collected Works of James Hogg (Edinburgh: Edinburgh University Press, 2004–   ), II, 10–12. For Hogg's account of his grandfather Will Laidlaw of Phaup, see 'General Anecdotes' in *The Shepherd's Calendar*, ed. by Douglas S. Mack, The Stirling / South Carolina Research Edition of the Collected Works of James Hogg (Edinburgh: Edinburgh University Press, 1995: paperback reprint 2002), pp. 94–117 (pp. 103–12).

14 'A Wilderness Station' in Alice Munro, *Open Secrets: Stories* (Toronto: McClelland & Stewart, 1994), pp. 190–225 (p. 197).

15 *Open Secrets*, p. 204.

16 See *The Shepherd's Calendar*, ed. Mack, pp. 27–28, 112–14.

17 L. M. Montgomery, *Anne of Green Gables* (London: Harrap, 1925; repr. 1941), p. 53.

18 Alistair MacLeod, *No Great Mischief* (London: Vintage, 2001), p. 259. Future references are to this edition, and are given in the text.

This book is dedicated to
Maureen Hamill
without whose encouragement and support
it might never have been completed

SCOTTISH FICTION
AND THE BRITISH EMPIRE